SuperB...

AND THE 70s

DAVE SHEEHAN

FOREWORD BY LES WILLIAMS

Dave Sheehan 2012

Panther Publishing

Published by Panther Publishing Ltd in 2013

Panther Publishing Ltd
10 Lime Avenue
High Wycombe
Buckinghamshire HP11 1DP
www.panther-publishing.com
info@panther-publishing.com

© *Dave Sheehan*

The rights of the authors have been asserted in accordance with the Copyright Designs
and Patents Act 1988

Drawings on the cover and accompanying the chapters are the copyright of the author,
Dave Sheehan

Inside front cover photos courtesy of (top to bottom) Norton Commando - Ian Kerr,
Kawasaki Z1- Copyright Kawasaki, Honda CB750/4 - Derrel Weaver, and Triumph
Hurricane - Craig Vetter.

ISBN 978-1-909213-12-8

ACKNOWLEDGEMENTS

Although writing a book is a largely solitary endeavour, my research and this book's eventual publication has come about through the help and support of many other people.

I am grateful to Suzuki GB, Crooks Suzuki in Cumbria, and the Suzuki Owners Club of Great Britain. The club proved especially helpful when I was researching technical details about the RE-5 rotary. Martin Lambert at Kawasaki UK was kind enough to spend his weekends trawling through his archive of Seventies publicity photographs (did we really dress like that?).

I am indebted also to the Z1 Owners Club. My thanks to club President Jerry Humpage, and club member Mark Hutchinson who very kindly entrusted me with an original copy of *Bike's* 1973 Giant Test of the Kawasaki Z1 and the Honda CB750/4 from his personal collection (an issue so rare that *Bike* magazine themselves don't even own a copy). Fellow club member Malc Anderson very kindly furnished pictures from his personal photographic record of the 'V-bikes' - the pre-production versions of the Z1. Dave Marsden at Z-Power in Leigh was also extremely generous with his time and advice.

I appreciate, too, the help and support I received from Dennis Lodge at the Vintage Japanese Motorcycle Owners Club (who, at one point, went so far as to take a tape measure to his Honda CB750 in order to verify a specific detail!). I have Dennis to thank, too, for putting me in touch with Honda CBX1000 guru, Ian Foster, author of the definitive book on the model, *The CBX Book*. Ian shared with me his incredible collection, which includes an example of the Honda Six from each year of its production.

My thanks, too, go to Kerrie (Lane) Bartzi of Nelson Ledges Race Course and Jim Sublet in Cuyahoga Falls, Ohio. As part of his research into my questions about Nelson Ledges, Jim sent me a copy of a cloth patch from 1969 as evidence that the track did indeed host America's first twenty-four hour motorcycle race!

Another American who was equally gracious with his time was Craig Vetter. Vetter is the man who designed one of my all-time favourite motorcycles: the Triumph Hurricane. Craig allowed me access to his personal archive and photographs, some of which feature in these pages. He also took time out to read my manuscript. This book benefited greatly from his input.

Dave Ekins, brother of Bud Ekins, the famous motorcycle racer, stuntman and friend to the actor, Steve McQueen, very kindly set me straight on a story about his brother Bud and Triumph supremo, Edward Turner.

Someone else who also knew Edward Turner is Les Williams. Les worked in Triumph's Experimental Department alongside Doug Hele, and was behind the team who raced the TT-winning 'Slippery Sam' Trident. Les is a real gent, and I am deeply indebted to him for applying his engineer's eye for detail to my manuscript (any errors that remain being entirely mine and confirmation that I am indeed no Les Williams). Les also kindly agreed to write the Foreword.

I'd also like to thank John Warr, the Managing Director of Europe's oldest Harley-Davidson dealer. When I'd hit a brick wall tracking down some information about Harleys in the UK in the early 1970s, Warr's was able to provide answers to all my questions.

Thanks are also due to my friend and fellow Triumph nut, Alan Evans. Alan was this project's earliest supporter who helped mould it from its roughest form right through to the book you hold in your hand. Colin Whaley too, who is stricken enough in years to recall the Seventies, was a mine of information about the cultural landscape of the decade.

All of the motorcycle clubs I approached were so generous and patient in answering my questions. Such curators of our motorcycling heritage - many of whom do it for free - are guaranteeing that future generations will continue to enjoy the superbikes of the 1970s. My research benefited greatly from their sage counsel. Any errors in this tome, however, are mine, not theirs.

My riding buddies in the Seventies also played their part in this book's gestation. Phil Parsons, Perry Slade, Bernard Daley and Pete O'Callaghan - all had a hand in colouring my rose-tinted motorcycling memories of that Day-Glo decade.

~ ~ ~

I am also very grateful to the many people and organisations who have helped me with the photographs in this book. Particular thanks must go to Craig Vetter, Dave Marsden at Z-Power, Malc Anderson, Ian Foster, author of *The CBX Book*, Geert Versleyen at Yesterday's Antique Motorcycles in Holland, Ian Kerr, David Koup of Koup's Cycle Shop Inc, the TR3OC, and the many other owners clubs who have been so supportive of this project. I am indebted also to Jacqui Harris, Archives Manager at Bauer Media, Cynthia Blackmore from the Reynolds-Alberta Museum, Brad Jones from The Power and the Glory (www.bsa1971.com), Bill Jackson at the Harley-Davidson Motor Company Archives in Milwaukee, and Honda UK's Glen MacMahon. I am especially grateful to Martin Lambert at Kawasaki UK who spent his weekends searching through his archives for material. Occasionally, even after extensive enquiries, I regret that I have not always been able to identify or make contact with the copyright holder. In other cases, the source I have cited in the caption to a photograph may not actually be that of the photographer whose name has been lost to posterity, but just the source of the photo itself.

~ ~ ~

Finally, I'd like to thank my family: my wife, Angela, our daughters Aimee and Emma, and Rusty, our ginger cat (de facto head of chez Sheehan). None of them share nor understand my passion for old motorcycles (particularly after yet another breakdown has left me stranded by the roadside). However, they've always smiled indulgently when I've read back to them some arcane motorcycling fact that it turns out only I have found interesting. I am especially grateful to my wife, who has suffered in silence (mostly) at my collection of ancient motorcycle magazines (which, despite her best efforts, have managed to follow us through every house move) and the smell of petrol on all her best linen. This book is for you.

See, Angela? I told you I'd put all those bike magazines to good use one day.

DEDICATION

This book is dedicated to the gladiators like Gary Nixon, Paul Smart, Percy Tait, Gene Romero, Dick Mann, Cook Neilson and Wes Cooley, whose exploits ennobled the story of superbikes in the seventies. The book also pays tribute to the designers and engineers who gave us the motorcycles in the first place - men like Doug Hele, Bert Hopwood, Fabio Taglioni, Don Brown, Craig Vetter, Yoshirou Harada and Gyoichi 'Ben' Inamura. Thanks, fellas: the Seventies would have been so much poorer without you.

~ ~ ~

During the writing of this book, two of the many larger-than-life characters whose names grace its pages passed away.

On 24 March 2010, Don Brown died at his home in Irvine, California aged 80. *MotorCyclist* magazine described him as 'the most influential person in the motorcycle industry that you never heard of.' Brown served as Editor of *Cycle* magazine, and co-wrote *How to Ride and Win*, which featured dirt and desert racer Bud Ekins.

As Sales Manager for Triumph's US West Coast distributor, Johnson Motors, Brown supplied Hollywood's glitterati with motorcycles, including personally delivering a Triumph to a young up-and-coming actor called Steve McQueen. Don helped establish the new US Suzuki Motor Corporation and, after Brown left BSA in 1970, he worked as a consultant to Kawasaki on their first long-range market study. In 2001, Brown was inducted into the AMA's Hall of Fame for his contribution to the sport.

~ ~ ~

On 5 August 2011, another Hall of Fame inductee, Gary Nixon, died. He was 70. The red-haired Oklahoman rode his 500cc Triumph twin to victory at the Daytona 200 in 1967, after trading first place with his team mate Dick Hammer fully 29 times. Nixon's win ensured Triumph prevailed at Daytona for a second successive year. 'We have the best machines,' said Dick O'Brien, head of the rival Harley-Davidson race team, 'spend the most money, try to get the best riders, and that little redhead comes out and blows us all off with 15 less horsepower!' His five victories that season secured Nixon his first AMA Championship, a title he held for two years running.

He earned the tag 'Iron Man' after continuing to race despite a series of injuries that would have laid up lesser men - like the time he broke his left leg on the Santa Rosa Mile flat-track. 'After I stopped slidin',' he recalled, 'I raised up to look around for my bike. When I seen that bone stickin' out, I knew there was nothin' I could do, so I laid back an' waited for the doc.' Nixon rode for three years with an 18-inch stainless steel rod holding his leg together.

Dave Sheehan
March 2013

What was scattered in many volumes, and observed at several times by eye-witnesses, with no cursory pains I laid together, to save the reader a far longer travail of wandering through so many desert authors

John Milton,
From the preface to
A Brief History of Muscovy first published 1632

CONTENTS

FOREWORD BY LES WILLIAMS

Race Team Manager of the TT-winning Triumph Trident nicknamed 'Slippery Sam'

Les Williams

When Dave asked me to peruse the draft of this book that day at Anglesey during the 21st Beezumph rally, I was so interested and duly impressed, that when I was asked to write the Foreword I had to read the book from beginning to end; and such is the detail, it did take some time, what with its fascinating facts on all the world's superbikes, and how the Japanese manufacturers too had their problems and disasters despite massive resources. It makes me realise all over again how our small team led by Doug Hele, on a comparatively miniscule budget, perhaps produced the first superbike of the era. Here, then, are a few details from me of our trials and tribulations in that endeavour.

'A potty idea' said Edward Turner when the rumours, drawings, and bits and pieces of probably the first of the world's superbike's prototypes started to emerge from the Triumph Experimental department, where I was one of the small team of experimental mechanics who were fortunate enough to be working there in the early 1960s.

The Triumph Superbike had been dreamed up by Bert Hopwood and Doug Hele in response to the growing demand for a successor to the Turner-inspired 650cc twins and the requirements from the USA dealers for more capacity. It was the time that ET, as he was known, was relinquishing his rule at Meriden and Mr Hopwood was the new ruler. So it was that the 'P1' came about.

We mechanics would gather round to see and discuss the bits and pieces being delivered from the tool room, the department that machined all the prototype parts (actually *three sets* of engine parts, as was usual with all prototypes). The usual experimental secrecy prevailed as components were laid out on one of the work benches up by the office (the department was off limits to most factory personnel). The mechanics selected to be involved in the assembly of this exciting new three-cylinder engine were Len Udall and Alan Barratt of Velocette fame, and Harry Woolridge of Triumph fame. I was not involved, as I was trying to extract more power from the lowly Tina scooter engine! But I did learn much about two-stroke development and had one of the fastest Tina's on the road!

The new three-cylinder engine, coded P1, was first intended for test bed work. Then, after months of work testing and modifying, the engine was installed in a modified T120 frame. The day finally came when, with 'Hoppy' [Bert Hopwood], Doug, Brian Jones and some of his drawing-office staff, plus all of us in overalls and a few invited worthies from the factory management, all gathered around for the birth of our first superbike, which was at last ready for its first teetering steps up the road in the hands of Percy Tait. Harry Woolridge tickled the first float chamber, and gave the kick-starter a mighty kick. The engine burst into life with a three-cylinder roar. Instantly, however, faces changed - from gleeful anticipation to utter dismay, as the noise from the gear-driven primary transmission with the plated clutch was absolutely terrible, even drowning out the exhaust note. The disillusioned worthies rapidly scuttled back to their offices, perhaps to pour scorn on the new project. After some head scratching and discussion, Percy took our new, noisy baby for a blast up Meriden Hill, arriving back to say that, despite the noise, he was impressed. (Just to explain: when the engine was on the test bed it was coupled directly to the powerplant with no transmission fitted. Also, it seems the gear cutting section was not up to their usual standards!)

After a year or so, the P1 evolved into the P2 with a primary chain replacing the gears; despite many teething troubles, it is no surprise to me that the three-cylinder unit went on to become the success that it was. As time went by, I became more involved with the Trident in its production form and, of course, with our successes on the various racing circuits of the UK and across the world. When racing was discontinued, I was one of the team responsible for developing the Trident T160. I also had an interesting time with the Wankel development in the final days at Meriden, and finally at Kitts Green in Birmingham where, a year or so later, NVT made us all redundant!

Back to the Meriden days. Over the years, we did have a few of the rival bikes to evaluate. I remember a Harley-Davidson sent over from the USA. I had a couple of rides on that. Also a Kawasaki two-stroke triple, which caused me a mighty adrenaline surge, and nearly a surge of something else as it flew over the top of Meriden Hill, in a lock to lock wobble. Then, too, such was the importance of the early Wankel development that the factory purchased an NSU Prinz Spider, as mentioned in this book. Quite a few of us borrowed it at the weekends, which we were permitted to do for the test miles and opinions reported. Until one Sunday, when the chief metallurgist wrote it off after he drove into the front of a lorry. He was OK!

Cleverly, the author has not confined his endeavours to those Seventies superbikes alone. I was fascinated by his facts contained in the background of that decade.

Buy and read this book, and you too will be fascinated. Just to dip into some of the facts – why, for example, the little Velocette LE was known as a 'Noddy' bike; the relation of the Laverda Jota to the Sex Pistols; the creator of that well-loved cartoon biker, 'Ogri'; an interesting explanation of the rise of bare breasts; or how a totem pole gave Edward Turner the inspiration for the Thunderbird badge. Did you know that well-known Japanese tuner 'Pops' Yoshimura was a pathfinder pilot during World War Two leading those kamikaze pilots to their 'honourable' deaths?

You will also learn of the politics and economics of the era affecting the 'honourable' demise of the UK motorcycle production in general. Truly it was a halcyon decade for us that were involved. For those readers all these years after, *Superbikes and the Seventies* should be on your bookshelf, as the chapters on Harley-Davidson and the Wankel engine machines alone are well worth the cost.

Les Williams
October 2012

1

INTRODUCTION

'It was the best of times, it was the worst of times'
(Opening line of *A Tale of Two Cities*, Charles Dickens)

A TURBULENT DECADE, A GOLDEN AGE

For the British, the Seventies is generally considered to have been a grim time: economic decline, double digit inflation, rocketing fuel prices, civil unrest, and deep industrial strife, culminating in 1978-79's infamous Winter of Discontent. Things were no less traumatic in America where the dreams that the newly-inaugurated President Kennedy declaimed on a bitterly cold January day in 1960, had, by the following decade, slid into a nightmare as Vietnam finally proved a burden too costly to bear.

Yet this version of the Seventies, in which the decade becomes a sort of shorthand for failure, ignores some inconvenient facts. In 2004, the radical think-tank, New Economics

Foundation, eschewed the conventional indicator for assessing national performance - gross domestic product - and constructed an alternative means of analysis. By measuring economic, social and environmental well-being, NEF found that 1976 emerged as the best year since 1950 and that Britain was a happier country in '76 than in any year since.

According to Alwyn W. Turner, author of *Crisis? What Crisis? Britain in the 1970s*: 'To be young in that dawn might not have been very heaven, but sometimes it didn't seem too far off, despite the privations.'

Indeed, from being 'the decade that taste forgot', the Seventies is now viewed as something of a golden era for the arts and architecture. In Hollywood, it was the age of the auteur directors like Francis Ford Coppola (*The Godfather*), Martin Scorsese (*Taxi Driver*), and Stephen Spielberg (*Jaws*). Notable British films of the decade include *Performance*, *Get Carter* and *The Wicker Man*.

And despite television in Britain comprising just three channels - BBC1 and BBC2, both funded by license fees, and the independent station ITV, funded through revenues generated from advertising - it still produced some memorable TV. Programmes like *The Sweeney*, *Monty Python's*, and the *Morecambe & Wise Show*, whose Christmas Special of 25 December 1977, attracted a record-breaking audience of almost 29 million. More than half the British population tuned in that night to see Britain's favourite double-act, and heavyweight broadcasters like Richard Baker and Robin Day, singing and somersaulting to Rodgers and Hammerstein's *There is Nothing Like a Dame* dressed up as US Navy matelots.

Popular music in the Seventies ran from Abba to Zappa. There was the flamboyance and narcissism of Glam Rock, the indulgence of Prog Rock, the nihilism of Punk Rock and the rollicking good fun of Pub Rock. Classic albums of the '70s included *Bridge Over Troubled Water* by Simon and Garfunkel, Lou Reed's *Transformer*, The Clash's *London Calling*, the movie soundtrack (and the best-selling album of all time) *Saturday Night Fever* by the Bee Gees, Kate Bush's *The Kick Inside*, and Marvin Gaye's environmental tract, *Let's Get It On*. Northern Soul, Reggae, Ska and Two Tone music bridged cultural divides, whilst heavy metal bands like Led Zeppelin, Black Sabbath and Motorhead turned it up to eleven.

In architecture, important buildings in the 1970s included the 110-storey World Trade Centre, whose North Tower, at 1,353 feet - taller than its twin to accommodate its Windows on the World restaurant's high ceiling - made it the tallest building on earth when it opened in December 1970.

Other iconic buildings from the decade include Lloyd's of London, the Pompidou Centre, and the Sydney Opera House.

SUPERBIKES AND THE SEVENTIES

For motorcyclists also, the Seventies was a special time. It was a decade when worshippers of horsepower genuflected before the altars of motorcycle makers from the Far East, Europe and an embattled British industry (who nevertheless still managed to spring surprises from its stable of venerable marques), as manufacturers vied with each other to woo riders in America, the market whose vast size exerted a lunar-like influence on the tides of change.

It was the decade of vivid hues; a time when the serried ranks of motorcycles in a dealer's showroom bore peacock-like liveries of lurid purple, pink and green, alongside classy silver or autumnal gold (as well as scatological brown).

Superbikes and the '70s explores why the 1970s were halcyon days for motorcyclists. The book tells the story of the dawn and early evolution of the modern superbike. It examines how success led to failure for the British motorcycling industry's once dominant brands and the growing hegemony of the Japanese manufacturers during the decade that has otherwise become a byword for decline in the UK, if not the rest of the world.

The book charts how competition between marques, environmental concerns, war in the Middle East and changing customer expectations, shaped and redefined the superbike. It relates the contrasting stories of the gestation and early development of some key models, revealing the markedly different approaches some manufacturers deployed in bringing their products to the market. It also provides an account of the final days of Britain's motorcycle industry, including the collapse of BSA, the Conservative Government's efforts to salvage a sector they recognised it was in Britain's national interest to retain, and the story of the Labour Government's efforts to support the Meriden Workers' Co-operative, one of the most bizarre episodes in British industrial relations.

Finally, the narrative travels back in time to visit two young pioneers in turn-of-the-century Wisconsin to learn the origins of the Harley-Davidson Sportster, before leaping forward six decades to the horsepower war between Japanese manufacturers, which resulted in 'megabikes' like the six-cylinder Honda CBX1000 and Kawasaki Z1300 displacing superbikes as the apex models of the 1970s.

BRIGHTON, 5 APRIL, 1969: THE SEVENTIES START HERE

A decade's trends seldom begin and end as neatly as its opening and closing dates on a calendar. Seventies motorcycling was no exception. However, in Britain at least, Saturday 5 April 1969 stands out as a strong candidate for the day the blue touch paper was lit that ignited motorcycling's most explosive decade. As the UK basked in the record-breaking sunshine of the Easter Bank Holiday weekend, both Triumph and Honda launched their ground-breaking 750cc multi-cylinder offerings to the British public in the English seaside resort of Brighton.

The tale behind how the Honda CB750/4 and the Triumph Trident made their British debuts in Brighton's Metropole Exhibition Hall is an elegy to a bygone trade war between two combatants: one from the Far East, whose fortunes were inexorably rising; and the other, from the West, fighting a rearguard action for its very survival.

~ ~ ~

My story, however, begins more than thirty years earlier, with Triumph supremo Edward Turner. The architect of Triumph's success home and abroad (most especially in America, a country he loved and visited often), Turner famously designed what he himself considered his 'masterpiece' - the seminal Triumph Speed Twin 5T.

The impact on motorcycling of the Speed Twin's vertical twin-cylinder layout would not be matched until the advent of Honda's CB750/4. Yet the very success of both Turner and his beloved Speed Twin would come to exert a baleful influence on the introduction of a successor, which engineers Doug Hele (pronounced *Heel*) and Bert Hopwood were forced to develop in secret, delaying by almost half a decade the launch of the first superbike of the modern era.

Ironically, it was rumours of a British multi-cylinder superbike which convinced Honda to increase their challenger's engine displacement to 750cc; coincidentally, just as stories of Honda developing a large-capacity motorcycle spurred the head of the BSA and Triumph combine to green-light Hele and Hopwood's secret project for a three-cylinder replacement to the ageing Triumph Bonneville.

When Honda unveiled the CB750 Dream Four at the Tokyo Motor Show in 1968, it changed the industry forever. It also very nearly put paid to Kawasaki's plans to launch a 750cc four-cylinder superbike of their own.

Bloodied but unbowed, Kawasaki regrouped to research the market's appetite for large-capacity motorcycles, returning in 1972 with a machine which *Cycle* magazine described as 'the most modern motorcycle in the world [and] the first of a generation of new bikes...'

Like the Honda CB750 before it, the Kawasaki 903cc Z1 was a paradigm shift, which introduced sophistication to performance motorcycles.

Of course, there were four-cylinder motorcycles available long before the CB750 and Z1. Moreover, not all superbikes in the Seventies had four pistons. Several had only three; some, just two; and in the case of the Suzuki, DKW/Hercules, and Van Veen rotaries, none at all.

The Superbike 7

In attempting to cover a whole decade and more than just one marque, I have inevitably had to leave some bikes out and concentrate on the stories of just a few of the machines from that decade. My starting point has been the machines the US magazine *Cycle* selected for the very first superbike comparison test ever published (something this book revisits as a leitmotiv in successive chapters, but each time from a different standpoint).

In 1970 the magazine evaluated the 'seven strongest motorcycles available for sale in the world.' The line-up comprised the three-cylinder BSA and Triumph 750s, the Harley-Davidson XLCH1000 Sportster, the Honda CB750/4, the Kawasaki 500 MACH III two-stroke triple, the 750 Norton, and the Suzuki T500 Titan two-stroke twin for a series of tests carried out at the Orange County International Raceway in Los Angeles.

Two years later, *Cycle* returned to Orange County to test the 1973 season's contenders for the 'Superbike which offered the most absolute performance'. But two years on and the line-up for the second of the magazine's Big Seven looked a little different.

The BSA 750 was no longer available, and *Cycle* decided against including the Suzuki 500 this time round. The Kawasaki MACH III 500 had been 'shouldered aside by its high-intensity big brother, the MACH IV 750', and the H-D Sportster, Honda 750/4, Norton 750 Commando, and Triumph 750 Trident were now joined by 'the new-dimension Ducati 750 and the frontier-stretching Kawasaki 903cc Z1'.

Cycle's second comparison test demonstrated that superbikes were changing and that raw data and quantifiable performance was not the most important measure of a superbike. Riders no longer had to sacrifice civility and comfort - and very often reliability - in the pursuit of handling, speed, and acceleration.

As the decade wore on, and times changed, so too did the superbike; a roster which now included the Laverda Jota and Yamaha XS750 four-stroke triples, the Honda Gold Wing and Suzuki GS750 and GS1000 fours, and towards the end of the Seventies, the Honda CBX1000 and Kawasaki Z1300 six-cylinder megabikes. All of them changed the game in some way or other (and, in some cases, arguably not always for the good).

Three machines, however, dominate the decade: The Triumph Trident, the Honda CB750, and the Kawasaki Z1. Each one forms a strand that weaves in and out of this book's multi-narrative thread, and each in its time makes its entrance and its exit to and from the stage, a player in the story of *Superbikes and the '70s*.

2

EDWARD TURNER AND THE SPEED TWIN

THE TEMPLATE FOR AN INDUSTRY

'a somewhat frightening spectacle'
(Triumph's Managing Director, Edward Turner, on the emerging Japanese
motorcycle industry)

Edward Turner

THE AMERICANS DEMAND A 750

The Trident was a motorcycle conceived at the right time, but born too late. The reason for its belated appearance was largely down to one man: Edward Turner. Triumph's dapper but diminutive managing director was against developing a multi-cylinder superbike.

'Ambitious', 'determined', and an 'engineering dictator', the red-headed and imperious Turner was wedded to the layout of the seminal 500cc Triumph Speed Twin he had designed three decades earlier. And with good reason: by the Sixties, the company's signature parallel twins were hugely successful on track, road, desert, dirt, and - most importantly - in US showrooms. In 1967, for example, Triumph's 650 outsold its single-cylinder 200cc Tiger Cub stablemate by nearly twelve to one. Turner had also toured the Honda, Suzuki and Yamaha factories in 1960, where he found their manufacturing capability a 'somewhat frightening spectacle.' He saw for himself that Triumph's production facilities were hopelessly outdated and couldn't match those of the Japanese. He was particularly impressed by Honda, reporting back to the BSA Board that Japan's 20 plus motorcycle companies were producing 'more motorcycles than the whole of the British industry put together... well over half a million motorcycles a year (against 140,000 British) of which Honda produces approaching a quarter of a million...'

Yet he did not view the Far East as direct competitors. As Lindsay Brooke and David Gaylin put it in their excellent book, *Triumph Motorcycles in America*, Turner 'continued to believe that when it came to building large, sporting machines for the true enthusiast, the Japanese would not eclipse the British'. Sales figures in the US supported his contention: Triumph's exports to the US rose from 6,300 machines in 1963 to 24,600 just four years later. Moreover, between 1967 and 1969, just 30 per cent of new bikes were bought by beginners, the majority being trade-ups to larger machines.

Nevertheless, North America (BSA and Triumph's biggest market, and home to the dictum: there's no substitute for cubic inches) was demanding a motorcycle that could deliver something in the region of 60bhp. US dealers pressed their British suppliers to increase their twins' capacity to 750cc. Unfortunately, BSA and Triumph engineers were reluctant to accede to American dealers' demands, justifiably nervous about the stresses and hard-to-cancel destructive levels of vibration such an increase in capacity would inflict on an already stretched design. Yet, ironically, despite Turner's lack of support for a multi-cylinder engine, it was a multi-cylinder engine that gave him his entrée into the industry back in 1928. More ironically still, it was Turner's Speed Twin of 1937 that gave his engineers their answer to the problem of meeting US demands: namely, do what Turner himself had done three decades previously to turn around the then ailing company's fortunes and fit an engine with one extra cylinder into a chassis already in production.

Edward Turner Joins Ariel

Turner was born in London on 24 January 1901, the very first day of the Edwardian era. That same day, Queen Victoria's son and heir, 'Bertie', was proclaimed King Edward VII, sovereign head of the richest nation on earth at a time when to be born an Englishman, according to the colonialist Cecil Rhodes, was to win first prize in the lottery of life.

In defiance of his middle-class family's expectations, young Turner ran away from his Camberwell home to serve in the Merchant Navy - aged just fourteen - as a wireless operator during the Great War. After he was de-mobbed, he turned his back on university for night classes at a technical school, studied art (informally), worked as a boiler maker, fitter, turner and blacksmith, before purchasing in 1923 a small, two-storey cycle repair shop, Velocette agency and showrooms called Chepstow Motors.

Situated in Dulwich, south London, on the corner of Peckham Road, the first floor boasted large windows through which traffic passing on either side of the modestly-sized showroom could peer at the motorcycles on display. By day, Turner fixed pushbikes and motorcycles in the workshop behind the showroom counter. But at night, he would climb a set of rickety stairs and retire to a second-floor studio where he would pursue his lifelong passion: designing motorcycles from scratch. By January 1927, he had built a single-cylinder, 350cc overhead cam engine - many of its components Turner himself having machined - which he housed in a frame he had fashioned, bicycle-style, from sections of steel tube.

The Turner Special sold for £75. Engineering drawings of his patented engine and photographs of the complete bike appeared in *The Motor Cycle* and Turner entered the machine in endurance races (without success). More importantly, press coverage of this one-man motorcycle manufacturer brought Turner to the attention of industry leader Ariel, its head Jack Y. Sangster (whom employees always referred to as Mr. Jack) and the company's chief designer, Valentine Page.

Turner attended a meeting with the two at Ariel's Selly Oak offices in Birmingham. However, whilst single-cylinder engines were the most popular configuration at the time, overhead cam engines were considered fragile and costly to manufacture. The meeting was winding to an inconclusive close when, in an afterthought, the 28-year-old Turner took a drawing from his coat-pocket of an idea he'd originally sketched out on the back of a Wills Woodbine cigarette packet (and which he'd already hawked around the Midlands motorcycle industry only to have it turned down by one factory after another). The drawing showed his nascent design for a four-cylinder engine.

Even back then, four-piston motors were not new. Founded by brothers William (known as Bill) and Tom, the eponymous Henderson motorcycles in Detroit, Michigan, manufactured a 1,068cc single-speed straight-four as early as 1912. In 1917, bicycle tycoon Ignaz Schwinn purchased Henderson as a prestige addition to his company's Excelsior V-twin range, moving production to Chicago, and appointing Bill and Tom to executive posts. Initially, the only visible difference to their four was the badge, which now featured Henderson's outstretched wings superimposed over Excelsior's famous Big-X. Two years later, Excelsior brought out the Model Z, a more sophisticated 1,168cc version of brothers Bill and Tom Henderson's increasingly popular four, and the first Henderson to be designed in Chicago. In 1920, Bill Henderson left Excelsior to form Ace and launched a 1,229cc in-line four. He and Tom (Bill being the engineer and Tom the business brain) managed Ace until Bill was killed in 1922 test-riding the new Sporting Solo Ace model. Ace folded in 1924. However, Bill Henderson's design, much improved by his successor at Ace, Art Lemon, was to reappear in January 1927 at New York's Motor Cycle Show in Madison Square Garden when Indian - who bought the rights to the Ace name and the tooling to manufacture the four - displayed the Ace four in the Springfield-based company's familiar red livery, but badged as an Indian/Ace.

All of these fours had their engines arranged longitudinally - that is, mounted front to back. The bikes were heavy, weighing between 450 and 540 lbs. They were long (the first Henderson straight four had a 65 inch wheelbase and 33 inch seat height), and although they broke records for riding long distances (in 1917, Allan Bedell beat former record holder 'Cannonball' Baker's time of 16¼ days on an Indian by chopping nearly four days off the 3,296 mile journey from Los Angeles to New York)* the bikes handled poorly. But Turner's idea for a four offered a solution. His design had the pistons arranged not inline, but in a rectangle, each cylinder situated upright in the corner of single block. Sangster was intrigued enough to give Turner his own office - separate from his new boss, the 39-year-old Val Page. Page had been head of design at engine builder JAP** before Sangster lured him to Ariel and the young Turner greatly valued Page's sage counsel. Turner also had an assistant, a very young draughtsman named Herbert Hopwood.

Turner's Masterpiece: The Triumph Speed Twin

The bike that emerged from Turner's office was revolutionary. The 500cc Ariel Square Four was effectively a pair of parallel twins, one in front of the other, with their crankshafts coupled together by gears. The motor was so light and compact that testing could be conducted by installing it in the standard chassis of Ariel's 250cc single. The 'Squariel' that went into production, however, and which proved the sensation of London's 1930 Olympia Show, used the same frame as their 500cc sloper single. The Square Four would remain a fixture in Ariel's range (in 500, 600 and 1,000cc variants) for nearly four decades - albeit at a rate of no more than 830 units a year - until the last of the breed, the Mk IV, rolled off the line in April 1959. (Despite its longevity, the Square Four's production figures were always 'minute', according to Hopwood who was very damning of the model in his book *Whatever Happened to the British Motorcycle Industry?*).

In 1932, Turner's boss, Val Page, left to join Triumph to develop a range of new engines. Sangster appointed Turner as Ariel's chief designer, assisted by the Birmingham-born Bert Hopwood, whereupon he applied his creative flair to Page's single-cylinder models, transforming them into the Red Hunter series by decorating them bright red, reshaping and chromium-plating the tank, to which he added a set of tank-top instruments. But in 1936, Turner threatened to leave unless Sangster bought the Triumph motorcycle division, put up for sale by Lloyds Bank to safeguard their interests as the company struggled to cope with the Depression. The bank's nominated manager, a man named Graham, decided the company must concentrate on making cars and sell the Priory Street plant in Coventry. Sangster could see Turner was serious. But he and Triumph also had some shared history: after graduating, Jack's father sent him to the continent to train as an engineer, during which time he worked at Triumph's German subsidiary in Nuremberg.*** Not only that, Jack also had recent experience of turning round an ailing motorcycle manufacturer.

---

* Cannonball would recapture the trans-continental record in September 1922. Riding an Ace and getting by on just nine hours sleep, Baker covered the journey from Los Angeles to New York in under seven days, beating Allan Bedell's record by seventeen hours.

** JAP built the propriety motor fitted to the Brough Superior, most famously ridden by T.E. Lawrence of Arabia (and the marque on which he suffered a fatal crash in 1935).

*** In 1896, a decade after setting up its bicycle-making factory in Coventry, the Triumph Cycle Company's founder, German émigré, Seigfried Bettmann, opened a subsidiary in his birthplace of Nuremberg. Triumph-Nuremberg went on to build a version of Triumph's popular lightweight two-stroke, the 225cc Junior (known as the Knirps or Nipper) until 1929, when the German branch lost its subsidiary status following a disagreement with Bettmann. Unable to use the name 'Triumph' outside of

Ariel had been producing motorised vehicles as far back as 1898. Jack's father, Charles, took control of the company in 1905; Jack joined in 1923. But, after becoming one of Britain's largest motorcycle producers in the Twenties, Ariel were hit by the slump precipitated by the 1929 Wall Street Crash. In 1932, as unemployment in Britain reached 17.6 per cent, the company went into receivership. Using his own personal fortune, Jack bought outright the Selly Oak works, plant and equipment, renaming the privately owned business Ariel Motors (JS) Ltd - the 'JS' denoting the initials of the new company's chairman and owner.

So, during the course of a two-hour train journey from Birmingham to London, Sangster negotiated a deal with Graham whereby they leased the Triumph plant and factory, but did not purchase the spares (which they sold on commission). Relying on considerable financial backing from Lloyds Bank, Sangster purchased the company for a reported £50,000, signing the agreement on 22 January 1936. From that point on, Triumph motorcycles and Triumph cars went their separate ways. (The bicycle division had been sold off several years earlier, eventually ending up with Raleigh.) Sangster made Turner general manager and chief designer of the new business - renamed Triumph Engineering Company - with 5 per cent of net profits plus a 4.9 per cent share in the company itself (although finances were so parlous that Turner was obliged to pay the first week's payroll from an overdraft!).

Emulating much of what Sangster had done to revive Ariel's fortunes, Turner immediately set about re-organising Triumph's rambling Coventry city-centre-based site (which Sangster called a 'rabbit warren'). He concentrated manufacturing on the right-hand side of the Priory Street works, transferred the service department from Much Park Street, and exercised an option to buy the Dale Street end of the complex, turning what had been the competition and development section into new offices and registering it as the company's official address, severing Triumph's last connection to its birthplace. He implemented take-it-or-leave wage cuts (most employees took it and stayed). He abolished the central sales office, divided the country into three sales areas, each with its own manager, leaving Priory Road to collate and co-ordinate each area's paperwork. In mid-April, he announced three new models. Derived from the Val Page designed Mark 5 models, the new 250, 350 and 500cc overhead-valve singles received a makeover from Turner involving chrome-plated fuel tanks and headlamps, silver side panels, as well as tweaks to the engines, which included polished cylinder-head ports, stronger valve springs, and new cast-iron cylinders 'hardened and oil-tempered to prolong life and improve friction surfaces'. The final flourish was to re-brand the range, which Turner evocatively renamed as Tigers 70, 80, and 90 respectively, nomenclature intended to hint at their speed potential. But the changes were interim. In 1937, Triumph announced a new 11-model range based around two types of frame, and a new, standardised, four-speed, foot-change gearbox. The three

---

Germany, they re-badged themselves as 'TWN' (Triumph Werke Nuremberg). TWN continued to manufacture motorcycles right up to 1957, after which they switched production to typewriters.

Tiger models were cosmetically looking sleeker than ever, graced as they were with high-level exhausts and new, contoured fuel tanks. The T70, T80 and T90 helped Triumph's production jump to 6,000 bikes a year and its finances go from broke in 1935 to a £7,000 profit in 1937.

Sangster transferred Hopwood to Coventry to accompany Turner as his design assistant, where he would carry out detail work on the Speed Twin. Hopwood, though, resented having to work up the mathematical elements of Turner's raw engineering concepts, which were frequently technically lacking (and would become more deficient still in the years to come). And, whilst Turner thought himself smarter than everyone, the less overtly arrogant Hopwood nevertheless considered himself smarter than Turner! Hopwood conceded, however, that Turner 'was an inventive genius and had a flair for pleasing shapes and an uncanny ability to "smell out" what the buying public would readily accept'. This was never truer than in the bike Turner himself called his 'masterpiece': the Speed Twin.

The Speed Twin was not Triumph's first parallel twin.

Amongst the bikes Val Page drafted when he left Ariel to join Triumph to develop a range of new engines, was the company's first 650cc twin, the model 6/1. Two years before Sangster appointed Turner to helm Triumph, Page had designed a twin-cylinder motorcycle specifically for sidecar duties. It evolved from an idea Page had hatched at Ariel, where he developed a 250cc parallel twin using one of the Square Four's dual crankshafts.

When Triumph introduced the model 6/1 in August 1933, most of its contemporaries were 500cc. Page's 650cc twin therefore stood out. It was also a more economical alternative to the 1,000cc fours and one litre V-twins of the time. The bike won several sidecar competitions, and a sleeved-down, supercharged version lapped Brooklands at over 105 miles per hour. Despite this, the 412 lbs model 6/1 was a commercial failure. Expensive to manufacture, and sporting hand-gear change (until its four-speed transmission gained a foot-shift mechanism in 1935), Triumph produced fewer than 500 units during the course of the 6/1's three-year production run. According to Bert Hopwood, however, the model's full potential was never realised. He felt its end was undeserved, and that Page's 6/1 actually owed its demise to Edward Turner's caprice.

Singles, though, remained Triumph's and its competitors' mainstay format. The overhead-valve single-piston engine was light, compact, simple, and inexpensive to produce. Yet, although Turner's revamp of the new Tiger range had been a great success, for Turner it was still much of the same old thing. During 1936 and '37, he worked on a replacement.

The result was a 500cc parallel twin, weighing just 353 lbs dry. Its engine copied the 360 degree firing order and side-by-side crankpins (with pistons rising and falling in unison), which Page had employed on the model 6/1. Disdaining the use of steel con-rods prevalent in nearly all car, motorcycle and even aircraft engines back then, the Speed Twin, also known as the 5T, used Hiduminium RR56, (the 'RR' indicating that it was forged to Rolls-Royce specification),[*] the same light alloy Ariel had used in the Square Four. Such measures resulted in a motor that was both lighter and slimmer than the single-cylinder Tiger 90 unit and therefore compact enough to fit into the T90's chassis (indeed, from the side, the 5T's engine looked like any twin-port single of the day). This 'modular concept' to manufacturing saved money. It also ensured that the Speed Twin, although innovative, did not look unconventional. It did, however, look attractive.

In an eleventh-hour move, probably intended to disguise the chassis' T90 origins and distract customers from the fact that the engine was the only aspect of the Speed Twin that was truly new, Turner took a bold decision: he eschewed Triumph's usual silver and black livery and had the whole bike painted a rusty plum colour, which Triumph dubbed Amaranth Red (after the poetic term for an imaginary flower that never fades). It was a colour that, up till then, the factory only applied to their De Luxe model tanks.

Launched at Earls Court in 1937, the Speed Twin cost £77 15s 0d (with a speedometer), a mere £5 more than its single-cylinder stablemate, the Tiger 90 (despite boasting twice as many valves, pistons, and connecting rods). Moreover, at 365 lbs fully laden, the 5T weighed 5 lbs less. The Speed Twin produced 26bhp, could top 90mph (*The Motor Cycle* recorded 93.75mph in their 1937 road test), and could achieve terminal speeds of 74mph at the end of a standing quarter mile.

The machine was an immediate success. With the Speed Twin, Turner had laid down the template for a long line of 360 degree vertical-twins. Its impact on the industry would not be matched until the launch of the Honda 750/4, some four decades later.

Hopwood Leaves Triumph

Hopwood eventually left Triumph in 1947 for spells at Norton and BSA. He returned to Norton in 1952; but, unhappy with the Board of Norton's then parent company, Associated Motor Cycles (AMC), he rejoined Turner at Meriden in 1961 to design the unit-construction 650cc twins - and in the expectation that he would succeed Turner as head of BSA/Triumph when Turner retired.[**]

---

[*]   Engineers preferred steel because it had calculable fatigue limits, unlike the softer, more ductile alloy which has no fatigue limit so was not trusted for reciprocating components. Alloy, however, conducts heat better and weighs less.

[**]   Triumph's Priory Street works - located just 200 yards from Coventry cathedral - were destroyed during the Luftwaffe's 400-plane bombing raid of the city on 14 November 1940. Although they were able to salvage some components and machine-tools, allowing them to continue production in a disused cement-mixer factory in Warwick and a few of the lesser damaged shops at Priory Street (which suffered further bombing in April 1941), the War Damage Commission considered rebuilding the factory on the Priory Street site would leave the factory vulnerable to further raids. Moreover, Coventry council had plans for the site as part of its post-war redevelopment of the city-centre. In May 1942, Triumph relocated to its new location some four miles outside the city on the main road between Birmingham and Coventry, in a field between the villages of Allesley and Meriden.

During Triumph's sojourn in Warwick, Turner - who had been noticeably upset at the bombings - left to join BSA following a long-running dispute with Sangster about royalties on all the patents Turner had helped create (he also disagreed with Sangster's keenness to keep the factory in Coventry). He returned to Triumph two years later as managing director, where he remained until his retirement in 1964.

3

HOPWOOD AND HELE

SECRETLY DEVELOP A THREE-CYLINDER SUPERBIKE TO REPLACE TURNER'S TWINS

'A 'potty' idea'
(Edward Turner's opinion of BSA/Triumph developing a three-cylinder engine)

Doug Hele

HELE AND HOPWOOD CONCEIVE A TRIPLE

Bert Hopwood, together with his fellow Brummy, Doug Hele, had conceived a three cylinder 750 as far back as 1961 while both were at Norton. Hopwood had been Hele's boss during Hopwood's time at Norton before the latter left to join Triumph. The two met occasionally of an evening to talk shop. It was at these get-togethers that they first mooted the concept of a large-capacity triple. Hele, however, knew Norton couldn't afford to develop the idea, so after the AMC Board decided to move production from Birmingham to Woolwich, just outside London, Hopwood was able to entice his former colleague - who didn't want to move south - to leave Bracebridge Street in October 1962 and join him at Meriden as Triumph's development engineer and race-shop chief and where together they could work on the triple.

When Hopwood presented Edward Turner with their idea, Turner dismissed the concept of a three-cylinder engine as 'potty'. As the Triumph chief did not give Hopwood a logical reason, he presumably feared it would be too expensive to manufacture or that Americans would not accept an engine with an odd number of cylinders. Yet thirteen years earlier, in early 1955, Turner had been similarly obdurate when he turned down proposals from the 21-year-old racer John Surtees and Norton race team manager, Joe Craig, urging Triumph to build a four-cylinder works bike to take on Geoff Duke and the Gilera four. Craig had pleaded for the most powerful figure in motorcycling at that time to 'Bet on the future, man'. Turner's objection back then was not that Meriden could not build a three- or four-cylinder engine - that was, in fact, no problem - but that they had no need to race, as Triumph was selling every bike they made.

In late 1963, after everyone in the factory had gone home,* Hopwood was in Hele's office where, for amusement, the two sketched out a basic outline of what a three-cylinder 750 engine might look like. Hopwood deemed the result 'very encouraging indeed' and although they filed the drawing away, aware of their Managing Director's dismissive opinion of a triple, Hele and Hopwood remained undeterred.

Even so, as taken as they were with the layout, the two were not sure how evenly a three-cylinder engine would run.

THE TRIPLE TAKES SHAPE

Only the year before, in response to Norton's American distributor, Joe Berliner's demands, Hele had led on the development of the company's 750cc twin-cylinder Atlas, a bike which in development its tester Fred Swift said delivered 'fantastic' performance, but vibrated so severely Hele was worried it had damaged Swift's hands. By the time Norton launched the Atlas in the States in 1962, Hele had had to dramatically detune the engine to quell its roughness. Hele, however, knew that a triple, with its crankpins spaced at 120 degree intervals, would offer perfect balance - yet remain barely wider than a twin. All the same, he harboured reservations after noting the irregular pulse of a three-pot Ford tractor at an agricultural show shortly before joining Triumph. Nor did Hopwood and Hele gain reassurance from discussions they instigated with a senior technician from the car maker, Rover, itself investigating a three-cylinder engine: he was simply unable to provide information on what levels of vibration the Meriden engineers might expect from such a power unit fitted to a motorcycle.

Hele therefore conferred with the distinguished consultant engineer Donald Bastow, who back in the Thirties had worked with W.O. Bentley, co-founder of the famous

---

* Hele felt there was more value from time spent discussing a design than could be gained from any formal written proposal. One night, Hele's wife grew so concerned at her husband's lateness that she phoned and asked the police to check in on him at his Bracebridge Street office. The investigating officer was unable to gain access to the Norton works, so had to throw pebbles at the one lit window to attract the occupants' attention - whereupon a reluctant Hele had to be persuaded to leave for home.

Bentley Motors Ltd. Both Hopwood and Hele had known Bastow from his days as head of research at BSA. Armed with Bastow's calculations for optimum size, weight and balance factors, in early 1963, Hele began secretly sketching a prototype unit and the triple's 120 degree crankshaft, at the same time as holding down his 'day job' developing the unit-construction 650s.

Senior Meriden designer Brian Jones translated Hele's concepts into detailed 'sharp pencil' drawings from which Meriden's Experimental Department could ask the Tool Room's precision engineers to work up into drawings that General Production could use to produce components (or buy them in from suppliers).

By 1964, the triple began to take shape. Using a modified six-cylinder automobile distributor, the project (codenamed P1) had its first cast-iron barrelled prototype engine running on the factory dynamometer within 12 months and installed in a stock '65 T120 chassis for road testing (chassis engineers had added 100lb in excess weight to a Bonneville to test its handling whilst Hopwood's team worked on the engine). Clothed in its Bonneville cycle parts, Hopwood claimed that the crudely constructed test bike (which, according to authors Brooke and Gaylin, 'looked like a proper Triumph and performed even better'), produced 58 horsepower and topped 120mph and could have gone into production that very year using BSA's existing machine tools.

In April of that year, Edward Turner retired. His health - he suffered from type II diabetes - and previously strong commercial instincts had begun to fail him. Although retiring as head of Triumph, he stayed on as a Board member with Triumph's parent company, the BSA Group, for a further three years.[*]

Hopwood - now Deputy Managing Director - officially unveiled the layout of the triple to Triumph's management, and Turner's successor, the recently appointed BSA Group Chief Executive, Harry Sturgeon.

Sturgeon had not been a universally popular choice. He did not have Turner's motorcycle background (he had been a senior executive at the De Havilland Aircraft Company, and latterly, Managing Director at the Churchill Grinding Machine Company from where, following the machine tool company's acquisition by BSA, he gained the positions of both Chief Executive and Marketing Director of the BSA and Triumph motorcycle divisions). He refused to move to Birmingham. When he did visit the company, he stayed in hotels. Otherwise, he remained ensconced at home on his Hertfordshire farm. Despite these reservations, and Hopwood's indignation at being passed over for the post he thought was more rightfully his (although many associates were not convinced of his managerial capabilities, including Turner who had sometimes been frustrated at Hopwood's passivity), the smartly attired Sturgeon was not an aloof man. Les Williams, later to find fame campaigning the Trident race bike known as

---

[*]   Turner stepped down in 1967 to form his own consultancy company, ET Developments, one product of which was the design for a DOHC 350 twin, which he sold to BSA. BSA would go on to develop his idea into the stillborn BSA Fury and Triumph Bandit. See chapter13, pages134-136.

'Slippery Sam', recalled from his days as a charge-hand in the Experimental Department that Sturgeon occasionally called in at eight in the morning to see how everything was.

Sturgeon was also something of a marketing genius, using attractive young men and women in a series of expensive adverts which pre-dated Honda's famous 'you meet the nicest people' campaigns. TriCor (Triumph Corporation originally) executive, Earl Miller, who met the BSA Group Chief Executive during Sturgeon and Turner's tour of Triumph's East and West Coast distributors in September 1964, thought that Sturgeon - who was now also the (absentee) president of America's east coast distributor, TriCor - was 'sales-orientated in a more vigorous way than Ed Turner.' Sturgeon subscribed to the maxim: 'race on Sunday, sell on Monday' - which was why the factory returned to Daytona.

Under Sturgeon's stewardship, Meriden's US sales rose from 6,300 in 1963 to 28,700 in 1967. Around 6,200 of that total were T120s going to the West Coast and 13,800 to the East (and this, in spite of the latter's short, 10-week April to mid-June sales season). Sturgeon responded by raising production and increasing Meriden's workforce to 2,200. In 1965, Triumph won its first Queen's Award for Export (helped in no small part by the company offering perhaps its most aesthetically prettiest range of twins yet). 1968-69 saw Meriden sales hit a peak, when the US took 24,407 motorcycles (compared to just 2,143 for Triumph's UK home market). Sturgeon would secure the group its second Queen's Award for Export in 1966. But his dependence on the US market (and the East Coast in particular), his chase for more sales, and his abhorrence of haggling, meant he too readily acceded to union wage demands (sometimes offering workers *more* than they demanded). It would set the pattern for ultimately fatal industrial relations.

Stung by rumours presented during a meeting of BSA Group's senior executives that Honda were working on a multi of their own, and anxious to kick off his appointment as Chief Executive with a marketable new model, Sturgeon was so taken with Hopwood's layouts for the triple that he green lit the project for development without even asking to see Brian Jones's technical drawings first - but only as a stop-gap model. (Reports of Honda's multi varied - it was either a 650 or 750cc four cylinder, with Honda themselves deliberately misleading rivals into thinking they were developing a 750 parallel twin. Rumours abounded, too, that Suzuki had a 750 triple of their own in the pipeline, albeit a two-stroke, and that BMW had still another 750 to follow - the R75/7 'boxer' twin.)

By 1966, engineers were testing a more production-based engine. Codenamed P2, the three prototypes - like the example of their T120-chassised P1 antecedent - still resembled three-cylinder Bonnevilles (so much so, in fact, that the experimental team's test rider, Percy Tait, racked up many miles aboard the P2 on the roads surrounding Meriden without any of the locals noticing his twin's surfeit of cylinders!). However, to combat heavy wear to the P1 engine's centre main bearings, and distortion to the cylinder head joint due to overheating, engineers replaced the original iron barrel with an alloy cylinder block to improve the P2 powerplant's cooling (and squared-off its finning to give the engine a narrower profile).

To prevent the rider's footrests from being spaced too widely apart, Hele reduced the engine's width by fitting a car-type single-plate diaphragm clutch instead of the more usual wet multi-plate unit. Further automotive influences included a car-type distributor and gear-driven primary transmission. Unfortunately, when Triumph demonstrated the prototype to the Metropolitan Police at MIRA's testing facility, the clatter and rattle from the drive's pinions and clutch so put off the prospective fleet buyer that Triumph were compelled to replace the P1's noisy primary gears with a triplex chain. For the P2, Hele also moved the oil pump to the primary drive case, and changed the engine's bore and stroke. The move from the P1's 63mm x 80mm (the same as Triumph's pre-unit 500 rather than the short stroke unit T100) to 67mm x 70mm, reflected Hopwood's modular design principles. Thus, the P2's more over square engine resembled a trio of C15s, BSA's 250cc single-cylinder motor, rather than a 'T100 and a half'.

Although barely wider than the 650 twin, the triple engine was around 40 lbs heavier and 15 per cent more powerful than a Bonneville, so Dunlop were invited to develop a new rear tyre specifically for the new model, the K81 series (also called the TT100 in honour of Malcolm Uphill's exploits on the Thruxton Bonneville in 1969).[*]

With BSA and Triumph organised around quite distinct and fiercely tribal dealer networks, especially in America, at the insistence of those dealers the Board's decision from the outset was to produce the bike in both BSA and Triumph guises - 'each demonstrably different.' The BSA A75 Rocket 3[**] would have transverse, 15 degrees from vertical, forward-inclined barrels (a nod to BSA's pre-war Sloper engine) and a timing side reminiscent of the 'power egg' shape of BSA's A65, the Triumph Trident T150, would have vertical pots and a timing side redolent of the Bonneville's 'heart-shaped' cases. However, far from rationalising production, the result was 16 main castings instead of just 8. So, whilst the engine and gearbox units were identical, the differences demanded that each bike had its own crankcase, gearbox and timing covers. Despite these brand-related styling licks for the engine, the BSA Group insisted on marking out the 750 triples as distinctly different from the 650 twins. Naturally, all those in Small Heath expected the new triple to emulate the lines of the A65, whilst everybody in Meriden involved in the project thought it would follow the contours honed by Turner and chief designer, Jack Wickes (the draughtsman often referred to as 'Edward Turner's pencil').

In the event, neither camp proved correct. The Meriden-based development team's expectations, however, were perhaps the more understandable.

In 1967, of the 33,406 British machines imported to the US, 24,700 of them were Triumphs (of which, over half were T120Rs). The figure was Triumph's best-ever total and represented about 60 per cent of the factory's total output for that year, a clear indication of the American market's importance to Meriden.

---

[*]   Triumph was so proud of the tyre that it provided the central strap line in magazine ads for the Trident that they ran in the US during 1969: 'So powerful we had to develop an entirely new concept in tires to carry it!'

[**]   The Rocket 3 had originally been christened the A75 Tri Star. However, Lockheed and Rolls-Royce had claimed that name for their triple-engined airliner. The 'Rocket' nomenclature had considerable currency with US motorcyclists due to BSA's popular Super Rocket and Rocket Gold Star models.

BSA Ask Ogle To Re-Style The Triples

However, the BSA board saw Turner's retirement as the opportunity for change. They ignored his advice to them following his visit to the Japanese factories in 1960 that consolidating product lines between the BSA Group's different brands meant customers would have no reason to choose one marque over the other. And despite the acclaim and success of Triumph's ageless styling, the Board saw how popular the very different-looking Japanese motorcycles evidently were with the motorcycle-buying public. They also realized how expensive it would be to fund two design teams. Moreover, they wanted to tap into the zeitgeist of the times, and Sixties' consumers' worship of *avant-garde* design. As a result, they went outside Small Heath and Meriden and commissioned a leading exponent of contemporary design to style BSA and Triumph versions of the triple (overlooking Meriden's long-standing resident stylist, Jack Wickes).[*]

The company, Ogle Design in Hertfordshire, whose credentials included 'the timeless Dualit toaster', had experience working with the British automobile industry (they had styled the Reliant Scimitar), but - fatefully, as it turned out - *not* motorcycles.

Toward the end of summer 1966, BSA supplied Ogle with a T120 rolling frame and Triumph-styled triple engine (less its internals) fitted with the test mule's Bonneville cycle parts, together with an A65 chassis and the essentials of the BSA inclined three-cylinder motor to work on.

~ ~ ~

At around the same time Ogle were sketching out their ideas for clothing the stripped-off Bonneville and A65 P2 prototypes, 6,000 miles away in Japan, at the world's largest motorcycle manufacturer, the man in charge of developing Honda's CB450 twin-cylinder 'Black Bomber' was considering reports he'd picked up on a trip to America that BSA and Triumph were set to launch a 750cc three-cylinder motorcycle.

---

[*]   Norton also enlisted an outside design agency to style their new flagship, the Commando. Launched at the Earls Court Show in September 1967 the Model 20 M3 was a stop-gap model that Norton rushed to market by upgrading its venerable 750cc Atlas engine (prototypes of their double-overhead cam, unit-construction 800cc P10 engine had been running for some years but were proving unpromising and its readiness for production was clearly some years off).

4

HONDA AND TRIUMPH

THE RACE TO LAUNCH THE FIRST 750 MULTI-CYLINDER SUPERBIKE

'Why make small when you can do big?'
(Message from US Honda dealers to Yoshirou Harada, the CB750/4 project leader)

Soichiro Honda

THE BLACK BOMBER

In 1966, Honda's sales in the US had begun to drop. As a result, Yoshirou Harada visited America the following summer to learn more about the US market and promote Honda's flagship, the CB450, the bike he had designed to satisfy dealers' demands for something bigger than Honda's phenomenally successful CB77 305cc 'Hawk'. Launched in 1965, the CB450 was Honda's largest capacity motorcycle prior to the arrival of the CB750. However, despite a CB450 holding the distinction of being wheeled off the production line by Soichiro Honda himself in January 1968, to mark his company's 10 millionth motorcycle, sales of the Black Bomber - dubbed so by a UK advertising agency because, like Henry Ford's Model T, it only came in black (although, in truth, its bodywork sported silver accents) - had been disappointing, and not just in the US. A Honda dealer in Leicester repainted some of his inventory of 450s red in an effort to shift them off his showroom floor. Changing the bike's livery, however, could not disguise the CB's styling or its ungainly 'tuna-shaped' fuel tank.

Yet, in spite of Harada detailing to staff at American Honda the 450's clear advantages over the British 650s - it was more powerful, more reliable and technically superior to its English and American competitors[*] (its short stroke engine boasted a five-speed transmission, an electric start, torsion-controlled valves and double-overhead camshafts; its twin 36-mm constant velocity carburettors were a first for a production bike; and it developed a claimed 43 horsepower and a top speed of 112mph[**]) - the US dealers kept asking Harada: 'Why make small when you can do big?'

Honda's own authorised history summarised what Harada's US visit had revealed: 'The majority of American riders, it seemed, did not judge motorcycles simply by how fast they could go. They also wanted responsive torque performance so that they could get the power they needed without downshifting.'

The American dealers' push for bigger motorcycles echoed that of the company's co-founder, Soichiro Honda. During a visit to Switzerland, Honda claimed that he had noticed how small a Triumph motorcycle appeared with a policeman on board. However, when the rider dismounted, Soichiro quickly realised that it wasn't the bike that was small but the European rider who was big.[***] Honda now understood that in spite of his company being the largest motorcycle manufacturer in the world, if the Honda Motorcycle Company was to grow, it must make bikes specifically designed to suit an international market rather than sell to those markets bikes made for Japan's smaller-sized customers.

SOICHIRO HONDA: RACER, METALLURGIST, MANUFACTURER

Soichiro Honda was born in Komyo Village (today called Tenryu City), in Iwata County on 17 November 1906. He was the eldest son of Gihei Honda, a bicycle repair man and blacksmith, and Mika, a weaver. In April 1922, Soichiro left elementary school aged just fifteen to start an apprenticeship at one of Tokyo's top automobile repair shops, Art Shokai. Under owner, Yuzo Sakakibara, the young Soichiro learned how to repair cars (and motorcycles), deal with customers, the importance of taking pride in your work, thinking for oneself, improvising solutions, and developing new ideas.

[*]   The FIM banned the CB450 from production racing because they considered its double-overhead camshafts 'too advanced'. They lifted the ban after they eventually accepted that it was indeed a genuine road bike.

[**]   In their August 1965 issue, *Cycle World* reported a maximum speed of 102mph for the CB450.

[***]   According to Honda's official history, Soichiro's trip to Switzerland took place in June 1968 and the Triumph in question was a Triumph 750cc. Honda's account appeared in the January 1969 issue of the company's newsletter (No. 124). However, the only 750 Triumph produced at that time was a homologation special for the US, and BSA/Triumph did not launch their 750 triples until September of '68. Moreover, according to Mick Duckworth's excellent book, *Honda CB750*, the project team had already settled on the Dream Four's 750cc capacity by February 1968.

In 1923, Sakakibara, his younger brother, Shin'ichi, and some of the apprentices, including Honda, began making racing cars. Their first car employed a second-hand Daimler engine. The Art Daimler was soon followed by another utilising the chassis of an American car, a Mitchell, into which they installed the engine from a Curtiss 'Jenny' A1 biplane. On 23 November 1924, the car won its first race with 17 year-old Soichiro, accompanying Shin'ichi Sakakibara, as engineer. The success led to Soichiro becoming a successful racing driver and builder.

In April 1928, aged just 21, Honda finished his apprenticeship and was given the distinction Sakakibara awarded to none of his other students, of opening a branch of Art Shoki in Hamamatsu. However, following a near-fatal car crash in 1936 at Tamagawa Speedway, and a growing dissatisfaction with repair work, Honda set up Tokai Seiki Heavy Industries in 1937. The company manufactured piston rings for Toyota and the Nakajima aircraft company.

In his endless pursuit of improving the product, he went back to school to study metallurgy. During the war, Honda - who was colour-blind and had been deemed unfit for military service when, aged 20, he was called up in the mid-1920s - produced aircraft propellers, but his factories were destroyed by bombing raids and earthquakes and he sold the company to Toyota. After considering manufacturing textile machinery, he chose instead to make bicycles, 500 of which he adapted and installed military-surplus engines. Two years later, and short of funds, Honda secured the financial backing of 38-year-old Takeo Fujisawa and together they founded the Honda Motor Company in September 1948. In August the following year, Honda became the first post-war Japanese manufacturer to produce both an engine and a frame. Called the D-type Dream (after someone at a party to celebrate the first prototype described the machine as a 'dream'), the 98cc single-cylinder two-stroke became a massive success, due in no small part to co-director Takeo Fujisawa's marketing acumen.

Honda operated a meritocracy, he encouraged innovation and free thinking in Japan's still post-feudalist society. The results were simply phenomenal: between 1961 and '63, Honda's exports grew from 50,000 to 338,000. By 1967, they had amassed 16 World Championships and 137 Grand Prix victories. At their peak, Honda was making more motorcycles per hour than Vincent produced in its entire 28-year history.

HONDA THINKS BIG

In February 1968, as Honda's sales recovered from the recession of 1966-67 (thanks largely to the Z50 Mini Trail and newly-launched CB350 twin), Soichiro appointed Yoshirou Harada to head up a project to build a 'big motorcycle'. Harada assembled a youthful team of about 20. His team included Masura Shirakura to oversee engine development, Toshio Nozue as frame designer, and Hitoshi Ikeda as chief stylist. Soichiro urged his engineers to think big, telling them: 'the bigger the better'. However, whilst Honda's message was emphatic, for Harada it was hopelessly vague.

At that time, the biggest displacement, large-scale production motorcycle manufactured in Japan was the twin-cylinder W650, a thinly disguised copy of the BSA A10 (originally manufactured by Meguro, then Kawasaki after the latter bought the factory).* At the outset of the project, the decision on engine capacity remained unclear. However, that did not prevent the team from setting themselves very clear targets for the new machine, the main objective for which was to manufacture a motorcycle that had 'superior output' but would make 'long-range, high-speed touring safer and more comfortable'.

To facilitate the collaborative process, the design engineers and production staff established some common goals, all of which were to incorporate the newly emerging science of ergonomics.

The bike had to remain stable at high speeds (140 to 169kph), yet be manoeuvrable in traffic. Its brakes must be reliable and capable of resisting 'high loads'. To reduce rider fatigue, Honda's engineers had to minimize engine vibration and noise and the designers were tasked to provide a comfortable riding position and easy-to-use and simple-to-learn controls. Lights and instruments were to be large and reliable. They had to be designed to help the rider make sound judgments and ensure they were easily visible to other vehicles. The team also had to extend the service life of each component and ensure the bike was easy to maintain. Finally, the design had to be original - yet still easy to mass produce using newer, better materials and production technologies (and it had to be particularly cutting edge in its use of surface-treatment technologies).

After capturing five consecutive World Grand Prix championship titles in 1966, Honda retired from racing the following year to concentrate on designing a new range of road bikes. Their years of campaigning meant the company could call on a wealth of knowledge accrued from developing sophisticated, multi-cylinder GP race-winning machines. But in developing their first large-capacity motorcycle, Honda were not only looking back to their past, they were also looking ahead. The team introduced computer systems - initially to streamline the various steps in the project bike's development. Eventually, however the system would help them achieve greater efficiency in planning modifications during the prototype stage. It also helped reduce the time taken in designing the production line for the manufacture of the bike.

After considering the merits and demerits of various configurations, including V, horizontally-opposed, and parallel-twin layouts, the decision to proceed with a four cylinder in-line engine reportedly followed a meeting Soichiro Honda had with the head of Honda's Californian office, Bob Hansen, in early 1968.**

---

*   The W650, however, was not the largest-capacity motorcycle ever made in Japan up to that time. Until 1958, Rikuo Harley made a 750 and 1,200cc under licence, which continued to sell into the '60s.

**   Four-cylinder motorcycles were not new. In North America, Henderson manufactured a longitudinal four as far back as 1912, with Ace following suit in the Twenties, and Indian doing likewise from 1927, through the Thirties and on into the early 1940s. Companies such as Cleveland, Gerhart and Militaire also marketed longitudinal fours. Over on the other side of the Atlantic, Brough Superior experimented with a 'stacked' flat-four whereby cylinders are paired one above the other on opposing sides of the engine, and Matchless a V-four, Vauxhall and Wilkinson produced inline fours, as did FN across the English Channel and Nimbus in Denmark (whose longitudinal four was in production from 1920 until the 1950s, but with few going abroad). But

Hansen and three other regional managers had been invited by Honda to visit the Japanese factory. After a tour of the plant, the delegation was told that Soichiro was having his English lesson and would be late. Their guide therefore took them to see the research and development department, but not the test area as that was where they were developing the new engine. When Hansen eventually met with Honda, the conversation turned to the new bike. Bob, a plain speaking man who was perhaps bristling a little at not getting to see the rumoured 750 twin, turned to Honda who was sat next to him and responded to the great man's declaration that they were going to build the 'King of Motorcycles.' 'That's good,' said Hansen. 'I hope it's not a twin.' Honda was puzzled. He asked why Bob would say that, and Hansen - mindful of the company's successful GP-winning multis - told him that it 'had to be a four, not just another twin'. BSA/ Triumph, he explained, were set to launch a triple very soon. The very least Honda could do, urged Hansen, was to go with a bike that had three cylinders, preferably four. Project leader Harada later wrote to Hansen acknowledging Bob's influence on Honda's decision in February of '68 to go ahead with a four cylinder.*

The first prototype was a four-cylinder 650 based on two CB350s. They also tried doubling up Harada's double-overhead cam CB450, but found twin-overhead cams made the engine too large. Harada therefore elected to begin with a single-overhead camshaft design with a view to upgrading to a DOHC layout in about three years' time. (The news that BSA/Triumph were developing a 750cc multi also settled the question of the Honda's capacity.) Harada's eventual choice of SOHC layout would be the basis of both the CB750's phenomenal success and its eventual usurpation. The engine proved so successful, that it wasn't three, but ten years before Honda introduced the DOHC engine, by which time several pretenders to its crown would emerge.

Testing took place at the Arakawa circuit near Tokyo and at the Saitama factory. Pictures of that first prototype appeared in a Japanese magazine in 1968 and show what looks like the SOHC engine fitted in a CB450 chassis.

---

probably the era's most enduring and successful four was Turner's Ariel Square Four, which was revived as the 1,000cc Healey in the 1970s.

Honda themselves had produced a series of four-cylinder motorcycles, but for racing, not road use. In August 1959, at Japan's Asama racetrack, Honda debuted its 250cc double-overhead camshaft, sixteen valve four-cylinder RC160 racer. It won on its first outing and went on to help Honda secure their first world championship in 1961. In 1966, Honda introduced the 85bhp Honda RC181, an evil-handling 500cc four-cylinder GP racer, which took that year's manufacturer's championship for its class.

* According to Honda's official history, Honda had determined the new power plant's specification by October 1967. 750cc, to match Triumph's rumoured three-cylinder 750; and a maximum output of 67bhp (one more than the 66 horsepower of Harley-Davidson's 1,300cc engine), with Harada appointed to head the project in February 1968. Mick Duckworth reports in his book, *Honda CB750*, that Bob Hansen visited the factory and spoke to Soichiro Honda 'in early 1968' and that the project team's 'decision to go ahead with an in-line four-cylinder design came in February 1968', which suggests that the decision on the engine's number of cylinders - if not its displacement - was made very close to the project's inception. Indeed, Honda's own official history says the development team's code name for the CB750 was *Nanahan* - Japanese for 750 (a term later popularised in magazines to represent a category of large displacement motorcycles).

Road Testing The Ogle-Styled Triples In America

Back in England, Ogle Design had completed drawings and mock ups of their makeover of the BSA/Triumph triples. Head of the company, Tom Karen, had assigned keen motorcyclist Jim English (owner and rider of a Triumph Trophy) to Ogle's first motorcycle project. English told author Mick Duckworth in an interview thirty years later for the journalist's definitive history of the triples that when, in summer 1966, Karen took him to the back of a workshop and removed the covers off a P2 prototype at Ogle's office in Letchworth, the designer, who had joined the company the previous year after training in vehicle design with automobile manufacturer Ford, was excited. English saw what at first glance looked like a Triumph Bonneville. Then he noticed that the bike had three exhausts. It was clear to him that this 'must be something a bit special'. Karen informed English that this was Ogle's next project. English was to work alongside a specialist in industrial design, Australian, Byron Fitzpatrick.

BSA's brief to Ogle indicated that they were after 'a very flashy American look, like a Cadillac car' English's own preference was the aesthetics of the Café racer, a look very popular with. British motorcyclists at that time. Nevertheless, as English would recall many years later, he and Fitzpatrick were really to let their hair down 'doing futuristic stuff', out of which would emerge the triples' signature feature: the silencers. Despite their later notoriety, when English presented early renderings of his ideas to the BSA committee, the triple-piped end pieces to the silencers proved the element they liked most. And although English never actually thought BSA would put his design into production, it did meet Doug Hele's brief that their volume should be big enough to install reverse-flow internals to mute the triple's characteristic howl. Both the BSA and Triumph triples would share the ray-gun silencers (as they were later dubbed); and the angular shapes of the fuel tank, seat and side panels - which echoed the Sixties idea of ultra modernity, Ogle's trademark boxy style, and picked up on Hopwood and Hele's squared-off engine finning. And Fitzpatrick brought to bear his knowledge of ergonomics for household appliances to the machine's ancillaries. He designed push-button, handlebar-mounted horn and lighting controls (set into the front brake and clutch lever housings), and direction indicators comprising a single pair of winkers visible from both the front and rear (mounted each side of the headlamp).

Ogle Design's sister company, Ogle Models, completed mock ups by March 1967. Triumph's Chief Development Engineer, Doug Hele, was horrified at what he saw (especially the Trident's square tank). BSA's Assistant Export Manager, Peter Glover, whose job it would be to sell the Rocket 3, was called to Meriden to choose the best of three designs hanging on the walls of Bert Hopwood's office. Not finding any of them to his liking, he selected the one he 'disliked least'. Don Brown, BSA's East Coast Vice President, was also a vocal critic of Ogle's designs (he took particular exception to the Ray-gun exhausts, which reminded him of the 1959 Cadillac owned by Triumph's West Coast distributor, Johnson Motors' titular head, Bill Johnson). Yet the older Ted

Hodgson, a senior BSA executive based in New Jersey, liked them (they reminded him of the pre-war BSA Sloper's 'fishtail' silencers).

In October that year, Doug Hele and his mechanics (Alan Barrett from Triumph and BSA senior engineer, Clive Bennett, and Graham Saunders from Small Heath's Experimental Department) shipped two Tridents and two Rocket 3s to the home of Triumph's Western US distributor, Johnson Motor's vice president, E.W. 'Pete' Colman in Claremont, California for secret testing. Using Colman's home as a base, Johnson Motor's (JoMo) technicians racked up 2,000 miles on the triples on twisty mountain roads and the scorching desert highways around Palm Springs, San Bernardino and Mexico, with Rod Coates and Ed Nemec of the East Coast distributors, TriCor, flying out of Baltimore to join them. Factory racers Gary Nixon and Gene Romero carried out speed tests at the Orange County Raceway drag strip outside Los Angeles. Key US Triumph and BSA sales staff also got to view the prototypes. The tests highlighted various issues, mainly electrical. However, whilst the Americans praised the triples' handling, speed, and smoothness, according to Hele, they did not like their 'bizarre styling'. Be that as it may, whichever components might have to change as a result of the Stateside findings, the tank and silencers could not be amongst them.

All the same, manufacturing requirements and the results from testing meant that not all of Ogle's designs made it to production (such as Fitzpatrick's handlebar switches, rejected in favour of Lucas items, which, though antiquated, came with the requisite federal clearances for use in the US; the air scoops on the oil cooler, which testing showed were inefficient; and detailing such as the BSA tank badges, the grab rail and some softening of the edges to the flat-sided side panels). However, not everybody agreed with the changes to Ogle's design.

Triumph draughtsman Brian Jones told author Mick Duckworth that he thought diluting Ogle's designs 'seemed a bit unfair'. Jones felt that making a break from BSA and Triumph's traditional styling made sense, given that Japanese designs were threatening to make British motorcycles look as archaic as the plants in which they were made (precisely how archaic was being amply demonstrated half a world away).

CB750 PRODUCTION HITS A PROBLEM

By 1969, Honda had selected the Saitama Factory (today known as the Wako Plant) to produce the CB750 Four's engine and the Hamamatsu Factory to manufacture the body. Because Honda considered the CB750 strategically important to its plans to increase sales of other models in the US market, Honda America sent two engineers to join the staff at the Saitama Factory to test and check 300 items from a US rider's point of view. Honda's ambitions for the American market, however, were not new.

American Honda Motor Corp's sales manager, Hirobumi Nakamura, shocked Triumph's West Coast distributor's Bill Johnson early in the decade when the JoMo boss invited Nakamura to a meeting with him and Don Brown, Pete Colman and Johnson's business partner, Wilbur Ceder, to discuss Honda's sales targets for the US. At that time,

Triumph's distributor was selling between 2,000 and 2,500 new motorcycles a year across its Western Territory of 19 US states. Johnson therefore considered Nakumura's figure of 5,000 - which Johnson described as 'a lot of motorcycles' - unfeasibly high. Nakamura flabbergasted the American, however, when he clarified that this was 5,000 new motorcycles a *month*, not a *year*.

Honda, though, was much less certain about forecasting the CB750's sales. As a result, and to keep investment to a minimum, each plant utilised production facilities currently lying idle, overhauling and modifying them to build the CB750.

At the ultra-modern Saitama Factory near Tokyo, where Honda elected to produce the Dream Four's engine, staff were wrestling with the myriad challenges posed by manufacturing components for a powerplant quite unlike anything they had produced before.

Honda's previous models used a split-type, press-fit crankshaft with needle bearings. However, the CB750's four-cylinder engine employed an integrated crankshaft and metal bearings. Moreover, it wasn't just a question of identifying the machining equipment they required. The team also had to decide on what assembly line configuration was right for manufacturing parts for which they had no experience making. They visited automobile manufacturers to acquire the knowledge they needed to plan the line. All the same, things began badly and efficiency was poor. Against initial production forecasts of 25 units a day, Honda were at first achieving daily volumes of just five (and less).

Things were also not going well in the English Midlands.

PRODUCTION OF THE TRIPLE BEGINS

As part of BSA Group Chief Executive Harry Sturgeon's strategy to maximise efficiency, Meriden was to concentrate on producing its twin-cylinder range, particularly Triumph's cash cow, the 650cc Bonneville (the plant was at full stretch anyhow trying to meet the massive overseas demand for its twins). Anything else the Group produced that wasn't a Triumph twin, BSA was to manufacture at Small Heath (where, unlike Meriden which relied heavily on outside suppliers for plating and pressing, the Armoury Road plant could produce almost every metal component on a motorcycle).* However, nearly a fifth of BSA's plant was up to 20 years old. According to Alistair Cave, the general manager in charge of production: 'Some of the machinery to be used for three-cylinder production was the same as had been used to make the M-series BSA side-valve singles and C-series lightweights back in the Fifties.'

Also, despite the Board's clear edicts at management meetings that the triple was a stop-gap model so production costs were to be kept to a minimum, their decision to produce two engine variants caused Cave headaches. Inclining the cylinder head for the Rocket 3 engine meant the company had to furnish the foundry with two sets of patterns.

---

* Meriden would make some engine components that were common to both the A75 and the T150, such as camshafts (for which the factory bought modern cam-grinders), cam follower tappets, and cylinder heads and barrels which came in as raw castings from outside foundries for Meriden to machine; both Meriden and Small Heath made gearbox components.

It also doubled the number of machining operations the large and complex gravity and die-cast aluminium alloy castings required (the crankcases and covers were supplied by outside contractors). The centre section of the crankcase shells alone needed 56 individual machining operations and 48 jigs, settings for which had then to be changed when the machinists switched from milling, drilling, reaming and tapping the A75 castings to swop over to T150 cases. It all added to time and costs.

Cave also lamented the company's continued adherence to vertically split crankcases, which he and senior engineering and design staff had wanted to abandon for pressure die-cast horizontally-split cases as used by the Japanese. This would have simplified production and helped make engines oil-tight. Unfortunately, the Board over-ruled them, insisting they persist with antique designs based on the capstan lathe machining techniques used to produce the single-cylinder engines from motor-cycling's earliest days.

Production processes were equally antique. Bob Heath, the racer and visor manufacturer, told *Classic Bike* magazine that when he worked on the Rocket 3 assembly line at the BSA factory, 'One of my jobs was to rub the splines in the primary drive shock absorber chainwheel with a carborundum stone, by hand. It had to be done because the splines were slightly undersize, and wouldn't fit on the clutch shafts. It was a boring job, but if I could do four a day, they could finish four more engines.'

Production of the triples began on 23 August 1968, after staff had returned to work following the plant's summer closedown. To begin with, BSA set Armoury Road a modest target of 50 units a week, building up to 150 units (which would comprise both BSA and Triumph variants). Meanwhile at Meriden, already working flat out trying to meet demand for its twins, a track was laid to assemble twenty-five Tridents a day. As Cave and his team prepared for production of the triple during the spring, the BSA Group's development centre in Umberslade Hall instigated a switch from the traditional British thread sizes to the American Unified system being adopted by the UK automotive industry. The move was intended to reduce costs. Instead, it caused disruption and simply added to Cave's problems as taps, dies and thread gauges had to all be changed and assembly line staff spent time sorting out the correct fastener from amongst an array of similar looking but different thread forms.

UMBERSLADE HALL

BSA Group's research and design base (or Group Engineering Centre as it was officially known) was situated in a large, brick- and limestone-built country house in Hockley Heath near Solihull. Established by Lionel Jofeh at the suggestion of private consultants McKinsey, staff could peer through its leaded glass windows to see peacocks roaming the grounds and gardens. Jofeh had been appointed Managing Director in February 1967 following Harry Sturgeon's departure due to ill health (he would pass away of a brain tumour just two months later). Jofeh joined BSA from Sperry Gyroscope's aerospace division. Like his brainchild, Umberslade Hall, he was remote from most of the staff in Small Heath (which he thought a 'muck heap') and Meriden where he was rarely seen (no doubt shocked at the plant's primitive facilities, especially if compared to what he was used to in the aerospace industry).

The R&D centre was a move to bring modern industrial practices to the BSA Group. However, Umberslade proved ruinously expensive (it cost the BSA Group around £1.5 million a year). Its technicians were non-motorcyclists who worked at a leisurely pace - wags called it 'Slumberglades' - producing ideas that paid scant attention to production requirements or customer needs. Although such a facility was an idea Bert Hopwood had wanted to introduce at each of the marques with whom he'd worked, he and his chief engineering assistant, Hele, never actually moved there (Hopwood thought the rooms too dark for draughting, and he missed the noise and din of the factory, which he felt were a useful reminder of where his designs would become reality).

BSA INVEST IN PLANT FOR THE TRIPLE

Manufacturing Hele's 120 degree throw crankshaft - the biggest BSA had ever dealt with - set the man in charge of production, Alistair Cave, challenges of its own. A one-piece forging, the crankshaft emerged from the drop forge with the three crankpins on a single plane. Following some machining, the crank was then heated up and twisted 60 degrees at a time, a practice which considerably reduced the number of machining operations. As ingenious, unorthodox, and time consuming as the process was, the finished crankshaft proved tremendously strong - if expensive. BSA had to buy a German-made grinding machine at a cost of £80,000 (around half-a-million pounds at post-millenium prices) to eliminate variations in web thickness encountered in early production.

Each of the 150 triple engines BSA were producing at their Armoury Road factory every working week was run briefly on a static test rig, oil was flushed through, drained, and the oil filters replaced. In addition, they checked one in every twenty engine's output on a dynometer. Later, when production at Armoury Road was fully up and running, the plant selected completed machines at random and took them to the MIRA (the Motor Industry Research Association) testing facility near Nuneaton for comprehensive testing. Triumph had similar arrangements for monitoring the performance of the 200 to 250 Trident powerplants Armoury Road trucked the 12 miles to Meriden for installation in the chassis. Yet, despite the factories' checking and testing, the early Rocket 3s and Tridents were to be blighted by a catalogue of manufacturing faults that only became apparent after the bikes were in the hands of the press or had left the showroom.

In contrast to producing the engine, manufacturing the triples' chassis and cycle parts proved straightforward (if needlessly inefficient and expensive).

Each plant made its own frame following its own processes and traditions. BSA MIG-welded the Rocket 3's chassis from steel tube just as it did for their 500 and 650 twins. Meriden, on the other hand, stuck with hearth brazing forged lugs and lengths of A-grade mild steel tube pre-shaped by Reynolds Tubes of Birmingham (because Meriden didn't have the equipment to bend them themselves), which, as with Triumph's twins, they would make up into front and rear frame sections that bolted together.

Production of the Ogle-designed fuel tanks that Doug Hele hated so much was carried out by the BSA Group's usual supplier, the Homer Company of Birmingham, whilst the Armoury Road plant manufactured the triples' ray-gun silencers using a 600 ton flat-bed press purchased specifically for the task. With its seamed joins along the top and bottom, Ogle's design was actually easier to produce than the traditional cigar-shaped mufflers whose joins required considerable polishing to produce a seamless finish before passing to Small Heath's in-house chromium plating shop. The finished silencer's large surface area was, however, susceptible to showing up the slightest knock, and its weight, coupled with problems manufacturing the manifolds accurately, made it difficult and fiddly to handle on the assembly line.

BSA/Triumph Unveil Their 750 Superbikes

Rumours of a BSA/Triumph triple had been circulating in the press for some time, but, in early 1968, the US magazine *Cycle* found evidence of their development in the most unlikely of places. They were testing a BSA 650 twin and found it had *three* holes in the holder for its *two* condensers. For the magazine there could be only one 'possible explanation'. The surplus hole was evidence that Lucas already had hardware in production for a three-cylinder motorcycle and that the two-wheeler itself could not be far behind.

In September 1968, the BSA/Triumph combine ended the years of speculation when they officially revealed the BSA Rocket 3 and Triumph Trident. Small Heath and Meriden had beaten the world's largest motorcycle manufacturer to the market with a multi-cylinder 750. As the American magazine *Cycle World* said in their first road test of the Trident in its October issue: '... there isn't another bike like it'.

Six thousand miles away, the Dream Four's project team had just weeks to finalise the 'King of Motorcycles' before its debut at Tokyo's Motorcycle Show on 25 October... and Harada still hadn't secured Soichiro Honda's sign-off of a key (and what would prove signature) component of the bike's specification.

5

THE HONDA CB750 STEALS THE SHOW

BUT BSA/TRIUMPH HIT THE MARKET FIRST!

'We aren't sure we can meet the completion target'
(CB750/4 project leader Yoshirou Harada to Soichiro Honda)

Don Brown

THE TRIDENT ENGINE MAKES FOR A 'STIRRING SIGHT'

Production of the A75 and T150 triples began in late August 1968, after line workers had returned from holiday following the factories' summer closedown. As had been planned from the outset, the first bikes to roll off the line were reserved for export. The domestic market would have to wait until April 1969 before British dealers would receive supplies of the new model (and even then, numbers would be limited).

As a result, and in recognition of Triumph's most important market, the US, Meriden gave the American motorcycle magazines the honour of the 'World's First Test' of the Trident.

The Californian-based *Cycle World* and its New York-based rival *Cycle* held between them the largest circulation of the US's half dozen monthly motorcycle magazines. Three-quarters of buyers of bikes over 500cc bought either *Cycle World* or *Cycle* (whose circulation was around 450,000).

Established by anglophile, Joe Parkhurst in 1962, *Cycle World* ran the Trident as their cover story for their October issue.* The as-delivered test bike managed a none too shabby 13.71 second standing quarter mile (a stock T120 Bonneville ran quarters at around 14.6). The magazine, however, went on to better that time by nearly three-quarters of a second after factory engineers corrected the centre cylinder's timing, which had been set up poorly in the manufacturer's rush to give *Cycle World* the exclusive. With AHRA 'pro' drag record holder, Bob Ebeling, now riding the bike, the Trident 'set a shattering time' of 13.028 over the quarter, breaking through the 100mph barrier to reach a terminal speed of 102.73mph. (This bettered a T120 Bonneville by nearly a second and a half.)

The magazine felt the bike's unique engine configuration made for a 'stirring sight' and deemed the Triumph something of a 'showstopper'. Testers also observed that the exhaust note singled out the triple as 'the most exciting motorcycle to be heard today'. They were less fulsome on the system's appearance, however (described in BSA Incorporated's press release as 'the futuristic Tri-Pak muffler'). The report noted that it had blued at the junctions where the centre cylinder's headers join the outer exhaust down pipes. They also suggested Triumph should replace the siamesed system with three separate exhausts, which *Cycle World* thought would not only be a more efficient system, but would look 'sharper', too. But testers heaped particular scorn on each silencer's 'three little outlets', which they thought more suitable to a scooter!

Whilst the magazine praised the front-brake actuated rear stop light, they deemed the single leading shoe rear brake inadequate to its task. The test bike also proved incontinent, leaking oil from both the cylinder head and its vertically-split crankcases. The test was also critical of the cheapness of some items on a vehicle costing over $1,750 - such as the rubber bands the factory used to attach the handlebar switches. (On the west coast, the Trident cost $1,765, on the east coast it cost $1,750 - nearly a third more than a BSA 650 Lightning, making the triple one of the year's most expensive motorcycles.)

Cycle World also lamented the fact that whilst the triple's engine and running gear were 'unmistakably Triumph', they questioned why the factory hadn't made the Trident look like a Triumph.** And, although they acknowledged that such a heavy bike could never match the agility of Triumph's 500 and 650cc twins, they judged the triple 'a keen machine' at long distances, capable of delivering 'effortless' highway cruising. *Cycle World* concluded their report by summing up the triple as 'a big, fast, groundshaker of a motorcycle. And [that] there isn't another bike like it.'

---

* For its inaugural issue, Joe Parkhurst revealed his predilection for British motorcycles when he selected a Triumph Bonneville for *Cycle World*'s very first road test.

** The press release BSA Inc. issued in October 1968 for the US launch described the Rocket 3 as having 'unprecedented beauty' and that the triple's 'sleek styling... provides less wind drag and easier handling'.

As testers and riders were sampling BSA and Triumph's new triples, now rolling off the Meriden and Armoury Road production lines at an initially modest rate of 50 units a week (climbing later to 150 units), with just weeks to go before Honda planned the launch of its CB750 at the 1968 Tokyo Motor Show in October, a key component of the Dream Four's specification had still to be cleared by Soichiro Honda: its brakes.

Mr Honda, Disc Or Drum?

Bob Hansen recalled that several years earlier, during testing of the CB72, Yoshirou Harada had asked to see the hydraulic brakes the pioneering engineer and racer Al Gunter had developed for his single-cylinder BSAs. Gunter had adapted these from the Hurst Airhart units which constructors fitted to the midget race cars US drivers raced at oval tracks. After coming across a set of after-market disc brakes in a motorcycle accessory outlet during his visit to America, Harada - having satisfied himself of their effectiveness following tests on the CB450 - visited the company who had developed and manufactured the brakes, Lockhart. Harada was convinced that the new model they were developing offered the perfect platform for disc brakes. After consulting with Lockhart's technicians, Harada departed with a batch of their products.*

With the fifteenth Tokyo Motor Show fast approaching and the specification for the CB750's brakes still undecided, Harada brought two different set ups to Soichiro Honda and asked him for his advice. Harada knew that Honda could be brusque and irascible. The great man favoured practical experience over academic qualifications, and was known to show his irritation with employees by flinging tools around or even clouting his technicians. For example, although much of Honda and Fujisawa's attention at the time was being taken up with developing the Honda 1300 car, a problematic project that tested even their strong relationship, Honda had made sure to check in periodically to find out how the Dream Four was coming along - one time with painful results. He'd asked a technician to demonstrate on an early prototype how easy it would be for an owner to replace the engine's oil filter, which at that point was located behind the clutch cover. Honda was furious to see that the filter was contaminated with grease so struck the hapless engineer across the head! Takeo Fujisawa described his business partner as '... a great person playing a leading role, so those of us who played supporting roles had to build a great theatre that would suit the leading actor'.

'We've designed two separate specifications,' Harada told Honda. 'One uses conventional drum brakes and the other [has] disc brakes. Of the two, the disc-brake specification [has] only recently been developed, so it will need more tests. If disc brakes are adopted, we aren't sure we can meet next spring's completion target.'

Mr. Honda's response was unequivocal: 'Well, of course we'll have to go with disc brakes.'

Despite approaching Lockhart to commission the US company to manufacture the brakes, in the end Honda elected to develop its own system alongside the Japanese

---

* Some accounts cite the company Honda consulted as Hurst Airheart. I have relied on Honda's own official history which states that the company Harada visited and consulted, and whose products he took away with him, was Lockhart.

hydraulics specialist Tokiko. However, testing with front and rear drum brakes continued right up to the CB750's unveiling at the Tokyo Motor Show.

In what was a first for a Honda road bike, chassis designer Toshio Nozue housed the CB750's powerplant in a double cradle frame. The CB250 and 305 had their twin-cylinder engines hung beneath pressed-steel spinal members, and the CB450 cradled its engine using a single front downtube arrangement. The CB750 employed twin downtubes wrapped under and around the Four's large engine cases, in a layout which followed the pattern set by the Northern-Irish McCandless brothers' Norton Featherbed frame of the late Forties and early Fifties.

Even if the 750/4's suspension was conventional - Showa rear shock absorbers (made under licence to a de Carbon design), and telescopic front forks comprising internal springs, polished alloy lower sliders, and flexible rubber gaiters - the bike still managed to break new ground in other areas.

Whereas Honda's early twins had the speedometer mounted in the headlamp shell (and the CB450, its tachometer also), the CB750 had separate clocks. These were green-faced, with plastic lenses and angled at 45 degrees to lend them a more purposeful stance and make them easier for the rider to read. Instruments were back-lit - the first production bike to incorporate this now standard feature. It was a small but telling example of the thought the project team put into delivering on their objective: to manufacture a motorcycle that would make 'long-range, high-speed touring safer and more comfortable'.

This focus on functionality went beyond the Dream Four's ergonomics. It extended to its aesthetics too, as the project team's designer, Hitoshi Ikeda's philosophy was that a vehicle's styling must complement its function. And, unlike the BSA Board's directive to Ogle to distance their flagships' styling from its corporate past and stablemates, Ikeda wanted very much to pay homage to the company's Grand Prix-winning antecedents. He focused, too, on 'an image of an ideal motorcycle as an American rider might envisage it.'

Hitoshi paid particular attention to the Four's fuel tank and exhaust system. As he explained: 'If a motorcycle's engine is on view, it needs to be imposing. One way of helping achieve this is to design a fuel tank that is slim and does not overshadow the engine.'

US dealer, Bob Hansen told Soichiro Honda that whilst a four-into-one exhaust system would probably be quieter and more efficient, for 'maximum sales appeal it needed to have four mufflers (silencers).' Ikeda investigated employing rolled-tube silencers, but, like Meriden, the team eventually opted for two-piece pressed-steel sheets, which were easier to form into complex curves and keep the four-pipe arrangement compact. Downpipes were double-skinned to prevent discoloration (known as 'bluing').

As late as August 1968, Honda continued to lay down a smokescreen ahead of the Dream Four's debut. During a visit to South Africa, Kiyoshi Kawashima, Honda's managing director, revealed that Honda was 'developing a 750cc twin' for America's big bike market. Only six weeks before Honda unveiled the Four at the Tokyo Show, *Motor*

Cycle, a UK weekly, reported that the Japanese company was developing a twin-cylinder 750cc. A few weeks later, and just one week before the show was to open, spy-shots of the Four appeared in motorcycle magazines across the world. Fuzzy as they were, the photographs clearly showed a large across-the-frame four-cylinder motorcycle sporting a quad of black exhaust headers exiting into two separate rolled-tube megaphone silencers, also finished in black, on the bike's left and right flanks. The machine had drum brakes front and back, and wore a fuel tank with chromed panels and rubber knee grips, to which the rider had strapped test equipment. The accompanying narratives confirmed the machine's capacity as 750; most estimated 80bhp, and some said it had the gear-driven primary drive of Honda's GP race-winning multis.

On 16 October 1968, the UK's *Motor Cycle News* announced the Honda 750/4's arrival, which they expected 'to be on sale in early 1969'. One week later, on 25 October 1968, the CB750 made its debut at the fifteenth Tokyo Motor Show. Honda's stand was dominated by a Candy Blue and Gold Dream Four (a finish developed in the US using a metallic gold or silver base coat beneath a translucent tinted lacquer). The pre-production model was mounted on a revolving turntable alongside a display engine.

Honda also provided the media with a press release of the bike's finalised specification, citing amongst the Dream Four's key attractions its 'specially developed tyres [offering] sound roadholding without shimmy or patter'; a 'Disc front brake - for strong and reliable braking, yet with feel at the lever.' Top of the list, however, was the new bike's engine: 'Four cylinders, four carburettors, four silencers - to provide outstanding performance with rapid acceleration for quick take-offs and overtaking while controlling noise output'.

Although back then the Tokyo Motor Show was aimed more at Japan's domestic market than the international platform it became later, the UK's *Motor Cycle News* nevertheless covered the Dream Four's debut in its 30 October issue.

Two months later, in January 1969, Soichiro Honda himself unveiled four examples of the Dream Four at a dealer convention held in Las Vegas to celebrate both Honda's first decade in North America and sales of a million motorcycles there.[*] That same month, the CB750 made the cover of the January issue of *Cycle World*.

On Saturday 8 February, the CB750 made its first public appearance on European shores after Honda Motor Imports of Eindhoven two days earlier flew a pre-production machine from America to Holland. On that Thursday, Honda had given Dutch dealers a preview - with strict instructions not to start up the Four's engine. Publicity photos of the bike being ridden (by Honda importer's manager, Rins de Groot) were shot with the bike coasting in neutral.

A few days later, the BBC featured the Four - alongside the Munch Mammut and other large-capacity two-wheelers - on its TV motoring show *Wheelbase*. Filmed in Hampshire on Lord Montagu's Beaulieu estate, former road racer and Honda UK service

---

[*]   In Colorado, Steve Shaw of the Sand Cast Only Club has identified the four exhibition bikes as what he calls 'late-pre-production' machines. Wearing engine numbers 2110 to 2113, the bikes featured non-production items, such as a different-shaped alternator to the model later sold to the public. Other differences included a flatter seat, fork mounting stays for the front mudguard, indicator lenses and the front brake's hydraulic pipe work.

chief, Alf Briggs, performed 'spectacular' tyre-spinning getaways on what was possibly the very same bike the Dutch were prohibited from starting!*

The following month, Honda France invited the French motorcycle press to view the CB750 on show at the prestigious *Pré de Catalan* restaurant in the Parisian district of Bois de Boulougne. The road show then crossed the Channel.

Shortly before the CB750 made its UK public debut, Honda arranged a press preview at its London HQ, hoisting 'the massive machine', as *Motorcycle Sport* described the Honda, to an upper-floor room where Honda's advertising manager, David Palmer, his assistant Ian Catford, and Arthur Carter from Honda's service department, briefed journalists on the Four's finer details. Honda also organised a junket for the press at London's Charing Cross Hotel where journalists from the monthlies could have details and photos in advance of the bike's unveiling at the Brighton Motor Show during the forthcoming Bank Holiday weekend.

Just a few days before the show opened, at the Brands Hatch race track in Kent, *Motor Cycle News* magazine's sports editor, Mick Woollett, became the first UK journalist to ride the new Honda. Acutely aware of the display model's value, Woollett admitted that he rode the Four very 'gingerly'. He was therefore only able to report his general impressions in the quarter-page piece he penned for the weekly's Show issue. All the same, Woollett clearly came away impressed. He thought the Honda 'delightfully smooth and comfortable', deeming the Four more tourer than sportsbike. He praised the slickness of its five-speed gearbox, but was critical of the bike's front disc brake, which he thought would benefit from bedding in. He did not, however, think the machine would sell in large numbers.

BSA/Triumph Unveil A 750 Triple, Honda A 750 Four

Under the clear blue April skies of 1969's Easter Bank Holiday weekend - temperatures by the Sunday had topped 18 Centigrade and several weather stations bested their all-time sunshine records - both Triumph and Honda launched their ground-breaking 750cc multi-cylinder offerings to the British public in the English seaside resort of Brighton, whilst just over a hundred miles to the west, the British-built version of Concorde was counting down to its historic 22 minute maiden flight from a test runway in Filton the following week.

Admission to the Motor Cycle Show at Brighton's Metropole Exhibition Hall was five shillings (25p) for adults, and 2s 6d (12.5p) for children. The four-day show opened at 10am on Saturday 5 April. Every day from 10am until 9pm through to 9 April, show-goers had their first opportunity to compare both versions of the home-grown three-cylinder 750s on display at BSA/Triumph's stand against Honda's 750cc Dream Four, whose show stand was sited immediately next to that of the British combine.

---

*   Reports vary. Mick Walker, in his brilliant history *Honda Production Motorcycles from 1946 to 1980*, says that the bike featured by the BBC was one of the four CB750s that Soichiro Honda presented to US dealers in Las Vegas and had been flown in directly from America. In his excellent tome, *Honda CB750*, Mick Duckworth says the machine featured on *Wheelbase* was the one flown in to Holland from America, which Dutch journalists were forbidden from starting.

To supplement the Japanese company's still quite small British operation, Honda UK chief Jim Harrison drafted in several members of the Owners' Club to help set up the stand's two pre-production Dream Fours for display: one in green and the other in gold.[*] They placed the gold-liveried model at ground level, and exhibited the green model at head height propped up on a special stand above a map of the Isle of Man's TT race track[**] (scene of many Honda GP-winning races). A board cheekily invited show goers to 'Look around the Honda CB750, there's nothing to compare it with'.

When Honda announced at the Brighton Motor Show a UK price tag for the Dream Four of £650, it marked the 750/4 as the most expensive bike on exhibition. After press speculation back in October that the triples would cost around £550 (which, even at that price, *Motorcycle Mechanics* magazine deemed 'an expensive lot for the average rider'), BSA/Triumph used Brighton as the platform from which to announce the Rocket 3 and Trident's domestic- market price of £614.

BSA's production manager, Alistair Cave, had estimated that each triple cost the Group between £400 and £500 to manufacture and, to be competitive, needed to retail at around £600. The £36 difference between the triples and the Honda (equivalent to several weeks' wages back then) afforded a degree of comfort to the beleaguered Small Heath and Meriden plants who had been hearing reports that Honda's Four would actually undercut the triple's price in BSA/Triumph's biggest market, the US.

Don Brown, a market analyst and head of sales at the New Jersey-based BSA US headquarters, had already put on record his concerns about the triples' looks. He had pushed, too, for electric starting. But his greatest misgivings concerned the triples' high ticket prices in the States of $1,750. His projection that BSA would not sell more than 2,000 A75s was not received well in Birmingham, whom Don suspected were relying on a return on their investment within a year. When Honda announced its prices for the Dream Four - initially $1,295, but later increased to $1,495 when, as Don commented, 'they realised they had the best game in town' - US dealers, many of whom also held Honda franchises, understood that they suddenly had a tough sell on their hands shifting the British triples. Brown, however, had an idea.

Several months before the Brighton show, at a final pre-launch meeting in England, Brown revealed to BSA plans he had been secretly developing to pull the rug from under Honda. In the same month as Honda and BSA launched their new multis in the UK, Brown had arranged an American Motorcycle Association (AMA) sanctioned event at Daytona International Speedway. Hiring racers Dick Mann, Yvon Duhamel, Ray Hampstead and *Cycle* journalist Gordon Jennings to ride four stock, straight-from-the-crate Rocket 3s, Brown's audacious plan was to put the Rocket 3 in the record books. Unfortunately, BSA's East and West Coast managers Pete Colman and Earl Miller did

---

[*]   According to *Motor Cycle News* journalist John Nutting, the gold-finished CB750 that Honda displayed at the Brighton Metropole was one of the four 'late pre-production' machines. Carrying engine number 2110, the bike was later sold to the then chief of the UK's Motor Cycle Industry organisation, the Earl of Denbigh well ahead of going on general sales.

[**]   The Isle of Man covers an area of just 227 square miles and nestles in the Irish Sea between Northern Ireland and Cumbria on the north-west coast of the British mainland. It hosted its first Tourist Trophy (TT) motorcycle race in 1907.

not receive Brown's idea well. Indeed, Brown himself understood all too clearly his plan's potential for embarrassment as he had *Cycle* magazine's Gordon Jennings agree to shelve the story if they failed to set any records. In the end, BSA Group's Managing Director, Lionel Jofeh, assented and 'approved the plan as it had been presented, and that was that'.

All that remained now was to take the four, box-stock Rocket 3s and do what had never been done before.

HONDA'S FOUR FORCES A CHANGE OF PLAN IN KOBE, JAPAN

Honda's Dream Four wasn't causing consternation just in the English Midlands and amongst BSA and Triumph dealers on the east and west coasts of the US. In Santa Barbara, California, in the studio of a small design firm, McFarlane Design had a full size mock up of a 750cc four-cylinder motorcycle they were styling for a major Japanese client - a firm who manufactured trains, helicopters, ships, aircraft, robots, and, since its production of military aircraft ended when World War II finished, motorcycles.

McFarlane's mock-up was part of a secret project to design a large-capacity four-stroke tourer to capture the US market. Codenamed N600, the Japanese company's Kobe-based motorcycle division had initiated the project in 1967 under the stewardship of Gyoichi 'Ben' Inamura.

Inamura's team presented the wooden mock-up of a four-cylinder double-overhead camshaft 750 to his company's board in September 1968, who approved the design for production the following year. The launch in Tokyo the following month of Honda's Dream Four therefore landed a body blow to Inamura and his team.

Inamura felt there was nothing they could do in the face of Honda's coup but to cancel Project N600, study the CB750 in close detail, re-evaluate the market, and come back with something bigger and better.

They named the new project T-103 (later, codenamed 'New York Steak'). In the meantime, whilst Inamura's team developed their answer to Honda's CB750, his company would just have to rely on its existing flagship motorcycle to take the battle to Honda: the Kawasaki H1 500cc two-stroke triple, a motorcycle the UK's *Bike* magazine later described as 'Thanatoid'.*

---

*   'Thanatoid' - *noun* deathly; deadly (Chambers English Dictionary).

6

KAWASAKI DEVELOPS A SUPERBIKE

BRITISH TRIPLES BREAK SPEED RECORDS, AND CB750 SALES SOAR

'New York Steak'
(Kawasaki's codename for its four-cylinder superbike)

Gyoichi 'Ben' Inamura

THE ROCKET 3 BREAKS SPEED RECORDS AT DAYTONA

Despite Pete Colman's and Earl Miller's reservations over Don Brown's proposal to take four stock Rocket 3s to Daytona's high-banked racetrack for a two-day tilt at the record books, having secured Lionel Jofeh's approval, Brown was now free to proceed.

He rented Daytona International Speedway in Florida and got the AMA's executive director, Bill Berry, to sanction the event, which he'd arranged to take place in secret the same month as BSA/Triumph unveiled the A75 and T150 triples to the UK market (and Honda its Dream Four).

Carved from Florida swampland, with 1,000 feet radius curves banked to 31 degrees at its East and West ends, straights more than a third-of-a-mile long, and a reputation for running higher than average speeds, Daytona's 3.81 mile tri-oval circuit made it the perfect venue for BSA's record-breaking attempt. Many, however, considered the track *too* fast. It also had a bad rap for being tough on tyres.

The four gunslingers Brown hired for the task included the French Canadian racer, Yvon Duhamel, a rider with a reputation for hard riding and who had won the 250cc class 'show-opening' race at Daytona the year before, and the American racer Dick 'Bugs' Mann. The two other riders were racer Ray Hampstead and *Cycle* journalist Gordon Jennings (who had agreed with Brown that he wouldn't file the story if their record-breaking attempt should not prove successful).

Under Florida's baking April sunshine, and against a backdrop of Daytona's empty grandstands, the four stock Rocket 3s performed flawlessly, taking various AMA time and distance records: Duhamel averaged 127mph in one hour, and 123.4mph over 200 miles, whilst Mann tore round the track at over 125mph to set records for 100 and 200 miles. The fastest time recorded by AMA's official timekeeper, Paul Shattuck, was 131.723mph over a five-mile flying start, set by Duhamel; a simply astonishing speed for a standard production motorcycle. Gordon Jennings had his story.

Some AMA members, such as H-D's William Harley, however, were unhappy when they learned of Don Brown's privately arranged session. But the records stood, the AMA classifying them under 750cc Stock Machines. *Cycle* magazine put the story on their May 1969 cover. And, naturally, BSA made sure to feature the Rocket 3's achievements in its advertising on both sides of the Atlantic. Yet the Rocket 3's success came at a cost to its sibling, the Trident. For the next few months, the Rocket 3 outsold its Triumph stablemate.

Later that year, in a move typical of the intense rivalry in the States between the two marques, Triumph's West Coast subsidiary responded by offering $25,000 prize money to anyone setting a new record on a stock or modified Trident-powered machine during Bonneville Speed Week held on the Salt Flats in Utah. By the end of Speed Week, Tridents had established fifteen out of a possible sixteen new AMA 750cc class speed records (BSAs didn't manage one). The new records included Geoff Gough's two-way average of 169.331mph on an alcohol-fuelled, partially-faired 750cc machine, and Rusty Bradley's one-way best of 169.891mph on his stock-engined, partially-faired gasoline-fuelled 750 Trident tuned by Jack Wilson. Triumph placed two-page advertisements in magazines headlined, 'Triumph Sweeps Bonneville.' Yet the Rocket 3's record-breaking achievements in Daytona continued to overshadow the Trident's success and cemented the myth that the BSA was the faster of the two triples.

In the end, although the triples were demonstrably fast, it didn't seem to matter. In 1969, whilst BSA/Triumph sold less than 7,000 triples, American Honda shifted over 30,000 CB750s.

US Best Sellers

In spite of its success, Honda's best-selling motorcycle in 1969 *wasn't* the CB750. That accolade went to their 50cc Mini-Trail. All the same, the Dream Four signalled the frontier of a changing landscape in motorcycling. Between 1969 and 1970, sales in the US of bikes over 600cc nearly trebled, a trend that would continue into the new decade, with the 750cc category making up the majority of that increase.

For motorcycle makers, the US in the 1970s was a marketplace of considerable duality. Alongside increased sales in large-capacity motorcycles (evidence of the Japanese manufacturers' growing dominance), dramatic increases in sales also occurred in the 100 to 299cc category. This was largely down to the dual-purpose sector. Between 1972 and 1976, the two best-selling motorcycles in the US were the Honda CB750 and the Suzuki TS185.

Then, in 1972, Meriden's stranglehold on a sector they had come to view as their own was finally broken when Japan's second largest manufacturer, Yamaha, outsold Triumph in the 650 twin class. The XS650 would go on to become Yamaha's best-selling motorcycle, a position it would command for four years in a row - from 1977 and on into the early Eighties.

A Vintage Year

Just as film buffs commonly cite 1939 as cinema's best ever year, 1969 was to prove a vintage year for motorcycling.*

Not only did BSA/Triumph make their Rocket 3 and Trident triples available to the British public, and Honda their CB750 Dream Four, 1969 also saw the release of Kawasaki's H1 500cc three-cylinder two-stroke. Producing 60bhp, the Mach III was claimed to be the most powerful road-going machine in the world, a bike the US magazine *Cycle World* said would 'raise the hairs on the back of a rider's neck, and turn them gray in 13 seconds flat'.

1969 was also the year Yamaha first released its Brit Twin challenger, the four-stroke 650cc twin-cylinder XS-1. Either because they saw no sense in bringing coals

---

*   In 1939, MGM released David O. Selznick's *Gone with the Wind*. Based on Margaret Mitchell's best-selling novel, the Civil War epic starred Clark Gable as Rhett Butler and Vivien Leigh as Scarlett O'Hara (the British actress Selznick cast following his famous nationwide search across America). John Wayne became an overnight star (after years of trying) in John Ford's Western, *Stagecoach*. Merle Oberon played Cathy and Laurence Olivier Heathcliffe in William Wyler's classic version of Emily Brontë's tragedy of love and loss, *Wuthering Heights*. Other films released that year include Frank Capra's *Mr Smith Goes to Washington*, with James Stewart as the titular hero; *Destry Rides Again*, again starring Stewart, but this time paired with Marlene Deitrich; and, of course, that modern Christmas TV perennial, Judy Garland's evergreen *The Wizard of Oz*.

1969 wasn't too shabby a year for filmgoers, either. Thirty years after his breakout role as the Ringo Kid in *Stagecoach*, John Wayne won his first and only Oscar playing one-eyed US marshal, Rooster Cogburn in *True Grit*. Indeed, Westerns featured prominently that year. They included: George Roy Hill's *Butch Cassidy and the Sundance Kid* starring Paul Newman, Robert Redford and Katherine Ross; *Paint Your Wagon* with Lee Marvin and Clint Eastwood; and Sam Pekinpah's violent elegy to the passing of the Old West, *The Wild Bunch* featuring Ernest Borgnine, William Holden and Robert Ryan. Even a film set in modern-day America was an allegory of the West and its frontiersmen: Dennis Hopper's *Easy Rider*, starred Peter Fonda and Jack Nicholson riding customised Harley-Davidsons. The movie would spawn countless Athena posters and prove the ruin of many a motorcycle's headstock in a bid to emulate Hopper's 'Captain America' H-D chop.

to Newcastle or perhaps be seen as administering the fatal blow to Britain's domestic manufacturers, Yamaha demurred from selling the bike in the UK for fully six years. It wasn't until 1975 that the 'Japanese Bonneville' landed on British shores, by which time it had reached its fourth incarnation and had the appellation XS650B. Having progressed from XS-1 to XS-2, the somewhat confusing (well, to British buyers, at least) 'B' suffix was to distinguish it from the previous year's model 'A' - a bike Yamaha sold in the US, but not in the UK.

MAKER'S TOP-OF-THE-RANGE BIKES GET LARGER

Up to the introduction of BSA/Triumph's triples and Honda's Dream Four, the largest displacement motorcycles available from the Midlands combine and its rivals from the Far East was 650cc.

BSA had its A65 twin-cylinder 650cc variants, such as the Thunderbolt, Lightning, Firebird or Spitfire. Triumph had its cash cow T120 Bonneville and Trophy 650 twins. Before they launched the Dream Four in Tokyo, Honda's largest capacity motorcycle was its CB450 Black Bomber. Until the advent of the XS-1, Yamaha's biggest bike was the 350cc YR-3 twin-cylinder, five-port two-stroke (forerunner to the RD400 and LC350 pocket rockets). Despite the 250 and 350cc versions of the air-cooled twin making the front page of the 9 April 1969 issue of *Motor Cycle News,* because of Rod Gould's trio of double victories over the Easter weekend, the YR-3's British debut at the Brighton Motor Show that same week was overshadowed by Honda's launch of its CB750/4.

Although Suzuki were to launch a multi-cylinder 750 of their own in 1970, at the time BSA/Triumph's triples and Honda's CB750 made their UK debuts in Brighton, the biggest bike in Suzuki's range was its 500cc twin-cylinder two-stroke T500. Introduced in late 1967, the T500/Five (500ccs and five gears) gained a reputation as one of the most reliable two-wheelers of the Sixties. Arriving in the UK in April 1968 as the 'T500 Mark 1' and costing £423 10s 4d (compared to £355 for a Triumph T120 Bonneville), British riders only really took to the bike when it started winning road races - ironically, just as the street version was turning into a 'budget workhorse' as its initially steep price remained virtually static.[*]

Soon the bike, renamed the T500 Cobra for the UK market, garnered further plaudits, this time for its handling (*Cycle World* magazine had been critical of the first T500's suspension in their road test), after Suzuki extended its wheelbase from 52.7 inches to 57.3 inches by lengthening the bike's swinging arm. The Cobra is also notable for introducing Suzuki's Posi-Force Lubrication. The system dispensed with the rider having to pour measures of two-stroke oil directly into the fuel tank by automatically metering the oil with the petrol (Yamaha had debuted a similar system, which they called

---

[*]   Suzuki 500s were victorious at the Isle of Man TT 500 events in 1970 and 1972. Barry Sheene made his one and only appearance at the TT on a T500 (retiring after a crash). He did better on the mainland's short circuits, raising the 500cc lap record to 99.42 mph on a T500-engined road racer at Oulton Park in 1973. That same year saw Sheene take the Suzuki to victory in the 341-1,000cc 40-lap Mellano Trophy race at Brands Hatch.

Autolube, back in 1963). Such devices became a common feature in the Seventies, as manufacturers, particularly the Japanese, domesticated and 'house-trained' the two-stroke engine. In 1969, the now T500 Mark II underwent a re-style - the rounded, chrome-panelled tank giving way to a more angular item - along with a name change from Cobra to Titan* (although most people simply referred to it as the T500). Weighing 408 lbs dry and capable of 105mph (down on the Cobra, which topped out at around 117mph), with its high gearing, torquey, well-mannered, and relatively vibration-free 47bhp motor, the T500 Titan proved a very competent tourer. Production of the Titan finally ended in 1976.**

Of the Big Four Japanese manufacturers, only Kawasaki had a bike larger than 500cc: the W1, a twin-cylinder, overhead-valve four-stroke 650. Originally produced by Meguro Manufacturing Company, Japan's oldest motorcycle maker and a factory dedicated solely to four-strokes, the 650W1 was re-badged as a Kawasaki-Meguro after Kawasaki Heavy Industries (KHI) bought them out in 1961.

The W1's design owed more than a little to BSA's 500 and 650cc Star Twins. The 50bhp 650cc W1, and its successor, the W2, sold well in Japan right up to the end of production in 1975. However, its engine's close resemblance to BSA's A10 probably accounted for its poor sales overseas. As a result, the W1 underpinned British manufacturers' misapprehension that the Japanese were unable to develop a bike capable of seriously competing with their large-bore offerings. It was a misconception to which Honda's CB750 would land a stunning blow. And more blows were to follow. During the course of the next decade, a succession of Japanese bikes would deliver a protracted *coup de grâce* to the UK's once dominant motorcycle industry.

New York Steak

If the British triples were motorcycles conceived at the right time, but born too late, Honda's launch in 1968 of their CB750/4 resulted in Kawasaki's 900cc Z1 being very nearly stillborn.

Early in 1967, 32-year-old 'Ben' Gyoichi Inamura was asked to head up a team of research engineers at Kawasaki's Akashi works to develop the world's first large-capacity four-stroke across-the-frame four, which they codenamed N600. The team examined the European manufacturers' motorcycles of the day. 'My impression of British bike engines at that time,' Ben said later, 'was that they were old fashioned designs - especially crankshafts, valve gear and lubrication systems.'

Throughout the whole of 1967 and well into 1968, the motorcycle division's Marketing Manager, Sam Tanegashima, approached dealers and journalists in the US for

---

*   Suzuki reportedly dropped the Cobra name after the Ford Motor Company threatened legal action. Ford allegedly claimed a legal entitlement to the name through their long-standing association with Texas racer and muscle car maker Carroll Shelby and his Mustang-engined AC Cobra. Suzuki evidently thought better than to challenge the automotive giant. However, difficulties arose with the successor name, Titan, after Suzuki learned that the Leystone-based British aftermarket company Read Titan had registered its use for their cafe racers.

**   The Titan remained available as late as 1977, just a year after Suzuki had introduced its first four-stroke in over two decades: the ground-breaking GS750.

their thoughts on this successor to the Vincent HRD. Given that Sam worked for the motorcycle arm of Kawasaki Heavy Industries, a company which built Japan's 125mph Bullet Train, journalists such as *Cycle World*'s Ivan J. Wager understood that suggesting something as otherwise outrageous as a four-stroke four was not a pipe dream beyond KHI's capabilities.

By March 1968, Inamura was bench-testing a twin-cam four-cylinder 750cc four-stroke engine that was revving to 9,000rpm and realising 75bhp. Meanwhile, taking what he'd learnt from the feedback, Sam Tanegashima had a mock-up built, which he escorted personally across the Pacific to stylist Don McFarland's offices in Santa Barbara, California where Don's company, Design Associates, could begin to explore ideas for designs. Photographs taken at the time show a double-overhead cam transverse four-cylinder engine in a conventional twin cradle frame. Its slab-sided tank and side-panels are styled remarkably like Ogle's modish angular designs for the BSA and Triumph triples. More remarkably still are the mock-up's silencers. 'Fish-tail' in style, and each ending in twin-pipe outlets, they look uncannily similar to Ogle Design's 'ray-gun' exhausts.

When Honda revealed the Dream Four at the Tokyo Motor Show in October 1968, the finished mock-up, which Kawasaki's board had just a month earlier signed off for production to commence the following year, was sitting in Sam's West Coast bachelor apartment. At this point he received a telex notifying him: '... drastic review of our project inevitable.'

For Ben Inamura and the N600 project team, Honda's CB750 - of whose existence Kawasaki was completely unaware - came as massive blow. 'I'll never forget how shocked I felt,' Inamura recalled. 'At that time we had no idea what was being developed in each others' companies, so it was a real surprise. We were developing virtually the same concept, and it was almost complete.'

Work on the N600 was immediately suspended, while Inamura analysed the CB750 and considered the team's next move.

Kawasaki was nevertheless convinced that the concept Inamura had been working on was fundamentally correct. By 1970, a working prototype, known as 9057 (and within inner circles by the much less prosaic tag of 'New York Steak')* was undergoing secret tests at the company's Akashi proving ground. On 1 April 1970, following intensive and promising testing during the spring at the Yatabe circuit near Tokyo of a 750cc prototype (and fresh research conducted the month before with US customers, dealers and editors from leading motorcycle magazines confirmed that there was a market for a big performance tourer), the company reunited the project team to develop what Kawasaki Motorcycle Division's General Manager, Mr. Yamada called 'The King Motorcycle' (a term very similar to that which Honda themselves had

---

* At a reunion of the Z1 project team to mark the model's fortieth anniversary, former president of Kawasaki Motors Yoji Hamawaki told *Motorcyclist*'s online magazine: 'You know we called the Z1 project "New York Steak," but do you know why? We knew,' he continued without missing a beat, 'that in America the best meal on the menu was New York steak. In our minds, the Z1 was going to be the best motorcycle we could make, the top of the menu.'

applied to the CB750). Drafting from within the company's ranks the best staff in their field, the team included Ben Inamura, John Watanabe, Tom Togashi and Ken Tada.

The aim now, however, was a 1,000cc four producing 85bhp and capable of 130mph - and all for the same price as the Honda.

There was just one problem.

Japanese manufacturers had kept to a 'gentleman's agreement' not to exceed 750cc, which would have put them head-to-head with Harley-Davidson and the European manufacturers. But then Honda introduced the CB750. Kawasaki knew it had to do something more than simply match Honda. Despite deep cultural trepidations about breaching the agreement, they saw the immense opportunities of developing a large-capacity motorcycle capable of a taking on all comers. 'There was a lot of debate,' Yoji Hamawaki told *Motorcyclist*, 'but we decided it was critical to our survival... to make the Z1.'

Alan Masek, general manager for Kawasaki's US importer, recalled: 'We had some information that Honda was working on a larger engine than the CB750's, and we realised that this was our chance to leapfrog. If we waited, did a 750 also, we might be beaten again.' The team did, however, have one constraint to any planned hike in displacement. With the castings for the engine cases of the existing 750 already set, bore and stroke had to be compatible.

Ben Inamura headed up the new project and led on engine development for Kawasaki's challenger to Honda's crown, to which the team assigned the codename T-103 (Ben had worked on the 650W1 parallel twin during his time with Meguro before it was bought out by Kawasaki). Watanabe was in charge of basic research and testing. Togashi and Tada were responsible for the new bike's chassis and styling respectively (the pair had also developed the chassis and styling for Kawasaki's H1, H2, and S2 two-stroke triples). The team also included Lyndon Yurikusa who was responsible for testing. Yurikusa would later be joined in Japan by Jim Corpe and Randy Hall from American Kawasaki in September 1971 to help with further testing and serviceability.

In charge of testing the prototypes Stateside was Bryon Farnsworth. His Santa Ana, California-based Research and Development team comprised Virgil Davenport, Gary Scott and British racer, Paul Smart. Smart had raced in the American Nationals for Bob Hansen, pitman for Dick Mann's Daytona-winning Honda CR750 (the racing version of the CB750 road bike).[*] The race shop was next to Kawasaki's Santa Ana R&D site. 'I was keen to do some testing in order to make money,' recalled Smart in an interview with *Classic Bike* magazine's Ben Miller. 'I didn't get paid anything for racing - I had my own mechanic to pay, Hurley Wilvert, so what money they gave me went straight to him. I earned cash through bonuses for winning races and leading laps.' Testing took place in

---

[*]   Despite being a commonly used appellation in books and magazines, Honda never officially applied the 'CR' prefix to the CB750. According to Mick Duckworth's definitive work on the model, *Honda CB750*, the term only ever appeared once in official literature - and that was in a US parts book listing RSC components for converting roadsters for competition.

the summer. Over the course of fourteen days, on a quartet* of test bikes wearing Honda nameplates, CB750 fuel tanks and diamond-shaped side-panels badges, plus gaffer tape over the 'DOHC' castings on the engine cases, the riders averaged 500 miles a day on highways across 17 states, with two big Dodge support trucks in tow. (Only one person in the whole of the 8,000-mile round trip from Los Angeles to Daytona and back - a young man in Shreveport, Louisiana - saw past the Honda badges: 'What the hell izzat? That ain't a Honda.')

Piloting machines capable of 135mph, and with two bikes riding at any one time down roads restricted to just 55mph, Smart confessed that 'there were speeding tickets'. And testers didn't just fall foul of traffic cops, either. They also managed to get themselves in hot water with their Kawasaki bosses.

During the California leg of the trip, testers stopped by a club race at Vacaville on their Honda-badged Kawas. 'Me and Hurley Wilvert sneaked one into an eight-hour race just outside San Francisco,' Smart recounted. 'The circuit was pretty typical,' he recalled, 'a few 50-gallon oil drums and some hay bales. At the end of the race we were ahead by miles on this strange looking Honda.' Kawasaki - who had tried to keep the testing secret - were none too happy. 'We got a proper bollocking for that,' remembered Smart, '... but you could tell they were also secretly pleased - publicity like that you can't buy.'**

The bikes were achieving 40 to the gallon at 70mph, and 32mpg overall. After travelling 13,600 miles, the bikes hadn't suffered a single failure. However, the testing programme wasn't finished.

Kawasaki shipped the bikes to, firstly, Willow Springs - then just a track with barbed wire round it - and later the scalding hot Talladega race track in Alabama, where the riders simulated a 250-mile road race and ran them flat-out for an hour (at Talladega, the track lets riders run with throttles wide open virtually the whole way round). Each machine racked up 5,000 miles, reached speeds of 125-130mph, and averaged 122mph. (Paul Smart observed that: 'The bikes could have finished in the top ten at this year's Daytona, even if the big two-strokes hadn't dropped out!')

Farnsworth recalled for *Motorcyclist* magazine many years later that: 'Bill Huth [Willow Spring's owner] said he'd stand guard and make sure nobody drove across the track.'

The next track, however, presented Farnsworth *et al* very different challenges.

'Talladega was prone to having those heavy thundershowers,' remembered Farsnworth. 'We were down there testing with Gary Nixon, Hurley Wilvert, Paul Smart, some fast Texas guy whose name I can't remember, and three or four hot Japanese riders. Yvon Duhamel and Art Baumann were also present.'

---

*   Reports vary as to how many machines undertook the journey. Paul Smart told *Classic Bike* magazine in a January 2012 article marking the Z1's fortieth anniversary: 'We headed off with *four* bikes in a couple of vans on a trip of 6,000 miles or so' (author's italics). In his preview piece of October 1972, *Motorcyclist* magazine's Bob Greene who, along with US journalists Ivan Wager, Cook Neilson and Bob Braverman, was amongst the first in the world to ride the Z1, reported: '*Three* test machines lived 5000 miles each through scalding runs at Willow Springs and Talladega race tracks...' (author's italics).

**   Smart's words are a combination of interviews with the racer reported in *Classic Bike* and *Classic Motorcycle Mechanics* magazines, January and November 2012 respectively.

'What we were trying to do was just hold the thing wide open through a whole tank of gas. If you could just hold it wide open, you could run right up there against the wall, doing about 140. It'd wobble some, but if you just kept the gas on, it was OK.

'So I sent out one of the Japanese guys. It started to rain one of those big rains, and he pulls in. I was in charge of testing, so I walked over to him to ask, "What the hell are you doing?"

"It's raining," he says, "too dangerous."

"Bullshit," I said, and jumped on the bike myself. I scared the absolute hell out of myself that day next to that wall. In the rain, it was really dodgy.

'Still, for the amount of power [the engineers] shoehorned into what was really basically an H1 frame, the thing worked pretty well. I mean, you could feel the head moving in relation to the swingarm pivot whenever you twisted the throttle, but it all worked. Frames then were pretty much all the same; here's where the engine goes, and there's a place for the seat and gas tank.'

Smart remembered one particular run in which he was flat-out on the banking, one hand on the fork leg, with his wife Maggie riding pillion! 'Even two-up the early bikes would hit 130mph. We rode three-up on the road sometimes, with Maggie on the tank.' As he told *Classic Motorcycle Mechanics* magazine: 'At one point, in fact, I had Maggie and Barry's girlfriend Lesley[*] on the bike. We rode a fair old way three up!'

Engine oil temperatures reached 150 Centigrade. By the time testing was over, the most significant problem engineers were able to discover was that the rivets securing the clutch hub to the reduction gear had worked themselves loose.

'But occasionally the engines would spit out a shim,' recalled Smart, 'which would hole the cam box and put oil everywhere. They'd get through clutches if you pulled endless wheelies, too, of course.'

The team ran the bikes through rain, snow and on scorching hot desert roads. To test the machines' lighting and electrical components, they ran the bikes with the lights on - day and night. Rear tyres lasted no more than 6,000 to 6,500 miles; drive chains half that. Engineers tore down the test bikes' motors, both during and at the close of the test programme. By the end of two months' testing, the bikes had travelled coast to coast twice on nothing more than routine maintenance.

Inamura recalled that 'working conditions were not so good in those days. The computer systems and test apparatus in particular were quite basic. But we had a lot of fun.'

Paul Smart: 'It wasn't test riding like it is now, where you ride it around and give it back all nice and shiny. They wanted to find out what broke so we were brutal with the bikes. We'd do standing starts until the clutches and gearboxes broke. And we'd hold the engine flat-out for a tank of fuel, come in, fill it up and do it again.'

Fellow test rider, Masahiro Wada, was, according to Smart, simply brilliant. A martial artist, who the Brit described as 'fit as a butcher's dog,' Wada won Smart's

---

[*]   Barry Sheene and his girlfriend at the time, Lesley Shepherd.

admiration as a 'bloody good rider' and 'tremendous crasher.' He was, said the Brit, 'very loose - wheelies were the big new thing and everyone was going for it, so he tipped one over backwards.' Curiously, perhaps, Kawasaki didn't seem to mind: 'And when we broke a bike they were stripped there and then, in the dirt and dust roadside, not back in the workshops. They'd lay a blanket out and start unbolting everything... it helped them work out what was broke.'

Forty years on, Smart recounted for *Classic Motorcycle Mechanics*: 'It was a lot of fun. These were 130mph motorcycles, they didn't exist before this. And for all our efforts they were incredibly robust. Sure they weaved about - they were a right handful until you got used to them. For the American racers, brought up on dirt track, they didn't think anything of it, they were used to everything wriggling about. For me, for British racers, we were used to more refined race bikes so back in the UK we'd put the motors in special frames. In America (and Australia) they just raced them the way they were. They were a lovely bike.'

Meanwhile, speculation amongst journalists about the new Kawasaki engine was rife. It was a transverse-mounted V-four. It would be water-cooled. The motor would be fuel-injected. Rumours abounded, too, about its displacement, which ranged from 750 to 1,300cc. The project team themselves had tested various capacities, including 1,000cc and a 100bhp, 1,200cc version. The team eventually settled on 903cc and 82bhp as offering optimum power, smoothness and reliability. As Inamura put it: 'I was never involved in racing, but a bike has to have the ability to be ridden sportily, or even have race potential.'

However, as Kawasaki's General Manager, Mr. Yamada, later explained to journalists at the Z1's press preview in Monterey, California in August 1972, the machine's 903cc engine capacity was down to no more than the fact that 'it turned out that way.' When asked why Kawasaki had not elected to go for a full litre, Yamada told journalists that 'we'd rather not compete just yet in a displacement class with anything Milwaukee Harley-Davidson builds. And 'besides,' he added, 'we don't *need* any more displacement.'

Cycle World had already reported almost a year earlier the Japanese manufacturers' unwritten position. 'It's not that they are afraid of the potence of the Milwaukee Twin,' wrote Jack Yamaguchi, 'but that they do not want to push its maker. The US-Japan trade relationship is strained tight enough.' Moreover, as the 'outspoken' Terry Yamada told the magazine back then in response to speculation that Kawasaki was developing, not a 650cc version of the MACH III, but 'a more sober' 750-850: 'We would go four-stroke for anything over 650.'

By February 1972, as the first pre-production Z1s (codenamed 'Model X') underwent final testing, the bike that forced Kawasaki to re-think its plans, the CB750/4, had enjoyed a level of sales that so surprised its maker that Honda was forced into a four-fold increase on its initial forecast of 25 units a day and push daily production to over 100 units (in America, Honda sold 30,000 Fours in 1969 alone). Even so, despite the CB750's phenomenal success on the track and showroom floor, Kawasaki had already ensured Honda was not going to have everything its own way. Whilst Inamura and his team prepared their heavyweight challenger for release, Kawasaki had already let loose its dogs of war - the H1 500 and H2 750cc two-stroke triples.

A CB750 EVERY THREE MINUTES

After disappointing sales of the CB450, Honda were understandably cautious in their projections for the CB750. To keep investment to a minimum, they overhauled and modified production facilities that were lying idle. They re-configured the Four's body-assembly production line in the Hamamatsu Factory automobile plant from L-shape to straight. At the ultra-modern Saitama Factory near Tokyo, the plant Honda selected to produce the engines, staff visited automobile manufacturers to acquire the knowledge they needed to plan the line for building a powerplant unlike anything the company had ever produced before. Yet, in spite of all their planning, production did not start well. Against initial production forecasts of 25 units a day, they were at first producing just five (and less).[*]

Back orders soon began to pile up. After building less than 7,500 Dream Fours, Honda had to abandon the gravity die casting method it employed to produce the CB750's main engine casings (the so called 'sand cast' models, later much prized by collectors) and re-tool to a high-pressure die-casting process in order to meet the phenomenal worldwide demand.[**] A projected production figure of 1,500 units a *year* had to be quickly revised so that that figure became the factory's output per *month* - which Honda were later obliged to double to *3,000* units every month. By the time the CB750 made its UK debut in Brighton, a new Four was reportedly emerging off Honda's production line at a rate of one every three minutes.

And it was not difficult to understand why the CB750 was so successful.

Although at £650, the CB750 cost £35 more than the Rocket 3 and Trident, the British triples' specification simply couldn't match that of their Japanese rival. Honda claimed 67bhp for the Four compared to 59bhp for the BSA and Triumph 750s. The Honda had both kick *and* electric start, front disc brake, and five-speed transmission. The Midland-made triples wore drum brakes all round, were kick start only, and had a four-speed gearbox. Unlike the Rocket 3 and Trident, direction indicators and rear view mirrors came as standard fitments on the Honda. And, of course, the Honda trumped the British 750 triples with its four cylinders. The Honda also scored in the area that had long been Triumph's strength: styling. With its four chrome-plated silencers prominently on display and a fuel tank suggestive of the company's Grand Prix-winning

---

[*]   Honda eventually transferred engine production from Saitama Factory to the Suzuka plant in July, 1971, and body production from Hamamatsu to Suzuka in the October of that year. At that time, Honda was building the CB500 at Suzuka, using a production line within its automobile plant. However, the plant's production line had a restrictively narrow corridor which hindered the smooth flow of parts. Honda decided that manufacturing the CB750 Four warranted the factory taking a long-term view. They therefore re-configured the body assembly's production line from L-shape to straight. The change resulted in a better work environment and vast improvements in employee safety.

[**]   CB750 expert John Wyatt of Yorkshire-based Rising Sun Restorations told *Classic Bike* magazine in October 2011 that Honda chose the cheaper, gravity die-cast method because they were uncertain how many 750 Fours they would actually sell.

antecedents, the Dream Four's designer, Hitoshi Ikeda, was unabashedly paying homage to the CB750's proud lineage (in contrast to the BSA Board who chose to distance their new triples from past successes). Yet the Four's Candy Ruby Red and Candy Blue Green liveries were utterly contemporary; as were the raised handlebars, specifically intended to appeal to American riders by emphasizing the bike's 'wild' image. Most ironically of all, some saw in the Honda's styling a very British influence, whilst BSA and Triumph enthusiasts thought the triples' angular styling was 'too Japanese'.

Early reviews of the Four were unfailingly fulsome. Although they all expressed reservations about the machine's intimidating size and weight, testers' concerns soon evaporated once the bike was underway. In one of the very first road tests of the CB750, US magazine, *Cycle Guide*, in its March '69 issue, said of the Four that 'a good portion of the weight vanishes the minute you release the clutch and move away', which they attributed to how Honda's engineers had distributed its weight. Of the Honda's handling, they observed that the bike felt 'quite comfortable both at high speed on the freeway, and at the same time manageable in heavy traffic'.

The project team's designer, Hitoshi Ikeda had styled the Four to ensure that its engine remained on view and appeared imposing. Yet his colleague responsible for developing the powerplant itself, Masura Shirakura, had sought to make it more compact.

Although doing so would mean sacrificing the motor's revs (and therefore peak power), to contain the motor's width, Shirakura elected to make the bore two millimetres smaller than its stroke (61mm to 63mm, respectively). He canted the cylinders forward by ten degrees to reduce the engine's height. To gain more ground clearance, he departed from the usual Honda practice of a wet sump, whereby the oil is retained in the lower part of the main crankcases, and installed a separate, frame-mounted six-pint oil tank instead. The under-seat tank was linked to the engine by two hoses, which supplied and returned oil to and from the motor (and, to avoid that bogey of British dry sump engines, Honda's technicians installed a valve to prevent oil draining back into the sump). In a first for a Honda motorcycle, the CB750 had a car-type twin-rotor trochoidal pump fitted, which was capable of supplying lubricant at high pressure (90 lbs).

The net result was an all-alloy engine that weighed a creditable 176 lbs (compared to, for example, Triumph's positively anorexic 650cc T120 unit's 130 lbs), measured just 21½ inches from alternator case to points cover, and, according to a Honda ad at the time, could perform standing quarters in 12.6 seconds and reach a top speed of 125mph.

The first consignments of the Four arrived on British shores in January 1970 (North America had been receiving supplies since the spring of 1969). Dubbed simply the CB750, only 36 of the 126 manufactured in total were imported into the UK - with all 24 of the initial batch pre-sold. By now, the cost of the Four had climbed to £679 19s, a rise of £30 since the price quoted at its UK unveiling in Brighton. There were differences, too, between the motorcycles the press had sampled at the time of the Four's launch (which themselves were different to the bikes exhibited in Tokyo) and the production machines arriving at Honda showrooms. Early pre-production models had the legend 'Honda' embossed on the cam cover, before it was changed to the more familiar 'OHC 750'. The side panels and badges on the display models at Tokyo were integral with the Four's air-box shrouds and sported oval badges. By the time of Honda's dealer convention in Las Vegas and shows here in Europe, the side panels had morphed into something closer to the louvred panels of the early production machines. Less obviously, Honda substituted the bar-actuated carburettor mechanism of the display models for a cable-operated system.

Further modifications occurred following several dealer recalls - most notably, to cure a serious problem with throttles sticking on early models.

In the US, the recently established Four Owners Club wrote to American Honda several times requesting the company recall the CB750 to correct the problem. The company refused. Then, thirteen days after the *Los Angeles Times* responded to frustrated club founder, Bill Robinson's suggestion to run a story on the issue - which was picked up and carried by newspapers across the US - American Honda instigated a recall. The Four Owners Club, however, had less success getting Honda to address final drive chains breaking and inflicting major damage to the crankcases on early models. It was a problem not properly cured until Honda re-designed the rear drive system on the next version of the Four, upped the standard 16-tooth engine sprocket to a 17-tooth item and installed a guide to direct broken chains out of harm's way.

'K' For 'Improvement'

Between June and August 1970, Honda produced a small batch of an interim model, which became known as the K0. The suffix was never an official appellation. It was an affix adopted later to distinguish the machines manufactured to original CB750 spec, but which incorporated modifications that formed part of the next generation Four, the K1.

The 'K' stood for the Japanese word Kariyo, meaning 'improvement'. However, refining the Four had started long before Honda launched the K1[*] in the US on 21 September 1970.

Since its debut in Tokyo, Honda's engineers had changed from eight valve guide seals to four, then back to eight, and changed the crankcases three times! Dealers would also routinely replace the smooth-surfaced oil-filter housings of the early models with the more robust finned housing of the later bikes. With the K1, Honda replaced the CB750's raised cow-horn handlebars with a flatter, European-style tiller. They ditched the snag-prone one-cable per carburettor and single-cable operated twist-grip system for a twin-cable, push-pull arrangement and bar-operated carburettors, first seen on the interim K0 machines. The speedometer's and tachometer's fragile acrylic lenses were replaced with

---

[*]   K1 production ran from August 1970 through to November 1971. Frame and engine numbers - which start at 1053399 for frames and E1044806 for engines - can differ by up to 2,000. This is because Honda manufactured the CB750's engine at its Saitama Factory, and its frame in their Hamamatsu plant before transferring production for both to its Suzuka plant (engines in July 1971 and frames in October). The K1 proved to be the biggest selling variant of the CB750 - 77,000 compared to the second most popular, the K2, at 63,500. Worldwide sales for the original CB750 and the interim K0 rank them fourth at 53,400 units. Despite the Four's global success, from its first appearance in British showrooms in January 1970 to the K7 of 1977-78, Honda UK sold only 7,960 four-piper CB750s (compared to America where Honda sold 30,000 Fours in 1969 alone).

glass, the clocks were now housed in sealed metal casings, and the clock faces went from green to black.

The smooth bodied, colour-coded air-filter assembly was replaced by a black ribbed box to avoid the original moulded item's tendency to crack. The side panels lost their air louvres, became slimmer and more rounded (slightly reducing the under-seat oil tank's capacity), and the saddle was deepened and re-shaped; all moves to address owners' complaints about comfort. The original, diamond-shaped badge was replaced by a large, calligraphic '750 Four'. The K1 also introduced new brown, green, and blue colour schemes (labelled Candy Garnett, Valley Green, and Polynesian Blue Metallic, respectively) to supplement the existing Candy Ruby Red and Candy Blue Green liveries.

Power output remained unchanged at a claimed 67bhp. Yet, in their March 1971 test of the K1, the best standing quarter *Cycle Guide* could achieve was 13.05 seconds - nearly half a second slower than the original CB750 Four - and a top speed of 121mph (down from 125mph). But by now, there was a new performance king on the street. At 500cc, it was two-thirds the size of the Honda. Yet what it lacked in capacity, it more than made up for in charisma. Its name was H1.

Very soon, it would be joined by its bigger brother...

7

Kawasaki's Mach III

The World's Quickest Motorcycle, *Cycle's* 'Superbike 7', And The Trident Gets A Makeover

'The World's Fastest Camel'
(*Bike* magazine road test of the Kawasaki 500cc H1)

Cook Neilson

The Kinkiest Streetbike Ever

As Lady Caroline Lamb said of Lord Byron, the Kawasaki H1 was 'mad, bad and dangerous to know'. In its April 1969 issue, US magazine *Cycle World* said of the white H1 adorning its cover* that the half-litre two-stroke (also known as the MACH III) was 'the kinkiest street bike ever!' and that the triple's quarter-mile acceleration would 'raise the hairs on the back of a rider's neck and turn them gray in 13 seconds flat'.

---

*   *Cycle World*'s front cover headline for the Mach III read, somewhat incongruously perhaps, given the H1's reputation, 'Kawasaki Three! World's Fastest Touring 500'.

Under development for two years, Kawasaki introduced their air-cooled piston-ported two-stroke triple in the same month that the Honda and BSA/Triumph multis made their UK debuts at the 1969 Brighton Show. Kawasaki's engineers had experimented with a two-stroke rotary-valve twin, along the lines of their successful 250cc Samurai A1, but found that a three-cylinder engine made more power with a lighter drive train. In a press release issued on 5 July 1969, Kawasaki said its aim was to build the world's best motorcycle ('Not the world's best small bike. Not the world's best medium-displacement bike'). And they defined what that meant. 'The world's best motorcycle should be able to outperform any other motorcycle regardless of displacement. It should be a good handling machine. Comfortable to ride. Yet the price should be reasonable and it should get good gas mileage.'

The UK magazine *Motorcycle Sport* found 45mpg was attainable, even when that included 'some very quick riding'. Other magazines found that around 23mpg was a more usual test figure. Oil consumption via Kawasaki's 'injecto-lube' mechanism eked out around 103 mile per pint.

As for price, in 1970 the 500cc Kawasaki retailed at between £575 and £589 19s 11d ($999 in the US), compared to its half-litre two-stroke rival, the statically-priced Suzuki T500's £448 10s. In performance terms, however, the H1 bore comparison with the new 750cc multi-cylinder offerings from Honda and the English Midlands, which sold for £679 19s and £614 respectively.

In fact, in many respects, the H1 outgunned them.

THE WIDOWMAKER

According to Kawasaki's press release, the H1 - or MACH III as they referred to it (MACHs I and II being the 250 and 350cc triples respectively) - was 'the world's fastest moving, fastest accelerating stock motorcycle'. Producing a claimed 60 horsepower, the H1 was, they declared (in a clear swipe at the BSA and Triumph triples), 'as powerful as the new three-cylinder 750s from Europe', despite being 'only a 500cc machine'.

Weighing 382lbs dry (174kg), the H1's 'resulting power-to-weight ratio'. according to Kawasaki, 'is the highest of any bike ever built, a fantastic 0.345hp/kg'.

It meant that in the right hands, the H1 was capable of sub-six second zero-to-60mph launches, accelerate to a quarter of a mile from a standing start in less than 13 seconds, and reach a claimed top speed of around 125mph. Indeed, Chas Butterworth broke several British national speed records for a 500cc street machine piloting a MACH III, achieving a top speed of 127.67mph (the average of two flying start kilometre runs), and 12.945 seconds for a quarter-mile standing start.

Yet, impressive as these numbers are, they do not fully explain the H1's fearsome reputation - or its nickname: *The Widowmaker*.

Its brakes - at least by the standards of the day - were good. *Motorcycle Sport* thought the H1's front 8 inch twin leading shoe amongst the very best, and its cable-operated 7 inch single leading shoe brake at the rear (the first road bike to the tester's knowledge to sport a cooling duct) just as good as its rivals. Indeed, *Cycle* magazine deemed the Kawasaki as second only to the disc-braked Honda CB750 in deceleration tests conducted during a March 1970 head-to-head between the Honda, the MACH III, the Rocket 3 and Trident, the Suzuki 500 Titan, a Norton Commando and an H-D Sportster.

The H1's problem was not its brakes. Its problems lay elsewhere.

Kawasaki described the H1's frame design as 'the best in the world' (and as their press release put it: 'The tough racing-machine type double cradle tube frame is solid, but light'). Cynics, however, felt Kawasaki had concentrated all their energies on developing the triple's marvellous engine, and that the company had neglected the H1's chassis, which they dismissed as little more than the frame from the 250cc Samurai. Likewise the H1's suspension. Kawasaki claimed the H1 used the 'famous Ceriani front forks… for smooth handling and control' (expending as many words in the press release on how they looked as to how they performed!). However, both wheels and forks appear to have had far less illustrious origins, taken, as they were from Kawasaki's own workmanlike W650 twin.

Motorcycle Sport noted that the frame was 'not as heavily gusseted at the steering head as some we have tested'. The result was a frame that many considered inadequate for housing a 60 horsepower engine. The forks were too spindly, rear shocks too weak, the wheelbase too short at 55 inches, and the chassis too easily overwhelmed by the motor's vicious powerband.

At least that is the received wisdom. In their June 1970 review of the MACH III, the UK's *Motorcycle Sport* magazine put the H1's rapidly-accumulating reputation for wayward handling to the test. In a report written in faintly Edwardian prose, they described negotiating an 80mph bend as though the Kawasaki was 'on tramlines'. They considered the rear suspension 'perfectly matched to the machine'. The magazine accepted that the addition of a hydraulic steering damper alongside the standard friction damper may have played a part in the bike's straight line steering 'almost imperceptibly ironing out' the front end's 'tendency to deviate' as it tried to lift under hard acceleration. The test also explored the H1's reaction when the machine *wasn't* travelling in a straight line and the rider grabbed a handful of throttle. Their advice is best summed up as: 'it's probably best not to!' Under these conditions, the Kawasaki 'was apt to pick itself up and come down to the right or left, leaving the rider pointing not quite where he wanted'.

Motorcycle Sport concluded that driven like any other machine, the triple 'is a good-mannered Mr. Hyde'. They acknowledged, however, that 'Dr. Jekyll is lurking in the background waiting to grab you by the throat'.

Britain's *Bike* magazine famously dubbed the ill-handling H1B they tested in 1972 'The Fastest Camel in the World'. The magazine's road tester Mike Nicks, recalling that encounter with the triple, later described it as *Thanatoid* - a word meaning 'resembling death, poisonous, deadly'. It was, he said, a 'piece of two-wheel demonry'. It would be fully two years before *Bike* girded itself to ride another Mach III.

The Kawasaki's demonic aspect was lent further credence by its ignition system. The CDI electronic ignition - the H1 was the first multi-cylinder production motorcycle to have one - didn't use contact breakers. The unit was set at the factory and required no further adjustment. The system also dispensed with conventional spark plugs, employing instead a high energy plug whose electrode ran down its centre. The spark ran between the electrode and all the way around the surrounding shell, firing so hot that the plug was self cleaning. The unit worked by using magnetism to build high-firing energy, then transmitting a sharp surge of some 20,000 volts to the odd-looking plugs in an attempt to jump the gap before the current leaked away (despite Kawasaki employing various forms of insulation to contain it during the course of the model's lifetime). As *Cycle World*'s technical editor Kevin Cameron recalled from his days as a dealer in Boston, the result was that starting the bike at night could produce a 'spooky blue corona... spiderwebbing all over the distributor side of the engine'.

The ignition box's malignancy didn't stop there, either. It also scrambled the reception of any nearby TV sets and is alleged to be the reason that UK bikes reverted to points for 1970.

Designed to adapt to the owner and the market in which it found itself, the H1's transmission had a double-ended output shaft so that the gear lever could operate on either the engine's left or right side (the MACH III pre-dated US federal law standardising brake and gear lever location). Less helpfully, neutral was at the bottom of the MACH III's five gears, something that riders - already struggling with the sensory overload a rapidly accelerating H1 induced - might easily forget (adding a new dimension to the rider's problems).

Such a potent, ill-tempered beast conferred instant hero status on the owner - and the H1's success on the track simply fuelled the MACH III's growing legend.

The UK's *Motor Cycle News* tested Cliff Carr's H1-R (the road-race version of the MACH III) in April 1970. Martin Hodder's piece described the Kawasaki 500 as 'the fastest racing bike available... a real exotic Japanese masterpiece... three cylinders of pure pleasure'.

'Acceleration,' he went on to declare, 'is incredible, the brakes are superb [ten inch double-sided twin leading shoe at the front] and handling is well up to the mark, even with the standard Japanese rear suspension units fitted to the test machine.'

Carr's bike delivered between 70 and 75bhp and had been electronically timed hurtling round Daytona's speed bowl at 156mph. Fuel consumption was equally dramatic, its 34mm Mikunis consuming it at a rate of just 11 miles a gallon.

One of the MACH III's earliest track successes was also one of the most unusual.

In January 1970, 26-year-old Peggy Hyde won her event riding her 500 Kawasaki at that year's Australian TT near Melbourne, becoming the first woman to win a road race in Australia. More remarkably still, after winning her event, Peggy refitted the MACH III's headlamp and rode her H1 eighty miles back home to where she lived.

In the same year, Ginger Molloy piloted his H1-R racer to second place in the world 500cc road race series. More successes followed. Works rider Dave Simmonds rode an H1-R to victory in the 1971 Spanish Grand Prix. Three years later, Keith Martin won the 500 Production TT in 1974 on a bike prepared by *Motorcycle Mechanics* magazine (his fastest lap being a remarkable 95.21mph).

The H1's high specification, aesthetics, performance, racing pedigree, and berserk behaviour all marked it out as quite unlike the slow, oily and proletarian two-strokes of AMC, BSA and Villiers.

But if motorcycles were changing, so too was the world they inhabited.
By 1970, nearly half of all households in Britain had access to a car (compared to only 13 per cent just twenty years earlier). Between 1970 and 1977, the second largest increase in consumer spending was on transport and vehicles, and daily traffic flows on UK motorways increased by some 65 per cent between 1965 and 1975.* Motorcycles were becoming less the utilitarian transport of previous decades and more and more a leisure vehicle. They were also becoming more affordable.

The Brough Superior SS100 was the speed king of its day. Launched at Earls Court in December 1924, each machine came with a certificate guaranteeing 100mph plus performance. At a cost of £175 new, the SS100 represented about 84 per cent of an average skilled worker's annual wage.

Twenty-four years later, Stevenage-based Vincent launched the Series B Black Shadow, a 1,000cc overhead-valve V-twin. Its 55bhp engine made it the first production motorcycle to achieve sub 15 second standing quarters. At £381, the Black Shadow cost the average-waged worker 106.5 per cent of their annual salary.

Twenty years on, and in 1968 Honda's CB750 Four cost just 73 per cent of the average gross yearly wage. By the time Kawasaki released its spiritual successor to the Vincent, the cost of the Z1 as a percentage of the average wage had, by 1972, fallen to just 60.6 per cent.

TRIPLE TROUBLES

Honda was not the only one to suffer teething difficulties with their new flagship. According to former Norton-Villiers Triumph sales director, Mike Jackson, in an interview published in *Classic Bike* magazine in 2001: 'The triple cost us a third more in warranty claims than the 500 twin and the bean counters were furious. It ought to have been a more profitable bike with a price premium, but it wasn't. It was a good stopgap and that's all.'

As the British triples rolled off the lines at the Armoury Road and Meriden plants, each factory randomly selected completed machines for testing at the Motor Industry Research Association (MIRA) facility near Nuneaton. However, problems began to emerge during testing when a batch of Tridents suffered catastrophic engine failures. Worse still, some of these very early machines had already been shipped to the States.

---

*   By 2008, the daily flow of traffic on motorways had increased fourfold over its 1965 level - from 18,300 to 76,900 vehicles a day - with average daily traffic rising by 150 per cent on all roads in those same four decades.

Meriden quickly dispatched Triumph foreman and trouble-shooter, Alan Barrett. Barrett was well acquainted with the Trident. He had worked on the P1 prototype as a fitter in the plant's Experimental Shop, and was part of Doug Hele's team of mechanics who accompanied four pre-production triples to the Californian home of Johnson Motor's vice president Pete Colman for secret Stateside testing back in October 1967.

Joining Barrett in his investigations was Mick Crowther, a young engineer from Meriden's Experimental Department. In Los Angeles, Barrett examined hundreds of machines destined for sale to the public and was appalled at what he and Crowther found. Among the litany of faults he recorded, Barrett listed swarf in the carburettor, seized pistons, misaligned threads for the alternator nut, incorrect cam timing, poorly punched oil pump gaskets that blocked the engine feed, and sand in the motor's oil (presumably left over from casting the crankcases). After taking a photographic catalogue of the defects to pass to Small Heath, Barrett and teams of American technicians set about rectifying the faults.

But early production models were afflicted by a series of other manufacturing issues, too. Misaligned teeth on the primary drive (which could cause the triplex chains to snap, leading in some cases to damaged crankshafts); weak chain tensioners; incorrectly machined sprockets and cush drives; poorly adjusted triple contact breakers resulting in holed pistons; blued layshafts, gears and selector forks; and inconsistently balanced crankshafts, a problem Mick Crowther identified as the reason some engines vibrated more than others, due to variable machining on the crank webs (in an engine that Triumph's own advertising said 'lets you forget about vibrations' and which in a magazine ad replete with language straight from NASA - 'Blast Off', 'Countdown', 'You're in orbit' - BSA invited customers riding the Rocket 3 to 'feel the smooth acceleration).'

When Barrett returned from the US, Hopwood relocated him and a contingent of Meriden engineers to Small Heath to address the manufacturing errors at the plant responsible for producing the three-cylinder engines. However, Triumph was culpable, too, as Meriden supplied transmission components also found to be at fault, along with engineering drawings that later had to be changed.

As a result, the factories made 24 alterations to the 1969 models. They included a revised gearbox, strengthened connecting rods, and various upgrades to the primary chain tensioner.

However, sales remained sluggish. Unsold triples began piling up at both Small Heath and Meriden. Something had to be done.

Blaming poor sales, BSA laid off 1,200 employees at the end of July 1969 and used the stockpiled bikes as a kind of flood barrier to buy time to rearrange production systems at both plants and implement changes to the A75 and T150 1970 model year's specification.

During the winter of 1969-70, Armoury Road constructed a new assembly section. Costing £250,000 and covering an area of 50,000 square feet, it housed four main assembly tracks, three of which were employed building Rocket 3s. Overhead conveyors supplied assembly workers with components manufactured elsewhere in the factory. Fully assembled machines were received at conveniently located rolling road stations, thereby precluding outdoor testing (Meriden also installed rolling roads). Here, motorcycles were tested and either deemed fit for despatch and sent to the warehouse, or passed to the rectification team to remedy any snags.

Barrett's findings in the US and feedback from the Baltimore and Duarte service departments forced Triumph to introduce 124 major engineering changes to the 1969-1970 models. To ensure crankcase joints sealed better, Small Heath installed new precision lapping machines to true the faces. New gasket materials also helped, as did coating castings with shellac to reduce previous problems with porosity.

To address complaints about vibration, Small Heath purchased a German-made crankshaft grinding machine. At £80,000, it was the most expensive piece of equipment bought expressly for manufacturing the three-cylinder motors. Previously, the BSA plant had machined the triple's crankshaft just as it had its twin-cylinder models, confining precision finishing to the crankshaft's journals and bearing surfaces. But to cure inconsistent crankshaft balancing, the plant acted on Mick Crowther's findings and now also machined the crank webs and balanced the crank electronically. They continued to machine and balance the cranks, even after BSA closed its Small Heath forge in 1970 and outsourced the task to a specialist company in Bromsgrove, Worcestershire (the contractor, Garringtons Ltd, supplied forgings to the car industry and could produce crankshafts at a rate Armoury Road simply couldn't match).

Bit by bit, Armoury Road and Meriden were overcoming the triples' early problems. As a result of the changes introduced by the factory, the triples were becoming more reliable - so much so that by 1971 *Cycle* magazine declared the new Threes 'bulletproof.' Yet the most obvious of the newly introduced changes had nothing to do with reliability or performance.

At a time when Meriden was operating at full pelt to satisfy US dealers' demand for the 500 and 650 twins, Jack Wilson, from Big D Cycle in Texas, complained that they 'couldn't *give* those 1969 Tridents away, they were so ugly'. Meriden, whose products were famed for their good looks, had no choice but to respond.

THE TRIDENT GETS A MAKEOVER

In February 1970, Triumph exhibited a very different looking T150 at that year's Southern California's Anaheim Show. Dispensing with the Trident's 'breadbin' fuel tank and ray-gun silencers, the display bike modelled a kit which dealers could retro-fit to T150s gathering dust in their showrooms. Comprising a traditionally-shaped 3.5 gallon fuel tank, T120-style dual seat, cigar-shaped silencers, rounder side panels, and replacement air filter and mudguards, the easy-to-install kit converted the T150's slab-sided cycle parts to the more popular look of the Trident's Trophy and Bonneville stablemates. The 'beauty kit', as it was later dubbed (or '1970 North American Variant' as it was described in the parts list for the Trident), transformed unsold '69-model Tridents so that they more closely resembled, but were not identical to, the upgraded three-cylinder machines Meriden was set to launch in two months time.

Exactly how unloved Ogle's designs were with US dealers was demonstrated in dramatic fashion by Jack Wilson who confessed that once he had his hands on the makeover kits, he flattened thirty brand new angular-styled tanks with a sledgehammer. Dealers such as Detroit-based Bob Leppan disposed of the original fibre-glass side panels and square-edged tanks by offering them to customers who purchased facelift-kitted bikes. Few, however, accepted Leppan's offer.

Then, just a month before American dealers were due to take delivery of Triumph's 1970 models, the Trident took part in the very first motorcycle magazine group comparison test. The 'Big 7 Superbike Shootout' appeared in the March 1970 issue of *Cycle* magazine and tested the Trident, the Rocket 3, Honda CB750, Kawasaki MACH III, Norton Commando S, Harley-Davidson XLCH, and Suzuki Titan against one another in a contest comparing price, acceleration, braking and handling.

The Trident acquitted itself well and staffers ranked it second only to the Commando as the easiest bike of the group to ride fast (despite the Triumph's heavy clutch, limited lean angles, and annoying vibration at 5,000 to 6,000rpm).

Its quickest time on the drag strip was 12.78 seconds at 103.92mph (editor Cook Neilson - pronounced *Nelson* - said the triple 'came out of the hole like a freight train'). The Triumph was the second quickest of the group, just behind the Norton, which posted 12.69 at 103.68. The Trident also performed well in the handling test, negotiating the road race course 'like it was on rails', although Technical Editor Jess Thomas noted that his lap times suffered due to the triple's poor front brake. (In deceleration tests, *Cycle* ranked the disc-braked Honda CB750 top and the two-stroke triple Kawasaki 500 second.)

~ ~ ~

Favourable reviews, improving build quality and reliability, and the Trident's facelift all helped sales. So too did the triple's phenomenal success on the track (proving the truth of the late Harry Sturgeon's marketing adage: 'Win on Sunday, sell on Monday').

8

THE TRIDENT WINS USA'S FIRST 24-HOUR RACE

AND DOUG HELE HAS FIVE MONTHS TO PREPARE THE TRIPLES FOR DAYTONA

'Win on Sunday, sell on Monday'
(BSA Chief Executive Harry Sturgeon's marketing maxim)

Gene Romero

THE TRIDENT ENTERS THE FIRST US 24-HOUR MOTORCYCLE RACE

In 1970, Jim Cotherman of C&D Incorporated, a Triumph and BMW dealership in Freeport, Illinois, selected a brand new metallic green Trident from his shop, rode the bike 500 miles to break it in, then completely dismantled it for inspection. What Jim found was pretty typical of Tridents manufactured around that time: a fractured valve spring, loose cylinder studs, misaligned pushrod, and an oil seal in the inner primary case that the factory had put in back to front. Still, there was nothing there that couldn't be corrected - or halt Cotherman and *Cycle* journalist Phil Schilling in their plans for this bike: take the Trident to Ohio's Nelson Ledges circuit and compete in America's first 24-hour motorcycle endurance race introduced just a year earlier.

The triple had already proved itself capable of withstanding ultra-high speed thrashing over long distances. In April 1969, the German motorcycle magazine *Motorrad* arranged for British press bike registration number SAC 341G (stock except for S&W racing valve springs) to re-run the 767 mile journey from Hamburg in Germany to Vienna in Austria, which the magazine had tackled before on a two-stroke Yamaha. However, after reaching speeds of between 90 and 110mph on Germany's unrestricted autobahns, the Trident's rider, Hans Ehlert, was forced to abandon the attempt south of Munich when he ran into snow blizzards.

At 4.45am on 2 May, the Trident set off again, this time piloted by Peter Karlau, but now heading in the opposite direction - north from Vienna to Hamburg. After eight hours and forty-three minutes actual riding, the Trident averaged 88.85mph, beating the Yamaha's average speed by more than 11mph (*Motorrad* felt the T150 might have done even better had its tank been larger and they'd not had to stop to refuel so often). The next day, the magazine rode the bike a further 1,740 miles from Hamburg to Stuggart. In all, the bike got through two tyres, a rear chain, half a tank of Castrol R, and lost a couple of fasteners along the way.

Eight weeks later, *Motorcyclist Illustrated* rode a near-stock Trident to its first win on a UK mainland circuit when, on 29 June, journalist Ray Knight won at Thruxton - not once, but twice!

Borrowing a bike from Stan Brand of Hughes Motorcycles, Knight entered and won both of the programme's seven-lap races aboard the same bike Hughes had campaigned to seventh place in that year's Isle of Man 750 class Production TT.

Schilling, therefore, had good reason to consider the Triumph up to the task. And, in spite of the Trident's known failings - oil leaks and indifferent build quality - the T150 also had its virtues: superlative handling and a fast, mile-munching engine.

He approached Cotherman's Midwestern shop with his idea. Cotherman (the titular 'C' in 'C&D') agreed with Schilling's plan and set about preparing the Trident. He narrowed the valve seats to aid gas flow, swapped the stock valve springs for American-made S&W items, and machined the carburettor manifolds to match the intake ports. He also balanced the conrods and pistons, and was meticulous when re-assembling the engine. He took similar care with the triple's chassis, removing the bike's side and centre stands and raising the ray-gun silencers to improve ground clearance. Apart from fitting lower handlebars, the Trident was otherwise box stock, right down to its Dunlop tyres.

Meanwhile, Schilling had chosen his riders for the four-man team: two AMA-licensed students at Wisconsin University named Finlayson and Schoville; Canadian Richard White who raced a Ducati single; and Cotherman, who was the only one amongst them who had raced anything larger than a 250. Each would take a one-hour stint at the throttle. Because he was the fastest, they elected White to go first so that he could grab the team the lead.

At 3pm on a July Saturday in 1970, at Nelson Ledges circuit[*] north-east of Grantsville, Ohio, the competitor's bikes were lined up for a Le Mans-style start. Riders sprinted to their mounts at the drop of the starter flag. White, however, couldn't get the Trident started after flooding the carbs. He kicked away uselessly whilst the other riders roared off. Eventually, the Trident fired up and White went chasing the pack. Within twenty minutes he'd not only caught up but had passed them all to take the lead.

But the Trident's cornering clearance remained a concern. To avoid wearing a hole in the exhaust, the team rode 'European style', hanging off the bike to keep it as upright as possible.

They refuelled at every second rider change. Over the course of the race they adjusted the chain twice, swapped the rear wheel for one with a fresh tyre, and disabled the rear brake after realising they had completely worn down the brake shoe. Even after Schoville ran wide and came off at 75mph in the pitch dark, cracking the Trident's headlamp, they managed to maintain the lead White had secured at the beginning of the contest.

By the time the race finished at 3pm the following day, the Trident was 20 laps ahead of second place Dennis Coply and Dick Mankamyer's Harley Sportster. They beat Skip Eaken and Rowland Kanner and their Norton Commando into third place, and a Honda 450 to fourth. Finlayson felt that even the bike which ran the Trident closest, a Kawasaki MACH III, was doing so whilst still laps behind them.

The Trident remained reliable while rivals, including Honda Fours, were having their engines rebuilt under lanterns. It was a remarkable achievement and the Trident's success gave Cotherman's dealership lots of publicity. Ever the salesman, Cotherman brought the triple back to his shop, returned it to road trim and sold it as a used bike. Moreover, the metallic green endurance-winner gave its local owner trouble-free service for many years afterward.

Impressive as the Trident's track successes in the hands of dealers and journalists undoubtedly were, the triple's most memorable campaigns were fought by the factory teams.

Daytona!

In the autumn of 1969, Triumph's race-shop chief, Doug Hele, initiated a four-month programme to build a three-cylinder 750 capable of beating all comers on the race tracks of America. The bike was to be ready to compete in Daytona in five month's time. Fortunately, the facilities for the project were already largely in place at Meriden.

When Harry Sturgeon was appointed Chief Executive in 1964, he encouraged the Group to officially participate in road racing. Such campaigns could be hugely expensive and it was an activity that up till then both BSA and Triumph had always approached rather tentatively. Sturgeon, however, was very marketing orientated and an adherent of the maxim: 'Win on Sunday, sell on Monday'. He firmly believed that victory on the track won customers in the showrooms. Unlike Honda, though, who garnered sales from

---

    *   Nelson Ledges circuit was also known for a while as the Steel Cities International Raceway.

the reflected cachet of their exotic race-winning grand prix machines, Sturgeon felt that campaigning road-based bikes would persuade customers that supremacy on the circuits translated to superiority on the highway.

Hele, who had been enticed by Bert Hopwood to leave Norton and join him at Triumph to head up the race-shop (as well as work with Bert on finalising the unit-construction twins and develop the ideas the two had for a three-cylinder engine), was delighted. Hele had hoped to develop a multi-cylinder racer when he was with Norton, but left when he realised that Bracebridge Street simply didn't have the funds (and, besides, AMC - Norton's parent company - were transferring production to London and Hele had no intention of leaving his beloved Midlands).

He threw himself into the task (albeit developing the twins for racing rather than the triple, which was still some years away from readiness). He used Sturgeon's modestly-budgeted race programme to extend the Meriden development department's usual experimental work. Then, in September 1965, TriCor's racing manager Rod Coates and Cliff Guild, his chief tuner, flew from the US to England to discuss Meriden's response to Honda's entry of their new 450cc DOHC twin in the middleweight event at Daytona the following spring.

There were just five months to go before the race. With both time and money tight, Hele and his team had to be resourceful. Although they had just one man, Jack Shemans, on the factory test bench, that didn't pose Hele too many problems as he dusted off data from his days at Norton developing the Domiracer and managed to apply it to the very different architecture of the Triumph.

Against the odds, Hele's team succeeded in getting the new 500s ready for the 1966 Daytona races held in early March. Taking standard roadsters off the assembly line, Hele personally tuned the four T100 Tiger-based racers that Triumph took to Florida. The bikes had lightened, strengthened frames, and the motors boasted hard-faced BSA A65 camshafts, a process Coates and Guild had brought to Hele's notice (as Hele explained to *Cycle World* in 1967: 'It pays to have the same size cams at the end of the race as you start with').

Meriden's race chief greatly valued Rod Coates and Cliff Guild's expertise - 'We learned from each other on that trip' acknowledged the then 46-year-old Hele, 'not least being the use of hard-faced cams which Cliff Guild had been using'. All the same, he arranged for the 500s to be shipped to the States as close to race time as possible because he said American tuners would lose two brake horsepower every week they had their hands on them.

At Daytona, Buddy Elmore rode his considerably reworked half-litre twin to victory against Harley's side-valve 750s. After working his way up from forty-sixth to first place, the Texan crossed the finish line one minute ahead of the second-place KR750. It was an historic win and Elmore's victory inspired a new model: The Daytona. BSA's factory team, on the other hand, hit up against all kinds of problems.

The following year, both factories returned to Daytona - but now with six machines each; whilst all six BSAs were forced to retire, every one of the Triumphs finished the course - Buddy Elmore taking second place this time, with the Oklahoman Gary Nixon clinching top spot (Nixon would go on to take the Number One plate from Harley that year and the next).

In 1969, works tester Percy Tait took a 500cc twin, which was very similar to the Daytona-winning machines, to second place at the Belgian Grand Prix, runner up to MV Agusta's three-cylinder twin cam works racer ridden by the Italian, Giacomo Agostini. But, it wasn't just the 500s that were doing well on the tarmac.

John Hartle won the Isle of Man's first production TT on a T120 in 1967. Two years later, eight of the top ten machines at 1969's Production TT were T120Rs. At their head was Malcolm Uphill who won the event riding a Triumph 650 at an average speed of 99.99mph. The Welshman became the first man to lap the mountain course at more than 100mph on a production machine. Indeed, he exceeded 100mph on two out of his three laps - 100.09mph from a standing start on his first, and 100.39 in his second, clocking a top speed of 134.6mph. And, had he not backed off on his final circuit, he would have cracked the ton for the entire race.[*] In honour of Uphill's achievement, Dunlop later marketed the K81 tyres worn by the record-breaking Bonneville, and which originally were developed for the BSA and Triumph triples, as the TT100.

Yet, despite Triumph's track achievements in 1969 culminating in the FIM awarding the factory that season's *Coupe d'Endurance*, it was clear that Meriden needed a new engine if they were to remain competitive.

Uphill's feat had come at a price. After four laps, his bike was spent. In just 150 racing miles, not that far as TT distances go, the Bonneville's pistons were cracking up to such a degree that the bike was incapable of completing another circuit of the course. Team mate Rod Gould had been clocked at more than 140mph and was tipped to win, but had to retire after his Bonneville suffered a snapped crankshaft. The twins were being pushed to the edge of their capabilities and race teams were finding that they had to strip, rebuild and even replace main engine castings before every key race.

At Daytona, Harley had turned the tables on Triumph's 500s in both '68 and '69. Harley-Davidson's racing department ploughed a rumoured half a million dollars into recapturing the Number One plate in '68. And although the red-haired Nixon was lapping two seconds faster than when he won in Florida in 1967, H-D's ace tuner Dick O'Brien managed to get the prehistoric KR-flatheads to outgun the British half-litre twins by as much as 15mph on the top end.[**] Nixon ended up finishing nineteenth after his

---

[*]   Uphill was not the first man to lap the Isle of Man's TT Course at 100mph. In 1957, the 'Flying Scot' Bob McIntyre posted the first 100mph lap on a 'dustbin'-faired works Gilera 500 four in the year the TT races celebrated its Jubilee year. Uphill's distinction was that he was the first to break the ton on a production bike.

[**]   In 2012, *Cycle World's* technical editor Kevin Cameron revealed in his monthly column 'TDC' that Harley's remarkable gains in performance at Daytona in 1968 were down to more than the KR's Cal Tech wind-tunnel-designed fairing and dual Tillotson diaphragm carburettors as is generally thought. In the piece, Cameron relates a story he was told by dirt-track racer and frame designer Neil Keen about how he and C.R. Axtell studied the combustion chambers of flat-head engines from Graham, Auburn and Hudson automobiles and discovered that by dropping the KR's compression ratio to as low as three-to-one, they

T100R's ignition packed up. He won only two Nationals in 1968: the season's opener in Houston and the Columbus half-mile.* The following year, he only managed ninth place at Daytona. It was Triumph's worst result in the 200 miler since 1960, and Meriden was not best pleased.

Moreover, Milwaukee was scheduled to replace their side-valve KRs with the overhead-valve XR750 as the AMA lifted its Harley-friendly restrictions limiting overhead-valve engines to 500cc.** The AMA's change to its decades-old Class C rules now permitted any engine configuration or valve arrangement as long as the engine was available to the public in significant numbers. The change opened the door to two-strokes. It meant Honda could enter their overhead cam 750 four. It also allowed BSA/Triumph to campaign their A75 and T150 750cc triples - the engine the Midland combine now elected to lead the British charge on America's racetracks. (Perhaps somewhat curiously, the BSA Group had chosen not to race their 750 three-cylinder machines when they launched them in 1968. This, in spite of Norton doing so with their new 750 almost as soon the Commando went on sale.)

An important push in the triples' favour came when, over in America, Peter Thornton, the newly appointed president of the recently formed Birmingham Small Arms Corporation Incorporated, was approached by BSA's head of racing in the US, Pete Colman. Colman suggested that BSA and Triumph's respective East and West Coast race teams come together and work out of BSA/Triumph's joint facility in Duarte, California. Thornton agreed and approved an initial racing budget of $440,000 for the 1970 season. In return, Thornton gave his race chief a very simple directive. In July 1969, Thornton declared that Team BSA and Team Triumph would dominate dirt and track racing in the States in 1970.

increased airflow by almost 50 per cent. The reason for this impressive increase was due to the fact that in a flat-head engine the side-valve chamber performs both airflow and combustion-chamber functions because the valve is to the side of the piston, not above it. Air has to negotiate three 90 degree turns starting at the carburettor and upward to the underside of the valve. From there it must turn sideways to exit the valve chamber, then over and across the top of the piston before flowing downwards as the piston descends for its downstroke. According to airflow expert Kenny Augustine: 'You can make air go fast and you can make it go around corners, but you can't do both at once.' The optimum shape of the piston crown and combustion chamber should therefore be wide and smooth to achieve the best airflow (albeit at the expense of compression ratio and torque). After experimenting with quarter-inch thick head gaskets and re-shaped ports, Keen and Axtell presented their findings to Harley's race manager Dick O'Brien.

In just four months of development, the team saw horsepower gains of over 10 per cent as power output rose from 53bhp to more than 60bhp (with perhaps a further two horsepower available, according to Keen: 'If the factory had not had had a previously-signed contract to use those sorry-ass Tillotson chainsaw carburettors…').

* Despite only two wins, Nixon retained his Number One plate even though Harley won eighteen out of the season's twenty-three races. Nixon's consistent second and third-placings meant that the title went down to the very last race, where his fourth place at Ascot to his nearest points rival, H-D rider Fred Nix's seventh place handed Nixon his second consecutive Grand National Championship with a season total of 622 points to Nix's 613.

** With around a third of the US workforce unemployed in 1932, the AMA introduced Class C racing rules in 1934 to help club riders by permitting the use of stock street bikes. The rules limited overhead-valve engines to 500cc and a compression ratio of no more than 7.5:1, whilst the less efficient side-valve engines could be 45 cubic inches (750cc). Machines had to run on pump gasoline. Competitors couldn't tow or trailer the bike, but had to ride the bikes they raced to and from the meeting. Modifications were limited to bobbing the rear fender and removing street equipment such as lights (and the front brake's internal components for machines competing in dirt oval races). And to stop manufacturers entering works bikes, competitors had to provide proof of ownership.

The AMA Grand National championship was America's premier series. Comprising up to 25 rounds in a season, it was mixture of dirt racing - where the British twins were able to hold their own - and track racing.

Doug Hele wrote to the company's managers suggesting that the factory should shift its focus from production racing to the new F750 open class. In a confidential memo dated 10 September 1969, Triumph's chief development engineer argued that 'Production racing has restricted development'.

Hele contended that, 'Instead of using in production something that has been used in development, the [F750] rules ensure no changes can be made, other than secret internal modifications of a minor nature.'

He believed that 'F750 would provide a competition department which would create a vast store of information on new approaches to problems, as a guide to our designers.'

The BSA/Triumph Board agreed. In spite of the company's growing financial problems, they announced that BSA/Triumph would mount a serious assault on America's new 750cc formula class and develop the triple to take on the Honda Four.

There were just two problems.

The shotgun marriage of BSA and Triumph and their East and West Coast distributors - whereby they were forced to move all race-bike development work to Duarte and share paddock space with their one-time rivals - was proving unpopular (some Triumph men speculating that Thornton was simply following orders from his bosses back in England to ensure the 1970 AMA Championship went to BSA).

The other problem was that Daytona was less than five months away.

HELE APPLIES LESSONS FROM THE DAYTONA-WINNING 500 TWIN

Work to develop a racing triple took place at Meriden. Staff and facilities normally employed developing prototypes of road machines were redeployed to work wholly on the race programme, as was nearly all of the Experimental Department. By November, the team was working till 10pm and, according to Les Williams, a chargehand in the department at the time, staff lived on Chinese takeaways. 'Sometimes,' he recalled many years later, 'my wife Joan would cook dinner for half a dozen of us.'

From the outset, the BSA Group's marketing strategy was to promote both marques and Hele had to build three BSA-branded machines and three others labelled Triumph. The Tridents kept their vertical cylinder heads; the BSA's retained their inclined barrels and timing covers (although cut down to improve clearance). All six engines were fitted with the curvier-shaped Triumph gearbox outer cover.

If, as has been suggested, Hele's work on the Daytona-winning 500s fatefully delayed the launch of the triple, he redressed this somewhat by applying much of what he learned developing the T100R to the three-cylinder race bikes. 'It must be emphasised,' wrote Les Williams in the foreword of Claudio Sintich's book, *Road Racing History of the Triumph 500 Unit Twin*, 'that the achievements of the little T100 racers and the wily race testing of Percy [Tait], contributed greatly to the world beating Triples.' For example, to achieve a better spread of power, Hele had adopted the BSA 650 Spitfire cam-form for the works Thruxton Bonnevilles; and a new cam, coded TH6,* the same cam Hele had first developed for the Percy Tait GP racers, was later used very successfully on the racing Daytona and production Trident and Rocket 3 three-cylinder racers (with the Experimental Department applying a Eutectic** metal-spraying process to the cams to extend their service life).

As the machines would be running at full throttle on the high-speed sections of Daytona's banked track, to aid gas flow, Hele replaced the road bike's standard 27mm Concentrics and installed a trio of rubber-mounted $1^3/_{16}$ inch Amal Grand Prix carburettors like those he'd used on the T100-based racers.

And, as with the Daytona-winning T100Rs, he raised the triple's compression to 11:1 (using high-compression pistons).*** In compliance with the AMA rules, Hele re-bored the cylinders to their maximum oversize, which increased engine capacity to around 760cc. Standard cylinder head castings were reworked by the race shop, modifications to which included resetting the centre spark plug hole to ensure compression read the same across all three cylinders.

Hele's attempts at a racing exhaust for the triple began as a three-pipe system. Before long, he started experimenting with headers that flowed into a single outlet, following reports he had picked up from America that such an arrangement showed real promise, modelling itself, as it did, on the two-into-one exhausts fitted to some dirt-trackers. Jack Wilson despatched from Triumph's Baltimore-based headquarters a system for Hele's scrutiny that the Texan had devised for the Trident. Having commandeered two of the Experimental Department's trio of dynometer test beds, Hele concluded the collector box was where most gains were to be achieved and set about working up a design that would be easier to produce than Wilson's system and which distributed exhaust gases more evenly. The resulting hand-hammered three-into-one system with four-inch megaphone, as well as saving weight, bettered Hele's own original three-pipe arrangement by up to 5bhp. It also became the first such system on a factory race bike.

All told, the changes resulted in engines that pumped out around 84bhp at 8,250rpm (with the best producing up to 86bhp) - an increase of around 25 per cent over the road bike.

---

* The 'T' denoted Triumph; the 'H' stood for Hele; and the 'G' indicated that it was the sixth variation.

** Eutectic process comprises a mixture of substances, usually alloy, with the lowest possible melting point of all the possible mixtures of those ingredient substances. According to Mick Duckworth's *Triumph and BSA Triples*, Experimental mechanic Arthur Jakeman applied the coating using a gas torch whilst turning the cams on a rig powered by a car windscreen wiper motor.

*** Engineers measure a four-stroke engine's compression ratio as the volume in a cylinder and combustion chamber when the piston is at the bottom of its stroke compared to the volume that is left when the piston has risen and is at the very top of its stroke (known as Top Dead Centre or TDC for short). The smaller the space that remains with the piston at TDC, the greater the difference or ratio will be. Usually expressed as a numerical value, the higher the compression ratio is, the greater the net power an engine is likely to develop. However, if the compression ratio is too high, it can induce pre-detonation. This condition is when the charge detonates instead of burning smoothly and progressively. Using a high-octane fuel raises the level that pre-ignition, known as 'knocking,' occurs.

All this power was transmitted through a close ratio five-speed gearbox, using the same internal components that transmission specialist Rod Quaife in Kent had provided for the race version of the 500 and 'Proddy' 650 race bikes. However, to comply with AMA rules, because the road versions of the Rocket 3 and Trident were four-speeders, Hele flew out fifty complete five-cog boxes to New York so that BSA Corporation Incorporated could add them to US parts books and inventories as a stock option available for sale to the public.

Presented with just six weeks turnaround time in order to be ready for Daytona, Ken Sprayson from Reynolds Tube in Birmingham, who had made the chassis for Percy Tait's 500cc Grand Prix racer, was obliged to turn down the job of designing and fabricating six purpose-built frames to house the three-cylinder engines - three for the BSA-badged racers and three for the Triumphs.[*]

Instead, at Percy Tait's suggestion, Hele commissioned independent chassis fabricator, twenty-nine-year-old Rob North, who was at that time based just a few miles from Meriden in a former colliery clocking-on shed in Bedworth. Working in close collaboration with Hele around an engine and front frame section supplied by Triumph, the six duplex triangular loop frames manufactured from Reynolds 531 tubing were built to the same pattern. Yet none were exactly alike[**] in size or geometry (although North charged BSA the same price for each: £145), so mechanics would not be able to swap components such as oil tanks from one machine to another.

A combination of disc and drum brakes hauled the whole plot to a stop. Up front was a massive Fontana 10 inch diameter double-sided, twin leading shoe drum brake (like the unit fitted to Nixon's 1967 Daytona-winning twin), batches of which Hele had ordered from the Milan-based company in October 1969. At the rear, a hydraulically-actuated two-piston calliper gripped a nine-inch cast iron rotor from Automotive Products (discs brakes still something of a novelty on motorcycles at that time).

Both brakes were laced to 18 inch alloy rims front and rear, shod with Goodyear tyres, as stipulated in the American riders' contracts. Forks were standard T150, but lowered and assembled with carefully selected stock components.

The Group's R&D centre, Umberslade Hall, was charged with developing the triples' aerodynamic glassfibre bodywork. Engineering Director, Mike Needham - whose background before joining BSA in 1968 included working for Scott motorcycles as a youth, the aircraft company Bristol, and on the Bloodhound jet-engined missiles - assembled a small group of technicians headed by Graham Nicholson and Trevor Winship.

An unfaired Rob North-framed prototype had circled the Motor Industry Research Association's high-banked test track near Nuneaton at 140mph. However, MIRA's track and its wind tunnel (which could only simulate speeds up to around 100mph)

---

[*]   According to BSA/Triumph's Chief Stylist Stephen Mettam, in a series of articles he wrote for *Motorcycle Classic* magazine in 1997, BSA/Triumph turned to Reynolds to build 'one-off' frames to avoid disturbing the factory.

[**]   Daytona rules required competing machines to be based on production models. However, they permitted the use of special racing chassis.

were both inadequate for testing the triple's streamlining at the velocities it was clear the triple could attain.

Needham's team therefore used the sub-sonic wind tunnel at the Royal Aircraft Establishment's research facility in Farnborough to develop the prototype's fairing and bodywork, which now comprised a taller than usual tailpiece to smooth airflow and reduce drag from the turbulence created in the machine's wake. Given the ultra-high speeds possible at Daytona International Speedway this was important.

Whilst the effects of drag at low speed are minimal, the air resistance a vehicle generates quadruples as its speed doubles. This means that a machine travelling at 60mph produces four times as much drag as it does travelling at 30mph. With the power required to overcome that four-fold increase in resistance being the *cube* of the speed, accelerating from 30mph to 60mph demands eight times as much power. The taller tailpieces gave the Beezumphs, as the triples were later known, an extra 200rpm, and another 3mph at the Speedbowl (provoking protests from the Harley-Davidson camp).

In January 1970, speed testing for the triples moved to RAF Elvington near York (MIRA's test track being too short to accommodate the machine's top speed), where the air force runway played occasional host to speed record attempts.

The test team took up position on a freezing cold Saturday morning. Snow covered the bomber base's two-mile long runway and the RAF refused to send out a sweeper to clear a path. By midday, however, most of the snow had cleared and Percy Tait took the faired prototype out for its first run. Hele clocked him at 164mph.

The race chief then prepared the timing lights to record Tait's second pass. It was nearly 3pm. Tait launched the triple down the strip, but this time in the opposite direction and with the runway inclined slightly downhill. To Hele's dismay, Tait fell off the bike as he approached the end of the run. Thankfully, Percy was unhurt, but the bike's top speed was down, Hele recording just 157mph on this run. Hele immediately assumed engine trouble - a closed tappet, perhaps. Tait's first surmise was that he'd lost speed due to clutch slip. Soon, however, he and Hele realised that the difference was actually due to rear-wheel slip as the tyre struggled to find grip on the icy runway (which also explained Tait's tumble at the end of the run).

Tait's two runs proved that the fairing worked - aerodynamically, at least; Elvington had been simply too cold to test the fairing's engine-cooling properties. Hele could therefore only guess at how they might perform under the heat of a Floridian spring sun.

It now was January. He had just six weeks to have the bikes ready for Daytona.

BSA/TRIUMPH ASSEMBLE A STELLAR RACE TEAM

The Beezumph's fuel tank and seat were made of fibreglass manufactured by Screen & Plastic, the same supplier who had moulded the bodywork for the 'Proddy' racing twins. The tank held five gallons (the underseat oil tank carried 10 pints). The marques were distinguished by contrasting liveries on the two variants of the fairing that the team brought to Daytona for testing during practice: red and white for the trio of BSAs, and blue and white painted bodywork for the three Triumphs.

To pilot the 375lb triples, BSA and Triumph assembled a stellar cast. Firstly, BSA pulled off a marketing coup by coaxing nine-time world champion Mike Hailwood out of retirement to ride the red and white triples in Daytona, a track at which in 1964 the British legend had set a world record of more than 144mph and where he also won the 500cc US Grand Prix (on both occasions aboard a works MV Agusta four).

Hailwood, who would turn 30 in a few weeks time, announced to the press - Sinatra-style - that this Daytona outing would be his last racing a motorcycle (he was scheduled to compete in Florida again the very next weekend, but this time at Sebring racing cars).

Hailwood's BSA Team co-riders were two Americans: Dave Aldana and Jim Rice. Aldana was just twenty. Both he and Rice were from the west coast and both usually rode BSA twins, the latter to three Grand National wins the previous year, all on dirt. (Having held back from approaching their former factory rider, Dick Mann, because at 36 they were worried he was past his prime, BSA eventually approached the 1963 Grand National champion - who had ridden the Rocket 3 into the record books at the Speedway less than a year earlier in April '69 - only to find they were too late. Mann had already signed up with American Honda to ride the Hansen Team CR750.)

Riding the blue and white Triumphs were three Americans. They included last year's runner up in the AMA Grand National, twenty-three-year-old Gene Romero. Nicknamed 'Burritto',* he and Aldana - who shared Romero's south of the border ancestry - called themselves 'Team Mexico'. The young Californian was a tenacious competitor who viewed himself primarily as a dirt-track racer although victory in Nebraska the previous year at the Lincoln TT proved he was capable on tarmac, too.

Also riding for Team Triumph was Oklahoman Gary Nixon, who had ridden Hele's 500cc Triumph twin to victory at Daytona three years earlier and secured the factory the AMA Championship two years running in 1967 and '68. Nixon, however, had broken his left leg half way through the '69 season when he crashed his bike racing on the Santa Rosa Mile flat-track. The third rider was the Californian rookie, twenty-year-old Don Castro.

Accompanying the team was factory racer and test rider Percy Tait. Tait was at Daytona *officially* as an adviser to the six riders, none of whom had any experience of the factory three-cylinder machines (although Nixon and Castro had dirt-raced Trackmaster-framed triples to second and third place last year at Pennsylvania's $1^1/_8$ mile Nazareth, giving the triple its best dirt placing). But, after having his ride commandeered by the

---

* A burrito is a Mexican dish comprising a meat, chicken, bean or cheese-filled tortilla, and Mexican Spanish for a young donkey.

Americans (the Brit racers' one-off rides being of no help to the Americans trying to achieve their season target of Grand National points), Tait contacted Rob North that Friday asking him to fabricate a seventh frame. Working right through the weekend, North delivered a newly minted frame to Meriden at one o'clock Monday morning, which the race shop built up in Triumph colours and shipped to Florida on the Wednesday, its engine not even bench-tested.

Supporting the riders were two teams of mechanics. US riders had their own American fitters and tuners, whilst mechanics working for Doug Hele included old hands from previous twin-cylinder racing campaigns, Arthur Jakeman, Fred Swift and Jack Shemans. Present also were BSA Group engineers, like Mike Needham. Wrenching Hailwood's bike was Mack Kambayoshi, who, to keep track of his work, would stamp 'MK' on his charge's crankcases.

In the week of training preceding race day, it was clear Florida's March weather was causing the triples problems. With spring temperatures in Daytona sometimes matching those of a hot summer in England, mechanics were having to remove ducting from inside the fairings to improve airflow to the engine.

Other problems also surfaced.

Pat Owens, Triumph's Western service manager in the US and Gene Romero's road race tuner in 1970, realised that Romero had the slowest of the three Tridents. With the three-lap qualifying sessions set to take place on Friday to establish each competitor's grid position for race day on Sunday, Owens had his work cut out to improve the bike's pace.

He swapped out the triple's 18 inch wheels and tyres for narrow ribbed 3.50 x 19 inch Goodyear hoops front and back, which Owens had inflated to over 40psi (compromising safety and the machine's suitability to the track's infield section). He had the fairing polished to cut down drag, and to reduce friction Owens removed grease from the wheel bearings.

Pre-race qualifying laps were run on the two-and-a-half-mile all-banked Speedbowl and not Daytona's infield section. A rider's first circuit of the track was a warm-up lap, the second their timed lap (their third circuit was a slowing-down lap).

Canadian racer Yvon Duhamel had set a new qualifying record when he reached 150mph on his open-class air-cooled two-stroke 350cc Yamaha the previous year, a speed the British triples had already proved they could top.

Castro, Nixon, Hailwood, Romero and Tait all posted average qualifying speeds that meant they were in amongst the first ten grid places on race day. And although Tait and Castro ran slower than Duhamel's 1969 qualifying speed, Hailwood and Nixon's 750 triples took the second and third spots with average speeds of 152.90mph and 152.82mph respectively, putting them ahead of Dick Mann's fourth-placed CR750 Honda at 152.67mph and Kel Carruthers' fifth-poled 350 Yamaha at 151.72mph.

Outpacing them all, however, was the Burritto. Gene Romero's Triumph averaged 157.34mph. Moreover, just seconds before Romero shut off the throttle to take a turn, the blue and white triple streaked through an unofficial speed trap to record an astonishing flat-out speed of 165.44mph. When Romero came into the pits after completing his three qualifying laps, Owens said the bike's skinny-ribbed Goodyear tyres 'had slivers of rubber hanging off, nearly shredded'.

Perhaps inevitably, Harley-Davidson lodged a complaint and AMA scrutineers forced the BSA and Triumph teams to cut down the triples' tall tail sections - thought to give the Beezumphs an extra 3mph - by a couple of inches.

Even so, the stage was set for the triples to put in a winning performance come show time on Sunday. It seemed that all BSA and Triumph had to do was to follow former actor Ronald Reagan's advice: 'Learn your lines and don't bump into the furniture'.

Dick Mann over at Honda, however, was rehearsing an altogether different script.

9

Dick Mann On The Honda CR750 Beats BSA/Triumph At Daytona 1970

And Wins Again In '71 For BSA/Triumph

'I had my race face on'
(Bob Hansen, personal mechanic to Dick Mann at the 1970 Daytona 200)

Dick 'Bugs' Mann

Daytona International Speedway

Daytona Beach lies on the Florida peninsula's east side, about 200 miles up the coast from Miami. To the west of the resort, sited at its outskirts, lies the Daytona International Speedway (or the 'Speedbowl' as it is also known). The high-banked, ultra-high-speed tri-oval tarmac circuit opened for business in 1961, the brainchild of local entrepreneur William H.G. France. Up till then, the 200 mile race had been run since the late 1930s on a 3.2 mile circuit comprising a narrow road behind the dunes and on the hard white sands facing out to the Atlantic Ocean.

The new Speedway was carved out of 455 acres of reclaimed swampland at a cost of three million dollars. Over a million cubic yards of earth were excavated to construct the Speedway's banked curves and carve out a 44 acre artificial lake. Boasting nine grandstands for 60,000 spectators, space for a further 75,000 people on its infield section, and parking for a like number of cars, and with tracks providing circuits varying in length from 1.3 to 3.87 miles, the Speedway was designed primarily for stock car racing and the AMA was slow in letting motorcycles tear round its 31 degree banked curves, initially restricting them to a rather unexciting two-mile circuit. That would change. As the Sixties wound on, Daytona International Speedway's 200 miler played host to some epic clashes and the race proved an increasingly important showcase for motorcycle manufacturers.

In 1969, the AMA's Competitions Congress scrapped its protectionist, decades-old rules that gave the big-bore American V-twins lawful parity with 500cc overhead-valve engines. The AMA's move opened up racing in the US to every type of production-based engine from 350 to 750cc. Only Harley-Davidson challenged the change and pushed for a twelve-month moratorium. They were unsuccessful. The new multis from Honda, BSA and Triumph, Kawasaki's 500cc triple and Suzuki's slim-line half-litre twin were free to take on the Milwaukee 750s at the 1970 Daytona 200.

Bob Hansen Lobbies Honda To Race At Daytona

Race day on Sunday 15 March 1970 dawned warm and sunny. With daytime temperatures in Daytona Beach reaching a high of nearly 65 Fahrenheit and light winds of about 8 knots, conditions for racing were good.

Gathered on the starting grid were 98 riders. As the Speedway's finish line is situated on a curved section of banked track, which slopes upward at 18 degrees toward the wall of the Cambell grandstand, race starts at Daytona take place on the flat 1,600 feet long pit lane.

Gene Romero's record-breaking Triumph 750 was at pole position. To his right, sat astride a red and white BSA triple, Mike Hailwood occupied second place; Gary Nixon on the blue and white Triumph occupied the grid's third place; and in fourth place sat Dick Mann on the red and white Honda CR750 Four. The Californian had ridden a good qualifying lap and he and his bike deserved their hard fought grid position, but the fact that man and bike were at Daytona at all was largely due to one man. That man was Bob Hansen.

After the AMA lifted its arcane restrictions to allow all production-model engine configurations to compete in the Nationals, Hansen - American Honda's parts manager - decided to approach his employers in Japan to propose that the company enter the CB750 in the 1970 Daytona 200.

According to Yoshirou Harada, the project leader who oversaw the development of the Dream Four, Bob Hansen's meeting with Honda during a visit to Japan two years earlier had been key in persuading the company to make its 'King of Motorcycles' a four.

Honda, however, was less receptive to Hansen's overtures this time. The company demurred from entering the 750/4 for fear that it might not win. Yet the bike had already proved its potential on the track. At its very first competitive outing in May 1969, at a meeting in Harewood, Ontario, Canadian Mike Manley led a production race for two laps on a straight-from-the-crate, barely prepped bog-stock CB750, before eventually finishing third behind a superior-handling Norton Commando and a Triumph Trident.

More significantly, Honda's own in-house staff racing club, Team Blue Helmet MSC, took their CB750 Fours to the Suzuka 10 Hour Endurance Race in August 1969, and after dominating the event, scored a one-two: Morio Sumiya and Tetsuya Hishiki taking first place and Yoichi Oguma and Minoru Sato coming in a close second.

The following month, on 13 September, a Honda CB750 won France's prestigious *Bol d'Or* (Golden Bowl) 24-hour endurance race held at Montlhéry's banked track on the outskirts of Paris. The French magazine *Moto Revue* had revived the event following the classic marathon's eight-year hiatus. Honda, who did not want an official factory-backed bike entering the French event, nevertheless shipped to the UK two race-tuned CB750s prepared by its top engineers Yoshio Nakamura and Hiroshi Uchida of the Racing Service Club (RSC) for Honda test rider Morio Sumiya to ride in the Japan-only Road Race series. And it was these two bikes that Cheshire dealer and road racer Bill Smith entered in the historic event (Smith's links with the manufacturer went back to the Japanese company's first forays to the TT). It was the first time in two years that Honda had fielded 'official' machines for a road race.

Yoshio Nakamura, fresh from the Honda Formula One car racing team, was made team supervisor. Meanwhile, Smith had pulled together a four-man crew to take on riding duties. His team comprised himself and three other British riders: former Honda GP rider, Tommy Robb; up and coming racer, John Williams; and Bill Smith Motors employee, Steve Murray.

When the team arrived at Montlhéry, however, race organisers explained that the event was only open to riders with a French racing licence. After it became clear that they were not going to budge on this, Nakamura loaned the Paris dealer Japauto one of Bill Smith Motor's factory racers in place of the nearly stock bike of the French team. Fitted with a special exhaust and hotter camshaft, clip-on handlebars, single seat, long aluminium fuel tank, and fairing, piloting duties for the specially-prepared machine fell to a pair of 19-year-old French students, Daniel Urdich and Michel Rougerie.

Japauto were the largest motorcycle dealership in Europe, selling over a thousand new bikes a year. In an effort to combine business with pleasure, Japauto's owner Christian Vilaséca instructed his mechanics to prepare a CB750 for entry to the *Bol d'Or* and show that the new Honda Four was both fast and reliable.

Vilaséca's shop manager and part-time racer, Robert Assante, quickly recruited Urdich to ride the Japauto machine following the teenager's unlikely success campaigning a 250cc twin-cylinder Honda CB72 to second place at that year's 1,000km Le Mans alongside his 18-year old team mate, Robert Gilloux. Assante would have signed Gilloux also, but, at eighteen, he was too young to race anything bigger than the quarter-litre CB72. Assante therefore drafted in Japauto's apprentice mechanic, 19-year-old Michel Rougerie in what was just his second year as a racer riding a 305cc CB77 twin.

After Japauto took over the Bill Smith factory bike, in a further example of *entente cordiale*, Steve Murray helped the French dealer's pit crew as Japauto were not familiar with a CB750 factory racer. To supplement the machine's existing headlamps, he installed an auxiliary spot light from a car (its switch later shorted the machine's lights forcing Rougerie to push the bike into the pits where Murray by-passed the blown fuse with a piece of metal foil).

Rougerie and Uldrich won after completing 445 laps, over a distance of 2,803km (1,742 miles) at an average speed of 116kph (72mph). Along the way, the Smith/Japauto Honda saw off stiff competition from a pair of Laverdas (one of which set the quickest lap), and a Kawasaki half-litre two-stroke triple that led the race just hours ahead of the event finishing, before it was forced into the pits to replace a broken chain. In the end, the Honda finished ten laps in front of a trio of H1s.

It was the first time a four-cylinder motorcycle had won a 24-hour endurance race and Honda's victory at Montlhéry made great marketing copy and boosted European sales, especially in Germany and the *Bol d'Or*'s home market of France. Success in America's 1970 Daytona 200 miler, however, promised even greater publicity and the prize of worldwide sales.

Bob Hansen had been behind Honda's first campaign in Daytona when the eponymous Team Hansen debuted a trio of CR450 factory racers there in March 1967 (the year Gary Nixon secured Triumph's second successive win at the 200 following Buddy Elmore's historic victory the previous season). Nevertheless, despite the twin's promising debut - the Black Bomber-based 450s finished a creditable tenth and twelfth under the rules limiting non-side-valve engines to 500cc; and Jim Odom's 450 broke the lap record in the Amateur 100 miler (before eventually crashing) - the factory dropped out of Daytona the following year to focus on developing the Dream Four.

Hansen therefore seized on the AMA's change to its rules and pressed Honda to return to Daytona Beach in 1970, but this time with the CB750. The Wisconsinite countered Honda's fears of the Four not winning by pointing out that 'out of our 1,200 dealers in the States some would be bound to enter Hondas at Daytona, and they wouldn't be likely to win'. Hansen turned the factory's argument back on itself. 'So it would be best,' he advised, 'if we made a really first-class official effort.'

The Dream Four's project leader, Yoshirou Harada, asked Hansen how fast the bike would need to be and what sort of lap times the American considered they would have to achieve. 'I picked numbers that were better than anyone had actually gone.'

A few days later Harada called Hansen back. 'He said they had fed horsepower and frontal figures through a computer,' Hansen recalled, 'and the top speed I quoted could be achieved.'

'We'll be there' Harada told him.

Hansen's gambit had worked.

Working to a copy of the AMA's technical rules that Hansen had supplied, Honda's RSC built four factory racebikes (twice as many as Bob was expecting). Testing took place in England, after which the Daytona campaign's coordinators, Honda UK and Nakamura, had all four bikes shipped to Florida. Numbered 101, 102, 103 and 105, the break in sequence was deliberate, the number 4 being considered unlucky in Japan (an omission that seems doubly odd given the bikes' engine configuration and the team's composition - a quartet).

The original roster of riders to race the 1970 Daytona 200 was entered by Honda UK and included Steve Murray and Bill Smith, Ulsterman Tommy Robb, and the 1965 50cc world champion, Ralph Bryans. As at Montlhéry, Yoshio Nakamura would supervise the team.

To correct the absence of an American rider on a team campaigning in the most prestigious event in the US Grand National calendar, at the factory's behest, Hansen invited his friend and veteran racer Dick Mann to an interview at American Honda. Mann's former works team, BSA, had failed to offer him a ride because of concerns about his age (he was 36).

Mann agreed a deal. 'The guys at Honda offered me generous terms for the one-off ride,' Mann recalled many years later, 'although most of the reward depended on me winning.' As the Californian's US racing number was 2, he was assigned bike 102 (Honda gave the Scotsman Ralph Bryans bike 101 because, according to Hansen, 'I think they figured Bryans would win'). Hansen told team leader Nakamura he was assuming responsibility for Mann's machine only, following tensions between him and members of the British crew.

Each machine varied slightly from the next in its use of weight-saving materials like titanium and magnesium, alloys which were wholly impractical for production vehicles (and, as a non-stock, un-homologated item, fell outside of the AMA's Class C rules). Also, apart from titanium being much too expensive and magnesium being dangerously combustible and corrosion prone, these exotic alloys brought other problems, too.

UK team mechanic and reserve rider Steve Murray recollected the factory ordering the Stateside team to remove the titanium lower fork yokes for fear of them cracking. Murray also recalled swapping out magnesium-cast crankcases which locked up the engine as they distorted during cooling.

During race practice, the danger of magnesium was spectacularly brought home when Bryans crashed his machine as he entered the banking, the new tyres he was running-in letting go when he introduced power too suddenly (but not before clocking an unofficial 164mph on the bankings). The machine burst into flames, the magnesium cases adding to the pyrotechnics. Fire crews attending the scene were slow to deal with the incident. As a result, many witnessed how the fire so completely destroyed the bike's engine cases that it was clear they could not be standard production items.

Bryans' bike was damaged beyond what was possible to repair in time for Sunday's race so Bill Smith was forced to surrender his ride to the Scotsman.

Further problems emerged during practice. The race-kitted Fours puffed smoke at each gear change; when mechanics changed the oil in Mann's bike, they found bits of metal and rubber from the camshaft drive tensioner. Taking no chances, Hansen had new components installed in Mann's engine for the start of the race.

Whilst Honda's use of exotic castings may have caused Team Hansen difficulties, they provided the BSA/Triumph team's Pat Owens the perfect rejoinder to Yamaha and Honda mechanics threatening to lodge protests about the legality of the British triples' five-speed gearbox. 'I quietly reminded those guys,' Owens said later, 'that their own bikes were just as questionable. For example, when Ralph Bryans' CR750 Honda crashed and burned, everyone saw its magnesium engine cases melt. No way were those magnesium cases available from any Honda dealer!'

Doug Hele, however, had a more delicate task in convincing a very anxious Lionel Jofeh.The BSA Group's Managing Director, Jofeh, had travelled to Daytona to be amongst the 60,000 plus spectators set to watch the race. The evening before, however, Jofeh had told Hele that the five-speed gearboxes had still not arrived in the US so all the bikes would have to be converted back to the standard four-speeds. 'I told him that was impossible,' Hele recalled later. 'It would have meant keeping the mechanics up all night, and then we would have had to start from scratch in calculating our gearing, with no practice whatever on four speeds. I risked the sack by not changing boxes.'

THE WIDOWMAKER MAKES DAYTONA

Also making its debut at the Florida track that year (courtesy of the new F750 rules) was the Kawasaki H1-R, with Rusty Bradley from Texas entering the 100 mile Junior race,* and Ginger Molloy the Daytona 200. Weighing 135kg and pushing out around 75bhp at 9,000rpm, the 500cc two-stroke triple was lighter and over 30bhp more powerful than a Manx Norton or a Seeley Matchless G50. However, when the Kawasaki arrived at Daytona it came with a major drawback - frightening fuel consumption, rumoured to be as low as 11 miles to the gallon. Even when the figure was later adjusted after it was realised Imperial gallons had been confused with American gallons, the H1-R still only achieved 16mpg.

Such a prodigious thirst necessitated installing aircraft-type fillers to expedite pit stops and converting the H1-R's under-seat two-stroke oil tank into a supplementary fuel container and displacing the battery and mounting a vessel in its place to store the two-stroke oil. Naturally, having around 30 litres of fuel sloshing about simply compromised even further an already dubious chassis.

Making Molloy's job still harder would be the 883 Sportster-based Harleys on which tuner Dick O'Brien had worked wonders to create the 750cc ohv KR race engines that recaptured from Triumph the Number One Plate two years earlier, and the Suzuki-backed 500cc air-cooled twins ridden by Ron Grant and Art Baumann.

---

*   Bradley would go on to win his event.

A War Of Attrition

When the flag dropped on race day, despite Romero occupying pole position for the start of the 53 lap event, it was Mann who spearheaded the charge down the pit lane by pulling out a 100 yard lead to the Speedway's infield section.

From the pit lane, riders enter the long sweeping left-hander that takes them onto the 1,600 foot long straight. This is quickly followed by a right-handed horseshoe bend, which brings competitors out onto another straight running parallel to the first. After this, the track sweeps to the left into a high-speed curve. A right-turn hairpin quickly arrives, then a mildly curving section ending in a sharp left eases riders into the 1,000ft, 31 degree-radius West wall. After which, the back straight brings riders hurtling into the West wall's opposite number, the similarly scaled East bank, from which riders are catapulted into the high-speed north straight, before they're forced to brake heavily in order to negotiate Turn One.

Before long, Mike Hailwood on the BSA and Gary Nixon on a Triumph took over lead of a pack comprising Dick Mann and Gene Romero with former 250cc world champion Kel Carruthers on the Yamaha in close company. The 350 Yams and 500cc Suzuki two-stroke twins were keeping the BSA and Triumph triples in sight, but the British four-strokes' superior handling gave the 750s the advantage on the track's infield section.

Fastest qualifier Romero, however, lost vital seconds when on the first lap he ran off the track and on to the grass. He quickly remounted to rejoin the fray, but was now down the field and forced to play catch up. Romero's Triumph team-mate, Percy Tait, retired after just nine laps, the engine of his hurriedly-prepared late replacement ride running too poorly to continue (he had also hurt his arm in a spill during race practice). For a while, first-year racer Gary Fisher acquitted himself well on his Honda Four till his machine gave up on lap twelve, to leave Hailwood as front man ahead of Gary Nixon and Dick Mann.

Although Nixon's Triumph had posted third fastest during qualifying, just behind Hailwood's second-placed BSA, out on the track his blue and white Triumph appeared to be the faster of the two. Lapping at 106mph, Nixon and Hailwood vied with each other for the lead - until flames spewing from the BSA's exhaust due to a broken valve tip forced Hailwood to pull out on lap fifteen after just 38 miles.

Frontrunner Nixon continued to edge down his lap times, but his Triumph gave up on lap 32 with terminal detonation problems, another casualty of the race's mounting attrition rate (which included fifth fastest qualifier Kel Carruthers when his Yamaha 350 seized on him).

Harley-Davidson was not exempt, either. As with the British triples, Milwaukee's V-twins were plagued by cooling problems, afflicting valves as rear cylinders overheated.

After Bryans and Robb also retired, as a result of their CB750s' cam chains failing, British expatriate Ron Grant on the Suzuki 500 twin took over the lead before he too had to pull out when his two-stroke engine suffered catastrophic damage after he ran out of fuel due to his crew miscalculating fuel loads.

Having earlier seen off Dave Aldana in a dice which forced the twenty-year-old to run off the track where he high-sided his BSA and had to remount to ride it back pit side for repairs, Mann now had the lead.

At a weight of 385lbs, Mann's CB750 was the heaviest machine in the field. With its 90bhp rated engine (compared to a stock motor's 67bhp) mounted in a standard frame, Mann's bike was actually the most mildly tuned of the four works machines, the other three Hondas sporting wilder high-lift cams. Even so, as the race wore on, Mann's engine began to lose power - the new cam chain Hansen had installed immediately prior to the race was starting to stretch, altering the engine's valve timing. Meanwhile, Romero had clawed his way back up the field. His Triumph was running flawlessly and with just ten laps to go Romero was trailing race leader Mann's ailing Honda by just 12 seconds. With the Burrito closing in on him, as the veteran racer later described it, Mann was now simply 'riding to finish'.

As the Four continued to slow, the Honda camp grew increasingly anxious. Mann's pitman, Bob Hansen, however, kept his head. He signalled his rider every time he passed, to let him know his lap position (Hansen had calculated that Mann could still win even if he lost one second on every remaining lap). At one point, Hansen was standing on the grass at trackside signalling Mann, when team leader Nakamura leapt over the pit wall to urge Hansen to tell his rider that he must go faster. 'But,' as Hansen later related, 'I had my race face on and just told him to get right back behind the wall.'

After almost two hours of racing at an average speed of 102.69mph, Mann - his engine firing on just three-cylinders and with less than half-a-quart of oil left in the sump - crossed the finish line just three seconds ahead of Romero.* Castro and his Triumph came in third.

Ginger Molloy's H1-R took seventh place (aboard a bike that was clocked on the banking at 159.83, but that had only been un-crated and assembled from a completely standard bike just days previously). Aldana's BSA came in twelfth. It had been a gruelling 200 miles. Of the original 98 starters, only 16 finished.

Whereas Honda team mates Robb and Bryson had kept their machine's rev-counter needle buried deep into the red-line, Mann knew that Daytona's layout was hard on engines, letting them run at maximum revs for sustained periods. He therefore went against factory advice and elected for a higher overall gearing. The technicians were concerned that he was now unable to reach the engine's optimum rev range. Mann, however, was riding to finish. He was to sum up his cool-headed approach many years later: 'Bob Hansen prepared the machine well and I rode it as best I could, just as I was contracted to do.'

---

    *   For BSA and Triumph, the 1970 season improved after the disappointment of the Daytona 200. At the next AMA road race, held at Washington State's Kent circuit, Gary Nixon clinched third place on his Triumph triple; but in May, Aldana won the 200 mile road race at Talladega in Alabama, his BSA's average speed of 104.589mph making it the fastest road race in the US. The following month, Nixon won the 100 miler at Loudon in New Hampshire, posting a Triumph-badged triple's only US Grand National win that season (Triumph not only won the 1970 American Racing Championship, riders of its machines took the first five places in the series). That same June, on the other side of the Atlantic, Malcolm Uphill won the Isle of Man production TT again, but this time on a Trident. The threes also took the 24-hour *Bol d'Or* that year.

BSA/Triumph Return To Daytona

After Mann's success in 1970 (in what was essentially a one-off US-based project), Honda did not campaign an official factory bike at the Daytona 200 again until 1973.*

Dick Mann, however, would return to the Speedway in 1971, this time riding a BSA triple (he had joined the team the previous spring), where he would score a second successive Daytona 200 win. With Gene Romero once again runner up aboard a Triumph Trident, and twenty-year-old Don Emde third on a BSA, the triples secured an astounding 1-2-3 (at one point in the race, the Beezumphs occupied the first five places, before Mike Hailwood's BSA dropped a valve at lap 14 and race leader Paul Smart's Triumph holed a piston on lap 41).

Mann's performances in '71 earned him one of the most impressive records in AMA history. After starting the season with a win at Houston's Indoor TT, 'Bugs' went on to score victories that year at Kent and Pocono. These wins, and second places at Atlanta and Talladega, were enough to make him 1971's Grand National Champion (eight years after he'd last held the Number One plate). Three decades later, in the foreword to author Mick Duckworth's history of the CB750, Mann acknowledged his debt to his victory at Daytona on the Honda: 'It put a couple of years on my career... because I'd proved that I wasn't over the hill, as some people seemed to think.'

The '71 season proved Triumph's pinnacle year in US racing. Hele had raised the triples' engine power to 84bhp at 8,500rpm. The upgraded motors were housed in new frames. Built by Rob North, their modified head angle made them sit lower, earning them the sobriquet 'Low Boy' to distinguish them from the 1970 bikes now commonly referred to as 'High Boys'. Slots at the front of the fairing fed air through to the oil cooler now moved to just behind to the fairing's nose, and twin discs replaced the previous season's front drum brake. Weight remained unchanged at around 370lbs dry, but handling was better and reliability much improved.

This was evidenced by the season's stats. Norman Hyde, an experimental draughtsman in Hele's experimental department (who, in his spare time, raced a world record-breaking Trident drag-bike), had the job of maintaining records for the factory's racing activities. In 1971, the five new racers made 124 starts in all, and were forced to mechanically retire on only 12 occasions. Factory riders suffered just five crashes. The new triples placed in the top three on 77 occasions, scoring 35 victories. Moreover, this record excludes the successes notched up by the bikes built for the 1970 season.

---

*   Honda fielded three machines at the 1973 Daytona 200. Managed once again by Nakamura, the official factory team included Daytona winner and one-time Harley-Davidson team rider Roger Reiman, Steve McLaughlin who would go on to carve out a name riding Superbikes, and Morio Sumiya

Sumiya had ridden with the Blue Helmets team CB750s that won at Suzuka in 1969, and as a development rider for Honda Racing Service Centre (RSC) had been key to developing the four-into-one exhaust system and slimmed-down fairing of the 1973 CB750 factory racers.

Sporting their new race livery of red, white and blue, Honda's return did not prove auspicious. Their top-placed rider, Sumiya, came in sixth (two places behind the race's best-placed four stroke finisher, Dick Mann riding a BSA triple). The Finnish 250cc GP champion, Jarno Saarinen took the chequered flag aboard a Yamaha 350, with the two-stroke twins also securing second and third places as four-strokes relinquished their grip on Formula F750 racing.

Triples not only won at Daytona, the F750 and production TT and *Bol d'Or*, but twice beat Agostini and the MV 500 on British short-race circuits. To top it all, they finished the '71 season beating all comers at the AMA's biggest National, the Champion Spark Plug classic in Ontario, California, where Englishman John Cooper's Doug Hele-prepared Rocket 3 took the chequered flag just inches ahead of Kel Carruthers' 350 Yamaha in what proved the closest and richest road race in the US ever.

Outdoing even H-D's effort to recapture the Number One plate a few years earlier, it is estimated the BSA/Triumph combine spent nearly a million dollars on its Stateside campaign. Paul Smart claimed he was passed $1,000 in cash 'by some Triumph-American fellow, who explained that it was pocket change - and there was more where that came from'. Dave Aldana told *Classic Bike* magazine that 'Peter Thornton was spending money like you would not believe'. BSA/Triumph's US race chief, recalled Aldana, 'flew us to the races in a Lear jet to make sure we were getting enough sleep. The guys we were racing would turn up having driven non-stop for two days. I thought I'm going to be a BSA factory rider for the rest of my life, I didn't think it was going to come to an end. When they stopped at the end of '71, it was a shock.'

10

THE KAWASAKI 750 MACH IV AND THE SUZUKI GT750

TWO TAKES ON TWO-STROKE TRIPLES

'A steaming, purple-eyed monster'
(*Cycle* magazine's impression of the Kawasaki 750cc H2)

Paul Smart

KAWASAKI MACH IV: FASTEST ACCELERATING ROADSTER EVER

Launched in 1936, the 81,000 ton luxury liner *Queen Mary* won the Blue Riband when she made the fastest North Atlantic crossing on her sixth round-trip voyage. Nearly four decades later, having retired to Long Beach, California in 1967 after completing 1,001 crossings, the ship was the venue for Kawasaki's launch in autumn 1971 of the world's fastest accelerating production vehicle: the H2 MACH IV, the 750cc three-cylinder two-stroke piston-ported big brother to the H1 500cc MACH III triple.

Kawasaki had assembled journalists for the launch both inside and outside the ship, where they were briefed on the Japanese company's new flagship model and latest addition to its existing three-cylinder line-up (comprising former range topper, the three-year-old 500cc H1 and the 350 triple launched just a few months earlier).

Producing 74bhp at 6,800rpm (with a peak torque of 57.1ft-lbs at 6,500rpm), with its fuel tank half full, the MACH IV tipped the scales at just 450lbs - meaning it weighed around 50lbs less than a Honda CB750, was only 40lbs heavier than its half-litre sibling, the MACH III, and just 25lbs more than a Triumph 650. Indeed, of all the 750s on the market, only the Norton Commando at 426lbs with half-a-tank of fuel was lighter.

In their report of the H2's Long Beach launch, *Cycle World* magazine calculated that with a 150lb (10 stone, 10lb) rider on board, each of the MACH IV's 74 brake horsepower carried 8.1lbs of weight, bettering the 500cc H1's power to weight ratio of 9.0lbs and the Honda CB750's 9.7lbs.

The magazine anticipated the H2 would 'slash its way through the quarter mile in the low 12 second bracket with a speed trap speed of from 105 to 108mph. Top speed will be in the neighbourhood of 125 to 130mph, with the proper gearing.'

Ominously, the H2 came with *two* steering dampers as standard (a friction damper and a hydraulic damper).

When the UK's *Bike* magazine tried to obtain the MACH IV's top speed for its March 1972 road test, the test bike went into 'a horrifying tank slapper at 115mph'. Testers had to tighten down the bike's friction damper before they were able to get it 'safely through the timing lights at 120mph'.

Another UK road test at the time reported that the H2 accelerated so rapidly that the 'problem was hanging on'. With a 'seat and tank that afford scant grip, all you can do is to try and remain attached to the H2 in any way you can'.

The tester seemed particularly awestruck by the bike's propensity to wheelie merely by pulling back the twist grip, the engine's 'enormous' torque (a claimed 57ft-lbs) obviating any need to drop the clutch at 5,000rpm to get the front wheel pawing the air and the whole machine winding itself around its back wheel.

Nevertheless, the bike posted a standing quarter time of 12.4 seconds. The tester, however, seemed disappointed that he could only wring 123mph out of it, which he felt he could have bettered had the H2's handlebars been narrower, 'the magic 125' being otherwise perfectly attainable.

The MACH IV was, according to the magazine, the 'fastest accelerating roadster' they had ever ridden. Across the Pond, after posting an elapsed standing quarter time (ET) of 12.72 seconds, the 750 triple also proved 'the quickest road machine *Cycle World* has ever tested' - a record it held for nine years. In the second of *Cycle* magazine's superbike comparison tests conducted at the Orange County International Raceway near Los Angeles, the H2 bettered even *Cycle World*'s record-breaking time when it 'produced a heart stopping run of 12.283 at 110.29mph, mufflers, air-cleaners, stock handlebars and all'.

In fact, *Cycle* scored the Kawasaki 750 H2 399.6 points out of a perfect 400. Of the seven bikes on test, the MACH IV posted quickest over the quarter mile (notching up the second fastest terminal speed, just 0.41mph behind its four-stroke stablemate, the 903cc Z1's ET of 110.70mph). The H2 also recorded the fastest lap time, delivered the strongest brake force, produced the highest horsepower and torque readings, had the best power-to-weight ratio, and was the least expensive bike on test, whilst scoring the highest number of test points. But, as the magazine recognised, superbikes were changing. A new era was round the corner.

The MACH IV Becomes An Anachronism

Although *Cycle* magazine described the H2 in their second superbike comparison test as 'a steaming, purple-eyed monster that does everything with a shriek and whose only God is performance', the model in contention was an H2A, which *Cycle* acknowledged gave 'more sensible gas mileage, more accurate throttle response and slightly smoother running' than Kawasaki's first generation MACH IV.

The H2 had, in short, become more civilised. But so had its comparison-test rivals, every one of which had 'evolved beyond the [magazine's] 1970 definition'. Only the MACH IV and the lowest-scoring bike on test, the Harley-Davidson XLCH1000 Sportster, remained, in *Cycle*'s view 'legitimate, old-time Superbikes' (although in the latter's case, its absolute performance failed to match its image).

As the bikes in *Cycle* magazine's test demonstrated, customers and manufacturers had traded the sacrifices and considerations once synonymous with maximum performance, for 'reliability, civility, and longevity' - with the result that superbikes had become altogether better motorcycles.

Indeed, Kawasaki's technicians declined to fit a 'gumball' slick rear tyre to the 903cc Z1 for their machine's assault on the quarter mile - which *Cycle* were confident would see the big four become the first stock production motorcycle to break into the elevens - because the factory didn't want their flagship's straight-line performance to overshadow its finesse and tractability.

Even at the zenith of the MACH IV's success, two rival machines had emerged which underscored how the H2 was already an anachronism. The first was the Suzuki GT750, a water-cooled three-cylinder 750cc two-stroke that was 'the motor cycling equivalent of a jet liner'. The other was *Cycle* magazine's December 1972 comparison-test runner-up: the heir apparent from the MACH IV's very own house - the mighty Z1 900.

Suzuki Launch A Triple

Due to when the Tokyo Motor Show is held - the middle of November, just before the onset of Japan's cold and wet winter months - the event is primarily a car show. With little expectation of garnering two-wheel sales, motorcycle manufacturers demur from exhibiting new models and instead put on displays. At the 1970 Tokyo Show, Honda exhibited wall-mounted engines as if they were *objets d'art*, featured a 'thundering' waterfall at centre stage, and ran a road-safety film on closed-circuit TV. The most notable item on their stand was a 'delicious chocolate-coloured CB750'.

Rivals Kawasaki displayed a MACH III-powered kneeler touring outfit built as a one-off by a Tokyo-based firm, the Japan-only W1SS 650cc twin in its new colour schemes, and a couple of psychedelically-painted A-Series two-stroke twins.

Yamaha's display consisted of small bears and dwarves going 'ho-ho' whilst riding round on little bikes. (*Cycle World* magazine's attending journalist, Yukio Kuroda, reported that exhibitors explained Snow White's absence was due to her being upstairs with a customer.)

Suzuki, however, used the seventeenth Tokyo International Motor Show to launch its new flagship, the GT750 two-stroke triple, before embarking on a world tour. By the time the GT750 show bike reached Britain on Christmas Day, ahead of its appearance at London's Olympia Show early in the New Year, it was evident that the display model had led a hard life. When the electric motor for the exhibition stand's turntable burnt out, leaving Suzuki's flagship immobile, journalists could plainly see that the bike's fuel tank was badly dented.

Dented or not, Suzuki's new range-topper caused a sensation. British buyers, however, had to wait until early 1972 before supplies of the three-cylinder water-cooled two-stroke arrived in UK showrooms whilst the Suzuki underwent rigorous testing by the factory to ensure the new model maintained the company's reputation for reliability forged by its previous brand leader, the T500 twin.

In a full-colour ten-page magazine pullout stapled to the centrefold of the January 1972 issue of *Cycle World* in which Suzuki announced their new three-cylinder GT series, off-road, and two-stroke street bikes, more than half of the advertisement's copy was devoted to the company's rigorous testing and development regimes.

'It takes about three years for a new Suzuki to evolve from drawing board idea to finished motorcycle,' the brochure told readers before going on to relate how a team of experts from Japan visits the United States every year to find out 'what's new and needed... today and tomorrow' by studying trends in styling, riding habits and rider's preferences for size. After digesting and analysing all the information they collect, the team submits proposals to the company's board of directors for their approval, 'with President Shunzo Suzuki taking an active part in the decision.'

The brochure described how artists and engineers work together on blueprints, calculations for which they then test on a computer called 'Big Brain' at Suzuki's Research and Development Centre, before moving on to the next stage: a full-scale mock-up model. 'This is usually made of wood, done so realistically that the only way to tell if a gasoline tank or expansion chamber is wood or metal is to rap it with your knuckles.'

'Next comes the hand-built working model; built as close to the final production version as possible.' Under the sub-heading 'Testing: a tour through motorcycle hell', the brochure detailed what the prototype can expect at Suzuki's testing facility at Hamamatsu. The 1,400 acre site comprises a four-mile long test track boasting a two-mile straight and over two miles of 'the most tortuous road that man or Mother Nature has ever dreamed up'. Test riders, we're told, inflict every prototype to a catalogue of tests - acceleration, power, braking, torque, handling, comfort, and the machine's ergonomics such as 'ease of instrument visibility'.

'We *punish* Suzukis. In every way we know how.' Test riders, all of whom have 'highly mechanical backgrounds' analyse each machine and use their expertise to suggest changes. According to Suzuki's ad, 'It's a costly technique, and it means a lot of time and hard work, but the results pay off.' It goes on: 'We'd rather test our products at the factory than on the public.'

And testing, readers were informed, didn't end there. At Suzuki's four Japanese manufacturing plants - Ohuska, Toyokawa, Toyama, 'and the main facility at Hamamatsu' - totalling in all, around 20,000 acres and about 30,000 employees, of whom about 10,000 in total are inspectors (including 'some inspectors who check the inspectors').

Yet, whilst the Cobra twin set the GT750's engineers a benchmark for reliability, the T500's disappointing sales caused Suzuki to conclude that motorcyclists had no appetite for a large-capacity two-stroke. A year or so later, the success of Kawasaki's MACH III half-litre triple made them revise that view.

As Hele and Hopwood did with the Triumph Trident 750 triple, Suzuki based the GT750 on a half-litre twin from within their own stable (engineer Etsuo Yokouchi overseeing both designs). The new bike shared the T500 twin's 70mm x 64mm bore and stroke to give the three-cylinder machine an actual capacity of 738cc. The three's two-ring pistons and conrods were also virtually identical to the T500 Titan (although the 750's smaller diameter flywheels were closer in size to those of the TR500 road racer).

Moreover, applying knowledge garnered from developing the T500's porting helped the project team develop the early triple's characteristic low-revving grunt and torque, giving what a UK tester at the time described as 'one of the 750-3's greatest qualities... its ability to "dig in" on hills or when going into wind when being driven at high speeds.' The Suzuki, he reported, delivered 'at any rpm, in any gear, at any road speed... [an] instant and prodigious response.'

And, as with the T500, the GT750's designers canted the triple's transfer ports 60 degrees from the line of the crankshaft in a bid to contain engine width. Even so, viewed from the front, the GT's 19.7 inch wide (500mm) crankcases remained an imposing sight despite being some two inches slimmer than the Honda CB750 engine's 21½ inches (540mm) measured from alternator case to points cover.

But, whilst several aspects of the GT750's engine owed a debt to the T500, the triple's signature feature - liquid-cooling - was unique to the new bike and a first for a Suzuki production motorcycle. Indeed, according to a US sales brochure for the triple, the GT750 was 'the world's first water-cooled two-stroke'.

It wasn't.

Water-Cooling Pioneers

British manufacturer Scott* had built a water-cooled two-stroke motorcycle in 1908. Two years later, in 1910, Scott fielded the first two-stroke to finish a race at the TT; set the lap record a year later at 50.11mph, and each year thereafter up to 1914 and the breaking out of hostilities in Europe; and won the race itself in both 1912 and 1913. In 1926, Scott launched the 500 and 600cc Flying Squirrel two-stroke water-cooled twins at the 1926 Earls Court Show, and displayed a prototype of a water-cooled 750cc two-stroke triple as far back as 1934.

Birmingham-based Velocette had also produced a water-cooled two-wheeler: the 192cc LE200 ('Little Engine') four-stroke twin. First introduced in 1948, with its pressed-steel frame, telescopic forks, swinging-arm rear suspension, shaft-drive and built-in leg-shield and panniers, the LE was certainly innovative. Sales, however, were slow and it was only its popularity with UK police forces that kept it in production, until it was finally withdrawn in 1968.** By the time the GT750 went on sale, both Scott and Velocette were defunct - but not so the advantages of liquid-cooling. The benefits it conferred remained as valid as ever.

Suzuki claimed water-cooling reduced temperature by some 30 per cent over the GT750's air-cooled counterpart, increased torque by 6 per cent and allowed their engineers to reduce piston clearance from the T500's 0.0026-0.0030 inches to just 0.0019 inches.

The pressurised system held 5.4 US quarts (or around a gallon) of coolant. Circulation was controlled by a vane-type impeller in the crankcases pumping over 16 gallons of fluid a minute when the engine was running at 6,000rpm, the amount and flow being restricted by a thermostat. This remained closed up to 82 Centigrade, opening up further and further until the coolant's temperature exceeded 95°C, at which point the thermostat opened completely. Around 10 degrees later, should the coolant reach 105° C, a small fan behind the radiator kicked in until water temperature fell back below 100° C. (During a testing programme covering 180,000 miles in all, ridden along the lines of the Equator in 115° Fahrenheit temperatures, and around the Los Angeles area during the hottest part of the year, Suzuki's development engineers found it virtually impossible to get the triple's coolant hot enough to activate the fan - which, by 1974, was only available as an optional extra.)

---

*   The company was founded by Alfred Angus Scott. Born in Bradford in the North West of England in 1874, Scott - a trained engineer who had worked for a time on marine steam engines whose layout would have a lasting influence on his later designs - was one of the nascent motorcycle industry's pioneers. His patents include: the first rotary valves on a two-stroke, the first kick-starter, the first telescopic forks, one of the very first triangulated frames, one of the earliest parallel twin-cylinder engines (which he built toward the end of the 19th Century), and, of course, water-cooled motorcycle engines. Sadly, in 1923, Scott died of pneumonia aged just 48.

**   The LE's popularity with UK police forces for urban patrol duties led to the little Velocette gaining the nickname 'Noddy' bike. This was not, as might be first supposed, after the Enid Blyton character, but a consequence of a police directive releasing patrolmen from saluting a superior officer, as that would have required them to take their hands off the handlebars. Instead, riders were told that the required protocol was to nod.

At the other extreme, adding anti-freeze to the coolant gave a further 20°C of protection from frost and freezing temperatures.

The GT750's close mechanical tolerances made for a quiet engine. This was made quieter still by the deadening effect of the water-jacket surrounding the highly-polished cylinder block's largely smooth surface and the omission of noise-transmitting cooling fins on the barrels. Road tests at the time complimented the motor's quietness, smoothness and civility (which were so pronounced that *Cycle World* described the GT750's 'mechanical, intake and exhaust silence' as 'unnerving'). Compare this with *Cycle* magazine's description of the GT's rival three-cylinder two-stroke 750, the air-cooled Kawasaki MACH IV, whose engine US testers said 'sounded awful... rattling, wheezing, pinging, knocking and vibrating'.

Closer tolerances and greater control over the motor's operating temperature also led to more consistent power output - a claimed 67bhp. The GT750 matched the Honda 750 for power, but achieved it with 1,400 fewer rpm showing on its tachometer - 6,500rpm compared to the Honda's 8,000.

In fact, the Suzuki's powerplant, though ruggedly engineered, was in a relatively modest state of tune. Simple porting, three 32mm Mikuni carburettors, and a compression ratio* of 6.7:1 produced a virtually flat torque curve (55.7ft-lbs at 5,500 revolutions per minute) and overall fuel consumption of around 45mpg (and more than 60mpg if ridden with restraint), which *Cycle World* declared 'outstanding for a four-stroke of comparable size, and nothing short of amazing for a two-stroke'. Presumably they had the MACH IV's dipsomaniacal thirst in mind here, given that the Kawasaki's fuel consumption could drop below 20 miles to the gallon (forcing one UK journalist to conclude that the H2 'guzzled petrol at [such] an astounding rate... [that the] trio of Mikuni carbs must've been pumping unburnt fuel straight through the engine and out of the exhausts').

Like its stablemate, the T500, the GT750 triple metered two-stroke oil mechanically via Suzuki's Posiforce - or CCI - lubrication system. The pump, driven by a take-off gear from the five-speed gearbox, opened and closed in concert with engine speed and the degree of throttle opening. Controlled by a cam connected to the throttle cable's junction box, the pump was virtually shut off at cruising speeds, opened up as the revs rose, then reduced output again with the throttle closed to prevent the engine loading up with oil.

Testers at the time reported that the triple consumed very little oil. This was in part due to Posiforce's careful metering, but also a scavenging system the factory called SRIS.

The 'Suzuki Recycle Injection System' worked by utilising the difference in pressure between cylinders to force any oil that had accumulated at the bottom of the crankcase

---

* The common convention for measuring the compression ratio of a two-stroke engine differs to the one engineers use to calculate the compression ratio of a four-stroke. Whereas with a four-stroke engine the baseline begins when the piston is at the bottom of its stroke, for two-strokes, engineers measure the volume above the point at which the piston has travelled far enough up the bore to close off all the ports it controls in the cylinder. A low compression reading for a two-stroke engine can therefore be misleading if compared directly to a four-stroke. To be more properly analogous, an engineer would have to measure the volume above the four-stroke engine's piston at the moment the inlet valve closed, which happens much later than at bottom dead centre.

into the scavenging port of the adjacent combustion chamber where it was burned off. This not only minimised oil consumption, it also contributed to cleaner exhaust emissions.

The Japanese manufacturers' penchant for initials was also evident in how Suzuki described the triple's exhaust arrangement. According to its makers, Exhaust Coupler Tube System (or ECTS for short) helped boost the GT's bottom-end torque by around 20 per cent. The system, which linked all three down pipes to cross tubes, was also credited with reducing noise and deepening the tone of the exhaust note.

The triple also boasted four silencers, stacked two on either side. Each of the engine's two outer cylinders exited into one large silencer: one on the left, the other on the right. The centre cylinder's header, however, divided into two small silencers tucked in beneath and banked inward of the conventionally-sized left or right flanking muffler. Despite the triple's relatively low ground clearance - a shade over five inches - the V-shaped arrangement helped minimise grounding when cornering.

Besides granting the triple's hindquarters a Blake-like 'fearful symmetry', the quad of chromium-plated, tubular-coned silencers, each ending in a black cap, were extremely quiet (they were complemented in this regard by the GT's air-filter housing, which was designed to reduce intake roar).

It wasn't just the fact of a three-cylinder motorcycle with four silencers that flattered to deceive. What appeared to be a five gallon fuel tank actually held just 3.75 Imperial gallons (4.5 US gallons/17 litres), its capacity reduced to accommodate the radiator system's header tank, the pressure cap for which was hidden beneath a neat hinged flip-up cover.

But whilst *Cycle World* described the GT750J they tested in December 1971 as feeling 'deceptively light at any speed', the fuel tank's girth, wide handlebars and prominent instrument panel (which included a temperature gauge) betrayed the machine's true bulk.

With a dry weight of 472lb - or 524lb with half-a-tank of fuel - the GT750 came in 8lbs under the Honda CB750's 480lb dry weight. However, when fully laden with fluids, despite the Honda's extra cylinder, overhead camshaft and four-stroke paraphernalia, the triple managed to top the Four's 485lb kerb weight by a not inconsiderable 39lbs.

Small wonder, then, that journalists expressed surprise that Suzuki fitted drum brakes all round to rein this Clydesdale of a bike to a halt, at a time when disc brakes were fast becoming *de rigueur* on big-bore motorcycles.

The rear was an eight-inch diameter leading shoe. The front was an impressive-looking 8½ inch ventilated twin leading shoe - essentially, two units from the 500 Titan installed back to back. Both brakes, according to a British tester, 'were heavy to work but effective enough,' with a US journalist deeming the triple's front and rear anchors virtually fade-free even after heavy use, and able to haul the bike from 60mph to a stop in 118 feet. UK Journalist Mike Nicks, however, in his spring '72 road test for *Motor Cycle News*, condemned the triple's brakes as 'inadequate' and 'simply incapable of halting the Suzuki's bulk in any kind of emergency situation'.

An American sales brochure for the triple (which referred to it as the '750 Outlaster' but which was more commonly known in the US as the 'Le Mans') cited the GT750J's performance as: 'Acceleration 12.7 seconds'. More careful reading reveals that its sub-13 second posting was measured over 400 metres, a slightly shorter distance than the more conventional Stateside and UK performance yardstick of a quarter mile. Over a benchmark 440 yards, in a magazine pullout advertising their 1972 range, Suzuki claimed the 'GT-750J Le Mans... does the ¼ mile in 12.6'. *Cycle World*, however, timed the triple's standing quarter at 13.87 seconds. By the time it crossed the finish line, the Suzuki was travelling at 93.55mph. The UK's *Motor Cycle News* did slightly better, wringing 13.69 second standing quarters out of their 1972 test bike.

Suzuki's promotional literature for the GT750 claimed its top speed lay somewhere between 115-120mph, whereas *Cycle World*'s test bike clocked 107.27mph at 6,880rpm and *MCN* achieved 112.5mph (in top gear at 7,000rpm).

Whilst these numbers fell short of the market's other two-stroke three-cylinder 750 (Kawasaki's MACH IV H2, with its low 12 second standing quarters and 123-plus mph top speeds), the GT750 road bike's real virtues were not to be found on the track or drag strip. It was out on the highway where the big Suzuki truly excelled: 'Its superbness,' according to a UK tester, 'comes not from sheer speed.'

'Riding the GT750 is a joy which must be experienced to be fully appreciated,' extolled *Cycle World*. 'Riding it brings a sensation unique among the entire range of motor cycles on the British market', gushed *MCN*'s Mike Nicks when he tested the J model in spring 1972 (his criticisms of its brakes presumably notwithstanding).

FLEXI-FLYER

By and large, testers at the time praised the Suzuki's road-holding. *Motorcycle Mechanics* Editor, Charles Deane, in an October 1972 review of the GT750, described its high-speed steering as 'light and precise'. He was much less impressed at the triple's low speed handling. Taking his first slow bend aboard the bike, Deane said it felt like riding a 'reluctant camel' (the animal seemingly the UK road testers simile of choice when describing recalcitrant road-holding for wayward two-stroke triples - see Chapter 7, 'The World's Fastest Camel').

Another UK journalist deemed the big Suzuki: 'Very stable handling, especially at speed... [and] safe steering in the wet.'

He even praised its Japanese-made Bridgestone tyres. Whilst complimentary about the grip afforded by the rear tyre even in the wet, he judged the front tyre merely 'adequate' - qualifying even this less than fulsome assessment by confessing: 'I never give Japanese rubber the chance to let go on me in the wet.' Nevertheless, he acknowledged that 'Oriental tyres have come a very long way in recent years and I'd be happy to enough to run my own personal Suzuki 750-3, if I had one, on Bridgestones.'

That wasn't something *MCN* tester Mike Nicks was likely to do. In his test of the J model for the UK weekly, Nicks was in no doubt as to where the blame lay for the Suzuki's transformation into an 'evil handler' when conditions turned damp: its Bridgestone tyres. 'In the dry,' he opined, 'they were fine, but in the wet they gave you the feeling that you were riding on brittle plastic.'

In the drier climes enjoyed by the journalists in the Newport Beach-based offices of *Cycle World*, the US magazine's 1971 road test, conducted in the teeth of a Californian winter, perhaps unsurprisingly passed no comment at all on the Bridgestones' wet-weather road-holding characteristics.

They awarded the GT750 'top marks in the handling department', the bike tracking as if on rails even when accelerating hard during high-speed cornering. They attributed the triple's good manners to its 'massive double cradle frame'. Whilst they adjudged the 750's suspension to provide 'excellent control on all but the roughest surfaces', and thought the two five-way adjustable rear De Carbon-style sealed gas shock absorbers did a good job preventing yawing in fast corners and rear-wheel hop under hard braking, they concluded that the softly-sprung front forks' focus on comfort was the suspension package's one impediment to spirited cornering.

The bike's 'Flexi-flyer' nickname came later, when Suzuki launched the TR750, the race-version of the road bike.* Producing between 100 to 105bhp, the engine's massive jump in power caused the frame to flex, prompting factory racer Ron Grant to award it its alliterative tag. When the TR made its debut at the 1972 Daytona 200, factory rider Art Baumann hit 171.75mph aboard the 352lb two-stroke triple, smashing the previous qualifying speed record (held by Paul Smart riding a Triumph four-stroke 750) and scoring the first 170mph average around the Speedbowl.

But, as Mat Oxley put it in *Classic Bike*, the F750's new big bore two-stroke multis' (or 'stinkwheels' as they were unkindly dubbed) 'dramatic increase in speed overpowered every area of motorcycle engineering, from engine design to chassis technology and tyre construction.'

'Two-stroke riders lived in fear - if the engine didn't lock solid at 170mph, there was a good chance that either the machine would break into a terminal tank-slapper or the rear tyre would explode.'

---

*   The TR750 Suzuki race bike - or XR11, as it is also called - was based on the GT750 production road bike. The TR discarded the street machine's alternator, triple contact breakers and electric start, but retained its engine, five-speed gearbox and water-cooling, a feature developed specifically for the GT - a bike Suzuki conceived as a long-distance tourer at a time the AMA's Executive Committee had in place a ban on water-cooled engines in all AMA competitions (ostensibly, because of the risk of hoses splitting or radiators leaking and spilling fluid on the track, but doubtless reflecting its industry representatives' concerns of two-strokes usurping racing).

The AMA's rule-making Competitions Congress later rescinded the ban so that water-cooling was permissible where it was standard on the production model. But it remained illegal to convert an air-cooled model to liquid-cooling.

Water-cooling stabilises the expansion rates of an engine's components and permits tighter tolerances. The benefits to a race bike are that the engine will produce much the same power at the end of a 200 mile race as it did at the start (which in air-cooled engines can amount to as much as a 10-15 per cent drop in horsepower after a few laps in race conditions).

More crucially, by maintaining a uniform engine temperature, a water-cooled engine is less affected by shifting climactic conditions. A change in weather during a race can cause an imbalance between plugs and jettings, leading to piston seizure and potentially the rider and machine parting company.

Understandably, then, excitement was running high as race fans anticipated the clash between the Beezumphs, Hondas, and Harley-Davidsons and this new breed of superbike. Unfortunately, the TR's appetite for chains and tyres became so critical that Baumann was forced to lead the race with a shredding front tyre, only to retire with a dead magneto. Ron Grant fried his clutch trying to re-enter the fray too quickly after pitting to re-fuel (the TRs did 13mpg). Suzuki's hopes were now pinned on Jody Nicolas' remaining TR750, which evaporated when his rear tyre blew out on the twenty-seventh lap, just over halfway through the 52 lap 200 miler.

After the challenge from Triumph and BSA collapsed - Paul Smart's ending before it began when his Trident remained immobile on the grid; Yvon Duhamel retiring one lap after pulling in for fuel on lap fourteen following an intense duel with Baumann; Dick Mann's BSA suffering ignition problems; Gene Romero dropping down the field with a flat tyre; Gary Nixon suffering a broken gearbox despite hanging back to preserve his engine; and Eddie Mulder's Triumph finishing sixth on the best-placed Beezumph - privateer Don Emde (third-placed rider in BSA/Triumph's incredible 1-2-3-winning team of 1971) took the chequered flag, his one-year-old Yamaha 350 twin becoming the first two-stroke machine to win the Daytona classic.

The TRs would eventually find success in the hands Paul Smart's brother-in-law, a promising young racer from South London named Barry Sheene. Sheene would ride a Seeley-framed TR to victory the following year, winning the FIM750 and *MCN* Superbike titles in 1973 and the *MCN* Superbike title again in 1974.

He would also suffer horrific injuries aboard a TR750 following a rear-tyre blowout at 170mph during race practice for the 1975 Daytona 200.

For most riders, however, the GT750 street bike's handling was quite acceptable. An open-road tourer that wasn't designed for scratching, the triple proved a reliable mount capable of giving high-mileage service.

Rubber-mounted at eight points, the GT's three-cylinder engine - firing at 120 degree intervals on every other stroke (rather than every fourth) - had the same number of firing impulses as an in-line six-cylinder four stroke, and was eerily smooth.

Displaying an 'almost complete lack of vibration', GT riders and pillions were further cosseted by a wide, 'ultra-soft' dual seat; electric start (plus a back-up kick-start lever, which *Cycle World* complained bumped into the rider's right calf and transmitted the engine's vibration!); centrally-mounted ignition switch nestled within the instrument panel, speedometer, tachometer, and temperature gauges; and a vacuum-type fuel tap obviating the need to turn the fuel on or off.

Cycle World described the three's detailing as 'exquisite'. 'Heavily applied chrome and lavish use of the buffing wheel on aluminum parts'. White stripes over Candy Lavender* paintwork, muscle car power bulges and shark-gill air vents on its side-panels, and massive chrome and enamel badges displaying the legend 'WATER COOLED 750',

---

* The GT750J was also available in Candy Jackal Blue.

the GT looked like a two-wheeled Cadillac Eldorado designed by General Motors Chief Stylist Harley Earl.*

At the time of its launch in the UK, the GT - at £766.50 - was more expensive than its multi-cylinder rivals: The Triumph Trident cost £665; the two-stroke three-cylinder Kawasaki H2 750, £758; and the Honda CB750 £761.

The big Suzuki received plaudits from press and public alike, whose enduring affection for the model is evidenced by the nicknames they gave it: the 'kettle', 'hot water bottle', the 'water buffalo'. The UK's Suzuki Owners' Club lists it as their most popular model, and it has its own official owners club in America called 'Le Mans'. Yet the GT750, whilst by no means a failure, did not make the impact Suzuki hoped for.

Increasingly restrictive emission legislation, a global fuel crisis, and changing customer expectations, were all responsible. The bike Suzuki developed to succeed the GT, however, very nearly bankrupted the company.

~ ~ ~

In August 1972, journalists gathered in Los Angeles airport to board a chartered flight to Monterey in California. They had been invited by Kawasaki, the smallest of the Big Four Japanese motorcycle manufacturers, to attend the US press launch of their '73 season's models.

The new bikes included various small bore road and trail bikes, more civilised versions of the 500cc H1 and 750cc H2 two-stroke triples, and a new 250cc triple. Also amongst the bikes on show would be the company's much anticipated, much speculated new flagship dubbed the Super Four.

The conclusion of a project initiated in 1967, the new machine would prove a game-changer.

---

* Harley J. Earl (1893-1969) was the head of General Motors' Art and Colour Section between 1927 and 1959. He introduced the custom shop technique of clay modelling into mass-production design practice, an innovation that would change the shape of cars forever. Earl is credited with hiding the radiator behind a decorative grill, dispensing with the running board, replacing the bolted-on trunk with the first built-in luggage compartment, removing the spare tyre from outside the bodywork, the hardtop roof and the polychromatic two-tone paint job.

He took his influences from aeronautics - particularly the Lockheed P38 Lightning war plane whose twin tail booms inspired the famous tailfins on the Cadillacs of the 1950s. Harley believed that 'to compete successfully for buyers' dollars, manufacturers had to make more than a good product... they had to make them look attractive to the shopper.' He exhorted his team of stylists 'to go all the way and then back off'. To austere European eyes, his stylings were vulgar, and sophisticated New Yorkers treated them with disdain; but Harley was designing his cars for blue-collar workers in Iowa and, as design guru Stephen Bailey says in his book *Design Heroes: Harley Earl*, Earl's 1956 Chevrolet Bell Air was 'the American psyche made visible'. That psyche included a love of novelty, which General Motors' marketing men indulged with gadgets and hyperbole. The '55 Buick featured RSVP (Really Sensational Variable Pitch), whilst in 1956, Chrysler offered *PowerFlite Range Selector, Torque-Flight Transmission, Torque-Aire Suspension* and *Super-Scenic Windshield*.

11

KAWASAKI LAUNCH THE Z1

CYCLE RETURNS TO ORANGE COUNTY FOR A SUPERBIKE REMATCH

'Big American Bertha'
(Opening to a US road test of the Kawasaki 900 Z1)

'Pops'Yoshimura

A BIKE TO MAKE THE FINEST IN THE WORLD SHRIVEL

August 1972, and for Paul Dexler and two of his fellow editors at the California-based *Big Bike* magazine ('For the custom bike enthusiast'), reveille this morning was a full one-and-a-half hours earlier than usual.

A still half-asleep Dexler and his colleagues were groping their way through Los Angeles' smog and traffic-bound freeways as they headed toward LA International Airport to catch a chartered flight. The three were responding to a notice that had arrived at their Ventura Boulevard office in Encino. The note announced in 'quiet terms' that Kawasaki were having a press showing of next season's new models, including details of the company's new big bore flagship: Would *Big Bike* magazine like to attend? 'We would, indeed,' was Dexler's response (anticipating that it might be a chance to learn more about Kawasaki's long rumoured challenger to the company's own 'killer' 750!).

Gathered at the airport were other local motorcycle journalists (including, to Dexler's surprise, reporters from *Playboy* magazine), all waiting to board the plane Kawasaki's public relations people had charted to fly them to the Laguna Seca race circuit, where, in two days' time, Kawasaki were sponsoring a road race.

After an hour's flight, the plane dropped through the clouds, past an overcast Pebble Beach and swanky Del Monte country clubs, to land at California's Monterey Airport. Once their hosts had rounded up the stragglers, Dexler and his colleagues loaded their luggage on to two waiting buses, took their seats and were driven the five miles or so to the race course (the laden buses struggling to make the steep hill, which takes visitors into the course area).

After alighting, the passengers were herded toward a tent plastered with large signs emblazoned with the word 'Kawasaki', indicating that this was where they intended to conduct the press meeting. In front of the tent were a couple of Kawasaki Team road and sidecar racers and a collection of intriguing shapes hidden under sheets.

Reporters and journalists milled around for a while before the meeting was finally called to order and a speaker introduced executives from Kawasaki Heavy Industries in Japan, followed by an invitation to ask them questions.

Sat behind linen-draped tables in front of the assembled press were Kawasaki Project leader, 'Ben' Gyoichi Inamura; John Watanabe, in charge of basic research and testing; Kawasaki's Marketing Manager, Sam Tanegashima; Tom Togashi and Ken Tada, responsible for chassis and styling respectively (including the H1, H2, and S2 two-stroke triples); and the Motorcycle Division's General Manager, Mr Yamada himself.

'Considering Kawasaki's experience with the two-stroke concept,' postulated one of the hacks, 'and considering the critical and technical success of the 750cc water-cooled Suzuki, why has Kawasaki, of all companies, decided to introduce a four-stroke touring bike?' *

Wantanabe, Inamura, Tanegashima, Togashi and Tada all smiled at one another knowingly, but left it to Yamada to explain.

'There's lots of reasons,' he said. 'Kawasaki wanted to build the King Motorcycle, a bike beside which the finest motorcycles in the world would shrivel in comparison, a universal motorcycle.' And, he continued, clearly warming to his subject, 'you just can't do it with a two-stroke engine.'

It didn't matter, Yamada explained, that many of the prejudices against two-strokes were largely invalid: but, as he well knew, that didn't make them any less obdurate.

'In the first place, the King Motorcycle must have an engine that *sounds* right' (which a two-stroke's 'Yingangyingyangpoppoppop' - as a *Cycle* magazine's reporter characterised it - simply fails to do).

---

*   This exchange is a reconstruction based on several contemporary reports by journalists attending the press preview. All the participant's words are as noted by reporters in their published accounts of the Z1's US launch.

The H-D Sportster. The Honda 750. Yamada knew that both bikes owed an element of their appeal and sales success to their distinctive exhaust note.

'No less important is the way the engine looks,' said Kawasaki's General Manager. 'Who could imagine a King Motorcycle with an engine that looked like a two-stroke engine looks, all crankcases and cooling fins? The King... has to have an engine that *looks* impressive. And only a big four-stroke is right.'

Yamada then expounded on the relative merits of two-stroke versus four-stroke formats: the economic case - a high-end motorcycle demands the machine be a four-stroke because of the need to control emissions, performance characteristics, and rider preferences. 'Once a street-rider switches to a four-stroke,' Yamada told the reporters, 'he never goes back to a two-stroke machine'.

'Fair enough, but tell us why,' asked the journalist, 'the bike displaces 903cc, and tell us why it has so much horsepower, considering the problems with rear tyres and drive-chains that it is likely to face, and considering that the bike will be marketed in the United States as a touring bike.'

The 903 had been tested in the United States, Yamada said, 'more thoroughly than any motorcycle ever built.' He referred to Bryon Farnsworth's team who had racked up over 13,000 miles on prototypes disguised as Honda CB750s. Despite brutal treatment, none of the chains broke, they just kinked. In Yamada's view, chain life and rear tyre wear was satisfactory.

Addressing the journalist's question about the bike's displacement, Yamada reflected the Japanese indifference to rigid cubic-capacity categories: the 903's 55 inch displacement 'just turned out that way'.

'The plan now is to build an engine,' Yamada explained, 'that works, and whatever size it turns out to be is the size it turns out to be.'

'Why not make it a full 1,000cc?'

'Aha,' laughed Yamada. 'We'd rather not compete just yet in a displacement class with anything that Milwaukee Harley-Davidson builds.'

'Besides,' Yamada added, 'we don't *need* any more displacement.'

And horsepower: 82bhp at 8,500rpm?

'It's not that we set out to make an engine that could produce 82 horsepower,' Yamada explained. 'We set out to make an engine that would deliver the kind of power that a touring rider could use, the kind of power that would permit him, and a passenger, and saddlebags full of gear to pass comfortably on the highway. The engine makes good horsepower at extremely low rpm. The engine is tractable, flexible and willing. It runs on low-test gasoline, and it can run on lead-free. The engine breathes well. It is a *good engine*. It just happens to make 82 horsepower. Its ultimate horsepower figures were almost a side effect.'

The question and answer session lasted perhaps 15 minutes, but by now Dexler was impatient to get his hands on the bikes, which the PR staff at last began to unveil.

First to be uncovered was a 75cc mini bike. This was followed by the new 90, 100 and 125cc models. Removing the wraps off the new 250cc triple, the smallest multi on sale in the US, certainly grabbed the press's attention. The S1 was followed by a series of dirt bikes, which in turn preceded the unveiling of the new 350 triple, now boasting a front disc brake.

Next up came the H1 500cc triple. Kawasaki attributed the smoother-running engine and broader power band to detail changes.

They then revealed the '73 MACH IV 750 two-stroke triple, resplendent in next season's candy purple livery. As with its half-litre sibling, Kawasaki claimed the latest iteration of the H2 was smoother than before, but also that it handled better, too.

The journalists had greeted every unveiling with ripples of polite applause as Kawasaki introduced each new model in turn. Now only one machine remained covered.

Dexler could see his colleagues' 'tongues were hanging far out' in anticipation as the last sheet was removed to reveal the bike whose details had graced his invitation.

When they finally unveiled the Z1, the bike received a standing ovation due to its outstanding appearance (but also, thought Dexler, with the Z1's introduction out of the way, 'those present could get down to the serious business of riding everything in sight').

The 'V-Bikes'

Six months earlier, in February 1972, Kawasaki had given 29 pre-production models to US dealers for shakedown tests. Codenamed 'Model X', the machines did not wear Kawasaki badges. Instead, their identity was disguised beneath the Honda CB750 livery of blue with a gold stripe. Also known as the 'V-bikes' on account of their frame and engine numbers (standard production Z1 engine numbers start with 'Z1E' and frames start with 'Z1F', whereas the Model X machines start with 'V1E' and 'V1F'), dealers were instructed to test the new Kawasaki to destruction.

After around 8,000 miles, engineers then examined them, reworking any weak points before production of the '900 Super Four Model Z1' (as it was officially called) started in May.*

US press previews of Kawasaki's new flagship took place in August 1972, followed by the Z1's official unveiling to the public on 16 September, when it headlined the IFMA Motorcycle Show in Cologne, Germany.

Less than ten days later it won its first race.

On 24 September 1972, the Z1 took the chequered flag at a 250 mile production event at Vacaville in California, piloted by co-riders Paul Smart from Britain and Hurley Wilvert of America.

'It was reaching about 132mph down the half-mile straight,' recalled Smart. 'It is definitely the fastest production bike I have ever ridden in standard trim'.

After tours to Paris and Oslo, the Z1 made its British debut in November at London's Earls Court Motor Show.

---

* The V-bikes are distinguishable from the production bike by differences such as its MACH IV-sourced brake calliper and swinging arm, and yellow needles on its dials. Authorities such as Dave Marsden estimate only around four examples of the V-bike test mules may have survived.

Five months later, in March 1973, the Z1 set a new 2- hour world record for 1,000cc machines when it averaged 109.641mph around Daytona's Speedbowl.

Aware of their reputation for building two-strokes renowned for their 12 second performances over a quarter mile, Kawasaki wanted to demonstrate the new design's durability across altogether greater distances and timescales. Setting an endurance record would provide the emphatic proof. Standard except for a pair of Clubman handlebars and strange-looking Goodyear tyres - 'We had a lot of trouble with tires in early testing,' explained Bryon Farnsworth. 'Finally, Goodyear used the rubber from a NASCAR tire and we were fine' - the bike covered just over 2,631 miles in 24 hours, breaking a total of 46 US and world records. A second Z1 - also standard - despite losing 30 minutes to repair a broken rear chain, still averaged 104mph (bettering the previous 90.115mph record held since 1968 by a Suzuki 250 Super Six).

Yvon Duhamel riding a third Z1, which had been tuned by 'Pops' Yoshimura* and fitted with a race fairing, set an absolute record for a motorcycle on a closed circuit when his machine recorded a flying lap of 160.288mph. The hard-riding Canadian went on to also break the world's 10 and 100 kilometre records, with speeds of 150.845 and 141.439mph respectively.

The Z1 Displays Its Twin Natures

In what was only the second of *Cycle* magazine's Superbike comparison tests, the Z1 finished a close-run second to the MACH IV 750, scoring 399 points out of a possible 400 to its sibling's winning total of 399.6.

The H2 beat the big four-stroke by just a tenth of a second on the drag strip: running a 12.283 second standing quarter mile compared to the 900's 12.386. However, the Z1

---

* Hideo 'Pops' Yoshimura was the world's best-known and most successful engine tuner. After graduating from pilot's ground school at the age of 17, Yoshimura had missed Pearl Harbour due to a parachute accident. His injuries had ended his hopes of a pilot's licence, so he decided to study aircraft engines instead, receiving his flight engineer's licence in 1941. He flew 4,000 hours all over South-East Asia, and was shot at twice by North-American P-51 Mustang fighters (armed only with a pistol with which to return fire). Towards the end of WWII, he escorted kamikazes, his plane's tail-light guiding the suicide pilots to their target. 'At Okinawa, ships started to shoot at us,' Yoshimura told *Cycle World* in 1979. 'We climbed up and watched [the kamikazes attacking the ships]. I was crazy then. I wanted to hit the big ships.'

In the closing months of the war, Yoshimura was flying every day, drinking to excess in order to cope, and was hospitalised when he began to spit up blood. Unable to fly, his two-month stay in hospital saved his life as the Americans now commanded the skies and Yoshimura lost most of his friends to allied fighter aircraft.

After the war, he returned home to Fukuoka City on Kyushu Island. Life in occupied post-war Japan was tough and food hard to come by. He was jailed for six months for running a thriving black-market business. In 1955, he opened a dealership selling BMWs, BSAs and Vincent motorcycles to American soldiers. It was the GIs who nicknamed Yoshimura 'Pops' who had now turned his hand to tuning the bikes - mainly British - that the soldiers raced at the nearby airbase. When Honda built the Suzuka race circuit and hosted its first 18 hour endurance event, it was an unknown team from Kyushu Island which proved fastest in qualifying and held first and second places in the race until the second-place bike retired and the leading Yoshimura bike took the winning flag. Honda signed Pops up to tune their bikes for Japan's domestic-market races, but his reputation had now spread overseas, as GIs stationed in Japan began to return to the US with Yoshimura-tuning parts and engines.

In 1971, a Yoshimura Honda 750 racing engine led at Daytona until its cam chain broke. Later that year, Yoshimura fitted a collector system he had based on his Honda 800cc sports car to a motorcycle competing in the 250 miler at Ontario. 'I was the first in the world to put a 4-into-1 on a motorcycle,' Pops told *Cycle World*. 'The next year, 4-into-1 pipes were everywhere.'

finished the quarter mile a shade more strongly, with a terminal speed of 110.70mph to the two-stroke's 110.29. Indeed, the magazine thought the four-cylinder machine could have gone on to better its time.

After just four runs, Kawasaki's mechanics abandoned the Z1's assault on Orange County International Raceway's drag strip after it 'blew an enormous cloud of oil-smoke out of its tailpipes'. A mechanical strip-down found 'nary a blemish' so engineers bolted it back together again and the machine resumed the contest the following day (factory mechanics Jeff Shetler and John Bridges guessed that oil had made its way through the machine's emissions re-cycling system into the combustion chamber).

Due to the 'line between perfect traction and hopeless wheelspin' being particularly fine for the Z1, its rider for the four runs that the bike did undertake before retiring reportedly didn't consider *any* of them perfect. Yet each successive run improved on the time he'd achieved in his previous attempt. His quarter mile time aboard the Zed on its first run down the drag strip came out at 12.429 seconds. He recorded 12.415 on his second attempt, and posted 12.386 seconds on its third launch. The fourth, and as it turned out, final attempt, was 12.397, 0.011 seconds slower than the previous run, but coupled with a higher terminal speed than he'd achieved on any of the earlier runs: 110.70mph.

Had the Kawasaki camp elected to return to the strip and undertake a fifth run, but this time fitted with alternative gearing (albeit not yet actually available for the 903 at the time of testing) or the optional slick tyre which *Cycle* allowed all seven contenders to use, the magazine was sure the Z1 would have achieved the 'first box-stock 11 second run'. That Kawasaki's representatives chose not to was, postulated *Cycle*, because the factory preferred to promote their new flagship's tractability over its straight-line performance.

And, anyway, their MACH IV had that base covered.

One month earlier, in November 1972, the magazine had tested a battle-worn Z1 with replacement piston rings so new that they hadn't yet seated. Even so, the bike logged a 12.52 second/107.52mph standing quarter, making it the fastest accelerating motorcycle ever, and besting the 750 H2 by two tenths of a second and a mile and a half higher terminal speed.

Remarkably, after 23 runs and 69 power shifts, the bike's clutch hadn't changed by 'so much as a millimetre'.

It was an early hint of the Z1's robustness.

A year later, in their November '73 test of the Z1, the UK's *Motor Cycle News* recorded a best of 134.4mph, making the Kawasaki the fastest road bike *MCN* had ever tested. Brian Crichton, the first journalist in Britain to ride the Z1, had been amazed by its effortless acceleration, which he described felt like 'a non-stop crescendo of power'. He delighted in the Kawasaki's smoothness, how deceptively quick the Z1 was to reach 130mph, and how relaxed the motor felt.

He was snapped out of his reverie, however, after the machine unexpectedly switched character - from benign to malignant in an instant - and broke into a sudden and unprovoked high-speed wobble. The handlebars flapped violently from side to side for what seemed an age. Crichton fully expected the bike to pitch him off.

Eventually, the front end's violent oscillations slowed and Crichton gradually regained control. 'I had been taught a sharp lesson about the machine's nature,' Crichton said.

Whereas he had at first 'simply blasted the machine' (which resulted in a 120mph-plus wobble that came on instantly and without warning), with his 'sensors on red alert', a chastened Crichton now built up his speed gradually. Yet the bike remained unstable, a disconcerting weave emanating from the back end setting in at anything over 90mph.

The magazine eventually traced the main cause of the weave to the tyres: Dunlop TT100s fitted by the firm who had supplied *MCN*'s test bike. Once the original 19 inch ribbed front tyre was re-installed, the Z1's stability improved markedly. Even so, Crichton was still forced to abandon several runs because of an incipient weave.

To minimise suspension pitch - which appeared to trigger the weave - the magazine set up their speed trap on the smoothest part of the airstrip. By keeping to this path and changing gears at exactly the point when the needle touched the red line, Crichton clocked 132mph.

He was convinced, however, that the Z1 was capable of more. In a subsequent run, with the rev counter needle buried 500rpm into the red, the Kawasaki topped 134mph.

It was a remarkable achievement. *MCN*'s readers voted the Z1 1973's 'Machine of the Year', toppling the Norton Commando's record-breaking reign of five successive years. Moreover, the Z1 would go on to win the accolade again the following year.

But in exploring what test pilots call a machine's 'performance envelope', Crichton discovered that the Z1 could catch out the unwary.

Kawasaki Targets Honda

In the main, the machine's road-holding received praise from the motorcycling press. 'A nimble handler... Neither fast sweepers nor tight hairpins make it wiggle or do anything untoward,' said *Popular Cycling*.

Cycle Guide's Frank Conner reported that a fellow journalist found the Z1 'so stable he could take his hands off the bars at a hundred mph, and the bike would continue to track perfectly straight'.

'In fact,' the journalist wrote, 'the bike allows you a margin of error - at anything less than the highest possible speed through a corner, you can change your line in the middle of the corner to take care of problems like decreasing radius of pavement.' Conner said he felt more confident riding the Z1 at speeds over a hundred than on most of the other big bikes he had ridden.

Cycle Rider journalists Walt Fulton Junior and Len Weed, along with the magazine's Editor Bob Braverman, whom Kawasaki had invited to a preview of the bike at their Akashi test centre in Japan just before the company's August unveiling of the Z1 to the US press at Laguna Seca, had been so impressed by the press bikes that they went out and bought machines of their own.

Braverman bought his 903 in October '72. Boasting a serial number ending 006, Braverman's bike was the first Z1 to go on sale, Kawasaki retaining machines one to five for themselves. Fulton and Weed collected their bikes in December (Weed's machine's was serial number 000031).

In Fulton's opinion 'the handling characteristics of the Z1 are superior to any other production motorcycle today with the exception of the Triumph T150'. The Z1, he said, was extremely stable in a straight-line and displayed 'no tendency to weave from side to side,' and likened its road-holding to riding 'on rails rather than travelling down the highway'.

US journalists attributed the Kawasaki's assured handling to its frame and front suspension - but not its Japanese Kayaba-made twin rear shock absorbers, which, if its riders were to avoid their test bike wallowing in sharp or high-speed turns, *Cycle* magazine found they were obliged to sacrifice comfort for stability and keep the springs at the middle-setting to which Kawasaki's technicians had adjusted them (a conclusion echoed by another US magazine, *Popular Cycling*).

Road tests deemed the Z1's front telescopic forks - also made by Kayaba to the specification prescribed by the project team member responsible for developing the bike's suspension, Mr Hatta - near ideal; better even (according to one US road test) than the acknowledged leaders in suspension at the time, the British.

New York Steak Project team member Tom Togashi, who was responsible for the Z1's chassis, experimented with a series of ten prototypes - each one tested by the likes of Paul Smart and Yvon Duhamel - before eventually arriving at the frame's heavily gusseted Norton Featherbed-type arrangement. With its mild steel three-tube backbone, five-member supported steering head, and large, 'thick-as-your-wrist', 1.61 inch diameter swinging arm (pivoting just five inches from the gearbox drive sprocket to minimise the arc prescribed by the rear axle and the chain in an effort to reduce wear and driveline snatch), road testers praised the frame's 'flex-free' rigidity.

The sturdy and compact double-loop design, with its widely splayed front down tubes and solid front engine mounts, housed the Z1's motor, the power unit itself acting as an additional frame member.

And what a motor it was.

An in-line, across-the-frame four-cylinder engine displacing 903cc with a bore and stroke of 66 x 66mm: such over square dimensions signalled smoothness, performance and, according to *Motorcyclist* magazine, exceptional engine balance. Firing impulses were every 180 degrees, the two outer pistons rising and falling in unison and in alternation with the centre pair. This arrangement meant the reciprocating forces of each pair of pistons cancelled each other out, as one set was always travelling in the opposite direction to the other.

Even before the Super Four was unveiled to the US press in Monterey in August 1972, Kawasaki Motors Corporation had invited US journalists Bob Braverman, Ivan Wager, Cook Neilson and Bob Greene to Japan for an early, week-long preview of the Z1 at their Akashi Works test strip near Kobe. From his one-hour test ride within the confines of a half-mile, 15 foot wide straight asphalt strip with a yellow painted stripe running down the centre, enclosed by a chain-link fence and with a net at either end to catch anyone who might overshoot the short strip, Braverman's impression was that the 900 ran smoother than the Honda 750. The *Cycle Guide* reporter partly attributed this to components such as the foot pegs, fuel tank, headlight, indicators, gauges, and silencers being rubber mounted - but surprisingly, he thought, not the rigidly-fastened handlebars. Neither the Honda nor the Kawasaki, however, were a match in this department for the Suzuki GT750, which Braverman considered was 'hands down' more comfortable, its two-stroke three-cylinder engine producing 'far less vibration' than either of the 'overhead cam four's.'*

Mr Yamada, however, had made it clear at the Z1's US press launch that Kawasaki felt that the large-displacement sector was shifting away from two-strokes and toward four-stroke engines. And though no one from Kawasaki explicitly said so at the Laguna Seca press event, *Cycle World* thought it evident from the pages of the 903's comparative technical specifications and from the explanations the company's people gave as to why Kawasaki had built the Super Four that they were targeting Honda's CB750.

At 22.4 inches, the 82bhp engine was only half-an-inch wider than a Honda CB750's powerplant. Amongst the ways Kawasaki achieved this was by employing caged needle roller bearings on the crankshaft's four connecting rods. This setup not only produces less friction, and therefore less heat, it allows engineers to fit one-piece connecting rods. Such items have a narrower cross section than two-piece rods, helping reduce engine width.

According to Kawasaki, their all-alloy 903cc four-cylinder motor tipped the scales at 180lbs. This was the same as the Triumph Trident's three-cylinder unit, something *Cycle Guide* found frankly hard to believe. The magazine's doubts notwithstanding, 180lbs brought the Z1's engine in at just 4lbs heavier than the Honda's 176lbs.

Yet, whilst transverse four-cylinder motorcycles were no longer unusual by the time Kawasaki released the Z1 (Honda had three in their line up: the CB750, the CB500, and the CB350F),** the 903's powerplant still managed to break new ground.

---

*   Kawasaki gave each tester a personalised decorative gold key by way of thanks. In embossed letters surrounded by a curling border, the key Neilson received read: 'With thanks to COOK NEILSON of *Cycle* from KAWASAKI'. The factory also offered all four journalists a chance to purchase the test bike at around half retail price. They all declined. Cook, however, accepted Kawasaki's offer of a long-term loan, retaining the bike for a couple of years before he returned the machine.

**   Honda released the CB500 Four in April 1971, but the machine did not appear in the UK until January 1972 when it went on display at the Racing and Sporting Show in London. They launched their CB350F in June 1972 in America. The CB350F never went on sale in the UK.

It was the first to include a device in its breathing system for controlling hydrocarbon emissions. Called PCV (short for Positive Crankcase Ventilation), the system worked by re-circulating any unburned mixture that slipped past the piston rings and into the crankcases. Before these fuel vapours could contaminate the oil, they were routed to the rear of the engine casting where they exited into a maze-type canister sited behind the barrels and above the transmission. This polished alloy canister acted as a 'fall-out chamber', in which oil condensed and ran back into the crankcase, and air pressure piped crankcase fumes up an 'S'-shaped rubber hose connected to the floor of a plenum chamber in the air box. These gases were then inducted through the motorcycle's air filtration system, on into the carburettors and back into the engine for combustion. This simple arrangement reduced emissions by fully 40 per cent.

Further nods to the environment included three-ring, flat-top pistons running at a compression ratio of 8.5:1, which together with exhaust valve seats made from special sintered alloy, permitted the Z1 to run on lead-free fuel without the motor suffering premature detonation or abnormal valve seat recession.

The Z1's eight valves were operated by twin-overhead camshafts driven by a chain running from the crankshaft and up a tunnel between the two centre cylinders. The arrangement allowed engineers to set the intake and exhaust camshafts wide apart, giving greater access to the spark plugs. Cam lobes bore directly upon inverted cups placed over each respective valve stem. Valve gaps were adjusted using shims inserted between the cam lobe and the retainer cup or bucket (each shim calibrated by hundredths of a millimetre in thickness). This 'bucket and shim' arrangement obviated the use of reciprocating screw-type adjustable rocker arms, which are prone to flexing (altering timing and causing valves to float at high rpm). The Z1's cam-on-valve stem mechanism was five times more rigid than a push-rod engine, and over three times better than a single-overhead camshaft motor. Against the latter, the natural frequency offered by twin-overhead cams was 1.6 times greater at proportionally higher rpm. Moreover, the DOHC valve mechanism's reduced mass meant the valve springs had to absorb less inertia and were more lightly stressed - lessening cam wear, extending service intervals, and leading to higher performance and smoother running.

The Z1's 83-84 decibel rated four-into-four exhaust system was yet more evidence of Kawasaki's awareness of the US's growing environmental concerns. According to *Motorcyclist* magazine's Bob Greene, the Z1 was so quiet that it was 'out-hushed' only by BMW.

Unlike the CB750's crankshaft which ran on plain bearings, the Z1's nine-piece pressed together crank was built around six massive roller bearings, which allowed the wet sump engine (in another departure from the CB750's dry-sump, remote oil-tank arrangement) to run at lower pressure - around 6lbs per square inch.

Retardation was taken care of by a single 11.65 inch diameter front disc brake manufactured by Tokico for Kawasaki (the right-hand fork leg had lugs cast in to add a second hydraulically-actuated calliper); and a 7.9 by 1.4 inch rear drum in a polished aluminium hub containing a rubber vane cush drive for the rear sprocket.

Driving the 18 x 4.00 inch rear wheel was a ¾ inch pitch chain. An endless chain, it came without a master-link, and was the largest ever installed on a motorcycle - outdoing even that which Milwaukee fitted to the Electra-Glide.

To reduce chain wear, a one-quart oil tank hidden behind the left-hand side cover automatically metered lube to the chain at a rate of up to 5cc an hour via a pump driven by an output shaft turning at 1,500rpm.

With a claimed dry weight of 506lbs, or 542lbs 'fully gassed', the Z1 was, as *Cycle World* put it, a Big Bertha of a motorcycle. Yet its elegant lines belied its size. The Z1's styling managed to be, according to a US road test, both 'assertive' and 'subtle'. *Cycle Guide*'s Frank Conner thought the bike looked 'purposeful' and well proportioned (its sense of 'compactness' achieved by clever use of black paint on things like the engine, headlight shell, instruments and yokes). Even the teardrop fuel tank and duck-tail fairing's purplish maroon (actually Candy brown) and reddish orange paint job, which he thought 'weird at first', eventually grew on him. But because this 'unlikely combination' - whilst certainly distinctive - was devoid of 'cheap ornamentation or decals', Conner thought the machine retained its overall dignity.

The Z1 had all the presence and luxury of a grand tourer but was Spartan enough to appeal to sports-bike riders.

Cycle magazine summed the machine up thus:

> *The Kawasaki 903 Z1 is the most modern motorcycle in the world. It is also the fastest. It is above all the first of a generation of new bikes, a generation which will run quietly on the streets of America... solve motorcycles' tiny contribution to the world's dirty air... come close to being within reason all things to all people, capable of nattering down quiet country roads packing double one minute and rotating the earth with incomprehensible acceleration the next.*

THE KING IS DEAD, LONG LIVE THE KING

One year after *Cycle* pitted the Z1 against the CB750 and five other challengers in the second of the magazine's superbike comparison tests, the Kawasaki and Honda fours met again - this time, just the two of them - *mano a mano* - for the UK's *Bike* magazine Giant Test.

Launched in the summer of 1971 by Mark Williams as a one-off (cover slogan: 'All that's fast, furious and fun on two wheels'), *Bike* magazine's strain of gonzo journalism was quickly gaining a reputation with manufacturers and importers for brutally candid motorcycle reviews. As only BMW and BSA/Triumph kept full press test fleets for magazines to sample, *Bike* often had to rely on private owners to furnish machines for their reviews. The CB750 on test was a K3 model and the personal machine of Graham Gull from the Honda Owner's Club.

As the report acknowledged, the 1973 Honda CB750 K3 was a quite different machine to the first generation model launched four years earlier. Since 1969, the 750 had undergone 5,500 changes, which included re-designs to more than 1,300 parts. The upshot was that, in *Bike*'s view, the Honda remained a superbike, but one that was 'more docile… [and] easier to live with'.

Despite its milder state of tune, the K3's top speed of 121mph was actually faster than previous models *Bike* had tested, 'but,' according to now consultant editor Mark Williams, 'the engine has to work a little bit harder to get up there.' The magazine had to over-rev the motor in third to achieve their best quarter mile time of 13.67 seconds, confirming the tester's opinion that the Honda was better suited to 'effortless motorway cruising, which, by definition, entails accelerating potential in the high gears'.

The magazine deemed the CB750's engine marginally smoother than the Z1 (although the Honda's harder twin-seat transmitted more vibration than the Kawasaki did through its perch). Mirrors began to blur at just over 5,000rpm compared to 3,000 for the Z1.

Testers praised the 'British specification' handlebars fitted to the Honda, which were comfortable and 'engendered excellent controllability'.

For such a big machine, *Bike* thought the Honda handled well at low speeds ('but it's not in the Z1 league yet'). They noted the 750's change from gas-damped shock absorbers to hydraulic, but observed that the change had not fully cured the model's handling ills. The front end felt light above 85mph (though not 'flighty'), with the tester's sense of unease compounded by the bike's ribbed front tyre, which he said displayed 'a tendency to wander slightly on less than perfect surfaces'. A rider could 'stuff' the Honda into a corner and it would steer through just fine, but applying the brakes or throttle too injudiciously would cause the frame to flex.

This compared to the Z1 whose frame resembled a 'beefed-up Featherbed'. The Kawasaki's handling, according to tester Barnaby Williams, was so good that 'You'll be hanging right inside the nimblest of 350s on any corner.' Tight or fast sweeping bends, it was all the same. 'The 900 could be heeled over as far as you could want, steady and firm, holding the line.'

Williams quoted Paul Smart (one of the Z1 project team's development riders) who had ridden prototypes of the 903 flat out at Talladega and Willow Springs race tracks during Stateside testing in the summer of '71 (where they averaged 122mph): 'The bikes could have finished in the top ten at Daytona,' said the British racer.

The magazine thought Kawasaki had done a 'classic job' on the Z1's styling, pronouncing its 3½ gallon fuel tank a greater success in disguising its capacity than Norton managed on the Interstate; and the 903's 'long, but narrow, and cunningly curved' side-panels - being much smaller than those on the Honda - gave onlookers the impression that the Kawasaki was much less bulky. The Z1's sense of elegance was assisted by its lack of clutter and 'juke-box stripes', the tailpiece ('blends perfectly'), and the 'really beautiful mudguards.' Even the engine received praise for its looks: 'Handsome' in its matt-black finish with cooling fins hand-buffed to reveal the metal beneath, and beautifully-made polished alloy cases and housings.

The magazine adjudged the Z1 engine's performance 'fantastic'.

'Neck-snapping acceleration'.

'Quicker than the phenomenal Mach IV over the standing quarter - but it handles!' It wasn't 'tricky' like the MACH IV, or 'evil' like the MACH 1.

Even the Z1's chrome and paintwork was considered superior to the usual industry standard-setter Honda. Indeed, as Williams put it:

> The 750 Four, for so long the best machine in the world is now old, and dated. After that, you can't look at it again in the same way. The King is dead. Long live the King.

~ ~ ~

The Z1 went on sale at £1,088 in the UK, retailing for $1,895 in the US (the K3 CB750 cost £849). Since Kawasaki had not established a UK operation at that time, sales were handled by the Agrati Company in Nottingham. It wasn't until 1974 - amidst Britain's miners' strike and the Government-imposed three-day week - that John Norman (who Kawasaki had recruited because of his many years experience with BMW and Honda) set up the wholly-owned Kawasaki UK.

Working from a one-room office in London's Holiday Inn, often by candlelight due to power cuts, Norman collaborated with his Japanese bosses to master-mind the British operation - which, by 1977, had outgrown its first base and transferred to smart, purpose-built headquarters located in Slough near London. (Up till Kawasaki established their UK operation, dealers would sometimes have to fly to Kawasaki's main European parts warehouse in Holland for spares in order to honour a customer's six-month warranty.)

The 903's immediate success caught the parent company by surprise and Kawasaki was compelled to extend their manufacturing plant to cope with demand. Between August 1972 and August 1973, they produced 20,000 of the original black-engined model (of which Kawasaki allocated just 38 to the UK).

In 1973 Kawasaki spent £4 million on new production plant and equipment, raising Z1 production from an initial 1,500 machines a month up to 5,000 a month by 1975, plus a further £3 million on research and enhancing after-sales support.

'Let the good times roll' indeed.*

---

* Strapline to Kawasaki advertisements during the 1970s.

12

DUCATI 750 L-TWIN

WINS IMOLA 200, PLAUDITS AT THE SUPERBIKE 7, AND COOK NEILSON BEATS THE KAWASAKI FOURS AT DAYTONA

'My big worry was the bike - bits were always dropping off'
(Paul Smart on racing the Ducati 750 desmo at the first Imola 200)

Fabio Taglioni

THE DOCTOR CREATES A BIKE FOR ITALY'S DAYTONA

Amongst the Daytona crowd who witnessed Dick Mann nurse his ailing Honda CR750 to victory that spring Sunday in 1970 was an august delegation from Italy. They comprised the president of the Italian Motorcycle Federation, Ferrucio Colucci, Moto Guzzi's Chief Executive Officer Michele Bianchi, Ducati chief engineer Dr. Fabio Taglioni, and the man who had invested most of life and fortune to create the Imola racetrack - which in 1970 still included sections of the northern Italian town's public roads - Francesco 'Checco' Costa. The group had travelled to Florida to learn more about the most famous 200 miler in the world. Impressed by what he saw there, Taglioni, whose beautiful hillside estate overlooked the Imola circuit, urged his good friend Checco to hold something similar to Daytona back home.

A few months later, in the summer of 1970, Ducati test riders at the Bologna factory were readying the company's new Taglioni-designed flagship for production; which by the end of '71, the Doctor had determined should compete in his friend Costa's inaugural 200 mile event at Imola scheduled to take place the following spring. It would, Taglioni felt, provide the perfect platform to promote Ducati's new superbike.

Ducati's 750 GT was a 90 degree V-twin (or 'L-twin, according to Ducati) at a time when three and four cylinders were fast becoming the superbike engine layout of choice.

Fours produced around a quarter as much power again as a twin with none of the latter engine's destructive forces. A four-cylinder unit's output was positively velvety compared even to a 750cc Norton Commando whose power impulses were quelled by its patented Isolastic frame mounts, or a one-litre Harley-Davidson Sportster whose narrow-angled cylinders did little to offset the violent gyrations of its solidly-bolted engine.

To Phil Schilling, managing editor of *Cycle*, the world's number-one motorcycle magazine at the time, the 750 GT seemed an improbable candidate for success in the showrooms, never mind on its first race outing.

'Ducati,' he recalled many years later, 'had absolutely no record at all for building big motorcycles. Nor was Ducati some high-tech maker with an ongoing history of stunning innovations.'

Schilling also knew that the Italian company lacked the resources necessary to develop a completely new machine so would be compelled to utilise what they already had. The result made its public debut at the 1971 Olympia motorcycle show in London. Effectively two 350cc singles set at 90 degrees and bolted to a common crankcase housed in a chassis with a 59.8 inch wheelbase, the 750 GT looked, according to Schilling, 'strangely different' to eyes accustomed to the compact lines of the 'tightly drawn' Honda single-camshaft fours and the double-overhead cam Kawasaki Z1.

Reportedly, Taglioni instructed engineers from Ducati's race department to select machines off the production line and prepare them for racing (although some think it more likely that whilst the bikes followed the production machine's essential architecture, they were actually built from the ground up).

What is not in dispute is that the race bikes departed from the production bike's spring-actuated valve mechanism by utilising for the first time on a V-twin desmodromic cylinder heads[*], a system for opening and closing the inlet and exhaust valves using bevels and a

---

[*]   Fabio Taglioni, who joined Ducati in 1954, first used desmodromic valve gear in 1956 in the company's first 125cc racer. Ridden by Degli Antoni, the machine won the Swedish Grand Prix on its very first outing. The win was followed later in the year with victory at the Barcelona 24-hour Grand Prix d'Endurance by works riders Fargas and Ralachs.

Desmodromic (from the Greek for 'controlled track') valve actuation eliminates valve bounce, grants greater control of the valve train's actions, and permits much higher engine revolutions per minute whilst also reducing the risk of internal damage. The system, however, was not new - James Norton roughed out a design for such a mechanism as far back as 1909, which itself was based on the principle of using cams to control poppet valves going back to the late 19th Century. Norton employed them on some Manx engines and Velocette on their KTT racer. But Taglioni became the first to put the system into a production motorcycle with the 1968 Ducati Mk 3D.

vertical coupling. This, together with other modifications, such as accelerator jets in the 40mm Dell'Orto carburettors, and high-lift Imola cams, raised power to 84bhp at 8,800rpm.

Output like that made the Ducati competitive with the Beezumph triples (Honda had withdrawn their factory fours after Mann's 1970 Daytona victory); but not necessarily a race-framed MV Agusta 750 Sport prepared under the world-beating factory team led by Arturo Magni. Although performance was poor in the production bike, a race-prepped MV, especially one ridden by the current 350 and 500 world champion Giacomo 'Ago' Agostini, remained an unknowable proposition.

More worrying to Ducati than the MV was the 750 GT's reliability. The engine used pressed-together crankshafts whose assemblies were not always properly trued. But Bruno de Prato, an aerospace engineering student fresh from college in South Carolina, suspected another problem.

Recently hired by Ducati as their public relations and product consultant following his brief time at Alfa Romeo's aero-engines division, he identified that even if the cranks had been trued correctly, the ball-type radial bearings Ducati employed would collapse under the crank's axial loads.

Bruno consulted his books and catalogues and found high-velocity, angular-contact ball bearings that were capable of withstanding the radial and axial loads. 'They were expensive,' Bruno told *Cycle World* in 2006, 'but proved so reliable that they are still on duty in current twins.'

Race-department chief Franco Farné stripped down the cranks, installed de Prato's high-performance mains bearings, fitted high-tensile steel twin-rib connecting rods, and then carefully reassembled the engines before placing them into the rolling chassis (near stock, apart from twin Lockheed 290mm disc brakes at the front, a 260mm disc at the rear, steering dampers, bespoke Marzocchi front suspension with 38mm offset axle, and race-compound Dunlop tyres).

With aqua-painted frames, gel-coated Metalflake-grey fairing and matching 21 litre fibreglass fuel tanks sporting a broad unpainted strip running up both sides of the tank toward the petrol cap (the translucent band allowing rider and pit crew to instantly determine how much fuel remained), the bikes were perhaps handsome more than pretty.

At 395lbs the 750 GTs were relatively heavy machines; and with their near 60 inch wheelbase, short rear suspension, and leading-axle front fork, the bikes were 'super-stable', if a little heavy to steer. To avoid burning the rider's inside leg, the Imola race bikes had a unique exhaust layout: one pipe up, one pipe down. The rear cylinder's exhaust ran high up along the machine's left flank, whilst the front cylinder's header and silencer was routed more conventionally lower down, running along the bike's right side. The arrangement was tailored specifically to the Imola track with its single right turn (Acqua Minerale).

Taglioni assembled a five-man team to pilot the desmo twin racers: Italians (and factory 500 GP regulars) Bruno Spaggiari, a Ducati stalwart, part-time racer, Ermanno

Guiliano, and Gilberto Parlotti (who did not race); and Brits Allan Dunscombe, who had raced with some distinction a Vic Camp V-twin in the UK during 1971, and Paul Smart.

Smart was not race director Fredmano Spairani's first choice. He had wanted Saarinen and Sheene, but they declined, viewing the big desmo as lumbering and uncompetitive. A desperate Spairani turned to Vic Camp for advice. Camp's response was instant. He suggested Smart. A Kentish lad, Smart was racing in America for Team Hansen Kawasaki when he received a call from his wife, Maggie (sister to rising superstar Barry Sheene).

'All I knew about Ducati.' Smart told the *Telegraph* newspaper in 2008 'was that they made out-of-date singles.'

'Paul was racing the Kawasaki when Ducati called me in California,' recalled Maggie Smart in an interview with racer and journalist Alan Cathcart. 'They needed an answer right away, but I couldn't contact Paul, so I accepted. I knew he wasn't doing anything, and the money was good - so I said yes. When he called that night, he went mad.' "I'm not riding that bloody thing," he said - but we discussed it over the phone, and he changed his mind.'

The veteran racer didn't even know where Imola was, but, struggling to make ends meet on a basic annual salary of $12,000 riding the Green Meanies, and because 'Ducati paid my airfare and there was £500 wages win or lose,' Smart was, as he put it, 'up for it.'

He was released by Kawasaki's Hansen, a squad Smart had joined from Triumph just two months previously, to race the Ducati at Imola on a one-off basis, convinced that the machine was not competitive.

PAUL SMART GOES TO ITALY

Smart's plane had no sooner landed in Italy than he was met and driven straight from the airport to the Modena circuit right in the heart of the old town of Modena and near the Ferrari factory. Smart was amazed at what he found. 'There was this flashy new bus with plate glass sides, in which all the race bikes were transported so people see them,' he told Cathcart. 'And there wasn't just one bike, ten had been built - two for each rider, plus two spares!' Together, the sheer number of Ducati staff and the presence of Ingenere Fabio Taglioni himself convinced Smart that something big was afoot.

Taglioni impressed the Briton, the Italian engineer reminding Smart of Triumph's Doug Hele. Like Hele, Taglioni was a good listener and understood very clearly what was required to ensure the whole bike worked. 'This,' Smart said, 'encouraged me no end.'

But Smart was less enthused when he saw the machine he was going to ride.

'The first thing that struck me was that the bike looked awfully long. It was,' he observed, 'clearly a road machine and didn't look too exciting.'

Smart was surprised to see that the bike retained its centre stand brackets. He was more surprised still to see mechanics in the paddock slip a bolt through the lugs and use the centre stand exactly as one might on a road bike. 'I'd never, ever, seen this done on a race bike!'

Out on the track, the Ducati provided still more surprises. It felt slow compared to the two-stroke H2 race bikes he'd been recently campaigning, the Ducati revving to just 8,250rpm ('it seemed to be firing every other lamppost,' was how Smart described it many years later). Ground clearance was limited and its long wheelbase meant its handling was slow: 'It took an age to turn,' Smart said. 'I liked it a lot.'

Race team manager Farné asked Smart what changes he would like made to the bike. Smart told Farné he wanted the road-going TT100s replaced. The team had fitted them because they were concerned that race tyres would not survive a 200 mile race on Imola's 3.12 mile circuit. Smart, however, insisted they go because the Brit was quite certain that road tyres would limit how fast and how safely he could ride. He persuaded Taglioni to fit Dunlop KR83 and 84 tyres to his and teammate Bruno Spaggiari's bikes instead.[*]

'Ducati was confused about F750, thinking it was it was a modified production with tuned engines,' Smart recalled, 'whereas I knew from the USA that this was GP racing with big motors, and no half measures would suffice.'

With its 60 inch (1530mm) wheelbase, he saw no reason for the bike's huge steering dampers. Smart also asked for a faster-action throttle. He had damaged his right wrist in a crash in Ireland at the North-West 200 and had lost strength and movement in the joint. The mechanics improvised a solution by cutting strips of rubber from a tyre inner tube and lacing the strands to fashion a fatter throttle grip.

Even after Ducati fitted the race tyres, Smart thought the bike 'seemed slow' and 'wouldn't corner.' After ten laps of the very last track session, a tired and exhausted Smart - whose thoughts were focussed on just one thing: going to bed - was passing the pits where all his mechanics were jumping up and down and hugging each other. When he brought the bike in he found out why. 'I had just broken Ago's outright lap record,' Smart recalled, 'and he [Agostini] had been riding his 500cc Grand Prix bike.' Yet the Briton thought the Ducati hadn't felt that quick. It was, he said later, 'such a deceptive bike, faster than the Kawasaki though hardly revving.' (When the American journalist and racer Alan Cathcart tested Smart's Imola bike decades later, he ascribed the Ducati's 'outstanding' pick-up out of turns to the 40mm Dell'Ortos' accelerator pumps, its 'clean torque from as low as 3000rpm', and the sharp right-foot change, close-ratio five-speed gearbox.)

When the team rolled up at the Imola paddock in the large glass-walled cargo unit they had used to transport the bikes the 30km from Bologna to Imola (the team had sequestered the unit from its normal role as a mobile showroom for displaying motorcycles at events across the country), Phil Schilling, the only American journalist covering the race, looked on slack-jawed. After turning to Ducati's PR man, Bruno de Prato (who had been helping smooth matters between *Cycle* magazine's managing editor and the Imola event officials who had been caught out by the level of media interest), the two burst out laughing.

---

[*]   The Ducati team's concerns about tyre longevity proved well founded. Smart told Alan Cathcart in an interview for the UK's *Classic Bike Guide* magazine in 2011 that the Ducati nevertheless 'wore out front tyres quickly because it understeered'.

Despite he and team mate Bruno Spaggiari setting quick times during qualifying and securing first and second places on the start grid, just ahead of Agostini in third, Smart took nothing for granted.

'Ago was riding a shaft-drive MV and he was taking it very seriously,' recalled Smart, 'especially on home ground, where it was the first time he'd missed pole for five years or more.'

Agostini, however, reassured the Englishman that he need not worry about any challenge from him as the MV 'was certain to blow up, and in any case, it was shaft drive and didn't handle.'

'My big worry was the bike,' Smart told the *Telegraph*. 'There was always something dropping off these old things so they need to be constantly nursed. In particular, I thought that the big V-twin engine would knock the hell out of the clutch and I didn't want to destroy it before the first corner.'

Smart shared his concerns with Kevin Cameron who was pit side at Imola. 'They're telling me this Ducati can go to 9,750rpm,' an incredulous Smart told the American. 'That doesn't seem right.' (The racer's paradigm had been set by British parallel-twins of the period whose peak power was limited by destructive levels of vibration and which at just 6,700rpm would have shaken themselves apart.) 'They're telling me if I have to, I can go to 11,000.'

Race team manager Farné, however, demonstrated far more confidence in the bikes. He was so convinced that his riders would secure first and second places that he persuaded Spaggiari and Smart to pool their prize money and split it down the middle irrespective of who of the two took the chequered flag. At a meeting the night before the race, Ducati expected that they would win so comfortably, Smart says 'We were told we could circulate together to the last five laps, then it was every man for himself,' with Spairani promising that: 'Whichever one of you wins the race will keep his bike!'

On 23 April 1972 Europe's first major Formula 750 type race got underway in front of a crowd of 70,000 (whose enthusiasm remained un-dampened by the morning's drizzle). It was St. George's Day and Smart's 29th birthday.

'The start was typically Italian - as soon as Ago started, they dropped the flag for the rest of us!'

SMART VERSUS AGO

Also racing that day was Don Emde. The now 21-year-old had come third in BSA/Triumph's 1-2-3-Daytona-winning team of 1971. One year later, he returned to the Speedbowl and took first place aboard a Yamaha 350cc twin, the first two-stroke machine to win the Daytona classic. Carlo Galavotti had approached Emde as he exited the Speedbowl's Victory Lane that day to invite him to race at Imola the following month. In just a few minutes, the two had put a deal together. Although he was contracted to Yamaha to ride the 350, because the Italians were only allowing bikes between 501 and

750cc* to take part in the first European 200 miler, Emde - the only American-born rider at Imola - agreed with Galavotti that he would pilot the Gus Kuhn 750cc Norton Seeley Commando he had signed to ride for the Anglo-American Match Races (later re-named the Trans-Atlantic Match Races).

The field at Imola included nine different works entries. With Ducati campaigning four desmo V-twins, MV Agusta their shaft-drive 750-4 with suspension and frame patterned on their half-litre GP bike, and the Moto Guzzi factory entering near stock Sports Twins, race-kitted with fairings, disc brakes and megaphone exhausts, Imola 1972 was all set to stage a titanic battle between the Latin and Anglo four-strokes.

However, BSA's quickly-unravelling financial situation meant the British combine was no longer able to fund an official factory team. Instead, Triumph despatched Tridents to Italy, which they entered as private machines (with some support from Meriden) as mounts for John Cooper, Tony Jeffries, Ray Pickrell and Percy Tait.

When the flag dropped, Agostini raced ahead, with Smart and Spaggiari on the Ducati 750 GTs, Tait aboard the Triumph triple, Roberto Gallina (Honda) and British rider Phil Read riding the John Player Norton all in pursuit. Don Emde on the Gus Kuhn Norton had qualified twelfth fastest in qualifying and was sat on the third row of the grid his motor dead. Imola's race organisers had decided that the usual five-minute countdown to the flag would begin *after* the riders had returned to the start line following a one-lap circuit of the track. Just seconds before the race started, Emde's Norton quit on him, the fuel in its Amal GP carburettor developing an air bubble as the petrol boiled. By the time he had wheeled his bike back to the pits, his crew had figured out what had happened, and Emde was able to rejoin the race, he was some seven laps behind the race leaders.

Meanwhile, by lap three, Smart's Ducati team-mate, Bruno Spaggiari, had moved through to join him up front as the Brit pressed race-leader Ago on the MV. After following him for four laps, Smart could see the MV was proving a handful when flat-out on the Tamburello turn just after the pits. At around 130mph, Smart had noticed that Agostini was having to ease off the throttle to get through the flat-out left turn, whereas the Ducati, according to Smart, was 'using all the road but on absolutely the right line'. For the fifth circuit, Smart kept his throttle wide open and sailed past. By lap five, Smart and Spaggiari were in front, first and second respectively, averaging 98mph and running ahead of the MV by eight to ten seconds.

It stayed that way until Agostini retired on lap 42 with a faulty gearbox (described as 'electrical problems' by MV who, whenever forced to quit a race, always blamed the Magneti Marelli distributor). All Smart and Spaggiari had to do now was to preserve their machines and see out the remaining laps. Smart, however, had lost first gear at the Tosa hairpin, which he had to now take in second. 'This wasn't much of a problem,' he recalled, 'since the engine pulled so well, but what worried me was that there might be

---

*   The FIM left organisers to determine their own eligibility criteria for machines. Imola introduced their 501cc to 750cc displacement spread in part to eliminate Yamaha's highly-successful 350cc two-stroke twins, but also to encourage Italy's domestic motorcycle manufacturers to campaign race-developed machines based loosely on production 750cc models.

a piece of broken metal floating around inside the gearbox waiting to lock everything up and kill me.'

Moreover, the clutch wouldn't tolerate being slipped on the uphill exit, forcing Smart to 'drive the bike through'. Whilst this meant taking (as Smart later described it) 'a high, wide 'n' handsome line', the Brit felt 'it wasn't a handicap, because of the Ducati's torque'. Nevertheless, for several laps Smart's concentration suffered. As the contest went on, however, he regained his confidence. Mid-way through the race, both Ducati riders pitted to refuel, with Smart the quicker of the two to return to the track. Seeing Smart speed off, Spaggiari cut short his fuel stop, pushed his mechanics away and set off in pursuit.

According to Smart, when the five-lap board went out 'old Bruno went mad - started smoking tyres up the inside of the hairpin on me and such like. Two laps from the end, he made a do-or-die effort in a very strange place, round the long left at the top of the hill before the Rivazza - it was a 90-100mph corner, no way could he have pulled it off, so inevitably he ran out of road. I remember thinking, "I hope he doesn't fall off, it'll spoil things for Ducati." There were clouds of dust everywhere, but he got back on the road, after that his engine started misfiring.' Following Spaggiari's close call, the two traded leads a couple of times.

By the final lap, Spaggiari was inches ahead of Smart. So evenly-matched were their machines that it appeared that the Italian in first and the Briton a close second was the order in which the two would cross the finish line. However, with just seconds of the race remaining, Spaggiari's Ducati began to misfire (either as a result of fuel starvation or, according to Smart, muck in the carbs), allowing Smart - who had been 'saving it all for the last lap' - to pass him and take the chequered flag at the very first Imola 200 miler. Smart crossed the finish line just four seconds ahead of team-mate Spaggiari.

Italian Walter Villa was the highest-placed British-mounted finisher, coming third on his ex-works Trident entered by importer Bepi Koelliker. Phil Read took fourth place on the John Player Norton, whilst Ray Pickrell, at fifth, was the best placed privateer on the Trident he had retained from his factory-racing days - along with his regular mechanic Arthur Jakeman, who Triumph chief Bert Hopwood had 'loaned' him for the event. Jeffries came sixth, whilst Tait was lucky to escape unscathed when his Trident's magnesium rear hub disintegrated and he was forced to pull up.

Don Emde finished nineteenth. Even so, Mr Galavotti told him later that he appreciated the American's decision to continue when his late start made a high-placed finish impossible. 'He mentioned that a number of the big stars who were there,' Emde said afterward, 'would have just headed for their trailers had they suffered my misfortune. I felt good about that.'

Despite his troubles, the first Imola 200 remained a career highlight for Emde. Years later, he recounted with amusement collecting his prize money: 'For the first (and only) time in my life I was a millionaire. The trouble was, you had to count in Italian Lira - not dollars. Oh well.'

Race winner Paul Smart was also pleased with his day's takings. 'I think I took home about £5,000 - which was a lot of money'.

'Ducati had also promised me the bike if I won and with my past experience of manufacturers' promises, I didn't believe them. But I was wrong and sure enough they did give me the bike and I've still got it today and it's now on display in the Ducati museum in Bologna.' *

THE DUCATI 750 GT MAKES IT IN AMERICA

By portraying the first and second-placed 750 GTs as modified versions of the roadster, Imola provided the perfect promotion for the new 750cc V-twin (spring-valve) production bike. (It helped that Ducati kitted out both machines with a Seeley-based steel frame instead of equipping the race bikes with bespoke, lightweight, quick-steering frames as BSA/Triumph did with the Rob North-framed triples.)

Moreover, the GT consolidated its success at Imola with favourable reviews by America's biggest motorcycle magazine, *Cycle*. Phil Schilling described magazine staffers as 'simply astonished' by the GT when *Cycle* carried out the first US road test of the vehicle for their October 1972 issue. Above a full colour photograph of a speeding black and white-liveried example, the front cover headline announced: 'Ducati Springs the Most Startling 750 Yet.'

But it was its appearance two months later in *Cycle* magazine's much anticipated second superbike comparison test which ensured that the Ducati did not merely become an exotic motorcycling curiosity.

Cycle's very first head-to-head took place in 1970 and, according to Schilling, 'drew an immense following to the magazine'. The follow-up two years later tested the 1973 season's contenders for the title of best all-round superbike by running seven machines back-to-back at the Orange County International Raceway where *Cycle* staffers Jess Thomas, Dale Boller and Cook Neilson measured each entrant's acceleration, braking force, and lap times around the Los Angeles racecourse.

Success in the test conferred immediate celebrity on the winner. Victory, however, depended on the points each bike amassed at the end of four challenges. Testing took place over three days starting 28 August. Rider preferences didn't matter. Fuel consumption, build quality, comfort, or styling - all the things buyers usually take into consideration when choosing which machine to purchase - fell outside the test. Whilst this meant that scoring was, by the magazine's own admission, limited, it was nevertheless 'pure and absolute'.

The rules of engagement were simple.

---

* Smart raced his Imola-winning desmo just three more times: At Brands Hatch, where it came first in the Hutchinson 100; at Snetterton, where it retired with ignition problems as Smart contested the lead with Agostini; and at Silverstone, where the Ducati's long wheelbase made the bike feel like it was always trying to push out its front wheel, and the circuit's fast corners and the bike's tall gearing left a gaping hole in the power, which made it hard for Smart to catch up. The Englishman attributed his bike's success at Imola to the fact that it was designed for just one race, and a circuit that back then was virtually all sweeping bends.

Entrants could bring along as many mechanics as they wished. They could work on their machines at anytime during the tests, but they could not remove them from the test area ('unless to correct a major deficiency').

Each motorcycle had to be standard, but run-in. However, mechanics could swap final-drive sprockets as long as they were stock items available from any local dealer. They could replace tyres with racing compounds (but using stock wheels), and they could 'super-tune' engines using standard components (this included 'valve jobs', as long as they did not alter 'port shape, size or finish').

The 750 GT on test was identical to the machine *Cycle* had reviewed in their October issue. For the comparison test, chief mechanic A.J. Lewis from Bob Blair's distributorship ZDS kept the V-twin tuned for its three-day trial at the Raceway.

Testing Begins

The first of the magazine's quartet of tests was to measure each bike's stopping ability at 60mph (all seven machines sported front disc brakes).

Kawasakis grabbed the two top spots. The MACH IV 750 two-stroke scored the maximum 100 points by braking from 60mph in 128.417ft with a brake force of 0.922 Gs, beating its four-cylinder stablemate the Z1, which, although bettering the triple's stopping distance with an impressive 126.417ft, the 903 was shaded by the H2's superior brake force (albeit by just 0.002 Gs). With its brake force of 0.916 G and stopping distance of 131.958ft, the 750 Norton Commando came third with a score of 99.3 points.

Exerting a brake force of 0.902 G and hauling to a stop in a tad less than 138ft earned the GT a score of 97.8 points. Its score placed the Ducati fourth (ahead of the Honda and Trident 750s and the H-D Sportster, the XLCH1000 trailing in last place with a stopping distance of 145.250ft).

After a day and a half of 'nerve-wracking panic stops', things now moved to the race circuit where *Cycle* staffers would test the machines' handling.

First up was the Honda.

Since its appearance in the inaugural comparison test of 1970, Honda had raised the Four's overall gearing, installed lighter clutch springs, retarded cam timing, and fitted quieter exhausts - at 80.5 Db(A), the CB750 was the quietest machine on test, and fully 7.5 decibels below the maximum permissible under Californian state law. (At between 90 and 91 decibels, the Ducati was, by contrast, the loudest machine of the group, far exceeding the 88 decibel state limit.)

From the outset, it was clear that the changes Honda had wrought to broaden the CB750's appeal had softened and slowed the Four, leaving it in sixth place in the handling test.

The Kawasaki Z1 was next.

Despite the 903's rear suspension losing its damping after a few laps 'at incredible speeds', causing the bike to wallow in fast turns, the rear brake also getting hot and becoming useless, and the gear lever losing its rubber cover after oil from the generator case saturated the pedal, the Super Four's best lap time of 44.5 seconds meant it tied with its Kawasaki stablemate for fastest lap.

The three-cylinder two-stroke also lost its rear damping after just a few laps. The MACH IV broke into huge wobbles, too, when its silencers grounded and lifted the rear wheel off the deck. With its engine 'rattling, wheezing, pinging, knocking and vibrating', and despite its lack of civility, the H2's power, lightness and acceleration and excellent brakes, which 'held up to perfection for the whole of the 10 lap session', saw the 750 tie for first place with the Z1.

Next to try was the Ducati.

With its lorry-like wheelbase, a steering rake approaching 31 degrees, long, swept-back handlebars, and - according to *Cycle*'s testers - 'incredible' angles of lean and 'perfect' clutch, throttle and brake controls, the 750 GT was only let down by its Metzeler rear tyre. The V-twin was utterly stable on fast bends (if a 'bit clumsy' in the Raceway's two low-gear corners). However, just as riders exited a fast corner and accelerated, the Ducati's tyre would slide alarmingly. Its waywardness cost the Duke dearly. A 46.4 second lap time relegated the GT to fifth in the test, one spot behind the Norton whose Avon tyres testers said 'felt vastly better than those on the Ducati'.

Third place went to the Triumph Trident whose Dunlop TT100 tyres testers deemed perfect for muscling the high-handle barred four-stroke triple through tight corners and around Orange County's sweeping bends with the throttle wide open.

Last out (and, by test's end, last placed) was the Sportster.

Like the Ducati, the Harley-Davidson was let down by its tyres, which in the XLCH's case were Goodyears, the only tyres that would fit H-D's new safety rims. Designed to prevent tyres distorting and causing a blow-out if a sudden flat should occur, the Goodyears' square section would squirrel during hard cornering. The Sportster's suspension was excellent, however, and despite the front calliper dragging after a few laps, the bike's brakes continued to perform well. Testers complained about the oil tank jabbing into the rider's right leg and getting blisteringly hot; the oil-pressure warning light blinking during the whole ten-laps; and the motor's 'clanking and rattling and general commotion'. They also felt that the XLCH's new California-legal silencers were so restrictive that they cancelled out any power increases gained by the Milwaukee-made V-twin's hike in displacement to 1,000cc.

The Sportster's best lap was 48 seconds dead, 3.5 seconds behind the joint first-placed Kawasakis who both scored maximum points in the handling test.

Just one test now remained where entrants could still score points toward their final tally. Measuring each machine's acceleration and terminal velocity from a standing start to the end of a quarter mile, the drag strip was, as *Cycle* put it, the Superbike's 'Primal battleground'.

The first machine to take to the strip was the Honda CB750 Four.

Two years earlier, when it took part in the very first comparison test, the Honda was the only entrant with enough 'snap' to pull a drag slick tyre. But when Honda's mechanics tried to run it with an Avon gumball this time, *Cycle* found that it was simply 'too much tire' for the de-fanged but more refined Four. They re-fitted the original equipment Dunlop and after nine attempts - more than that seemed pointless, especially given that the MACH IV had still to run - testers took the Honda's best times from runs five and seven to record a standing start over the quarter mile of 13.485 seconds at 100.67mph.

Next on the drag strip was the Ducati 750 GT.

Clutch problems with the bike *Cycle* tested for their October issue had prevented the Ducati from posting its best times, but ZDS spannerman, the legendary mechanic A.J. Lewis, had prepared the GT this time. Throughout the day and during the course of twenty runs, Lewis experimented with his charge's final gear ratios. In the end, the bike achieved its best elapsed time (ET) and terminal speed on stock gearing and wearing standard tyres. Riders found the gearbox's accuracy a 'revelation' - once they stopped overshifting from first to second, and changed gear at an even 9,000 revs (the GT making its most useful power past 8,500rpm). And with the engine's impressive torque helping control any wheelspin, the black and white Ducati successfully reeled off five runs at 100mph or better. Nine of its 20 runs reached 99mph, three hit 98, and the remaining three 97. The very best time posted by the Italian V-twin was 13.289 seconds at 101.12mph.

(In an interesting postscript, when *Cycle* later tested the Ducati on the dynometer at Yamaha's Buena Park headquarters in California, they discovered that the rubber manifolds connecting the carburettors to the air filter housing were pinched near shut, seriously restricting air flow. After correcting the fault, testers immediately realised another 5bhp, leading them to ponder on how much better the GT's times at the drag strip might have been.)

The Ducati was followed by the Triumph Trident, a veteran of the *Cycle*'s very first comparison test when it ran a 12.78 second standing quarter at 103.92mph. Despite wearing more restrictive silencers this time round, the five-speed triple - 'the most perfectly-geared motorcycle in the test' - produced in the course of elevens runs, two at 12.72 and one 12.718 second standing quarter and 105mph terminal speeds at 8,000rpm in top gear. Then, just as the Trident appeared to be responding to mechanic Bob Ellison's fine-tuning and deliver the high 12.5 second quarters testers had anticipated the triple was capable of at the outset of the test, the Triumph shredded second gear on its twelfth run.

Runner up to the Trident on terminal speed at the drag strip two years ago, but beating all comers back then with its 12.69 second pass, the '73 season Norton Commando was next to face the starting lights.

This time round, in the course of ten runs, the 'beautifully prepared' but entirely stock Roadster never bettered the 104.77mph finishing speed it achieved on its very first pass. Nor was the Norton able to improve on its ET of 12.896 seconds nailed on just its second pass. *Cycle* attributed the 750's slower ET in the second superbike head-to-head to changes Norton introduced since 1970 to quieten the engine, but which hurt its times. Although the bike would surge in higher gears when hot (a trait *Cycle* had experienced with previous Nortons), testers praised the 750 vertical twin's 'light and accurate' four-speed gearbox, which shifted as cleanly as the Commando had in the 1970 comparison test. They felt, though, that like the H-D Sportster, the Norton's times might have benefited from a fifth gear.

After the Norton came the two Kawasakis.

The MACH IV went first. Although the two-stroke triple had the most willing engine, the bike proved a handful. It performed best when the engine was well below normal operating temperature. Riders wrung their fastest times from the bike if they ignored the engine's willingness to rev and shifted early - 7,000rpm or less. To keep the front wheel from lifting skyward or avoid hopelessly spinning the rear wheel, riders had to strike a delicate balance between engine speed and clutch engagement, all the time hunched forward to counter the triple's rear weight bias in an effort to keep the front end planted on or near the tarmac, whilst also trying to stay mounted, their feet on the pegs, and shifting from first to second as the bike rocketed out of the gate in a series of furious hops and convulsions.

By the third pass, testers had found the optimum combination: through first gear holding the throttle at three-quarters, slipping the clutch just a tad then changing up the cogs at 7,000rpm, the triple's motor a cacophony of ringing fins and slapping pistons. *Cycle*'s journalists recognised that to anyone with an ounce of mechanical sympathy, holding an engine at 7,000 or 8,000rpm then pinning back the throttle and dumping the clutch run after run after run seemed 'unnatural and abusive'. But the MACH IV was just so eager to rev and such a willing partner that, in spite of being the most demanding machine of the all to pilot down the drag strip it was also the most fun. It was also the quickest.

From a standing start to the end of a quarter mile, the H2 - stock apart from a change to its final drive ratios, which tuner Jack Murphy, mechanic to drag-racer Tony Nicosia, had raised from 3.13 to 3.21 - posted a best and winning time of just 12.283 seconds at 110.29mph.

It was now the turn of the second of the two Kawasakis. The 903 Z1 completed just four passes before prematurely retiring after blowing a billowing cloud of smoke from its exhaust. Even so, despite its weight and civility, and testers failing to nail the sweet spot between perfect traction and the 903's propensity to spin its rear wheel uselessly, nor tester's curtailed attempts to improve on its times (which *Cycle* was sure that had its pit crew elected to fit a slick rear tyre, the Z1 would have gone on to record the first box stock eleven-second standing quarter), the MACH IV's big brother still managed to produce the strongest terminal speed of all seven entrants: 110.70mph. It also posted an elapsed time just two tenths of a second behind its 750 sibling. The 903's terminal speed and ET of 12.386 seconds earned the Z1 99.2 points, placing it second in the last of the scored trials. A final tally of 399 points meant the Z1 finished runner up, 0.6 points behind the MACH IV (which scored 399.6 out of a possible 400).

Last up was the Sportster.

A participant in the magazine's first comparison test two years earlier, the then 883cc Sportster had chewed up the quarter mile in just 12.97 seconds, crossing the finishing line at 102.15mph. Two years later, its California-compliant silencers had dented the now one-litre V-twin's power at high revs. But its 'gargantuan low-end torque' remained intact. The Sportster just needed a tyre that would hook into the tarmac to lay down all that torque. Unfortunately, the stock Goodyear 4.25 X 18 fitted to its rear wasn't that tyre.

The H-D had to be 'tip-toed out of the hole to reduce wheelspin' only for testers to find that when they had the motor spinning in the higher reaches of its rev range, 'there simply wasn't a lot of urge left'. Moreover, just as they were nearing the traps, a huge gap between the four-speed box's third and fourth gears 'pulled the engine down from its peak power'.

Nor were the Sportster's ergonomics much help. The chopper-style handlebars stopped riders getting flat on the tank and out of the wind. Its tachometer's needle was so erratic that it was impossible for testers to know when to change gear or replicate shifts between passes.

The Sportster's times over the course of 22 punishing runs were, however, very consistent: six passes in the 13.6 second range and ten at 13.5; nine of its terminals reached 98mph, with seven passes trapped at 99mph. In the end, the XLCH's very best figures were 13.393 seconds and 99.98mph, making the Harley the slowest bike in the test and the only one of the seven not to crack the ton at the end of its standing quarter.

The Harley's ET bettered the Honda by just over a tenth of a second, but the CB750's 100.67mph terminal speed was a shade faster. With a final score of 365.4 points, the XLCH trailed the Honda 750 in the final points tally also, finishing last of all in only the second of *Cycle* magazine's superbike comparison tests.

The Ducati's performance on the drag strip secured fifth spot in the fourth test. By the end of the third day, the Duke's final tally of 377.4 (out of a possible 400) meant it finished fifth overall - one place behind the Norton, but ahead of both the Honda and the Sportster.

Yet, in spite of the magazine's avowal at the outset of the test that the yardsticks by which they would measure the '73 season's crop of superbikes were 'pure' and absolute', the eventual winner - the Kawasaki MACH IV 750 two-stroke triple - did not turn out to be the testers' favourite bike.

As *Cycle*'s report pointed out after bench testing all the entrants, it did not follow that each bike's performance on the road paralleled the margins of difference charted on the dyno graphs. To illustrate the point they compared the Z1's torque and horsepower readings with those of the 750 GT.

Despite the Z1's greater torque at 3,000rpm, by dint of the Ducati being far lighter (469lbs wet weight compared to the Kawasaki's 542lbs) meant the GT would 'kill the 903 in a high-gear throttle roll-on' from 3,000rpm, where for every foot-pound of torque the Ducati was producing it was carrying just 12.58lbs in weight. The Z1, by contrast, was carrying 13.75lbs for each foot-pound it generated. Moreover, the Ducati could maintain its lead because even by 6,000rpm it retained its torque-to-weight advantage right up to 7,000rpm. By then, the big Kawasaki's motor was producing some 45 foot-pounds of torque to the V-twin's 37, and overhauling the Italian's previous advantage so that the ratio per foot-pound was by then 11.95lbs for the Z1 and 12.75lbs for the GT.

Even so, in spite of the Ducati 750 finishing fifth overall in the comparison test and being by far the loudest bike of the group (its 90-plus dB(A) level shattering California's 88 decibel limit), it was 'the bike everybody wanted to ride home, points total or no,' said *Cycle* in its conclusions.

Very shortly afterward, two of the three authors of *Cycle* magazine's second Superbike comparison test went out and purchased GTs of their own, with *Cycle* staff eventually buying around half-a-dozen in total. 'Ownership,' observed Schilling many years later. 'Now that was the ultimate endorsement of the new Ducati V-Twin.'

'OLD BLUE' WINS DAYTONA

Five years later, Phil Schilling and fellow *Cycle* staffer Cook Neilson, would make history when they secured Ducati their first and only Daytona win. On 11 March 1977, riding a much modified 750 Super Sport, Neilson took on and beat the previous year's winner of the AMA's new Superbike Production Series, Steve McLaughlin and McLaughlin's second-placed team mate Reg Pridmore, both of whom were riding BMW R90Ss.

AMA rider's representative Steve McLaughlin from Pasadena, California, had been an early advocate of a Superbike Production class running alongside AMA road-race nationals. In 1973, as a support race to California's Laguna Seca AMA National in Monterey, racing promoters and publishers Gavin Trippe and Bruce Cox added a Superbike Production race to the card. Other promoters followed suit. Backed by Daytona International Speedway's Jim France and Ed Youngblood of the AMA, in 1976 the class finally gained national recognition to become a key component of every AMA road-racing national.

'The time was ripe for Superbike racing,' recalled McLaughlin in an interview for the AMA's Hall of Fame (an inductee since 2004). 'The AMA was beginning to make road-racing independent from the traditional Grand National Series and Superbike could draw from a large pool of production racers coming from growing ranks of road-racing organisations such as the AFM, WERA and others. Plus, the management of the AMA realised that Superbike racing was essentially a return to Class C (production) racing that the AMA had favoured since the 1930s.'

When 36-year old Neilson and the bike he and Schilling had nicknamed 'Old Blue' took the chequered flag at the Florida track in the following year's return bout, he not only put himself and Ducati into the record books, the *Cycle* editor also turned a humble housefly into a Daytona legend, too.

'OLD BLUE' VERUS THE DAYTONA-WINNING BEEMERS AND YOSHI FOURS

Since 1974, in between writing and editing *Cycle* magazine, Schilling and Neilson spent all their spare time campaigning and honing the bevel-drive 750 Ducati race bike they dubbed Old Blue ('It was blue,' Cook said later, 'And God knows it was old'.) Schilling, a fan of Ducatis since the Fifties and a self-taught mechanic of the Italian brand, acted as wrench (Ducati dealers being thin on the ground in the young Schilling's home state of Indiana). 'I spent all the money I had on the bike,' Cook recollected in an interview for the AMA (Neilson was inducted to the Motorcycle Hall of Fame in 2006). 'And what I couldn't come up with I was able to talk out of Schilling'.

Neilson and Schilling's machine was one of three pre-homologation Super Sport 750s that Ducati shipped to America in 1973. 'The reason we latched onto a Ducati to race,' Neilson explained later, 'had nothing to do with the fact that it was Italian or oddball... we figured we could take this bike, soup it up, and beat fours with it.'

But, as Neilson put it: 'Certain things were not exactly first rate.' He described the Ducati's electrics as 'ratty and unfinished', and the finish on the chassis as 'not that great'.

'For instance,' Neilson explained, 'the first 750 Super Sport we ever got had a fly cast into the fuel tank. The Italians had laid up this fibreglass tank and this critter got trapped in there.'

For two solid years they worked on it. By 1976, the year the AMA formally launched its Superbike Series,[*] Neilson, Schilling and Old Blue were ready. However, as results in the Series' inaugural race at Daytona would prove, evidently not quite ready enough.

---

* Under the AMA rules for the new Series, entrant's bikes could displace up to 1,000cc, had to use the stock frame, retain the rear light and headlamp shell, engine cases, carburettors and the outer shell of the standard silencers. Competitors could, however, make internal modifications. The rules also allowed for competitors to lighten their machine by up to 20 per cent below the homologated street version's dry weight. Observance was subject to whatever teams could get past scrutineers. Tuners like Udo Geitl - who had developed Steve McLaughlin's 1976 Daytona-winning Butler & Smith BMW R90S racer - interpreted the AMA's rulebook as licence to do whatever it did not specify he couldn't. McLaughlin's winning bike was monoshock, whereas the stock R90S wore twin Borge rear shock absorbers. Neilson told *Motohistory*: 'At least one competitor fabricated a four-into-two exhaust system which completely bypassed one of the two mufflers - and the dummy muffler was the one closest to where the AMA would set up its decibel meter.' Several teams saw the one-litre limit as 'merely a guideline'.

Neilson was therefore unapologetic of his and Schilling's use of an overly-optimistic rev counter, which read a few thousand more rpm than the engine was turning (thereby helping them get the bike though the pre-race sound-test), as Old Blue was running the smallest-capacity motor compared to its main rivals, its front suspension, chassis and hollowed-out silencers were AMA compliant, and even the bike's lights worked. All the same, Neilson harboured a secret doubt. 'I will admit, though, that we never knew if the 750 Ducati Desmo Super Sport was ever properly homologated.'

Butler & Smith fielded three BMW R90Ss in AMA's first race of the Superbike Series: the race winning Number 83 of Steve McLaughlin; Reg Pridmore aboard Number 163; and National racer Gary Fisher (one of the best 250GP riders around) who retired with a broken rocker. McLaughlin had been racing for Racecrafters Kawasaki in the Heavyweight Production class, the precursor to the Superbike Series. After turning down an approach to race for the Yoshimura team in the new AMA-supported race series (no money, just for the honour of racing for Pops was how it was put to him), McLaughlin - who made his living from racing - accepted Butler & Smith's considerably more generous terms of $500 per race, plus bonuses (Pridmore was getting $1,000 for the whole season). Having already raced in the Daytona 200 on a TZ750, McLaughlin understood about 'The Draft'. In a 2010 interview with Alan Cathcart for *Motorcycle Classics* magazine, McLaughlin explained how he spent his laps 'looking for where the draft is, until I finally found it, and the real tow is about eight or nine bike lengths behind [Reggie Pridmore's bike] - a lot more than on other bikes, probably because of those cylinders sticking out the sides.' Tailing in Pridmore's draft on the last lap, McLaughlin powered out of the final chicane. He had quite a gap to make up - plus, Pidmore's bike was actually the faster of the two - but the 27-year-old Californian managed to just inch past to take the flag by half-a-tyre's width. It was so close that the track announcer Roxy Rockwood put Pridmore centre podium in the winner's circle, despite AMA referee Bill Boyce advising him to wait for the results of the photo. When the photo evidence confirmed McLaughlin the victor, Pridmore handed him the trophy, suggesting they split the winnings. 'I said, "what are you talking about. Get outta here,"' McLaughlin recounted. 'Reggie's never talked to me since that day.'

Neilson placed third.

'I was sick about my finish at Daytona,' Neilson recalled. 'Phil gave me the best bike out there. We had a top-speed advantage over the BMWs and when you combine that with the other advantages of the Ducati, a good rider would have gapped those guys. I knew I had to improve.'

Money was tight. What sponsors they had covered little more than sparkplugs and oil. But Neilson and Schilling 'knew somebody who knew somebody'.

California in the mid-70s was a hot-bed of craftsman and artisans. 'Phil found the best of the best,' Neilson told *Cycle World* years later. With a lot of assistance from the renowned engine tuner Jerry Branch reworking the Duke's heads, plus ace fabricator Pierre des Roches' help with the chassis, Schilling set to work on improving Old Blue. Roches was actually busy building a Kawasaki for Reg Pridmore, but agreed to 'do stuff' for the California Hot Rod (as Neilson also called their Ducati), just because he wanted to. 'Titanium tower shafts; a magnesium rear calliper carrier; titanium axles and axle nuts; a reinforced chassis and swing arm - these things just would appear, courtesy of Pierre. He was,' Cook joked, 'almost like the Tooth Fairy that way - but he never took any teeth!'

Working without factory data, Schilling nevertheless managed to correct for preload rates and expansion factors and shim the desmo's gears and shafts so that the engine, according to Neilson, 'went together like a fine watch. Phil,' his friend observed, 'was the watchmaker.'

For Daytona 1977, Old Blue now displaced 883cc thanks to a pair of Venolia-built 87mm pistons with Yamaha XT500 rings and lightened Toyota wristpins that Schilling and Neilson designed to cure ring-sealing problems associated with earlier large-bore Dukes. Schilling had tried 926cc, but performance proved disappointing and he decided to keep displacement close to the capacity for which Bologna had designed the camshaft. Harley-Davidson XR 44mm intake valves (increased by 2mm over last season) and 38mm BMW exhaust valves helped take care of breathing, whilst power was transmitted through a five-speed gearbox built by Marvin Webster. 'I remember going to the airport to pick up the tranny and just staring at the silver-gold colour of the gears,' Neilson told *CW*'s Nick Ienatsch in 2007. 'It cost us £2,000, which was a lot of money back then, and I teared up at how beautiful it was.'

When a factory-ordered oil cooler didn't turn up, they made their own out of Volkswagen parts. The whole plot rolled on Morris cast magnesium wheels shod with Goodyear slicks. Retardation was provided by magnesium callipers and a trio of Harry Hunt plasma-sprayed brake rotors hauling down a bike that now weighed just 398lb (181kg), 25lbs less than it did a year ago. Meanwhile, as Schilling prepared and modified the Duke for the coming battle, Neilson was honing his track skills.

A keen motorcyclist, accomplished drag racer, and Bonneville Flats record-holder on his much-modified H-D Sportster, Neilson was an Ivy League graduate with an English major (he was suspended for a year from Princeton for taking his motorcycle on campus), who worked his summers as an assistant municipal bond tradesman. After serving in the National Guard, he resumed his studies at Princeton, but was deflected from an almost-certain career on Wall Street after being hired by Gordon Jennings in 1967 to join the staff of *Cycle* at its editorial offices in the magazine's Ziff-Davis corporate headquarters on New York's Park Avenue (where Cook would become editor in November 1969 at the age of just 26), on the strength of a few submissions he had penned on drag racing for publications such as *The Enthusiast* and *Cycle World*. Neilson, therefore, was a quick study. During the close-season, he competed in every club event in the West Coast area that he could in order to sharpen his proficiency in preparation for the 1977 Series.

For the opening race at the Speedbowl, however, Neilson was not just in contention with last year's Daytona victor Steve McLaughlin and runner-up Reg Pridmore. The success of the Series had attracted Kawasaki's attention. In addition to the BMWs, Neilson now found himself up against a brace of factory-backed Z1s. These included John Bettencourt and Wes Cooley on the Yoshimura Kawasaki Z1, Lang Hindle riding the Lester Wheels Kawasaki, and Keith Code aboard a Racecrafters-sponsored Kawasaki Z. Also in the mix were young up-and-coming talents, such as Mike Baldwin, David Emde (brother of Don) and Ron Pierce.

At the track, Schilling and Neilson were in the Goodyear garage bantering with their neighbours, the Yamaha factory team of Kel Carruthers and Kenny Roberts. The atmosphere was jovial. Old Blue was posting 2 minute 15 second lap times, equalling Roberts' Yamaha 250 GP bikes; whilst Cooley's Yoshimura Kawasaki may have clocked the highest speed in practice with 153.06mph - with Neilson second fastest at 149.50mph - Old Blue's times showed *Cycle*'s editor was lapping the track two seconds faster than anyone else. 'The thing must be making great power,' observed Champion Spark Plug's Bobby Strahlmann after examining the Ducati's plugs and exhaust pipes (it was said Strahlmann could discern from the burn pattern of a spark plug what the rider had had for breakfast).

It wasn't just Neilson's engine that was strong, either. Unlike the BMWs and the Kawasakis, Old Blue's chassis was rigid enough to handle the grip afforded by the Goodyear slicks. The Boxer twins and transverse fours flexed so much that they were forced to use DOT tyres, as the traction from slicks caused their bikes to buck and weave violently.

Qualifying was abandoned due to rain. Riders therefore took up their position on the starting grid subject to their previous season's points ranking. Neilson occupied third spot, flanked by last year's winner Steve McLaughlin and runner-up Reggie Pridmore's BMWs on one side and Mike Baldwin's Leoni Moto-Guzzi on the other. Behind them was Wes Cooley astride the Yoshimura Kawasaki Z1.

Old Blue was making 90.4 horsepower at 8,300rpm (up nearly 20bhp on the standard bike). That was good power for a twin, but around 30bhp shy of the Yoshimura Z1s, which were rumoured to be pumping out 120bhp. A fire at Pops Yoshimura's Hollywood site, however, just days before the Florida race, destroyed both the tuner's dyno and the 120 horsepower engine. Pops suffered terrible burns, and it fell to his son, Fujio, to assemble a replacement engine and rebuild a bike for Daytona with just days to go. The incident, however, prevented any further development ahead of the race. Even so, the Yoshimura Kawasaki still turned the fastest lap in practice.

'The Daytona Superbike was the one race I really wanted to win,' Cook told *Motohistory*. 'I know it sounds unsophisticated, but I always loved the track, especially Turn One, which I think is (or was, before they changed it) the most technical single corner in all of racing. There were multiple radiuses and camber changes, the final part of it has a decreasing radius, you're coming into it off the tri-oval at top speed, and if you do it right you have to be willing to use a lot of front brake while you're leaned over pretty far. But the whole place screams "Big Time!"'

When the flag dropped, Cooley took off like a rocket to seize the lead. As they passed Daytona's tri-oval for the first time, the 19-year-old from Los Angeles was 30 bike-lengths ahead of second-placed Neilson ('His Kawasaki had pulled about 60 bike lengths on me around the banking,' Neilson told *Cycle World* 30 years later, 'but I made it all up on the brakes'.) At Turn One, as the two men hit the apex, Neilson had caught up and was on Cooley's tail. He had managed to do so in such a short distance he allowed himself to think: 'Well now. This is gonna be good.'

When, on lap two, Cooley took the second horseshoe bend a little wide, through the visor of his open-face Bell helmet, Neilson spotted his chance. Entering the corner, Neilson executed a neat inside pass just before the apex. His elation was short-lived, however. In Cook's excitement, he fluffed his shift to fourth gear on the section between the horseshoe and the entrance to the West Banking. Cooley pounced. The young Californian grabbed back the lead. On lap three, Neilson overtook Cooley once again at the next pass. This time, though, he shifted to fourth without missing the change and began to pull away, leaving Cooley further and further behind.

Neilson crossed the line 28 seconds in front of second-placed David Emde. Cooley finished third by a fair margin.

~ ~ ~

After competing at Daytona four times previously, the first occasion back in 1975 riding a Ducati 750 GT, Neilson had finally achieved his goal. He was all set to hang up his leathers. Schilling, who was overjoyed at their Daytona victory, persuaded him to complete the season. He retired after Riverside, finishing the championship in second place, just three points behind the winner Reggie Pridmore.

Neilson's Daytona win, Ducati's greatest since Imola, the Ducati's creditable performance in Cycle's 1972 Superbike 7 comparison test, and the magazine's favourable reviews, coupled with Mike Hailwood's remarkable TT comeback in 1978 on a Bologna twin, all helped cement the Italian company's credibility with motorcyclists.

13

THE COLLAPSE OF BSA

THE OIL-IN-THE-FRAME FIASCO, AND THE MERIDEN SIT-IN HALTS PRODUCTION OF THE TRIDENT

'It became evident there is hostility in motorcycling circles'
(Letter writer to *Motorcycle Sport*)

Dennis Poore

ATTITUDES TO CHANGE

As *Cycle* Magazine observed in the conclusion to its second comparison test, 'Superbikes were changing.' Something similar could also be said of Britons' attitudes and expectations. In the UK, foreign tourism increased by 50 per cent as nine million Britons holidayed abroad, fuelled by the lifting in January 1970 of the amount of foreign currency travellers could take abroad (raised from £50 a year to £300).

In January 1968, six months after BBC2 transmitted Britain's first colour broadcast on 1 July 1967 (when the station showed four hours of tennis from Wimbledon), colour TV licences became available for the first time. At £10, they cost twice the price of a black and white licence, yet by 1977 - despite a brand new colour TV in the early Seventies costing around £400 (equivalent to about £8,000 four decades later) - the sale of colour TV licences overtook black and white licences (9.9 million to 8.1 million respectively).

Meanwhile, it was a TV situation comedy of all things that would push the boundaries of what TV could depict of people's changing lifestyles. *Robin's Nest*, a spin-off of *Man About the House*, was the first British sitcom to show an unmarried couple living together, portrayal of which required special permission from the Independent Broadcasting Authority - to ensure ITV maintained 'suitable standards'.

The highest rating shows of the day, however, suggest a society where unreconstructed attitudes also prevailed. The 1970 Miss World contest garnered BBC Television their highest viewing figure that year. (The swimsuit section, however, faced stiff new competition. Just a few weeks earlier, on 17 November, 20-year-old Stephanie Rahn from Germany became the first women to bare her breasts in a national newspaper when she appeared topless on page three of *The Sun*, launching a 40 per cent rise in sales in the space of a year.) *

Some TV shows reflected contemporary sensibilities to race. Shows like *Mind Your Language* in which a teacher played by the actor Barry Evans taught English to a class of caricature foreigners, and ITV's *Love Thy Neighbour* with its racist character, trade unionist Eddie Booth; or white comedic actors like Spike Milligan blacking up to play an Indian in *Till Death Us Do Part*, and Michael Bates doing likewise in *It Ain't Half Hot Mum*.

And, as if to confirm that the past is indeed a foreign country, one of the most popular shows in the Seventies was *The Black and White Minstrel Show*, in which white singers wore black greasepaint with exaggerated white-accented eyes and mouths.**

Yet, just as programmes like *The Minstrel Show* and *Dad's Army* looked to the past, shows such as *Tomorrow's World* and *The Burke Special* turned their gaze to the future. That future promised infinite possibilities following Neil Armstrong's small step from the Eagle landing craft onto the powdery surface of the Sea of Tranquillity at around 3am Greenwich Mean Time - scheduled to coincide with primetime TV in America - on 21 July 1969. The worldwide viewing audience for the event was estimated at 528 million.

Then, just a little over two months later, on 1 October 1969, Concorde exceeded Mach 1 for nine minutes, 36,000 feet above Toulouse.

But even as *Tomorrow's World* showcased the latest advances to emerge from the 'white heat of technology', as Harold Wilson called it, and recent relaxations on hire purchase

---

*   The twentieth Miss World contest became an unlikely lightning rod for militant factions. 'Women's Lib' protesters rose from the Albert Hall audience and threw flour bombs at that year's host, veteran US comedian, Bob Hope, whilst outside, the Angry Brigade set off a bomb underneath a parked BBC van. The contest also provoked protests from the Liberal Party, particularly the Young Liberals. Led by Peter Hain, they were furious at the organiser's clumsy response to South Africa's inevitable selection of white-only representatives. Mecca Ltd, headed by Eric Morley, who along with his wife Julia, owned the Miss World franchise, had that year introduced for the very first time a Miss South Africa and a Miss Africa South. Hain felt the move endorsed apartheid. It was probably therefore much to Morley's relief that the contest would go on to yield yet another first. The 100-1 outsider Miss Grenada, 22-year-old Jennifer Josephine Hosten, was the contest's first ever black winner - with Miss Africa South emerging as runner up.

**   By the time *The Black and White Minstrel Show* ended its 20 year run in 1978, it had collected both Gold and Silver awards at the first Rose of Montreux television festival in 1961 and its 1976 Christmas special ranked amongst the five most watched programmes of the holiday.

fuelled a boom in consumer goods, Britons seemed Janus-like as they straddled the threshold between the old and the new. Motorcyclists, too, seemed similarly afflicted - sometimes *neophobic* (fear of the new) and sometimes *neophiliac* (love of the novel).

BRIT VERSUS JAP

In autumn 1973, 'Britain's No 1 Motor Cycle Dealer', Coburn & Hughes (tel: Luton 26903), sponsored a full-page advert in *Bike* magazine. The London- and Luton-based dealer's ad offers a snapshot of motorcycling during a time when new machines from Britain's venerable marques shared showroom floor space - some of them for the last time - alongside their rivals from Japan.

Running down either side of Coburn & Hughes' price list were a series of small photographs of motorcycles, with the word 'DISCOUNTS' above each one and the bike's marque set out in bold capitals underneath. Every picture was surrounded by a badge-like circle. Arranged down the left-side of the price list were the Japanese manufacturers (Kawasaki, Honda, Suzuki, and Yamaha); down the right-hand side, British and European manufacturers (Norton, Triumph, BSA, and Bultaco, CZ, MZ, and Montesa).

As the list shows *(see below)*, even before discount, the British bikes compared well on price with their Japanese counterparts.

	LIST PRICE	OUR PRICE		LIST PRICE	OUR PRICE
KAWASAKI 500 H1B	£624	£579	TRIUMPH T140 V750CC	£625	£589
KAWASAKI 250 F11 TRAIL	£520	£469	TRIUMPH TR7 750CC	£597	£559
KAWASAKI 125 F16 TRAIL	£343	£299	TRIUMPH HURRICANE	£826	£749
SUZUKI T500K	£520	£489	TRIUMPH T120 V	£525	£479
SUZUKI GT 380K	£517	£489	TRIUMPH T120 R	£499	£459
SUZUKI GT 250K	£397	£379	TRIUMPH TR6 R	£479	£439
SUZUKI GT 185K	£315	£299			
SUZUKI TS 125J	£234	£219	TRIUMPH TR5T TRAIL	£479	£439
HONDA CB 750 4CVL (sic)	£849	£789	TRIUMPH DAYTONA	£474	£439
HONDA CB 500 4CVL (sic)	£699	£649	NORTON 850CC	£726	£679
HONDA CB 350	£405	£379	NORTON 750CC	£649	£599
HONDA XL 250 TRAIL	£425	£389	B.S.A. A65L	£474	£429
HONDA CB 250	£393	£369			
HONDA SL 125 TRAIL	£261	£249			
HONDA CB 175 SPTS	£320	£299			
HONDA CD 175	£269	£249			
HONDA CB 125	£255	£209			
SUZUKI GT 750K	£799	£779			
SUZUKI GT 550K	£645	£619			
YAMAHA XS2	£552	£519			
YAMAHA RD350	£455	£429			
YAMAHA RD250	£427	£399			
YAMAHA RD200	£320	£305			
YAMAHA DT175	£299	£289			

However, in the same issue as the ad appeared, a letter to *Bike* magazine's 'Write On' page summed up many motorcyclists' dilemma. The author, M. Hodder from Gloucestershire, was a 'die-hard' British bike lover, but difficulties sourcing parts for his eight-year-old AJS 650 meant he could now see why people like him 'who've stuck with the older British makes for so long are now turning to the Japs simply because we've lost faith in the home industry's after sales service'.

A reader from Kent wrote to *Motor Cycle Mechanics* bemoaning the difficulties he had finding a reasonably priced British-made learner bike. He ended up buying a Honda 125. But whilst such letters were tinged with regret at the domestic market's failings, others spoke of outright xenophobia.

In a letter to *Motorcycle Sport*, a Honda CD175 owner from Surrey related incidences he encountered with British-bike riding motorcyclists who, with monotonous regularity, would overtake him at full throttle whenever the author's 'rice-can' passed them. 'It became evident to me that there is some hostility in motorcycling circles.'

Returning to his bike one time, he was confronted by a gang of youths talking mock Japanese. Another time, he was admiring a Honda 250 parked outside a dealer when a chap going into the shop exhorted: 'Make sure you just look, but for heaven's sake don't buy it.'

In spring 1972, Lyndon Needs from Newport complained to *Bike* about an article written by Dave Minton entitled 'The Rise and Fall of BSA'. The correspondent felt the magazine 'brought BSA and other British bikes down real bad and you were all for that foreign rubbish'. Owner of a 12-year-old BSA A10 Rocket that had never let him down, the letter's author questioned the need for indicators and starter motors, defended his bike's propensity to leak a little oil - 'if a bike doesn't there's something wrong with it' - argued that there were plenty of British bikes capable of outperforming any Japanese makes, and suggested staffers 'emigrate to Japan and take your Honda, Suzuki etc with you'.*

Mr Needs' views did not go unchallenged. A letter in the next issue's letters pages accused Needs of pig headedness and 'being carried away with excess patriotism'. A long-time rider of British motorcycles, who had switched to Japanese machines because he had become 'sick and tired of spending all my spare time poring over the innards of my bikes just to keep them on the road', the respondent pointed out that the number of bikes

---

* Few contemporary commentators captured the tensions of motorcycling in 1970s Britain better than comic illustrator Paul Sample. His anti-authority cartoon hero Ogri was a fixture on the back pages of *Bike* from the magazine's earliest days. Dressed in leather jacket, denim jeans, boots and rolled-top white socks, with flowing blonde locks and pudding-basin helmet with wings (making him look like a cross between the Interflora man and Marvel Comics' Norse superhero Thor), the hard drinking, fast-riding Ogri was an unreconstructed champion of lost causes and inevitable saviour to his hapless friend Malcolm. Ogri was the kind of biker we imagine ourselves to be, whereas Malcolm was the kind of biker we probably are!

Richly drawn in a style reminiscent of beat-culture cartoonist Robert Crumb, Sample's storylines exposed and punctured the absurdities of bureaucrats, Brit-riding reactionaries, and the pomposity of the new breed of lifestyle bikers. With the throttle of his trusty Vincent-engined cafe racer pinned back, our stubble-chinned hero and his canine pillion, Kickstart, ran rings round the image-conscious owners of the latest multi-cylinder superbikes. Indeed, that, in fact, was Sample's recurring theme: it's how you ride that counts, not what you ride.

sold with refinements such as indicators and electric starting compared to those buying British machines was evidence that the bike-buying public disagreed with Mr Needs.

The debates and reader's stories went some way to explaining what lay behind the changes to British manufacturers' sales and market share. By the end of the Sixties, Meriden was producing a record 900 machines a week (mostly Bonnevilles and TR6s), beneficiaries of the boom in America, which saw US sales of motorcycles rise from 60,000 to 750,000 units. The Japanese firms' success with smaller machines had been, according to Don Brown, 'a blessing to the British', helping BSA/Triumph and Norton to secure almost 50 per cent of America's over 500cc market. Within the space of just three years, however, this slipped to just nine per cent, bringing down the curtain on what was one of the oldest and once the world's largest motorcycle manufacturer - BSA.

Money Problems

In May 1971, financial analysts were predicting losses of £1 million for BSA Group's Motorcycle Division. When, some two months later, BSA's directors finally announced the official figure, it proved far worse than the City had anticipated. On 30 July, the company revealed the loss for the previous operational year was actually £3 million.[*]

Managing Director Lionel Jofeh had resigned earlier that month. He was replaced as head of the motorcycle division by Bert Hopwood. Chairman Eric Turner declared that he himself should also step down. According to Hopwood, Turner felt his departure would help the company in its 'creation of a new image'. He would stay only until the company appointed a new Chair. BSA's British bankers, Barclays, made it a condition of its £10 million rescue package that the Board elevate fellow board member Lord Hartley Shawcross as its non-executive chairman. Born in 1902 in Geissen, Germany to an English father (a professor of English at a local college), Shawcross had been England's chief prosecutor in Nuremburg during the Nazi war crime trials, and although moneyed, his family's politics lent leftward (he was at one time Labour MP for St Helens in the North of England). Granted a life peerage in 1959, Shawcross served on various company boards, including EMI, Shell, and the Times Newspaper and had been a non-executive member of the BSA Board since January 1968. His appointment as chairman signalled just how important Barclays viewed the motorcycle industry to Britain's economy and national pride. Barclays further demanded that the President of US operations, Peter Thornton, the man who had authorised BSA/Triumph's lavish racing campaign, resign.

Thornton declined.

In the end, the company bought him out for a reported $400,000.

Long-time Triumph man, Dennis McCormack, was persuaded to come out of retirement and resume command of what was left of his old company. When he analysed BSA Company Incorporated's (BSACI) books, British-born McCormack was, according

---

[*]   These were difficult times. The BSA Board's announcement came just six months after two of the most famous names in the British automotive industry declared bankruptcy. On 4 February 1971, Velocette closed its factory gates for the last time. And on that same day, Rolls Royce went into receivership.

to Lindsay Brooke and David Gaylin in *Triumph Motorcycles in America,* 'appalled at Thornton's frivolity'.

After enjoying a sell-out year in 1970, Thornton's profligate spending had been contingent on a promise of receiving 50,000 motorcycles in 1971. All the auguries seemed good. By year's end, the US had already received a record 30,000 Triumphs. The BSA Group's Motorcycle Division was planning for a turnover of around £40 million. Triumph and Gene Romero were close to securing yet another Grand National Championship. And dealers were abuzz with rumours of new models, including a 'clean-sheet design' middleweight capable of taking on the Honda and Yamaha 350s.

But BSA and Triumph's joint share of the US market had fallen to just 6.9 per cent. Nearly half of all motorcycles now sold in America were Hondas. Yamaha's 30 per cent share placed them second. The Midlands-based combine came fifth, trailing both Suzuki and Kawasaki.

At a time when the company could not afford any more slip ups (like its disastrous foray into the scooter market with the BSA Dandy and Triumph Tigress and Tina, or the £2 million the Group lost on the Ariel 3 three-wheeler), two further ill-conceived projects combined to land fatal blows.

In November 1970, Peter Thornton invited journalists to the US launch of the '71 season's models at the luxurious La Quinta Hotel in Palm Springs, California. The British combine's operational arm in the US, BSACI, had hired the hotel to host motorcycling's most expensive ever media event.* On the first day of the all-expenses paid, four-day junket, at which the press would get to ride the new BSAs and Triumphs, Thornton unveiled the US's ten-model line-up.** As the BSACI President theatrically lifted the covers to reveal each new model, alongside street and dirt versions of the 250cc single, the carryover 500 twins, and revamped 650s, BSACI announced high and low-piped variants of a new double-overhead cam, 180 degree throw, 350cc four-stroke twin.

The Triumph Bandit 350 presented to dealers at La Quinta was the high-piped T35SS variant. Sadly, like the static example on display, the Bandit and its middleweight stablemate, the BSA Fury, would also prove to be non-runners.

---

* BSA Company Incorporated (BSACI) was set up by Lionel Jofeh in August 1969 and comprised the four former US distributors Triumph Corporation, Johnson Motors, BSA Western, and BSA Incorporated (East).

** Held the month before the US launch, at a cost of £15,000, the UK press event in October 1970 was equally lavish. Located in the heart of the capital, the recently-built Royal Lancaster Hotel, overlooking London's Hyde Park, played host to 350 guests. They included reporters and photographers from the mainstream media, industry insiders, distributors and dealers from across the world, as well as Government officials and senior civil servants. Guests were treated to a fully catered meal, entertained by comedian Dave Allen, dancers, and music from the Young Generation. The evening culminated in the largest model roll-out in motorcycle history (according to the BSA Group) as the company unveiled 16 new and improved models. Displayed in its own massive three-dimensional picture frame, illuminated by spotlights, and each model in turn revealed to a trumpet fanfare and commentary, whilst the whole affair was undeniably impressive, according to former BSA service manager Wilf Harrison, 'There wasn't a word of applause when [the motorcycles] were introduced.' The retired chairman of the BSA Group's board, industry veteran Jack Sangster, even before being told that several of the models would not actually go into production, flatly predicted the range would be unsuccessful, whilst Johnson Motors executive Don Brown observed the launch with a growing sense of dismay, increasingly upset at what he heard said in the introductions.

The model had come about in response to Honda's success with its Anglo-styled CB350 and CL350 twins launched in 1968. By 1971, the Honda 350 was the world's best-selling motorcycle. Of the 650,000 machines Honda sold in the US that year, nearly 22 per cent of them were 350 twins. According to Mick Walker's *Honda Production Motorcycles 1946-1980*, that figure comprised 64,350 CB350 roadsters, 42,900 CL350 street scramblers and 33,150 SL350 trail bikes. BSA Group Chairman Eric Turner commissioned semi-retired founder of the Triumph Engineering Company Ltd, Edward Turner (no relation), to produce a 350cc twin. Now running his own design firm, ET Engineering Developments, Edward Turner - with the help of designers on loan from BSA/Triumph who also gave him space in an old factory in Redditch - had a prototype running that same year. However, despite Doug Hele and Bert Hopwood's reservations about Turner's design, Triumph green-lit the DOHC twin. As a result, and much to Hopwood's chagrin, company executives suspended work on Doug Hele's 250cc triple authorised three years earlier by Harry Sturgeon.

According to Brooke and Gaylin's *Triumph Motorcycles in America*, Hele had designed the quarter-litre triple in two forms: a single-overhead camshaft six-speed road bike; and a DOHC head, eight-geared road racer. The authors cite an interview Hele gave to *Classic Bike* magazine in which the engineer recalled Meriden stopped work on the 250 in 1965 to concentrate on its road-racing campaign. (Bert Hopwood, however, in his book *Whatever Happened to the British Motorcycle Industry?*, attributed the 250cc Three's demise to Turner's DOHC twin, which, following a BSA executive's visit to the US, chimed with the executive's conviction that the factory needed to develop a 350 of its own.) In something of a postscript for the stillborn triple, Brooke and Gaylin relate the poignant recollection of Matt Guzzetta from his time at the Group's Engineering Centre near Solihull. An industrial designer, and the first American to work at Umberslade Hall, the Californian entered the drafting room and noticed one of the draughtsman resting his feet on a 'beautiful little double-overhead cam cylinder head'. When Guzzetta asked the draughtsman about his makeshift footstool, the man explained it was from Doug Hele's 250 Three and showed the young American a large closet filled with engine castings for the abandoned project.

THE BANDIT AND THE FURY

Hopwood thought Turner's design was so flawed that he wrote to Lionel Jofeh refusing to have anything to do with it. He eventually relented and after redesigning almost every aspect of Turner's original layout (bench-testing revealed the crankshafts were a particular weak spot in Turner's design), he and Hele discarded the overhead camshafts' gear-drive, replaced it with a chain, and beefed up the crankshaft.

Badged as the BSA Fury and Triumph Bandit, in both street and high-piped scrambler formats, the 350cc double-overhead cam twins boasted 34 horsepower, optional electric starting and five-speed transmission. A prototype, one of the twelve built for road testing, recorded a top speed of 103mph (beating the CB350's maximum speed of almost 95mph).

The chassis comprised an extremely light (23lb), Rob North-style frame (fabricated by renowned frame builder Ken Sprayson to replace Turner's fragile original), Ceriani-look-alike front suspension and a drum brake up front. One of the few magazines to test ride the twin-cam machine, *Motorcycle Sport Quarterly*, praised the 360lb twin's handling, but tester Rob Greene thought that, whilst pokey enough at high revs, the twin-cylinder Fury 'lacked the lugging power of its popular Japanese contemporary'.

BSA/Triumph procured components and tooling worth over £2 million, manufactured 26,000 pistons and con-rods, and got as far as producing a complete parts replacement book, leaflets, posters and magazine adverts for the 350, which was scheduled to begin production in 1971 for sale the following year: at first 'by March,' followed later by 'sometime in the summer'. Given that over 80 per cent of Triumphs and more than 65 per cent of BSAs were exported to the States (making the US models the 'standard' machines), that America's sales season started earlier, and that US magazines demanded longer lead-in times, the first of any new season's models were always those destined for the American market. One would-be US ad depicted a smiling Gene Romero, dressed casually in a smart tee-shirt and slacks, sat astride a high-piped Triumph T35SS in front of the doorway of a stuccoed ranch-style house. Behind the Burrito stands a blonde. Her right hand rests on his as he grips the Bandit's throttle; her left arm is draped around the Grand National Champion's shoulders. It was all very aspirational: buy a Bandit and you too can have the girl, the house, the racing glory…

What the ad's audience could not have known was that the 350s in the photographs were not production machines. BSA/Triumph's Chief Stylist, Stephen Mettam, had had to persuade the development shop to surrender their pre-production test vehicles for three weeks and prepare them for a Stateside photo shoot. This entailed stripping, cleaning, and replacing test components and installing and painting tank, side panels, and mudguards in next season's new liveries.

The machines featured in studio shots were more bogus still. Whilst the fuel tanks were actual plant-pressed production items finished in the factory paint shop, they arrived without centres or any holes for the petrol taps. Mettam had to sit the tanks on wooden blocks and balance them on the frame. As tooling for the exhausts was not yet complete, the young stylist - he was just 26 when he joined BSA/Triumph in 1967 as an Industrial Designer working directly to Bert Hopwood - had to cut 'n' shut pipes to get the bend right, camouflaging his handiwork with chromium Sellotape.

The Bandit and the Fury were certainly handsome looking machines (Mettam said that, as wholly new machines, the 350s were meant to host changes and trail the image to be adopted throughout the whole range). But when the prototypes were presented to BSA Incorporated's vice-president Don Brown and his colleagues, and the Group's accountants revealed that the minimum at which the 350s could be sold in the US was between $1,500 and $1,600 (when the Honda 350 was retailing at $800), Brown became depressed. He had been sure that if priced around $900 to $950, US dealers could have sold every bike the English shipped over.

Brown never got the chance to find out. The Bandit and Fury's uncompetitive price and the Group's dire financial situation forced the factory to abandon the 350.* Brooke and Gaylin summed it up thus: 'From that point on, Triumph had to stand and fight Japan's upmarket advance with three ohv engine families descended from Edward Turner's 1938 Speed Twin.'

THE BONNEVILLE GETS A NEW FRAME

Hopwood considered the change to an oil-bearing frame pointless. The executive head of engineering in the BSA Group contended that 'the average motorcyclist doesn't give a hoot where the engine oil is located'. Hopwood and Doug Hele did all they could to dissuade the company from developing the new chassis. They argued that the company's energies should be devoted to improving reliability, reducing costs, and standardising the frames across the range - particularly the Triumph's. BSA MIG-welded their chassis from steel tube, whereas Meriden hearth-brazed forged lugs onto mild-steel tubes (which, because Meriden did not have the equipment to bend them themselves, were pre-shaped by Reynolds Tubes), which the Triumph factory made up into front and rear frame sections, then bolted together to form a complete chassis.

Stephen Mettam, however, a proponent of the change to the oil-in-the frame chassis, felt the design held considerable merit. 'The advantages are obvious,' he told *Motorcycle Classics* magazine, 'you now have "for free" all the space once occupied by an oil tank, since the oil has gone where nothing was before - no loss.'

More restrictive silencing had helped BSA/Triumph's engineers reduce the biggest contributor to a motorcycle's noise emissions - its exhausts - to an acceptable level. However, new regulations compelled manufacturers to now address what constitutes the next greatest contributor to engine noise: induction roar on the engine's intake side. One solution is to fit a much larger air box.

A motorcycle engine can process as much air as a car twice its size. Engineers working on reducing induction roar had experimented with positioning air filters, pipes and plenum chambers behind the centrally-placed oil-tank, under the side covers, or fashioned to replace the side covers altogether. They even placed them in front and behind the rear suspension. The result, according to Stephen Mettam, was 'a real dog's dinner!' Siting the oil in the frame's backbone, however, released much needed space.

A further virtue of having the frame double as an oil reservoir was that it kept the lubricant cooler compared to a separate oil tank, due the frame's greater surface area.

Triumph draughtsman Brian Jones' first penning of the concept caught the eye of Umberslade Hall chief Dr. Stefan Bauer. Bauer, a scientist, was the former director for engineering at Norton (where he had developed the Commando's innovative Isolastic anti-vibration chassis).

---

*   According to Stephen Mettam, the reason for the Bandit and Fury's demise most certainly was not, as was later cited by BSA/Triumph, due to 'component failure' - in particular, 'breaking crankshafts.' In an article he wrote for the UK magazine *Motorcycle Classics* (August 1997), Mettam said: '[S]omeone made up a report about broken Fury and Bandit crankshafts as a (false) reason for not proceeding with this model. Somebody big did not wish to manufacture it.'

Codenamed P39, the new cradle was Triumph's first all-welded production frame (and their first twin-loop frame since 1960-62). Dispensing with cast-iron lugs helped reduce weight, and with the new frame's four-inch diameter backbone acting as an oil reservoir in an arrangement similar to the Trackmaster, Cheney and Rickman racing frames, as well as BSA's own competition frames, engineers eliminated a perennial service complaint: cracked oil-tank mountings. The large spine also made the new frame immensely strong, far stronger than its predecessors.

Problems with the new frame, however, soon emerged.

Meriden's shop floor was three months late receiving drawings for the new frame, as Umberslade Hall undertook over 1,200 changes to get them right. To keep the plant occupied, Triumph workers overlooked the usual production sequence and built the 500cc Daytona and Trophy models (which didn't use the new frame) until they had exhausted that whole year's inventory of components. They built and tested Bonneville and Trophy engines and gearboxes, stacking them wherever they could find the space. And still they waited. Small Heath continued producing the triples, but demand for the Trident was no match for the 650 twins.

September turned into October and still no drawings arrived (Umberslade had by now been working on the P39 for over three-and-a-half years). Receiving full 'average' earnings as management deemed they were idle through no fault of their own, Meriden's plant staff killed time playing dominoes and competing in chess tournaments (deploying oil pumps, valve springs and rocker arms as pawns, rooks, kings and queens on boards sketched out on top of packing crates).

When the drawings did finally arrive, having already missed the short American sales season, Meriden immediately set about reversing three months' lost production. Staff threw themselves into producing the jigs, tools, and processes the factory needed to manufacture the new frame in which to house the backlog of stockpiled Bonneville engines. First build of the pre-production frames did not go well. Placed in a large water tank and tested with compressed air, the backbone-housed oil tanks leaked like a sieve. Meriden drafted in welders from across the Coventry area to deal with the backlog, and those who had experience of MIG welding high-pressure vessels helped Triumph adapt its welding equipment to run on higher amperages, filler wire of a reduced diameter, and a mix of argon and CO_2 instead of just pure CO_2 shielding gas. The new methods cured the leaks, but when the first P39 chassis was ready for assembly, workers discovered that the T120 engine didn't fit.

The only way they could install the Triumph motor into the new frame was to remove the engine's rocker boxes - which they found were then impossible to refit. The factory itself developed eighteen modifications to Meriden's time-honoured arrangements for installing the 650 twin's cylinder head. The changes, however, allowed production to finally restart just before Christmas 1970.

The fiasco confirmed production staff's already poor opinion of Umberslade Hall. Sadly, the Group's Research and Development Department's new frame would give Meriden further cause for despair.

The P39 frame raised the T120's seat height by three inches, making the Bonneville taller than any other large capacity road bike. Umberslade blamed Meriden for not following their drawings. An angry Meriden Inspection Department took a frame off the production line, checked it against Umberslade's specifications and reported back that the finished item was indeed higher than the drawings - by all of twenty-eight thousandths of an inch. To correct the problem the factory implemented three modifications in the course of the 1971 model year - none of which were interchangeable - in an effort to restore the seat height to more manageable proportions.[*]

Engine vibration with the new frame was also more pronounced, the return to a twin down-tube layout probably acting like a tuning fork, with resonances similar to those Triumph had encountered when they introduced the duplex frame back in 1960.

To accommodate both the BSA and Triumph 650 engines, it was necessary to move the oil filler from the original design's position - just aft of the headstock - and reposition it further down the main tube, between the rear of the fuel tank and toward the front of the seat. Relocating the neck reduced capacity from three to just 2.2 quarts. As a result, despite its theoretical advantages, the oil-in-the-frame models tended to run hotter than their centrally-mounted oil tank predecessors.

At their lavish UK press launch in October 1970, guests gave the new models a muted reception. After more than three years development, all Umberslade had to show for its market research and 'clean-sheet' designs - results of which the Motorcycle Division's hopes were pinned and the bank's forbearance on its loans to BSA would prove justified - were upgraded suspension and brakes, questionable styling licks, a frame change customers didn't ask for, the same ohv twin cylinder engine - and, most conspicuously, no disc brake or electric start.

Still, road tests of the new Bonneville complimented its road holding, and a five-gear version (a factory option for the '71 season) was the first Bonneville which *Cycle World* magazine had ever tested to run a quarter mile in under 14 seconds (13.9). Problems with the early versions of the Triumph five-speed transmissions, however, emerged very quickly in the US. Cliff Guild, Triumph's Eastern service chief, recalled: 'The gears were so brittle that the teeth flew off like popcorn.' It seemed that the factory had omitted to carburise the drive dogs of first and second gears, a process in which the heat-treated metal is plunged into a bath of oil to cool it.

With some 1,000 five-speed 650s, worth a total of almost $2 million, affected, the Duarte and Baltimore warehouses set up makeshift assembly lines to replace the gears with items treated at a Los Angeles metallurgist. Meriden reacted quickly as soon as they learned of the issue, but as Triumph's Detroit-based dealer Bob Leppan explained to authors Brooke and Gaylin: 'You sell someone a new bike, the gearbox fails immediately, and then you tell them they won't have the bike back until the end of the summer. The

---

[*]   In April 1971, Triumph's service representative Stan Truslove toured Triumph dealers across France. The six-feet, four-inch Truslove's report makes clear that he spent much of his time disabusing French dealers that he was not the model around whom the P39's saddle had been designed.

customer's pissed, and he wants his money back. But we couldn't afford to give them a new bike. Our warranty claims as a result of those early five-speeds were just enormous.'

Yet it did sell, albeit not well. Sales of the BSA variant on the other hand, with its grey-painted frame (in emulation of BSA's titanium-framed works moto-crossers), fell off alarmingly.

THINGS GO FROM BAD TO WORSE FOR BSA/TRIUMPH

Having missed the spring sales season, the Group now found themselves by May 1971 with 11,000 1971-model year BSA and Triumph motorcycles left in stock in the USA. Dr. Felix Kalinski, appointed by Barclays Bank and the BSA directors to head the American operation after Denis McCormack stepped down to retire, this time for good, initiated an immediate 'fire sale'. The 50-year-old Kalinski, whose background was mathematics, engineering, and architecture, but *not* motorcycles (he promised Triumph's American senior management team at his first meeting with them in Baltimore in 1972 that he would become an expert on motorcycles in six months), also commissioned an expensive 'all-out, no holds barred' ad campaign, taking out space in both men and women's glossy magazines. As part of a fact-finding tour to US dealers, Kalinski learned that customers were becoming less accepting of an outdated model line-up and wanted the factory to increase the twin-cylinder 650s' capacity to 750cc (the demand was fuelled by some dealers enjoying success short-track racing with bored-out 650s). They also asked him to lobby Meriden to redress the shortage of service items (when the assembly lines were humming, the factory, according to Hopwood, 'tended to starve' the Spares Department). The paucity of spares was forcing US dealers, who had borrowed against the spring sales season, to abandon Triumph for other marques.

As sales of the heavily discounted '71 models began to rise, so too did warranty claims. Valve seats fell out. A batch of Lucas batteries sent to Triumph with plugged breathers split (some even exploded), leaking corrosive acid and damaging the motorcycles. Lucas despatched a rep from England to investigate, but refused to pay any reparation. The new front forks wept oil, as did outlets on the oil-bearing frames. Long-time Detroit-based Triumph dealer Bob Leppan commented sardonically: 'I thought that at last we'd done it. We'd developed a motorcycle that leaked oil where it never had for forty years!'

From an anticipated turnover of £40 million, the Motorcycle Division actually turned over just £26.7 million, whilst the value of its stockpiles had gone up from previous year's £9 million to £15.6 million. In short, the Division had negative liquidity, owing more than it could expect to generate in revenue. It meant that under British law and its own company articles, BSA was trading illegally.

Things went from bad to worse. In July, the Motorcycle Division declared a trading deficit of £2.5 million. BSA's shares fell by more than half - from a high that year of 87p to just 37p. One month before production of the 1972 season's model was officially due to start, BSA's Board of Directors announced job cuts. Small Heath's workforce went from

4,500 to 1,500. Production of BSA-branded models fell from 6,286 machines in the three months between August and October of '71 to just 202 bikes in the first quarter of 1972 (February-April), when manufacturing of complete machines effectively came to an end.

Various companies showed interest in buying BSA (including the Austrian motorcycle maker, Steyr-Daimler-Puch). But on 3 August, the *Daily Express* reported that negotiations had collapsed following the BSA Board's announcement that they anticipated losses of £3 million for the year, plus a further £1 million deficit as a result of rationalisation. Two months later, on 1 November 1971, the Board announced at an extraordinary General Meeting that the Motorcycle Division's trading loss now exceeded £8 million. As a result, share prices fell to an all time low of 7.5p.

At that same meeting, the Board appointed 49-year-old Brian Eustace to its main Board of Directors. As Chief Executive, Eustace's role was to act as 'Company Doctor'. He would be responsible for the Group's day-to-day operations; leaving Shawcross, as non-executive chairman, who would stay out of the daily running of the company, to sign off on all the important decisions. Having recently returned from three years in India where, as Chief Executive, he had tackled the problems of a strike-riddled company employing 13,000 people, Bert Hopwood considered Eustace well qualified to tackle BSA's problems. On his first day in his new job, Eustace addressed workers at Small Heath to tell staff - who had already been notified to expect redundancies - his first priority was to save the jobs of those remaining.

Eric Turner, who up to November's extraordinary Board meeting had been its Chairman, resigned. He agreed, however, to stay on in an advisory capacity. His last act as Chairman was to put in motion the Coopers Management Consultant's plan to reorganise the motorcycle division. The plan entailed concentrating production at Meriden, closing around three-quarters of the Small Heath site (the gun and general engineering sides of the business would be left to occupy what remained), and making 3,000 staff redundant. The task of laying 3,000 people off fell to Alistair Cave.

'I was proud of the co-operation I received from the workforce, many of whose families had worked at Small Heath for years,' recalled the plant's Works Manager for Mick Duckworth's book *Triumph and BSA Triples*. 'They took into consideration that the future of the 1,500 remaining staff depended on them.' There was no major dispute as a result, although a clerical union made its feelings known by refusing to issue staff the redundancy notices.

The day after he resigned, the outgoing Chairman endured an hour-long interrogation from an audience of around a hundred angry shareholders attending an extraordinary meeting to agree the Board's proposals to keep BSA afloat. The planned restructure was eventually accepted, with share and stockholders giving Barclays Bank charge of the company's assets in return for which the bank agreed a £10 million loan. But BSA really needed twice that if it was to survive into the 1972 sales season.

That same month, Brian Eustace persuaded Bert Hopwood to delay his plans to retire and return to work full time to support Engineering Director Mike Needham.

(Hopwood had relinquished his executive position on the Board early in 1970, and reduced his hours, disenchanted with Lionel Jofeh and Eric Turner's lack of response to the concerns he had voiced about Umberslade Hall and new models that did little to redress the company's desperate need for new products.) Much to Hopwood's surprise and delight, the following month (December 1971), the company asked him to join the Parent Board of BSA with executive responsibility for the Motorcycle Division's design and engineering.

For staff in Meriden, who felt their view point was often overlooked by the BSA Board, Hopwood's appointment came as encouraging news. His engineering expertise was rated highly, and long-serving employees respected him for his plain speaking and ability to argue through problems to find a workable solution.

In January 1972, BSA finally closed the Umberslade Hall Research and Development Centre, with the loss of almost 300 jobs after transferring selected personnel and equipment to Meriden. On the 28th of that month, BSA announced its half-year's trading figures. They showed a further trading loss of £1.5 million.

Despite the Board's interim Chairman, Lord Shawcross, announcing production of the new 350 and the existing 250cc ranges were to cease and manufacture of the 500, 650 and 750 BSA models to transfer to Meriden, Small Heath had retained around 1,100 staff who continued to produce BSAs and the three-cylinder engine units for installation at Meriden. Production of the BSA Rocket 3, however, ended in January (Small Heath shipped the very last example - a five-speed model - to Germany in May). It did not, however, signal the end of the A75 engine, which would see service again later that same year in a radically different guise.

In March, production of the ill-conceived Ariel 3 tri-cycle launched under Eric Turner's leadership finally ceased, incurring a loss to the BSA Group of around £2 million. Meriden, meanwhile, continued to produce its Tiger 100, the TR6 Trophy and T120 Bonneville.

BSA/Triumph Develop A Rotary

With heavy discounting helping clear stockpiles in the US of last season's models, and BSA/Triumph selling all the triples they could make (the re-organisation at Small Heath had seriously affected production of the A75 and T150 engines), the Motorcycle Division forecasted profits for March. However, 'petty' strikes reduced what should have been 20 days production to just 14, and transformed an anticipated profit of £181,000 into a £12,000 loss. Although industrial action continued, mainly at Meriden, the Motorcycle Division managed to turn a profit in April and May. Bert Hopwood thought this offered grounds for encouragement: "To me, there seemed little doubt that we could be on the way if our workforce would get behind us.' In Hopwood's view that most certainly was not going to come from the new management team's practice - however well intentioned - of gathering the workforce together at mass meetings to show them giant charts of projected and actual performance.

Hopwood was further buoyed by the Board's decision in June to take up an offer from Audi-NSU for BSA/Triumph to purchase a licence from them to manufacture and develop the rotary engine. For the last five years, the Group Research Department had been developing the unit in conjunction with Fichtel and Sachs, a German supplier who manufactured the Wankel engine's specialist components under licence to NSU. The Group had a prototype motorcycle under test. They knew, however, that should they decide to produce a rotary-engined machine, Fichtel and Sachs wanted to build and supply complete engines in order to offset the high cost of their licence with NSU. What BSA/Triumph also knew was that the licence F&S had did not extend to the power unit the Group were interested in manufacturing (NSU's Wankel licence was linked, not to capacity, but to the engine's power output: up to 20bhp - £54,000; 20 to 35bhp - £117,000; 35 to 50bhp - £78,000).

The Board eventually agreed to purchase a licence for an engine that could deliver between 35-60bhp at 5,000rpm (a specification deemed the most financially viable) at a cost of £129,000. The head of motorcycle design and engineering, Bert Hopwood, was delighted. Despite BSA's financial problems, the rotary engine's virtues of simplicity and smooth-running, and the fact that a very large British manufacturer had volunteered to pay the high costs of developing a Wankel motor, meant that the outlay for a licence to manufacture a rotary engine made good sense nevertheless.

By August 1972, production began on the '73 season's models incorporating the detail changes that had occupied the Engineering Department these last nine months. All the 650cc plus models received five-speed transmissions and disc brakes. The company launched a new half-litre twin-cylinder off-roader, the Triumph TR5T Trophy Trail or Adventurer, and a radically-styled limited edition three-cylinder 750 from the studio of a young American designer called Craig Vetter. With barely concealed disdain, Hopwood later referred to the bike's target audience as 'what I can only describe as the "trendy" type of rider whose numbers were increasing fast in the States'.

Feedback from Felix Kalinski's meetings with US dealers prompted Meriden to bring forward to September production of the new 750 twin, developed to replace the rapidly declining 650 market (the 750 version was originally scheduled for manufacture from December). Johnson Motors' assistant general manager Pete Colman told authors Lindsay Brooke and David Gaylin that Felix Kalinski sent him to England to press the case for an increase in the 650's displacement, but that Hopwood nixed the idea. It was only after Colman told Meriden's engineering chief that he should get on the phone to BSA Chief Executive Brian Eustace to explain why he was against the Americans getting their 750 twin that Hopwood relented.

John Barton, who worked for Doug Hele on the T140's development, told *Classic Bike* magazine that Meriden was unhappy about upping the T120's capacity by a further 100cc: 'It was a horrible form of engineering.' In fact, Meriden had very nearly rolled out the 750 the previous season. However, after querying with the Sales Department a very large despatch of crankshafts to the US, Hopwood discovered that the 650s raced in America as bored-out 750s commonly had major components replaced after each race. Although it made him unpopular, Hopwood insisted they thoroughly test any such conversion first (no doubt anxious to avoid a repeat of the oil-in-the-frame fiasco).

Meanwhile, the fire sale spread. In late 1972, Birmingham Corporation purchased part of BSA's Armoury Road site. The council also bought the BSA sports fields, which were famous with locals - all for £1 million.

Nevertheless, Lord Shawcross notified the Department for Trade and Industry that without the assistance of Prime Minister Ted Heath's Conservative Government, BSA would soon be unable to meet its obligations. The company would be left with no option but to ask its banker, Barclays, to call in the receiver. The Government, however, refused to help prop up the existing BSA Group. They were prepared, however, to support the formation of a new company. BSA's Board was in no position to argue. The Group was at the limit of its £10 million overdraft. And although Barclays Bank agreed to extend its £2 million bridging loan to the end of the next financial year, the Board was unable to secure an acceptable price for the Group's profitable Metal Components Division (which, if sold, would leave the motorcycling business in command of around 80 per cent of the group's activity), its bankers were threatening to appoint a receiver if Government support was not forthcoming.

THE GOVERNMENT ASKS DENNIS POORE FOR HELP

That autumn, the Department for Trade and Industry (DTI) invited the Chairman of Manganese Bronze Holdings (MBH) Limited, Dennis Poore, to private discussions with BSA and Barclays Bank. Poore had been a commander in the Royal Air Force, a successful amateur race car driver (he was the RAC hill-climb champion in 1950, came fourth in 1952 at the British Grand Prix, and won Goodwood's nine-hour endurance race three years later in a works Aston Martin). Poore also had offices at Love Lane working in the City. More relevantly, he was Chairman of Norton Villiers Limited.

In 1966, Associated Motor Cycles (AMC) - the conglomerate whose stable of marques included AJS, Francis-Barnett, James and Norton - had gone into receivership. Later that year, AMC merged with Villiers, supplier of the proprietary two-stroke engines fitted to several small British bikes (and more prosaic items such as lawn mowers and cultivators), and themselves the subject of an acquisition not long beforehand by Manganese Bronze Holdings, who were best known for manufacturing ship's propellers. AMC's merger produced Norton Villiers, a company which reported to MBH's chairman, Dennis Poore (sadly, Matchless, James and Francis-Barnett did not survive Poore's acquisition).

The DTI's recently-formed Industrial Development Unit asked Poore to merge Norton Villiers with BSA/Triumph whose annual turnover of some £40 million was under serious threat of being lost to the country. On the last day of November 1972, the principals convened in Birmingham for a meeting in BSA's grand boardroom. The talks were conducted in the strictest secrecy (papers and correspondence referred to Norton using the codename 'Zebra' and BSA as 'Longlegs'). DTI officials explained that under the provisions of section 8 of the new Industry Act, the Government could make public funds available. Up till then, the Department had only provided support under section 7 - to support employment in a development area. Funding granted under section 8 was for an altogether different purpose: 'the promotion of industry... in the national interest when for some reason adequate private sector funds could not be obtained.'

Edward Heath's Conservative Government had stepped in to save another major sector just two years earlier when it nationalised Rolls-Royce's aircraft division. The firm was locked into a contract with the American Lockheed Corporation to produce engines for the RB-211 Tri-Star airbus. Wholly unrealistic deadlines, coupled with crippling time penalties, meant the firm ran into trouble almost immediately. Despite successive Government subsidies totalling over £50 million and £18 million bailouts from the banks, by February 1971 the firm had run up losses of £110 million. In spite of a manifesto commitment to champion 'a vigorous competition policy', Heath had little choice but to nationalise the company - The Royal Air Force and the Navy, 81 foreign air forces and 200 international airlines depended on Rolls-Royce, as did 80,000 people whose jobs relied on its continued survival, as well as Britain's national security and reputation abroad.

On 7 March 1973, the *Daily Telegraph* published a letter from the former head of Triumph, Edward Turner. 'Lord Shawcross,' Turner wrote, 'is a distinguished lawyer, but this does not mean he is an expert on motorcycles.' He went on: 'Machines sell on the whim of fashionable young men. These fads are constantly changing. BSA Triumph are still trying to flog off the stuff I designed 30 years and more ago.'

One week later, on Wednesday 14 March, as details of the plan were circulated around the principals, BSA's share prices plunged from 18 pence a share to just 5 pence, immediately wiping £2 million off its value. Trading was suspended.

Whatever its causes (and an official government inquiry exonerated Poore from any involvement in what they concluded was a 'bear' raid by a syndicate of private investors who, to drive down BSA's share prices, offered to unload a large number of its shares - which they didn't in fact own - with the sole intention of buying them up later at greatly depressed value and deliver them to their own buyers at a pre-arranged price), the crash worked to Poore's advantage. 'BSA was not worthless,' as Abe Aamidor put it in his history of the rise and fall of the British motorcycle industry, *Shooting Star*, 'but it was worth less.'

On 15 March 1973, the Minister of State, Christopher Chataway, announced in Parliament that the Government had accepted proposals to form a new company. Norton Villiers Triumph Ltd (NVT) finally became a reality four months later on 17 July when the legalities were completed on a deal costing £10 million, almost half of which would come from the Government. Manganese Bronze would sell its subsidiary, Norton Villiers Ltd, to the newly formed NVT, with MBH acquiring a half portion of the new company and BSA shareholders the other half. The DTI agreed to inject £4.8 million financial support. The funds were an investment, not a grant, free of dividends for three years, and intended to create a competitive and profitable motorcycle industry.

Independent of Manganese Bronze, the NVT board of directors' brief was to focus solely on developing a sound, profitable motorcycle business capable of taking on the Japanese.

When Meriden's workers clocked off on the Friday for their annual two-week summer break, they did so in the knowledge that a deal had finally been struck, the uncertainty ended, and that the man now in charge had a proven record of turning round the fortunes of a famous British motorcycle factory. Or so they thought.

Poore had, with the Government's help, managed to offload the financially ailing Norton Villiers (whose balance sheet had not been available during negotiations). MBH had also acquired into the bargain the BSA Group's profitable non-motorcycle subsidiaries at a knock-down price of £3½ million. Moreover, since the recent voluntary redundancy of 300 staff at Meriden, the plant's staffing levels at last seemed in balance with the brisk demand for the factory's large-capacity machines - with the result that the Motorcycle Division produced a surplus for April '73 of £390,000.

Hopwood, who had not been present at the negotiations, was left wondering what it was about Poore that had spellbound Conservative Ministers. Years later, he commented acerbically that Ministers had so weighted negotiations that it felt like BSA should feel 'fortunate to be joining forces with a company... masterminded by [such] a brilliant individual'. Yet, at a meeting Hopwood had with Poore at the behest of the Board, it became clear - in contrast to BSA/Triumph's advanced plans for a new generation of modular engines ranging from a 200cc single cylinder to a 1,250cc five-cylinder unit[*] - that apart from a 750cc twin-cylinder competition engine being worked up by the external engineering consultant Cosworth, and exploratory designs by the Formula 1 racing car company BRM for a four-cylinder unit, Norton Villiers had no significant product changes planned. Hopwood's hope that Norton were 'nursing some winners, with which to rock the Japanese boat' and that the two companies combined would revive Britain's motorcycle industry, were dashed.

In August, Poore invited Hopwood and Hele to present the product strategy they had been working on for twelve months to a meeting attended by most of the top management. They rejected it forthwith. The strategy was too ambitious, they told the pair, and 'we do not intend to interest ourselves in the smaller machines which carry no profit margin'.

Bert Hopwood tendered his resignation.

---

[*]   Alongside the single and the 1,250cc five, Hopwood's plans included 750cc three-cylinder and one litre four-cylinder engines utilising components common throughout the range. Each unit could be upgraded in capacity by 25 per cent at negligible cost: the 200cc single-cylinder could be upgraded to 250cc; the 400cc twin-cylinder to 500cc; the 600cc three-cylinder to 750cc; the 800cc four to 1,000cc; and the five-cylinder unit from 1,000cc to 1,250cc. Each engine would be overhead cam with simple tappet adjustment, and available with either two- or four-valve cylinder heads and the option of electric starting.

Meriden Walks Out

Just before noon on 14 September 1973, twenty-eight-year-old John Rosamond was making his way to the Meriden canteen to attend a meeting Meriden's trade union officials had called with Dennis Poore to discuss the plant's future within NVT.

Rosamond was there as Shop Chair for the Sheet Metal Workers Union, which represented the factory's recently unionised welding section (the SMW was one of eight unions at Meriden). As he neared the canteen, he and some of the shop stewards noticed that newspaper sellers were hawking copies of the mid-day edition of the *Coventry Evening Telegraph* at the factory gate. Because that was unusual, one of the stewards went over and bought a copy. The headline read: 'Triumph Meriden factory to be closed on 1st February 1974 with the loss of 1700 jobs.'

Word spread quickly. Standing on top of a table in the canteen, Poore made a five-minute address to the assembled union officials, stewards, convenors and factory supervision staff. Also present was the Labour MP for Nuneaton, Leslie Huckfield. In an announcement that confirmed the headlines, the NVT Chairman declared the three-phase closure of Meriden, during which he expected workers to produce 7,500 motorcycles, and outlined the conditions under which they must do so. Full-time union official Andy Smart sprang to his feet: 'In all my years in the trade union movement, I've never heard such a callous statement! Can I ask a question?'

Poore didn't answer, stammering instead that he had a 12.30 train from Coventry to London to catch. He then departed, leaving the meeting in uproar and attendees with a two-page statement headed *Closure at Meriden - Basic Plan*.

The statement set out Poore's plan to reduce the workforce by a third on 30th November, a further third on 1st January, followed by Meriden's closure on 1st February 1974. Production was to continue uninterrupted: 7,500 machines between his announcement and February; 700 motorcycles a week up to the end of November. NVT would procure materials to manufacture at least 6,600 motorcycles, of which 2,200 would be Tridents and the rest, twin-cylinder 750s. After final closure of the Meriden plant, NVT would transfer production to Small Heath.

It all flew in the face of the Coopers Management Consultants' plan. Two thousand of the 3,000 scheduled BSA redundancies had already happened, a strong indication that Coopers' plan was in train. Dennis Poore's announcement therefore caught the Meriden workforce by surprise. Unknown to Meriden, however, the BSA Group Board had commissioned a second report, which favoured concentrating production at Small Heath. Moreover, as Poore later revealed, he never considered Meriden large enough to house his plans for NVT's manufacturing activities.

Despite their initial shock, the workforce's response was swift. Union officials hurriedly convened a meeting in the factory car park where, from a makeshift platform, they addressed the assembled workers. They pledged to mobilise the whole of the trade union movement and fight back against Poore's 'blatant asset stripping'. They would canvass local MPs and demand Parliament hold the Government to account. Poore had 'attacked the Triumph Meriden "family" and its way of life'. As soon as the senior managers left the site for home, workers padlocked the factory gates behind them.

The battle for Meriden had begun.

The Sit-In

Volunteers from Meriden's 1,700-strong workforce implemented round the clock pickets to secure everything within the plant (which included 1,000 fully assembled bikes). They worked six-hour shifts on a rota basis organised around sections (John Rosamond was on D-shift - the frame section). Pickets erected lean-to shelters at both the factory's main gate and the number two works gate about two hundred yards down the road, through which completed motorcycles and spares were packed and despatched.

Donations to the strike fund came in from all over the world. Local coalmen and miners (who hailed from the same communities as many of Triumph's workers) donated fuel for the picket's braziers. The women supplied pickets with hot food from the factory canteen.

The local Bobbies would share a cup of tea with the pickets when they stopped by to patrol the idle factory. (Good relations with the local constabulary were established early on when the union officially contacted the police immediately after workers padlocked the gates to assure them of the legality of the striker's actions, and this cordiality was bolstered further when pickets handed over to police a gang of thieves caught attempting to load six T150 engines from a trolley into a waiting van.)

With 1,200 members - out of a total workforce of 1,700 - the Transport and General Workers' Union (TG&W) led the occupation. TG&W district organiser Bill Lapworth, Meriden picket organiser Dennis Crowder-Johnson, and local Labour MP for Nuneaton Leslie Huckfield started to explore the idea of a workers' co-operative. They found support in the TG&W General Secretary and head of the Trades Union Congress (TUC) Jack Jones (the Liverpool-born, Spanish Civil War-veteran trade unionist was considered so powerful that graffiti during the 1974 election exhorted the electorate to: 'Vote Jack Jones, cut out the middle man').

The surprise was that Poore seemed surprised. Hopwood had warned him during a lunch the two had not long after Norton Villiers' merger with Triumph that the Chairman could expect a robust response from the workforce to Poore's then mooted proposals to close Meriden. Hopwood had argued that once complete, the three-phased reorganisation Brian Eustace had initiated made the Triumph plant a more viable prospect than Small Heath.

So, in an effort to counter the bad press he had received over his decision to shut Meriden, the NVT chief told the media he would consider any reasonable offer the Triumph workers made to buy the factory. His management team, meanwhile, were warning off US dealers from visiting Meriden by decrying pickets as communists who would stone them on sight!

Dealers in the States had been told of NVT's plans to move Triumph production to the old BSA plant on the same day as Poore had notified Meriden's workforce in the staff canteen.

The news came as yet another blow to Bob Myers, the owner of Free State Cycle, a successful Honda and Triumph dealership in Maryland, Washington DC. Already deeply unhappy at Norton's takeover ('We thought Villiers had died years before. Putting Triumph at the end [of NVT] seemed like an insult'), Myers alerted Triumph dealers across the Eastern states of the workers' blockade of Meriden, news of which BSACI had withheld and did not officially announce until 16 October.

When Les Huckfield and Bob Lapworth visited America to drum up support from US dealers for the Triumph Workers' Co-operative, Myers accompanied the pair to the first of the MP's many visits to the British Embassy in Washington. Myers also visited England, initially as one of 300 dealers taking part in a Buy and Fly promotion arranged by BSACI months earlier for traders who had ordered stocks of unsold BSAs, Triumphs and Rickmans.

Triumph workers picketed the hotel the dealers were staying in, and the visit's organisers warned traders to expect violence. Some of the workers even managed to make their way in and speak to the dealers, who for the first time heard the story of the blockade from the workers' side of the barricades. The picketing passed off peacefully, and when the Co-op's export chief Bill Roberton later called Myers in Maryland imploring him to help, Myers - still angry with NVT, upset at BSA Group's management of Triumph, and convinced by the 'rightness of [the worker's] cause' - began the first of more than two years of shuttling between Washington's Dulles International airport and London Heathrow in support of the Meriden workforce. Between 1973 and 1976, Myers made twelve trips to Coventry at a cost to his own pocket of around $40,000.

During Myers' visits to England, he met industry minister Christopher Chataway and NVT's boss, Dennis Poore.

Bob's meetings with Poore did not go well. 'I felt he was talking down to me, as though I didn't know the American market,' Myers told *Classic Bike*. 'He didn't care about the human side of Meriden. It seemed he had the Norton twin and just wanted to go with that. I was told Triumph's American dealers only wanted the Trident and that was just not true. Poore told me a lot of things that weren't true and put every obstacle in our way. He was dastardly!'

'At one meeting,' recalled Myers, 'he said the Bonneville had no future because the gearshift couldn't be changed to the left, as would be mandatory in America. But I told him I'd already ridden a left-shift bike at Meriden. Jim Barclay, a really clever engineer, had designed a cross-over system that worked well.'

Although Myers' business did not rely on selling Triumphs, Bob knew many small traders in the US whose survival did (he was a member of the US Triumph dealer's organisation, the National Dealer Advisory Council). It was vital, therefore, to ensure the 1974 models arrived in the spring for the start of the sales season. Whilst right-wingers in the UK viewed a workers' co-operative as communist inspired, union leaders on the far left considered them a betrayal of socialist principles. Ever the pragmatist, Myers simply saw the co-op as his best hope of getting US dealers the Triumph twins they needed.

At a discreet meeting with the Minister at his offices one evening, Myers read out some of the hundreds of letters he'd received from dealers citing the volumes of Triumphs they would take - if only they could get hold of them. 'He came round from behind his desk,' Myers recalled, 'looked through the letters and said with tears in his eyes, "Maybe we backed the wrong person." I said that was how we American dealers felt. He assured me he would try to help us, but not "out front".'

By the end of the meeting, the two discovered they shared more common ground: a love of athletics (Chataway famously acted as Roger Bannister's pace-setter during the historic four-minute mile in 1954, whilst at High School Myers had run the mile in a creditable four minutes forty-two seconds).

The Minister's assurances to Bob Myers may explain why, despite the unions' continued occupation of the factory, the police were not instructed to evict the men from the plant.

In December, Myers succeeded in persuading picketers to lift their blockade and allow desperately needed spares to be released and shipped to Baltimore.

But the workers' blockade wasn't just hurting US dealers.

Brian Bennett was part of Meriden's Key Dealer scheme and one of the UK's top 20 agents for Triumph. Trapped behind the pickets' barricades were lots of his customer's machines. Although Brian's relationship with the pickets was generally good, negotiations to release the machines proved difficult. Pickets eventually relented and allowed him to retrieve his customers' motorcycles on presentation of a document signed by both the machine's owner and Dennis Poore. The arrangement worked well, except one time when, as Bennett told *Classic Bike* for an article marking the sit-in's twenty-fifth anniversary: '...we had just gone through all of this fuss and loaded some bikes onto a truck, when this union official strolls out and demands that we unload them all again. I lost my rag, tempers flared and things started to get ugly. One of our lads was still outside the gates and when he saw what was going on, he ran and called the police. Eventually we were allowed out with the bikes and there was no real trouble.'

Bennett repaired the warranty bikes. However, he never got paid. He lost still more money on a cache of spare parts he discovered stored in the factory tester's room. After handing over a cheque in payment for the parts he needed, he returned later to collect them, only to find the items had been sold for scrap and his cheque cashed. Yet he remained on good terms with the pickets, always leaving a donation to the strike fund.

Hughie Hancox had much less truck with the blockade. Hancox had joined Meriden in 1966 and worked in the plant's service department. When the picket lines first appeared, he and his colleagues continued working. 'I remember arguing with the pickets when customers with service appointments would turn up from miles away, only to be refused entry to the works. I couldn't believe they would just turn away some poor fellow down from Scotland or somewhere. Later, when the blockade was complete, it just got worse.'

Hancox had little time for the unions. He recalled an incident for *Classic Bike* to illustrate their truculence: 'One time the polishers demanded more pay for polishing a batch of longer exhaust pipes. Of course, when they went back to working on the shorter pipes, they still wanted the increased rate!'

On the day pickets erected the blockade and refused entry to the factory, Hancox was unable to retrieve his tools and the riding gear that he'd left overnight in the service department. He lost the lot - along with his pension, the paperwork for which was never recovered when the factory reopened.

As dealers cried out for spares, Hancox knew that stuff was leaving the factory at night - 'sold for cash, no questions asked'. When pickets allowed Brian Bennett to enter the factory to buy spares, he noted the damage that had been caused during the sit-in: 'Machinery and fittings were smashed and water pipes were ripped out. It was a hell of a mess in there.'

TROUBLE AT HOME AND ABROAD

The siege at Meriden lasted 18 months. During that time, events occurred at both home and abroad that would change the political landscape in Britain, have repercussions for the motorcycle industry generally, and for Norton and Triumph in particular.

Triggered by Syria and Egypt's invasion of the Israeli-held Sinai Peninsula on 6 October 1973, the Jewish holy day of Yom Kippur, oil experienced a five-fold increase in price. The Arab-state members of OPEC (the Organisation of Petroleum Exporting Countries) started a four-month long oil boycott of pro-Zionist countries, principally the Netherlands and America, and cut oil production in an attempt to isolate Israel from its allies. Saudi oil minister Sheikh Yamani exempted the UK from the worst restrictions of OPEC's embargo due to the British foreign secretary Alec-Douglas Home's call in 1970 for Israel to withdraw from its illegally occupied territories. Even so, Britain was not immune from the rising price of crude, which, by January 1974, had climbed to more than $11 a barrel, compared to just $2 two years previously.

Four days after the start of the Yom Kippur War, the National Union of Mineworkers, buoyed by the oil crisis, rejected the National Coal Board's pay offer (around half of the 31 per cent wage increase the NUM was demanding in defiance of the government's wages policy). On Monday 12 November 1973, two days before the royal wedding of the Queen's daughter, Princess Anne to Captain Mark Phillips, Britain's 260,000 miners began an overtime ban. As a national miners' strike loomed (the second in two years), Prime Minister Ted Heath made a special broadcast to the nation announcing the introduction from midnight on New Year's Eve of a three-day week. The measures, aimed at conserving the country's energy supplies, lasted through January and February 1974.

BBC and ITV closed down after 10.30pm. The speed limit on motorways was restricted to 50mph.* The Government ordered street lighting to be cut by half and floodlighting was banned at sports events, forcing the football league to break a taboo and play matches for the first time on Sundays.

And although memories of the emergency remained fresh in the electorate's mind, when Heath called the election for February 1974, the far more pressing concern for voters was inflation running at 20 per cent, which the Chancellor Anthony Barber had tried to curb with the biggest credit squeeze anyone could remember. Some banks, who had overextended themselves during a short-lived boom fuelled by tax cuts, increased public spending, and a relaxation to the rules on lending, found their value drop by a third. House prices plummeted as the great property bubble burst (land halved in price in less than a year).

Interest rates rose to 13 per cent and growth came to a standstill. A stagnant economy, together with high inflation, saw a new word join the lexicon: 'stagflation'.

Nevertheless, the Conservatives remained ahead in the polls. So it was against expectations when Labour won, albeit without an overall majority. After Heath's overtures to the Liberal leader Jeremy Thorpe to join him in a coalition government ran aground (Heath was unable to accede to Thorpe's demands for electoral reform and his wishes to be Home Secretary, particularly untenable after the Secretary of the Cabinet alerted the Premier of 'matters in Thorpe's private life, as yet undisclosed to the public'), Labour's Harold Wilson avoided the first hung Parliament since 1929 by negotiating a pact with the Liberal's flamboyant leader, which saw Heath ousted and Wilson return to Number 10 as Prime Minister.

For his second government, a noticeably tired and uncharacteristically passive Wilson appointed the socialist firebrand Tony Benn as his secretary of state for industry.

TONY BENN AND THE SHIPYARD-WORKERS' WORK-IN

The novelist Kingsley Amis called Benn 'the most dangerous figure in British politics today'. Known as Anthony Wedgewood Benn up to 1973 when he told the BBC that they should henceforth refer to him as Tony Benn, the 2nd Viscount Stansgate - a title he had inherited following his father's death in 1960 and which he later dropped - earned Amis's

---

* America introduced similar measures to save fuel following OPEC's oil embargo, as gasoline in the US soared in price from 35 cents a gallon to 45 cents. Whereas in 1950, the country had been self sufficient in energy, by 1973 America was importing 35 per cent of its oil (rising to nearly 50 per cent just four years later). In January 1974, President Richard Nixon signed into law the Emergency Highway Energy Conservation Act, which restricted motorists to 55mph (former Van Halen lead singer, Sammy Hagar, capturing many Americans' exasperation at the 'double nickel' speed limit with his hit record 'I Can't Drive 55').

The Nixon and Ford administration also put in place price controls, promoted nuclear and solar energy, and cut down air line schedules. However, when the embargo ended in March 1973, Americans and Congress appeared unmoved by the crisis - until the US suffered a second oil shock at the end of the decade (as a result of the Shah of Iran persuading OPEC to double the price of oil overnight). The move took billions out of the Western economies. Inflation in the US rose to ten per cent, prompting President Carter's new chairman of the Federal Reserve, Paul Volcker, to raise interest rates to 20 per cent.

approbation for his support of the unions. A third generation MP from a family with a long tradition of radicalism, Benn's role as a tribune for the workers was an anathema for many sections of British society already fearful of the power trade unions wielded and who were convinced that the country was lurching inexorably leftward.

Benn had been a vocal champion of the Upper Clyde Shipbuilders' (UCS) work-in organised by the shop steward Jimmy Reid and his colleague Jimmy Airlie, and had arranged the shop stewards' visit to Westminster. In June 1971, the MP for Bristol South East headed a 70,000 strong march in Glasgow to protest the Heath Government's plans to close the publicly-owned yards, which had gone into receivership after ministers refused UCS a £6 million loan. Marchers were entertained by former shipyard employee Billy Connolly. A cheque for £5,000 arrived from ex-Beatle John Lennon. Even a Conservative association contributed.

'We are not going to strike,' the Govan-born communist trade unionist Reid told the 8,000 workers. 'We are taking over the yards because we refuse to accept that faceless men can make these decisions. We are not strikers - we are responsible people and we will conduct ourselves with dignity and discipline.' This included 'nae bevvying', for, as Reid pointed out: 'the world is watching us.'

Unable to find a private-sector buyer, coupled with rising unemployment across Britain, and a fear that closure of the Upper Clyde shipyards would turn Glasgow into another Belfast, the Government abandoned its policy of allowing 'lame ducks' to go to the wall. In February 1973, the Conservative Secretary of State for Trade and Industry John Davies announced to his Cabinet colleagues a £35 million rescue package (despite admitting that the yards were never likely to be commercially viable).

The shipyard workers' success was a Damascene moment for Benn.[*] He now saw the balance of power in industry had to shift in favour of, and be more accountable to, the workers and the community.

On Thursday 13 June 1974, barely three months after taking office, the new Secretary of State for Industry wrote in his diary: 'I [am] absolutely determined not to let the Meriden people down... I shall go flat out to try and get the independent Meriden cooperative working.'

THE MERIDEN IMPASSE

Three months earlier, an increasingly exasperated Dennis Poore issued a writ to retrieve tooling NVT needed to resume production of the three-cylinder Trident and recover a batch of up to 1,000 Triumph twins that had been built at Meriden before the blockade. Benn persuaded the pickets to release the equipment and the stock of Bonnevilles to Small Heath (NVT's Marketing Director Hugh Palin paid pickets £3 toward the fighting fund for each motorcycle they loaded onto a lorry).[**]

---

[*]   Reid quipped that Benn had 'more conversions on the road to Damascus than a Syrian long-distance truck driver'.

[**]   Alistair Cave told author Mick Duckworth that to preclude further layoffs, he had Small Heath's assembly workers paint the factory.

To show solidarity with the Co-op, on one occasion the Industry Secretary and his wife joined the Meriden workers on the picket line (Benn doing so anonymously three more times over the course of the blockade). But the head of the DTI was not the only one who had been busy. As the blockade continued and US dealers desperate for spares resorted to cannibalising models from their own showrooms, Bob Myers came up with an ingenious solution. He and his business partner in the proposal, Bill Kennedy, a dealer from Elyria, Ohio, would buy the factory.

The two very quickly dispensed with that idea, however. As Kennedy told authors Brooke and Gaylin: 'The floor sweepers had a union; the people putting the spokes in the wheels had a union. If one union had a problem, they'd all just sit down!'

Kennedy also explored relocating production to a site in Gassaway, West Virginia, but the deal collapsed as soon as Meriden got wind of his plans.

Myers also looked into buying the Triumph name. He had drawn up plans for a pricing and US distribution network when exploring the possibility of purchasing Meriden, and at his own expense had flown to the UK former head of TriCor, Dennis McCormack and two backers in the enterprise, Dale Yeager and his trucking industry business associate, Winfield Moon (Yeager's company transported the machines for TriCor).

'When Poore told me he wanted £4 million for the Triumph trademark I decided we could use Meriden instead,' Myers told *Classic Bike* magazine's Mick Duckworth. 'I designed a logo and even had some cloth badges made.'

In the end, the Americans backed out; Moon - according to Myers - found the British 'too shifty'.

Any solution to the Meriden impasse was going to have to be found nearer home.

14

CRAIG VETTER DESIGNS THE TRIUMPH HURRICANE IN SECRET

AND THE TRIDENT FINALLY GETS PUSH-BUTTON START

'Tridents are rolling again!'
(Headline from an NVT magazine advert)

Craig Vetter

NVT DEVELOP THE NEXT-GENERATION TRIDENT

When NVT unveiled The Trident T160V to the British press and motorcycle traders at a joint launch held in Ragley Hall in Warwickshire in March 1975, the first multi-cylinder superbike of the modern era finally had the specification and looks it lacked when BSA/Triumph launched the A75 and T150 triples nearly seven years earlier in 1968. The new Trident (which Americans had got to see two months beforehand at the Los Angeles dealers show on 16-17 January) now boasted hydraulic disc brakes, electric start and traditional styling. Moreover, the T160 was no longer a stablemate to the twin-cylinder Bonneville, but rather its co-debutante at the press launch, NVT's electric-start 850cc Norton Commando.

Up to the Triumph workers' sit-in, assembly of the three-cylinder 750 was completed at Meriden, where the factory installed the Trident engines manufactured by Small Heath at a rate of 300 a week. Following the picket's blockade and occupation of Meriden in September 1973, triple engines soon began to stack up at Armoury Road. This stoked resentment already simmering amongst some BSA staff still bitter that Meriden had been spared the large-scale redundancies Small Heath had suffered in 1971.

NVT Chairman Dennis Poore's shock announcement to workers in Meriden's canteen of his plans to close the plant and transfer production of the T150 to Small Heath had been confounded by the Meriden occupation, as blueprints, drawings, and tooling for the Trident's frame and many other components were held captive behind the factory blockade.

Two months later, with production of all Triumphs still at a standstill, NVT undertook a massive search to recover any drawings held by outside contractors. The company commissioned its draughtsmen to remake blueprints based on completed components, re-fabricated its own tools and jigs, and laid out a whole new assembly line. The cost of the exercise came to a reported £500,000, but by late April 1974, completed Tridents were rolling off the hand-pushed production track once more, in time for the American spring sales season.

The T150s emerging from Small Heath were almost identical to the '73 season models apart from their exhausts and new livery (black with Sundance Yellow panels). NVT placed adverts in magazines showing a phalanx of disc-braked T150s receding into the distance. The headline boldly proclaimed 'Tridents are rolling again!' whilst the copy explained: 'Thanks to the success of the Norton Villiers Triumph Birmingham factory in re-tooling to counteract the Meriden factory blockade, Triumphs - the experts' bikes - are here again. At first, demand may be hard to fill. *Reserve yours now*'.

NVT allocated dealers in the US stocks based on past sales. But what the bike dealers were clamouring for was not the triple nor the dual-purpose 500cc TR5 Trophy: the machine they wanted was the Bonneville. In September, NVT managed to negotiate the release of the completed twins held back by the siege at Meriden. Most of them, however, were 650s destined for other markets. Even so, the number that made it to American shores proved pitifully few. By October, warehouses in America were filling up with unsold T150s.

The statement Triumph-Norton Incorporated issued back in April (TNI was formed following Norton-Villiers' merger with BSACI) announcing a forthcoming electric-start version of the Trident may have been intended as a fillip at the start of the new sales season, but it probably didn't help shift what was obviously now just a stop-gap model.

An electric-start version of the Trident had been in development at Meriden as far back as 1969, when the Experimental Department rigged up some BSA and Triumph triples with a starter motor. However, it was after the factory cut its support for the race programme in early '72, that Meriden began work in earnest on the second-generation electric start engine.

Unlike the upright barrels of the Triumph, the BSA's inclined cylinders (canted forward from vertical by 15 degrees, in homage to the company's signature Sloper models) left space above the gearbox for engineers to locate a starter motor. The two configurations were the result of the BSA Board's original diktat that Hele and Hopwood produce the triple in BSA and Triumph guises in order to appease both marque's dealer networks and fierce tribal loyalties (particularly in the BSA/Triumph combine's biggest market, America). The answer to Triumph's brand-identity conundrum - developing an electric-start Trident that utilised the forward-canted engine more closely associated with its BSA rival - was provided by Don Brown, BSA's New Jersey-based sales chief, and a hip young designer operating out of Rantoul, Illinois called Craig Vetter.

DON BROWN DECIDES TO RE-STYLE A BRITISH BIKE TO SUIT US TASTES

Even before their public launch, BSA's East Coast Vice President, Don Brown, had expressed his misgivings at Ogle Design's styling of the triples in a report he submitted to Small Heath in 1967. 'The only way we were going to sell the Triples,' Brown told authors Brooke and Gaylin, 'was by restyling them - I was convinced of that. And because BSA Group executives approved the original Rocket 3's styling, I'd have to get the bike restyled on my own, in the US - and in secret.'

During dinner on his First Class return flight home from England following the pre-launch meeting for the new triples, Brown, a former sales manager at Triumph's Californian distributor, Johnson Motors (or JoMo, as it was commonly known), found himself thinking about 'specials' such as those from the likes of Paul Dunstall. He reflected, too, on the US custom bike scene. He also considered what had drawn him to his own first motorcycle - a sprung-hubbed Triumph Thunderbird, purchased when he was serving in the military in 1950. Brown - who was just 21 years of age at the time - bought the 6T on sight one Saturday while on a pass from Camp Stoneman after driving past Triumph dealer, Vern Gardner, in Oakland, California where the Thunderbird was on display in the showroom window. Gardner had customised the 650 twin, fitting, amongst other things, Flanders handlebars and a two-and-a-half gallon teardrop fuel tank.

'It had alloy sport fenders, a small James petrol tank, tachometer and speedo, a single big chrome headlamp, a solo saddle and a pillion pad. It was beautiful,' recalled Brown, somewhat wistfully.

That customised Thunderbird and his airborne reflections left a powerful imprint on Brown. He was convinced that BSA and Triumph had to develop strategies to counter the Japanese manufacturers' inexorable advances toward the big-bore motorcycle market. He concluded that the two British marques should develop models specifically for the US. Targeted at particular niches, Brown was sure that such an approach would boost sales and enhance their image. Triumph, he felt, should capitalise on its time-honed looks, leaving it to BSA, according to Brooke and Gaylin's book *Triumph Motorcycles in America*, to be 'the one to break new ground in styling'.

Brown returned to his office at BSA's East Coast headquarters in Nutley, New Jersey, and decided that what he needed now was someone who could render into metal his idea of how the triple *ought* to look. Rather than Ogle's heavy, slab-sided styling, Brown envisioned the 750-3 with the slim, sleek lines of Triumphs from the Fifties... or those of the customised 650 Thunderbird in Vern Gardner's Oakland showroom that so entranced him as a young man all those years ago.

When BSA/Triumph launched the Trident and Rocket 3 in October '68, the lukewarm reception to Ogle's styling dampened the excitement surrounding the long-rumoured superbike and confirmed all of Brown's fears.

He turned to his sales manager, Harry Chaplin. Without revealing the true extent of his disdain for the BSA triple, Brown asked Chaplin if he knew any motorcycle design specialists who could work up a prototype for a styling project he had in mind. Chaplin's response was almost immediate: 'Craig Vetter.'

Chaplin had met the Illinois University design graduate, who was just three years out of design school, a few weeks earlier at the Daytona Bike Show. Two of the products Vetter had on display at that year's Cycle Week caught the BSA sales manager's eye - a shapely one-piece fibreglass tank-and-seat unit installed on Vetter's own Suzuki T500, and a fairing fitted to a Triumph T150.[*]

Chaplin gave Brown Vetter's business card. Printed on it was the company name, Vetter Fairings; the address, Vetter Design Works, Champaign, Illinois; but the card gave no telephone number. 'We just did not make phone numbers public back then,' Vetter told this author. 'Long distance calls were too expensive.'

Brown nevertheless tracked it down, and on 21 April, 1969, he telephoned Vetter at his moulding business in Rantoul, near Urbana, Illinois to explain his idea and invite the young designer to fly out to BSA's headquarters in New Jersey for lunch with him. 'Don's offer was to fly to Nutley and meet,' recalled Vetter years later. 'If he liked me, he would give me the keys to a BSA Rocket 3 and I could drive it home to Illinois. I bought a one-way ticket.'

With the 27-year-old Vetter attired in blue jeans and a T-shirt and the 39-year-old Brown feeling overdressed in his shirt and tie, the pair met on June 3 to discuss the project in more detail (although Vetter's recollection of their meeting was that much of it was taken up discussing their shared passion for aeroplanes - Don's father, a Navy aviator who died in an air crash when Brown was just 17, flew the 1929 Travel Air Mystery Ship designed by one of Vetter's design heroes, Walter Beech!).[**]

'I liked Craig's mind right away,' recalled Brown. 'Sure, he was a long-haired, hippie-type guy - a free spirit - but he was a keen thinker and ambitious. He brought some drawings with him for the project, and they intrigued me. So I asked him right away whether he'd be interested in doing it.'

---

[*]   Accounts of Chaplin's encounter with Vetter report that the faired Triumph Vetter displayed at Daytona was a Bonneville. However, photographs taken at the time clearly show Vetter's fibreglass-kitted Suzuki 500 nose to nose with a Trident wearing one of the designer's Phantom III full fairings.

[**]   In 1980, Vetter would launch a limited edition Kawasaki KZ1000-based project bike he developed which he dubbed the Mystery Ship, after Beech's aeroplane.

Brown liked the fact that not only was Vetter a dreamer, but that he was also a practical industrial designer. At the time of their meeting, Vetter already had ten employees, was selling fairings nationwide, and from 1967 had run adverts in every issue of *Cycle World*.

Brown explained his idea. 'BSA is introducing a new triple, the styling of which isn't to my liking and may not be that well accepted in the marketplace,' he recalled telling Vetter in an online article for *Motohistory*. 'We can't change the styling of this model - it's done - but maybe we can influence the engineers in the UK how styling might be done'.

In an interview reported by Mick Duckworth in his book *Triumph and BSA Triples*, Brown recalled: 'I told Craig I wanted a design that looked like it was moving even when standing still. It ought to have a light, lean look and symmetry of lines was important. They were the fundamentals I had heard Edward Turner lay out many times when I was sales manager at Johnson Motors between 1956 and 1965'. Vetter, a motorcyclist since childhood, and himself a fan of the mid-Sixties Triumph Bonneville, saw that many of the dynamic qualities Brown sought were similar to those influencing the chopper movement.

As Vetter told *Cycle World* in 1970 when the magazine featured the bike on its cover for a story they ran on what at that point was a BSA prototype: 'Chopper people recognise, unconsciously perhaps, the animalness of a motorcycle. Look at the lion: deep chest, paws forward, the rear end light. There's something primitive in us that we associate with that and transfer it into motorcycles. I think there are some lean animal proportions in some choppers today. Some go too far. But chopper ideas are pointing in some direction; I feel that the BSA is an assimilation of some of these ideas, some of the stimuli around me - it is what's happening today.'

Brown had just one condition. Vetter couldn't tell anyone what he was doing.

The designer had to build the prototype in secret. To address the young designer's understandable concern that to do so might leave him vulnerable to the parent corporation stealing his ideas and denying him his rightful credit, Brown set down their arrangement in a letter dated 10 June 1969. (Brown made only three members of staff privy to the project. He told them that they should discuss it with nobody but each other. He did not share his plans with his fellow BSA managers, Group chairman Eric Turner or Lionel Jofeh, BSA's managing director, neither of whom was aware of what Brown was up to.)

Vetter was to submit progress reports to Brown each week - 'done in simple handwriting' if he so chose. He was to log how much time he spent working on the project (Brown having accepted the designer's proposed rate of $15.30 an hour).[*]

'If he [Brown] did not like the bike,' Vetter told this author, 'which I always referred to as the Vetter Rocket, I would not be paid. I could keep it and do anything with it I wanted. No matter what, I could keep it.'

The East Coast Vice President gave Vetter full access to the BSA parts store at Nutley, New Jersey and agreed to refund all of Vetter's 'out-of-pocket expenses'. As promised,

---

[*]   Accounts of the hourly rate BSA Inc. paid Vetter vary. Brown himself cites $27 in *Motohistory's* online interview with the former BSA chief. I have used the figure Vetter scribbled on Don Brown's letter dated June 10 1969 in his handwritten notes summarising a telephone conversation he had with Harry Chaplin about Brown's letter.

Brown also loaned Vetter an early production example of a Rocket 3 to take back with him to Illinois. The machine (engine number KC-00197 A75R) was probably one of the four Rocket 3s that had set speed and long-distance records at Daytona that April (yet another thing Brown had organised in secret). It was also the bike Lord Montagu had borrowed to cover the journey from the airport to the Empire State Building for the New York leg of a transatlantic air race sponsored by the *Daily Mail*.

The impression Vetter gained aboard the triple during the ride home was that the Rocket 3 was too heavy, its seat too wide, and its foot pegs poorly positioned. 'I loved the engine and the sound of the BSA triple, but not much else. Riding it was like sitting on an ugly board. In 1,000 miles, I pretty much knew what had to be done.'

When Vetter wheeled the bike into his fifty-foot-long by fifty-foot-wide workshop in Rantoul and removed the Rocket 3's tank and side panels, he found that, stripped of its Ogle-designed bodywork, the BSA in its nakedness revealed an already visually more exciting machine.*

VETTER GIVES THE ROCKET 3 A NEW LOOK

Even in the earliest sketches, scribbled on whatever came to hand (including Vetter Fairing company brochures), the element that would become the bike's signature feature - its integral seat and tank - was present in his tyro designs. With Vetter's friend Duane Anderson fabricating the Rocket's metal components, work on the seat and tank unit began on 2 July 1969 and lasted for twelve-and-a-half hours. But Vetter then spent endless hours sculpting and moulding body filler into the flowing lines of the one-piece bodywork before he was happy. Interestingly, the very bike whose swoopy body-kit was responsible for bringing Craig Vetter into Don Brown's orbit, the T500 that Harry Chaplin had so admired at Daytona, also included elements he would, on this bike, make sure not to repeat. Vetter told *Motohistory* that his Suzuki's 'zoomy' shape 'forced a viewer's eye right off onto something else - anything else. My next motorcycle design, I decided, would somehow keep a viewer's attention right there.'

The sensuous fibreglass bodywork for the BSA 750 certainly addressed that concern, succeeding instead in directing the viewer's gaze, not elsewhere, but toward the Rocket 3's powerplant.

In the notes he wrote at the time, he described the cylinder head as 'much too timid' and told Brown in one of his weekly updates that the stock head looked like a 'skinny weakling'.

'I already liked the looks of the triple engine, but somebody had emasculated it by shaving its cylinder fins off,' explained Vetter years later. 'I put them back on.' He fashioned mock fin extensions from plastic, then glued them in place to give the cylinder head a much bolder profile, accentuating their prominence still further by painting the barrels black. And, by deliberately leaving space around the engine, and

---

* Vetter subscribed to the maxim 'doing more with less'. The philosophy of another of his design heroes, the designer and mathematician, Buckminster Fuller, it was the motto Vetter adopted for his business cards after he sold Vetter Corp in 1978.

using the bodywork to frame it as one might a painting, Vetter made the powerplant the focus of attention.

The three-into-three exhaust system Vetter designed also played its part in bringing attention to the A75 motor. Positioned on the right-side only, the three-fanned silencers and triple-sweeping headers - like the curvy bodywork - help direct the onlooker's gaze toward the engine; whereas the bike's bare left flank means the engine dominates as a consequence of their very absence. Vetter had sketched several ideas, but remained uncertain. Then Brown sent him the exhaust system he thought had been fitted to Jim Rice's BSA three-cylinder flat-tracker, which had all three down-pipes swept to the right.* He also sent Vetter a trio of race megaphone silencers, which the director of BSA's eastern facility told the designer to use however he wished - BSA's engineers would take care of making them run quietly!

'The best I could come up with,' Vetter recalled, 'was the now famous, fanned-out configuration' (achieved by deploying the megaphones Brown had supplied).

Vetter, however, claimed to never like the finished arrangement.

'If you notice, most of the photos I took of the Vetter Rocket in 1969 were of the left side... not from the pipe side. But,' he admitted later, 'I was wrong.'

In order not to jeopardise the chances of his designs making it to production, Vetter fitted a pair of internally-sprung Ceriani front forks, which Don Brown had sent him because they closely resembled the items Brown knew the factory intended to fit to its own models very soon. But the units Brown had provided were short-length competition forks. On 23 July, in response to Polaroids Vetter had sent him, Brown wrote to the designer to say that 'the machine appears to me to be front end heavy, in that it seems to be slanting forward'.

Vetter's solution was to fabricate and install two-inch slugs, which extended the stanchions and restored the bike's rake and trail back to standard. It was a move that would cure one problem, but unwittingly create another later on.

Some ideas, however, never made the final cut.

On 24 July, Vetter noted in his log: 'the time has come to incorporate a fairing as factory equipment, but not a fairing that exists anywhere else.' He sketched an abbreviated quarter-fairing made from Plexiglas that curved up and over the instruments. It was a neat idea, but Vetter abandoned it for Brown's project.

After removing the Rocket 3's instrument binnacle, he installed separate instruments, which he had in mind could be adjustable to allow the rider to tilt them to whatever angle best suited them.

Yet another idea that didn't make it came from Brown. The BSA boss thought the bike should be yellow. Vetter did as his patron asked, and first painted it yellow. 'If you scraped the paint from the Vetter Rocket,' the designer told *Motohistory*, 'you'd find that it was once yellow... for about ten minutes.' Vetter elected instead to paint the integral tank and seat unit a reddish orange, actually Camaro Hugger Red, adorned with two yellow stripes.

---

*   Jim Rice later told Craig Vetter that the pipes were not his and that he had no idea where they had come from.

The AMA had recently published a bulletin exhorting designers to use Scotchlite in motorcycle products. Vetter was a big fan of the material, having deployed it on his Series 1600 Phantom Fairing. As he had replaced the federal-mandated side reflectors on the Rocket 3's oil cooler with end caps depicting BSA's piled arms logo (and because the bike was not now going to be yellow), to comply with road regulations, the designer applied light-reflecting Scotchlite in two broad bands along the top of the pseudo tank, each of which narrowed as they passed down to the side panels. On the tank, each stripe contained the legend 'BSA' and on the side panels they tapered off into a decal declaring '750'.

The seat (which Brown had briefed Vetter should be a 'one-and-a-half person design') was fastened discretely in place by Velcro. Vetter replaced the A75's flat-backed headlight with a traditional bullet-shaped chrome shell, a move guaranteed to sit well with Brown whose own fondly-remembered Thunderbird sported a similarly-styled unit. A chromed tubular Y-shaped bracket, fastened to the bottom yoke, held the Rocket's front lamp prominently in position.

By 5 September 1969, Vetter had a rolling prototype ready. Vetter sent Brown a Polaroid of the finished bike. 'It's not my bag,' replied Brown, 'but that's probably good.' *

'I had earned Don's trust,' recalled Vetter. However, word of Brown's arrangement with Vetter had reached BSACI's new president, Peter Thornton.

An MIT graduate whose background was in advertising not motorcycles (he had been president of Sales Communications Incorporated, a subsidiary of one of the world's largest advertising agencies, Interpublic), Thornton was a consultant to BSA before persuading Group Chairman Eric Turner and Managing Director Lionel Jofeh to appoint him as Chief Executive Officer over BSA/Triumph's US operations.

Thornton reportedly 'lived by the organisational chart'. He gained a reputation for being manipulative and condescending to his junior staff, amongst whom he inspired scant loyalty. Inevitably, he and Brown did not get on. 'But he put up with me,' explained Brown, 'because I had strong support from the chairman and Lionel Jofeh, my boss before Peter Thornton.' The BSACI president called Brown in to his office to explain himself.

'What's this about a secret project?' demanded Thornton, suspicious that Brown might be misusing BSACI funds.

'Oh that,' replied a disenchanted Brown (the sales chief had already decided it was time for a change of career following the reorganisation of BSACI and Thornton's appointment back in July). Thornton asked to see the files and Brown got his secretary to pass them over. 'He ordered me to arrange for him to see the bike. I called Craig and he put the finished prototype in his van and drove it out to Nutley from Rantoul.'

Vetter loaded the bike - unrideable due to its plastic stuck-on cooling fins and wooden mock-up oil tank - into the back of a friend's VW Microbus camper van and drove it east to New Jersey, arriving at BSA's headquarters on 31 October. He was completely unaware of the intrigue simmering away at BSACI.

---

* Years later, Brown told *Motohistory*: 'I think I was referring to the long forks, or something else. I liked the seat/tank design from the first time I saw it.'

After notifying Thornton that he had arrived, Vetter and the bike then waited several hours in the BSA service room (unbeknownst to him, the BSACI president and Brown were arguing because, as the latter recalled later, 'Thornton thought he had caught me with my hand in the pot and that I had absconded with corporate funds to fund the styling project!'). Staff passing by the bike made comments like: 'Sure is orange' or 'Never seen anything like that before.' Otherwise, the response was muted as people waited to learn what Thornton thought of the prototype. When he finally walked in, Vetter said, 'there was an audible gasp, then he blurted out: "My God, it's a bloody phallus! Wrap it up and send it to England!" And with that, everyone laughed and clapped and began to give me compliments. The boss had told them it was okay.'

Brown said: 'It was like, yeah, that's what we ought to do! Myself, I was ecstatic.'

The staff at Nutley did as Thornton instructed and cocooned the bike in bubble-wrap and air-freighted it that same day to Stephen Mettam, BSA Group's Chief Stylist, at his workshop in Umberslade Hall.

Brown, meanwhile, unknown to Thornton, had spoken to BSA Group chairman Eric Turner and tendered his resignation for his post as Vice President for National BSA Sales. He acceded to Turner's request not to discuss company business with the press (whose true financial situation the BSA Board was anxious to keep the Americans - their biggest market - from knowing). By way of *quid pro quo*, Brown got Turner's agreement that he would ensure Vetter received full credit for his work, that any production bike would remain faithful to the original design, and that BSA would recompense its designer.

On 5 January 1970, in his last telephone conversation with Vetter, Brown explained that Lionel Jofeh was in America to see Peter Thornton. 'Don asked me to draft a Project Summary in order to help him get the project accepted so I could get paid. I did and mailed it to him,' recalled Vetter.

Three days later, on 8 January, Thornton called Brown into his office. He accused him of misusing company funds to sponsor the Vetter styling project and fired him.

'I've already resigned,' replied Brown wearing a big grin. 'Just ask the chairman.' Whereupon he strode out of Thornton's office and began to collect his personal effects, bequeathing BSACI's president his files on the Vetter project.

It was the last official act of Brown's involvement with the Vetter Rocket. All too aware of the parent company's dire financial circumstances, he left BSACI pessimistic for the triple's chances of ever making it to production and available in the market place.

A few days later, Vetter wrote to Peter Thornton, on 11 January 1970, seeking payment and asking the BSACI president to call him and tell him what was happening with the Rocket 3: 'My best work is in limbo,' opined Vetter. For the next few months, Thornton and his executives stonewalled the designer. In a telephone conversation with one official, he asked if Vetter would accept less than the amount BSACI owed him. Exasperated, Vetter contacted Brown who had returned to California to start his own business from offices in the Hilton Pasadena. Brown duly contacted the Group Chairman, Eric Turner.

'Eric Turner called me at my office in Pasadena one morning to ask whether or not I had executed a valid contract with Craig,' recalled Brown in an interview he and Vetter recorded for *Motohistory*. 'I told him the contract was valid and after a brief reflection on BSA affairs, he said he would arrange for Craig to be paid. Peter Colman's secretary, Ruth Furman, also had called me a few days before the Chairman to ask me if I had a copy of the contract I had signed with you. I said I had a copy but it was still somewhere in my archives from the move. Actually, I wasn't certain I still had a copy but I was prepared to testify that my contract with you was a valid obligation of BSA Inc.'

Vetter received his cheque for $12,000 on 9 March 1970.

'Mr Turner was an honourable man,' Brown said, 'whom I liked very much despite his unwillingness to listen to his American managers and his propensity to hire senior executives who had no experience with the motorcycle industry.'

BUILD IT JUST AS VETTER DESIGNED IT!

The Vetter Three, as it became known during its seven-month residency in Steve Mettam's basement workshop at Umberslade Hall in Hockley Heath near Solihull, was one design to which the young styling chief contributed nothing. Indeed, Mettam worked hard to ensure that no one else did either.

'The [factory's] designers initially wished to use an existing steel tank and fibreglass seat pan, and mimic on these the Vetter colour scheme,' Mettam told the UK magazine *Motorcycle Classics* in 1997. 'I did not, and insisted that we use the integral tank/seat.'

Draughtsmen from Armoury Road measured up the prototype and produced detailed drawings for manufacturing the bike's special components. To address concerns about the legality of the prototype's fibreglass fuel tank, the factory commissioned a company called Homer to supply a steel item, which would be moulded into the tank and seat unit. Mitchenall Brothers in Wiltshire, makers of the famous Avon fairings, had the task of moulding the one-piece fibreglass tank and seat itself.

Mettam also had to fight to retain the prototype's three-into-three exhaust system. 'There was strong pressure to use the standard one,' said the stylist. 'Eventually, the only compromise was the use of larger silencers, with the consequential loss of power.'

But Mettam appreciated the prototype's less obvious features, too, which the stylist recognised demonstrated the sheer depth of thought that Vetter put into his reworking of the triple. The American redesigned the rear mudguard to make it easier to raise in the event of a rear-wheel puncture. He improved the toolkit, and repositioned the fuse box and oil dipstick. In specifying these changes, Vetter was simply trying to improve the bike as a whole, not just enhance his design's look or aesthetics.

The factory did make some compromises. When BSA Inc. shipped the prototype from New Jersey to England, they enclosed a note instructing the factory to build it just as Vetter had designed it. Apparently, in seeking to honour that plea, instead of replacing the prototype's massive front drum brake with the Lockheed front disc brake now standard on the '73-season's Trident and 750 twins, Umberslade Hall installed the off-the-shelf

BSA/Triumph conical-hub. In another change, Steve Mettam substituted Vetter's high-mounted rear light with the long polished unit intended for the 350cc Triumph Bandit.

In the meantime, Vetter's prototype returned to the States to take part in a *Cycle World* photo shoot, the result of a deal Don Brown had cut before he left BSACI. The magazine's editor, Joe Parkhurst, wanted the Vetter Three for a cover piece and feature in the September issue. However, when the designer collected his prototype from Chicago customs on 7 May 1970, he discovered that 'the bike was in very rough shape' with several pieces missing. Vetter had just three days to produce replacements, fix up the bike, and have it ready for its photocall.

On 11 May, the bike was on its way back to Chicago from where it was freighted by air to *Cycle World,* over 2,000 miles away in Los Angeles. Vetter and Duane Anderson, who had helped fabricate the prototype's metal components, flew out ten days later for an interview with the magazine's managing editor Dan Hunt, after which the pair rode back to Illinois on two brand new Kawasaki 500s.

For a short while after the photo shoot, Parkhurst kept the bike on display in the lobby of the magazine's offices. A few months later, that same bike could be seen on newsstands everywhere, adorning the cover of *Cycle World*'s September issue. The prototype, prominent in bright orange against the cover's white background, appeared above the caption: 'Is this the next BSA 3?' Inside, Vetter described his design philosophy - including how the flowing lines of the Three's bodywork acted as a 'buffer zone' between the hard lines of the machine and the softer outline of its rider. Elsewhere in the article, Don Brown's successor at BSACI, Tony Salisbury, explained that the bike was intended to test the market. 'People have seen bikes like this before - customs - but never from the manufacturer. We want to know if the consumers agree with the design. We want to get letters from people. If we get a positive reaction it may go into production.'

That month's edition proved the most popular in the magazine's history, with an additional print run also selling out. *Cycle World*'s office was inundated with letters from readers. One reader of the famous 'white cover' edition was Don Brown.

'I heard nothing of Craig's design until seven months later [after leaving BSACI] when I picked up a copy of the September 1970 issue of *Cycle World*. The bike was beautiful indeed, like a super model is beautiful. I smiled, again and again... that is, until I read the feature article about the creation of the project. It was a near-complete fabrication and that did get to me. But I didn't call Parkhurst, and the reason was simple enough. Upon resigning I had promised the chairman that I would not grant any interviews or otherwise communicate with anyone in the press about matters related to the Group or its problems, and I kept my word.'

BSA showed the prototype at the Houston Astrodome dealers' convention over the weekend of 29-30 January 1971 where it was on display as the 'Vetter BSA Rocket 3'. Vetter was invited back to the Astrodome a year later for a special presentation of a pre-production model that BSA had shipped over to display at the trade show in order to gauge audience reaction. The machine still wore 'BSA' on the tank and '750cc' on the side as per Vetter's original design.

In the twelve months between each show, Small Heath had built two pre-production vehicles, which in recognition of their five-speed transmissions, they coded V75V. In factory documents, however, staff referred to the bike as the Rocket 3 Chopper on account of their two-inch longer than standard forks (a literal interpretation of the two-inch slugs Vetter had fitted to compensate for the short-length racing Cerianis Don Brown had given him).

Writing in 2012, the designer explained to the author: 'The Vetter Rocket model I sent over indeed had one slug added to the top of each fork tube to bring the bike up to the original Rocket 3 height. While it was in England, somebody added a second set of slugs to the model. I was told recently that it was Pete Coleman. The extra slugs were there when it was returned for the *Cycle World* shoot. If you look real close on the cover shot, you can see them. Two sets of slugs remain above each fork tube on the model Vetter BSA today.'

In testing at MIRA in December 1971, one of the pre-production machines achieved a one-way best of 122.90mph. When, however, Small Heath ended production of the BSA Rocket 3 in January 1972, development of the V75V transferred to Meriden, where testers discovered problems with the triple's handling due to weaknesses between where the bottom alloy front suspension yoke joined the steering stem.

During a visit by Dr. Felix Kalinski to Small Heath later that year, Kalinski - who in May had replaced Thornton's temporary successor, Dennis McCormack (appointed after BSA's British financiers, Barclays Bank, had demanded that Thornton, the man who had authorised BSA/Triumph's million-dollar US race campaign, resign) - advocated that Meriden send 3,000 Vetter Rockets to the US for the '73 sales season. He suggested, too, that the factory should promote it over the Trident, and, moreover, that they should produce an electric-start triple with disc brakes.

Also attending the meeting was Bert Hopwood. Appointed to the Board the previous December as the executive responsible for design and engineering in the BSA Group's Motorcycle Division, he explained to Kalinski that despite curing the early problems with the steering yoke, the bike - which Hopwood still referred to as the 'BSA Vetter Rocket' as late as August 1972 (almost eight months after the last A75 had rolled off the line) - did not handle as well as the Trident. Hopwood and his testers attributed the Vetter Three's failings to its extended forks and ribbed front tyre (although some within Meriden felt that factory testers were riding it like it was a TT bike).

Vetter himself felt the problem lay with the forks. 'The ribbed tire on Brit bikes was a tradition. I had no reason to think there was anything wrong with it. Since the production Hurricane ended up with longer forks than the original Rocket 3 - and I changed nothing else regarding geometry - I can only conclude that any handling differences would have come from the extra fork length added in England.'

By the time the bike went into production in September '72, BSA was near to collapse. Umberslade Hall Research and Development Centre had closed at the beginning of the year, BSA had announced a half-year trading loss of £1.5 million, the Group was at the limit of its £10 million overdraft, and in autumn, the DTI asked Dennis Poore to merge Norton Villiers with BSA/Triumph. As a result, the Vetter Three was re-badged as a Triumph, although its new model name, 'X-75 Hurricane' (bestowed by Dr. Kalinski, according to Joe Parkhurst), maintained a weather-related naming convention established by BSA with motorcycles such as the Cyclone, Lightning and Thunderbolt twins. Vetter, however, was told that the names were airplane-related in their origin. He therefore liked the name as it continued BSA's practice of calling its models after British World War II fighter planes. 'I suspected that Don liked it too,' he told *Motohistory*.

Even Vetter had to admit that the production bike remained pretty faithful to his original concept. When the designer visited Meriden in December to discuss his suggestions about restyling the unloved oil-in-the frame Bonneville, he was pleased at how the factory had translated his ideas for reworking the triple. He didn't like the new wire-braced front mudguards, which were now standard fittings deployed across the model range. He was also disappointed at finding that the combined seat and tank unit had been made in two parts and that the seam where each of the halves joined was covered in adhesive tape. Otherwise, though, as he told the author Mick Duckworth: 'I thought it was executed reasonably well, especially considering I had not talked directly with England.'

For the first few hundred machines off the line, the factory retained the Hurricane's BSA V75V code for each bike's serial number, before later altering it to TRX75. And to finagle concerns that the triple's exhaust system might not comply with new American noise emission regulations coming into effect from January 1973, Meriden simply back-dated any US-bound machines they manufactured from the New Year onward.

From a planned run of just 500 machines, the factory built around 1,200 Hurricanes between September 1972 and January 1973.* The majority went to America. The UK market received just 34. A small number were sold in Canada and Europe; two went to New Zealand and 24 to Australia.

In the US, Triumph's asking price for the X-75 was $2,195 (compared to $1,900 for a standard Trident). In Britain, the Hurricane retailed for £895, plus purchase tax. Although a two-stroke, the market's only other three-cylinder 750, the Kawasaki MACH IV, cost £754 (plus tax). In their April 1973 road test, *Motorcyclist* magazine praised the X-75's looks, engine performance, comfortable seat, and 'bitchin' sound'. However, testers were critical of its top-heavy handling and 'absolutely atrocious' fuel consumption of 30mpg - which, with the Hurricane's small tank, gave riders a range of no more than 85 miles. To ameliorate the triple's handling ills, BSA/Triumph's Western Distribution Centre in Duarte, just outside of Pasadena, issued a fork kit to dealers comprising shorter

---

* The precise figure remains uncertain. Joe Parkhurst in his book *A Hurricane Named Vetter* says that 1,175 machines were made, whereas Meriden's records suggest the factory built 1,154 machines. Determining the exact number Meriden manufactured is made more difficult because Hurricane serial numbers were not always sequential, broken by the factory interspersing them with the T150Vs they also produced during 1973.

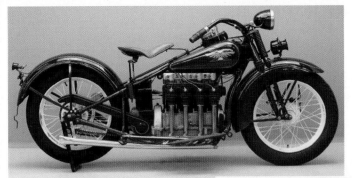

Left. 1931 4-cylinder Henderson KJ 1305 *(Photo: Yesterdays Antique Motorcycles)*

Below, 1940 Indian 440 1265cc. *(Photo: Yesterdays Antique Motorcycles)*

YESTERDAY'S SUPERBIKES

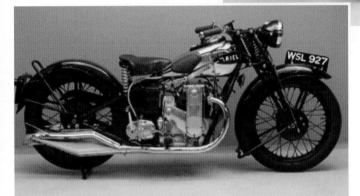

Left Ariel Square Four. *(Photo: Yesterdays Antique Motorcycles)*

Below. The flowing lines of a 1937 example of Edward Turner's Speed Twin *(Photo: Yesterdays Antique Motorcycles)*

TRIUMPH / BSA

The pre-production triples. Above, the Triumph T150 and below the BSA Rocket 3 *(Photos: TR3OC Archive)*

Left and below, Ogle design sketches for the Triples *(Photos: TR3OC Archive)*

Ogle chalk drawing of the Triple *(Photo: Craig Vetter)*

Left, Craig Vetter with the finished one-piece bodywork for the Hurricane *(Photo: Craig Vetter)*

Below, 1969 Craig Vetter and the BSA with the ugly stuff removed, working on his drawings *(Photo: Craig Vetter)*

Below, Vetter drawings - 'I could never produce such a finished sketch. [he is referring to the Ogle sketch shown earlier] For one reason, I don't have the talent. But I wouldn't want to, either. Can you see the difference in feeling? The Ogle refined sketch is quiet and still. My quick sketch is alive and flashy.' Craig Vetter *(Photo: Craig Vetter)*

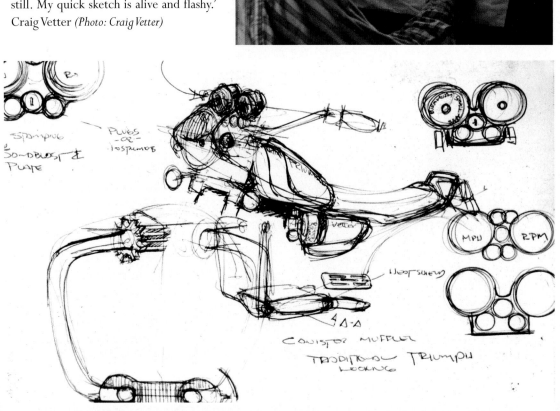

Above, 1968 BSA Rocket 3 and below, Craig Vetter's finished 1969 Hurricane *(Photos: Craig Vetter)*

Stephen Mettam, chief stylist at BSA *(Photo: Brad Jones Picture Library)*

Below, the Triumph 1,000cc 4-cylinder Quadrant ridden by NVT tester Neil Coombes *(Photo: TR3OC Archive)*

Triumph P1 prototype - first of the line *(Photo: TR3OC Archive)*

The Triumph P1 *(Photo: TR3OC Archive)*

The BSA Rocket 3 and, in the background, the Triumph P1 *(Photo: Author)*

HONDA CB750/4

A beautiful and original 1969 CB750 sandcast, registered on 1st January 1969. *(Photo: Derrel Weaver)*

Brighton, Saturday 5 April 1969: the day the blue touch paper was lit that ignited motorcycling's most explosive decade. *(Photo: Bauer Media)*

Above, the winner's circle at Daytona International Speedway, March 1970. Dick Mann (No 2) holds the winner's trophy after finishing just three seconds ahead of runner-up Gene Romero (No. 3) riding the Triumph 750/3. To the left of Mann third-placed Don Castro (No. 81) on board the Triumph 750 triple. *(Photo: Bauer Media)*

Dick Mann's Honda CR 750 on display *(Photo: Author)*

KAWASAKI 500 AND 750

Above, the Kawasaki H1, MACH III *(Photo: copyright Kawasaki)* Below, the Kawasaki H2 750/3 *(Photo: Author)*

SUZUKI 750

The Suzuki GT750J. Known as the Le Mans in the US, the 750cc triple made its debut in 1970 but British buyers had to wait until early 1972. Praised for its engine's quietness and civility, the Suzuki was a smooth and sophisticated three-cylinder 750 two-stroke - unlike Kawasaki's 750 two-stroke triple, the MACH IV! *(Photo: John Noble and Bauer Media)*

Close up of the engine of the GT750 Suzuki *(Photo: Author)*

Suzuki RE-5M in all its complexity! *(Photo: Rollo Turner)*

Above, clay mock-up of the Kawasaki X99 concept, Kwasaki's attempt at a rotary housed in Z1 running gear, which never saw production.

(Photo: Dave Marsden of Z-Power)

Left, the DKW W2000 *(Photo: Bauer Media)*

KAWASAKI Z1

1972 Talladega. Above, testing the first Kawasaki Z1 900 in the USA. Note the blue 'Honda' tank to hide its identity! Winner of the first Imola 200, Paul Smart (in green jacket) 'It wasn't test riding like it is now, where you ride itthen give it back all nice and shiny.' Below, stripping the engine by the side of the track *(Photos: David Koup of Koup's Cycle Shop Inc)*

Right, the Kawasaki V-bike disguised as a Honda.
(Photo: Malc Anderson)

Below, the Akashi test ride key.
(Photo: Malc Anderson)

The Kawasaki Z1 *(Photo: Copyright Kawasaki)*

DUCATI

Above, A Ducati line-up at Imola - these are all replicas of Pul Smart's race winning Ducati taken at the first Imola festival in 2010 *(Photo: Ian Kerr)*

Paul Smart on board a factory built replica of the race winning 750 Ducati at Imola *(Photo: Ian Kerr)*

The 1972 Ducati 750GT. Paul Smart's historic victory for Ducati at the very first Imola 200, the 750 'L' twin's performance in the second of *Cycle* magazine's Big 7 Superbike Comparison tests, and Cook Neilson's win at Daytona aboard 'Old Blue', all helped cement the Italian marque's credibility with motorcyclists. *(Photo: Patrick Gosling and Bauer Media)*

Close-up of the 750 engine *(Photo: Ian Kerr)*

HONDA GOLD WING

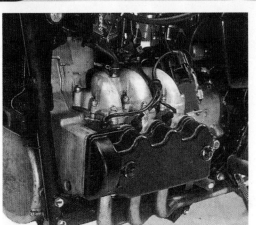

Above, two rare pictures of the prototype of the Honda Gold Wing, then a six cylinder. Left, some details of the engine. *(Photos: Copyright Honda)*

Above, the Honda Gold Wing GL1000 was the factory's first significant new model since the CB750. Honda described it as: 'Super Tourer or Superbike. It Just depends on the Way You Ride It.' *(Photo: Reynolds-Alberta Museum)*

Below, a close-up of the Gold Wing engine. Compare these photos with the prototype pictures on the previous page. *(Photo: Author)*

NORTON

Norton Commando at full chat. *(Photo: Ian Kerr)*

LAVERDA

Laverda Jota *(Photo: Rollo Turner)*

HONDA CBX

Clay model of the CBX with integral bodywork.

Rolling model without tail

An early clay model of the CBX *(All photos on this page: Copyright Honda)*

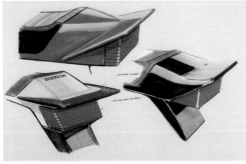

Above left, tail piece sketches for the CBX.
Right, CBX sketch with bikini fairing

A line-up of all models of the CBX. *(Photo: Ian Foster)*

Right, a cut-away view of the amazing CBX engine *(Photo: Alan Evans)*

Below, the bike itself, a CBX 1000 with a cut-down seat and aftermarket exhaust *(Photo: Ian Kerr)*

KAWASAKI Z1300

Concept sketch of the Z 1300 *(Photo: Copyright Kawasaki)*

The Z 1300 at Graceland! *(Photo: Copyright Kawasaki)*

HARLEY-DAVIDSON

Harley-Davidson Sportster, the 1973 XLCH *(Photo: Harley-Davidson Motor Co. Archives)*

Above, the Harley Sporter in 1964 *(Photo: Ian Kerr)*

The Yamaha XS750, seen here at its debut at the 1975 Milan Show. The three-cylinder 750cc four-stroke went on to become *Bike* magazine's Bike of the Year. *(Photo: Bauer Media)*

Concept sketch for the Yamaha XS750 *(Photo: Bauer Media)*

springs. The Americans also developed an 'Economizer Kit'. Available from late '73, the kit boosted consumption to more than 40mpg. Even so, the X-75 proved a slow seller.

In a preview of the 1972 Triumphs, the US custom bike magazine *Big Bike* opined in an otherwise complimentary piece on the X-75 - which they described as 'one of the best looking cycles around, for a stocker' - that 'The Hurricane, as Triumph calls the Vetter, is fitted with a drum front brake. How gross. Here they take their top-of-the-line machine, after they've put discs on their cheaper models, and use a drum binder. We won't even try to explain this, because it can't be explained. Archaic thinking such as this killed BSA; is Triumph next?' Over on the other side of the Atlantic, in a road test which put the X-75 750cc triple up against the Kawasaki 750/3, *Bike* magazine also questioned why Triumph fitted the Hurricane with a twin leading shoe front brake when the rest of the range had discs. *Bike* did accede, however, that the polished drum brake looked nice and did work, even if it needed 'a strong handful to haul it quickly to a stop'.

Bike magazine thought both bikes 'handled pretty well, though the Kawasaki plunged about a bit through the bumps… [while the] Triumph stayed rock-steady all the time…'

Neither test bike earned plaudits for their frugality. Ridden hard, testers found that the X-75 consumed a gallon of fuel every 35 miles, its 'meagre' tank compelling the rider to look out for a petrol pump after about 65 miles. The Kawasaki was even thirstier. The two-stroke triple drank petrol at a rate of 20 to 22 miles per gallon, but this was mitigated somewhat by its tank's greater fuel-carrying capacity (four gallons to the Hurricane's two).

In his summation, Editor-in-Chief Mark Williams declared the Hurricane 'the most exciting motorcycle built in Britain'. He might well have added: 'or Rantoul, Illinois in America.'

AFTERLIFE AND LEGACY

Vetter's prototype ended up parked in the dark corners of Vetter Corporation's storage areas, first in Illinois then later in California. During that time, his friends cannibalised the prototype, filching parts from inside the engine to keep their own triples on the road.

When he married his wife, Carol, in 1977, Vetter hung the prototype from the living room wall of his new home in San Luis Obispo, California. Strategically placed beneath the bike was a cat litter tray, because, even after ten years, the BSA somehow continued to leak oil!

In December 1998, Vetter donated the bike to the Motorcycle Hall of Fame Museum in Pickerington. (As Craig told this author in 2012, Don Brown had said when the two first met: 'No matter what, I could keep it, which is why it got saved intact, and is now on display in the AMA Hall of Fame Museum in Ohio.') Earlier in the year, the Solomon R. Guggenheim Museum had included the X-75 Hurricane for its exhibition, *The Art of the Motorcycle* (running from 26 June to 20 September 1998).

Almost four decades after its launch, *Motorcycle Classics* journalist Margie Siegal credited the Hurricane as having 'a marked effect on contemporary design. Motorcycle designers began blending in the lines of the tank and seat, while a new type of motorcycle, the cruiser, started to become popular. To be sure, the Hurricane has been called the first cruiser, and it was undeniably the first factory custom.'

VETTER AND THE BONNEVILLE TT 750

Following the excitement generated by the X-75, Triumph's Product Planning Director, Jack Redmond, contacted Vetter in early 1972 and commissioned him to develop a makeover for the Umberslade Hall-designed 650 twins. Taking his inspiration from the US-only T120TT 650 'desert sleds' of the Sixties ('When I was a kid,' Vetter told author Mick Duckworth, 'that was the hottest motorcycle you could get in America'), the designer studied pictures furnished by Pete Colman, Vice President and General Manager of BSA/Triumph's West Coast operations, of Gene Romero's twin-cylinder dirt track race bike.

Vetter constructed a prototype, which he had air freighted to England. He then flew over to join it in Meriden where in winter 1972 he met Bert Hopwood and Triumph stylist Jack Wickes. When he arrived in Wickes' office on 28 November, 'Jack,' recalled Vetter, 'had already faithfully reproduced the tank from my Bonneville TT. He had made two of them. One was on a five-speed twin; one was on a inclined 750 triple.' When Triumph later showed the prototype - dubbed the Bonneville TT 750 - to dealers in America in a hotel in Dearborn, Michigan, feedback from both dealers and customers on Vetter's reworked twin was uniformly favourable. Vetter had incorporated ideas that had been gestating with him for some time. The bike, displayed beneath an attractively lit corner of the hotel, incorporated the kind of modifications Triumph owners were making to their own machines - individual K&N foam filters and Sixties-style cigar-shaped silencers, sculpted tank and raised instruments. However, although well received, the bike never went into production, a victim of the parent company's upheavals following the NVT takeover.

Even so, the Bonneville TT 750 would not disappear entirely. Key aspects of Vetter's design would live on and reappear in the next-generation Triumph Trident, the T160.

THE THUNDERBIRD III

Although work on the electric-start Trident was well advanced, the project had fallen behind schedule. NVT therefore transferred development to its former BSA site, Kitts Green in south east Birmingham, where chief designer Brian Jones - who had been involved with the triples since the days of the P1 prototype - headed a team of around 25 designers and draughtsmen; Doug Hele led four engineers and about ten charge-hands and fitters.

The advent of the BSA-engined Hurricane in a motorcycle branded as a Triumph had neutralised previous arguments about maintaining marque distinctions. Still, in a move probably intended to bolster its credentials as a proper Triumph, the factory revived a model name from its back-catalogue and called the new triple the Thunderbird III (although wags at the factory had already nicknamed it the 'Rodent' owing to the engine's mix of Rocket 3 and Trident components).* The company even manufactured side-panel badges emblazoned with the legend 'Thunderbird III' before eventually dropping the name after colleagues in the US counselled Triumph to find an alternative, worried that the Ford Motor Company might sue (despite the fact that it was Triumph Engineering who first used the name and had granted Ford licence to use it on their 1955 sports car).**

According to Vetter, the 'Thunderbird III looked like my Bonneville TT and embodied most of the features of it. As far as I know, only one complete bike was made.'

In the meantime, the T160's development team explored chain-driven camshafts (Meriden registered an example for road use in 1973); duplex frames; and header pipes sweeping to the right and under the engine where it merged into a radical-looking 'double-decker' silencer. Although the Doug Hele-designed system combined good silencing with excellent power output, NVT directed the team to install the annular silencers fitted to the Trident's new corporate stablemate, the Norton Commando (but tuned to suit the triple engine).

One of Hele's engineers, the then 29-year-old Norman Hyde, told *Bike* magazine's Mike Nicks in 1974 that one of development team's main challenges for the new triple was to reduce noise. 'The early Tridents were really quick and would do mean two-way speeds of at least 120mph at MIRA,' he told the journalist. 'But their noise level was 98 decibels. We have to be down to 80 decibels to sell in the States in 1975, and the problem has been to get down to that level without losing performance, or at least to lose as little as possible.'

As Hyde explained, although similar-looking to the model it would eventually replace, the next-generation Trident still had 500 new items that required drawings. 'We have to test items such as plastic clips against metal clips, different brake pad materials, different generators, different makes of chain, just everything you can think of on a bike, really. You find some new parts don't fit and have to be remade, and when you get everything together you always want to alter something again.'

A very obvious difference between the T150 and the T160 was the latter bike's *quartet* of exhaust headers. The symmetrically-arranged down pipes comprised one each for the outer pots, and *two* from the centre cylinder. These branched out either side of the frame's front downtube via an alloy Y-shaped manifold fastened to the cylinder head's exhaust port.

Other notable differences included hydraulically-actuated disc brakes front and back, a ten-inch rear disc replacing the T150's seven-inch drum; an inclined cylinder head, canted forward by 15 degrees from vertical to accommodate the Lucas M3 electric starter sited above the gearbox; and the now federally-mandated left-foot gear-change

---

* It was Les Williams who christened the prototype the Rodent, the appellation he used for the header of the model's test-bed figures. Bert Hopwood eventually called Williams into his office and asked him to stop referring to the hybrid as the Rodent and henceforth only by its proper name, the Thunderbird III.

** Triumph's 650 Thunderbird was named after a giant mythical eagle-like bird which, according to some Native American tribes, unleashed thunder, lightning and rain. The name came to Edward Turner on a business trip to the US. After attending the New York Show in February 1949, Turner and Rod Coates (TriCor's Service Manager and head of the East Coast's competition department) were driving south to Daytona for the races. It was while passing through South Carolina that Turner spotted a huge totem pole topped out with the figure of a bird in front of the Thunderbird Motel.

mechanism developed at Meriden by engineer Brian Jones using a crossover shaft similar to the arrangement Jim Barclay had designed for the Bonneville.

Jack Wickes Styles The Trident So It Looks Like A Triumph

Styling for the T160 was carried out in-house by Jack Wickes, who adapted the fuel tank shape that Craig Vetter had brought over on the still-born Bonneville 750 TT. The new Trident's 4.5 gallon unit (20 litres)* was a fresh take on the traditional Triumph teardrop tank (*Motor Cycle*'s John Nutting described the T160 tank as 'a work of art'). The new bike also borrowed Vetter's tilted instrument cluster. Indeed, Felix Kalinski saw Vetter's Bonneville TT's grab bar, seat, tank, instruments and headlight as design elements he dubbed the 'Vetter Top Line', which he felt Triumph should apply to the rest of its line. By extending the swinging arm an inch to make room for the bigger battery, installing shorter springs in the front forks to preserve the Trident's 58 inch wheelbase, and discarding the cover for the centrally-mounted oil tank, the T160 managed to look longer, lower, leaner and more purposeful, despite a kerb weight of 552lbs.

T160s began rolling off the production line in November 1974. Unveiled to the press in March 1975 at Ragley Hall in Warwickshire alongside the new electric-start Norton Commando, NVT earmarked the first batch of triples for export, with UK dealers receiving supplies in the summer. Price in the UK was £1,215. In America, the recommended retail price was $2,870. However, when the Government withdrew NVT's export credit guarantee, the company responded by flying sales director Mike Jackson to its American distribution centre in Duarte where he immediately began telephoning Norton and Triumph dealers across the US. By offering discounts on batches of 50 or more - sometimes for as low as $995 per machine - Jackson managed to shift 1,000 T160s in a week.

Press reception to the new triple was mixed. When *Cycle World* tested the T160 for its September '75 issue, they welcomed the return to classic Triumph styling (unflatteringly comparing the original 750 as looking like 'something out of a Buck Rogers serial'). They also praised the new bike's handling. It was, they felt, the Trident's most impressive quality, describing it as 'nothing short of fantastic'.

'Without a doubt,' they declaimed, 'the Three handles better than most, if not all, bikes on the road today.' No matter how hard the magazine pushed it, the frame showed no signs of flex. 'It's rock steady and confidence-inspiring.' They attributed some of that to the triple's forward-inclined cylinders, which placed more weight on the front wheel. But the Dunlop tyres also helped. 'These are some of the best tires we've ridden on, short of a racing tread.' The one fly in the ointment regarding the latest Trident's road-holding was a lack of ground clearance, which meant the bike ground its footrests and centre stand too easily. (Ironically, the T160's frame was based on the T150-derived chassis that Triumph's Experimental Department developed for the factory production racers - most famously, the TT-winning Trident, 'Slippery Sam' - whose raised engine rails increased ground clearance by $1^3/_8$ inches.)**

---

*   A 2.5 gallon tank (3 US gallons) was also available.

**   Slippery Sam got its name from the Trident that factory production-class racer Percy Tait and Steve Jolly took to fifth

Whilst *Cycle World* felt sure that the T160's powerplant would be 'the same bullet-proof unit found in previous Triples', the magazine was dismayed at its more sluggish performance. They blamed the new annular silencers, which created too much back pressure, resulting in an over-rich fuel mixture, causing 'unbearable vibration' and poor performance. Experiments leaning out the mixture helped, but testers determined that 'if the engine weren't choked up as much as it is and were allowed to breathe, quarter-mile times could be improved by a full second or better'.

Yet, despite the magazine's complaint that 'the '75 Trident is much slower and more sluggish than its predecessors' (covering as it did, a quarter mile in 13.954 seconds at 95.64mph), in truth the T160 wasn't too far off the T150 Trident *Cycle World* tested in October 1968. Seven years earlier, their T150 test bike recorded a 13.71 second standing quarter at a terminal speed of 98.46mph, and bettered the T160's top speed by more than 8mph (117.03 to the later bike's 109mph).

However, the new triple's drop in performance was more apparent if one compared *Cycle World*'s T160 with the T150 Tridents that rival magazine *Cycle* had run at Orange County International Raceway during the course of two separate superbike comparison tests. In 1970, a stock, but professionally-sorted Triumph 750 triple ran a 12.78 second standing quarter at 103.92mph. Two years later, a five-speed Trident achieved 12.718 seconds at 105mph - more than a second quicker and fully ten miles an hour faster than the 1975 bike.

In Britain, however, UK testers somehow managed to find a few more miles-an-hour from their T160 test bikes. During pre-launch testing on a wet MIRA test track, factory riders wrung a one-way best of 118mph from theirs; in a comparison test with the Trident's NVT stablemate, the Norton Commando Mk III, *Bike* magazine coaxed 126.05mph from their T160 triple.* A year later, *Motor Cycle* recorded a two-way mean of 119mph and a one-way best of 124.8mph. That, the magazine said, 'makes the Trident one of the fastest machines of 1976'.

---

place at the 1970 *Bol d'Or* 24-hour endurance event at Montlhéry near Paris (Paul Smart and Tom Dickie's Triumph triple came first, beating the factory-backed Honda 750 fours and the Italian Laverdas). Tait's bike became smothered in oil when the engine began to wet sump and spew oil, causing the bike to slip and slide all over the track. The pair, however, refused to retire because, as Tait explained to author Mick Duckworth, 'the French importer told us that if we finished in the first six, we'd get money. So we went out finished fifth!'

Tait thereafter referred to that bike as 'Slippery', which, together with Tait's nickname among his Meriden colleagues - 'Sam the Transport Man' - combined to give the Trident its famous sobriquet. The bike later won five successive Isle of Man production TTs. The first was in 1971 when Ray Pickrell averaged 100.07mph. In 1974, Sam - now with disc brakes for the first time, although standard equipment on the road bikes - was up against Z1s, Laverda Jotas, one-litre BMWs, and Peter Williams riding the Norton Commando. Even so, Mick Grant, riding a bike entered by dealers A. Bennett & Son, took the chequered flag to notch up Sam's fourth consecutive TT victory; the Yorkshireman receiving the John Hartle Challenge Trophy for the fastest lap: 22 minutes and 28.2 seconds at 100.74mph.

Sam's last TT win was in 1975 in the Island's first ten lap race. The campaign was backed by NVT boss, Dennis Poore, in return for which team manager Les Williams agreed to paint the Triumph in Norton's 1975 race livery of red, white and blue, the colours of team sponsor, John Player, the cigarette manufacturers. Slippery Sam may well have gone on to secure further wins, but rules limiting production machines to just five years deemed the bike obsolete.

*   Some years later, it was discovered that Triumph's experimental department had blueprinted the test bike's engine.

But UK magazines also uncovered problems. *Motor Cycle* reported oil leaks from the rev-counter drive and where the clutch cable entered the primary chaincase. Another magazine, *Motor Cycle Mechanics*, reported in their July 1975 review that the clutch on their test bike let go at the drag strip, that the bike vibrated (a lot), drank fuel and burned oil (due to defective piston rings, a problem known to the factory and one that wasn't confined to the press fleet, but shared by some early machines sold to the public). What went unreported was that one of *MCN*'s two test bikes leaked oil from porous engine castings, and suffered electrical failure as a result of a chafed wire and broke down. The bike had less than a thousand miles on the clock.

NVT built and sold around 7,000 T160s in 1975. However, by the end of the year the company was in receivership. In a desperate bid to raise cash, NVT offered unsold bikes - usually worth around £1,500 - at the knockdown price of £1,211 (including VAT). The very last Tridents produced at Small Heath were single-seat police bikes destined for Saudi Arabia. To meet the order, NVT Motorcycles had to purchase the machines back from NVT Manufacturing's receiver. The receiver, seeing a chance to generate cash for NVT's creditors, recalled any Tridents the company owned. 224 US spec bikes about to be shipped abroad were diverted back to the UK market. Another 288 UK spec bikes were returned from Australia. Five shipments totalling 450 Tridents went to the Middle East. 130 machines remained in storage in the Midlands. These were badged up as the Triumph Cardinal* and sold as well-equipped tourers for £1,522.80 each (including VAT plus £16.20 delivery). Each all-white machine came with £150-worth of accessories, including a tri-point motoplas screen, a set of Craven panniers, 7 inch Maserati air-horns, Britax crash bars and a pair of 5 inch spot lamps. Owners also got a six-month or 6,000 mile warranty on parts and labour.

In April the following year, Small Heath ceased production of the Trident. Dennis Poore suggested that Meriden take over development of the proposed 830cc triple following the closure of Kitts Green, and in May 1977, he instructed Alistair Cave to sell the jigs and tools and return the rights to the Triumph name and manufacturing rights for the Trident back to Meriden. However, the recently formed Triumph Co-operative elected instead to continue producing the Bonneville twin.

Despite the Trident's remarkable achievements, success and glory on the racetrack, and countless speed records, after just eight years in production, the world's first modern multi-cylinder superbike was no more.

---

*   The name Cardinal followed a faintly ecclesiastical theme set by Triumph's previous police bike. As *Bike* journalist Peter Watson said in his May '77 review of the T160: 'Someone at NVT recalled that they'd called the police-spec the TRP6 the Saint, so... why not the Cardinal. Geddit? No, neither did we.'

15

THE RE-5 NEARLY BANKRUPTS SUZUKI

THE HERCULES W2000, VAN VEEN OCR1000 AND NORTON ROTARIES HINT AT A WANKEL-ENGINED FUTURE

'The rotary is the thing'
(*Motor Cycle Mechanics* article from February 1973)

Felix Wankel

BIKE SALES SOAR AS FUEL PRICES DOUBLE

When NVT unveiled the T160 Trident and electric-start Norton Commando to the press and motor trade in 1975, the two machines entered the market at a particularly turbulent time. In August, inflation in Britain hit 26.9 per cent. Pay awards that year were running at 30 per cent, house prices had fallen 16 per cent, and unemployment climbed to one million for the first time since the Second World War. As Britain's Gross Domestic Product declined, Government expenditure rose, peaking in 1975 as a growing welfare state consumed almost half of UK GDP. (Despite implementing cuts to public spending, the Labour Government's beetle-browed Chancellor, Denis Healey, was forced a year later to ask the International Monetary Fund for a $3.9 billion loan, up till then the largest sum the IMF had ever dispensed.)

Meanwhile, events abroad hurt the economy still further as OPEC increased the price of crude another ten per cent, bringing the cost of a gallon of petrol in Britain to 75p. This was almost double its pre-1973 price when war in the Middle East and oil boycotts had resulted in a 500 per cent increase in the price of crude, adding an extra £2.5 billion a year to the cost of importing oil into Britain. Rising fuel prices, soaring motoring costs, expensive public transport riven by walkouts and lightning strikes, fuelled a boom in motorcycle sales as Britons sought a reliable and cheaper means of transport.

Two-wheeler mileage rates in 1975 rose by 22 per cent. Registrations of new motorcycles went up 40 per cent over the previous year. In October alone, dealers registered 25,386 new machines compared to 14,572 for the same month a year earlier. Total new bikes registered for the whole year came to a staggering 264,814 machines (of which 97 per cent were of foreign manufacture). Sales of motorcycles, excluding scooters and mopeds, rose by 126 per cent.

For around £130 less than the price of a brand new British Leyland Mini, commuters could swap four wheels for two and buy a Suzuki GT750M for £969. For a tenner more, they could own a Honda CB750. The Japanese-made middleweights offered riders even better value for money.

Released in early 1975 following its debut at Cologne Show the previous year, at a list price of £669, the new four-cylinder Honda CB400F cost nearly £300 less than its now ageing 750cc stablemate. Nor did owners choosing the 400F find that the 45 per cent smaller capacity (408cc to 736cc) meant near half the performance. On MIRA's 1,000 yard test strip, *Motor Cycle* recorded a two-way mean of more than 104mph. This compared to 113mph for the CB750 K2 that *Cycle Australia* tested in March 1975. The 400 was also lighter (395lbs with one gallon of fuel against 510lbs for a similarly laden CB750). Against the 750's increasingly dated styling, the smaller bike was ground-breaking: the Spartan simplicity of its lines and graphics; its compactness, which made the 400's handling and steering simply a revelation; and refined, turbine-smooth engine - 'as quiet as a car' - which was good for 37bhp and 55mpg.

Other middleweights on offer in '75 included the Yamaha RD350 two-cylinder two-stroke, the venerable Suzuki GT500 twin and the three-cylinder air-cooled GT380 and 550 two-strokes - with 'Ram Air Induction' - launched three years earlier alongside the company's flagship liquid-cooled GT750J. Kawasaki's mid-capacity contenders included the three-cylinder two-stroke KH400 and the sanitised (and now reasonably well-mannered) 500.

All of them were good for 100mph-plus and although *super* bikes, they were not *superbikes*. And in 1975, the superbike *par excellence* was still the Kawasaki 900 Z1. The third generation Super Four - now called the Z1B - had lost little of its original potency. But the bike dubbed King was now stalked by pretenders to his throne, each with designs on stealing his crown.

THE YAMAHA AND SUZUKI SEVEN-FIFTIES

Having whetted appetites at the 1971 Tokyo Show, Yamaha disappointed many when they later demurred from putting into production their GL750. A liquid-cooled, fuel-injected two-stroke four-cylinder tourer, the GL show bike, resplendent in Metal Flake-painted tank and side panels, chrome fenders and white quilted dual seat, was a road-going version of the factory's all-conquering racer, the TZ700. However, increasingly restrictive emission regulations, oil-price shocks and rising fuel costs contributed to the GL being stillborn. Following Yamaha's cessation of production of its short-lived TX750 twin[*] in 1974 (cycle parts of which featured on the GL750), and until the newly-unveiled 750cc three-cylinder shaft-driven sports-tourer was available for sale in showrooms in late 1976, Yamaha's largest capacity motorcycle for 1975 remained its six-year-old 650cc vertical four-stroke twin. Released in 1969 as the XS-1, the 'Japanese Bonneville' went on sale in the UK for the first time in 1975, having by then reached its fourth incarnation: XS-1, XS-2, models A and B (and, briefly, a flirtation with the prefix 'TX' in the US during the Omni-Phase 750's short production life).

Suzuki's biggest bike was still its two-stroke three-cylinder GT750. The bike made its debut at the Tokyo Motor Show in November 1970 and was first glimpsed on British shores when it arrived by airplane from Europe on Christmas Day for its UK unveiling at the London Olympia Show. In 1975, three years after the GT eventually went on sale in Britain, the company released the M model, following the launch in autumn 1974 of its touring-oriented, rotary-engined RE-5. The factory decided to refocus the triple and engineered it to make the fourth-generation *Gran Turismo* into a more serious sports-tourer. Applying what Hamamatsu had learned campaigning its world-beating TR750 racing triple, the new road bike put out 70bhp, up 3bhp on the earlier J, K and L models.

When *Motorcycle Mechanics* tested the 750M in October, they noted that Suzuki had tamed (but not entirely eliminated) the feeling that previous bikes had 'a flexible coupling between the front and rear wheels'. They noted, too, its improved in-town, low-speed handling. Testers were also impressed by the triple's broad-power band (especially when

---

[*]   Yamaha announced the TX750 in 1972. A 360 degree, air-cooled, single-overhead cam, twin-cylinder tourer producing 65bhp at 6,500rpm, it weighed 518 lb and was capable of 110mph. To temper the bane of all big bore parallel twins - vibration - such units move with the centrifugal forces generated by the rise and fall of two large pistons, irrespective of how engineers may phase the crankshaft, the TX's engine had two balancers: one to counter the primary imbalances of the pistons; and a second balancer to counter the rocking coupling of the first. 'The result is smoothness beyond belief,' claimed *Cycle World* in their October 1972 report on the TX. The magazine's testers claimed: 'Shut your eyes and you are on a four. It couldn't be a twin.'

Riders were more ambivalent about the TX's on-board diagnostic system. This featured a set of warning lights housed between the speedo and tacho. Red lights flashed to warn riders if the bike's brake linings had worn below 2mm. They also glowed every time the brake warning light came on, and flickered insanely should the brake light bulb or rear lamp burn out.

A handsome bike, if a little gaudy in its Metal Flake Gold (and later, Burgundy Wine Flake), early TXs were plagued with problems due to the dry-sump engine's two counter-rotating 'Omni-Phase' balancers frothing and aerating the engine oil at high rpm and starving the roller-bearing crankshaft of lubricant. In addition, the balance chain could stretch, causing rough running as the counterweights went out of phase. Yamaha cured both problems on later models by fitting a deeper sump and an adjustable balance chain, but by then it was too late: whilst Yamaha could fix the TX mechanically, they could do little to repair the damage to its reputation, and after just two seasons, the factory withdrew the model from sale in 1974.

compared to the Kawasaki 750/3); the Suzuki's turbine-smooth delivery; and described the twin front discs as 'superb'.

Although the new bike received good press, it was the race version of Suzuki's triple that generated the biggest headlines following an incident at that year's Daytona 200.

In March 1975, Thames Television was in Florida filming a documentary about the 1973 FIM Formula F750 World Champion, Barry Sheene. During pre-race practise on Daytona's twin-banked ultra-high speed circuit - a track notoriously hard on tyres - Sheene's blue and white Seeley-framed TR750, sporting his trademark Number 7, suffered a catastrophic rear-tyre blow out as he entered the straight at 178mph.* The bike lurched sideways, Sheene tried to control it by turning into the slide, but the bike high sided, spat him off, and threw him 275 yards down the track. He sustained massive injuries, including six broken ribs, wrist, right forearm and right collarbone, as well as crushed vertebrae. To repair his shattered left thigh bone, surgeons inserted an 18 inch steel rod (which doctors described in a film taken of the operation as a 'nail'). Sheene suffered such extensive loss of skin that it threatened his kidneys. As a grim memento of the crash, Sheene later hung the remnants of his tattered racing leathers on his wall at home. Incredibly, the 24-year-old was back on a bike competing at Cadwell Park just seven weeks later, and would go on to score wins at that year's Dutch and Swedish GPs.

The publicity that followed Sheene's crash at Daytona made the indefatigable Cockney the sport's first media superstar. He modelled underwear for the *Sun* newspaper; advertised Brut aftershave with boxing champion, Henry Cooper; appeared in road safety adverts; courted and later married the Old Spice model, Stephanie McLean; pioneered body-protectors; won back-to-back 500cc World Championships in '76** and '77; appeared on *This Is Your Life* with Eamonn Andrews; and in 1977 was awarded the MBE. He was a tactical rider who understood the benefits of close racing to please the crowds, sometimes livening up a dull race by reining in his lead if he was too far out in front. Although not always popular with race-goers because of his uncompromising stance over track safety, Sheene probably did more to popularise motorcycling in Britain than any other rider at the time.

On sale alongside the GT750 was the RE-5, a bike about which company president Jitsujiro Suzuki said at the 1974 Tokyo Show: 'We see the rotary as the beginning of a new age in the history of two-wheel touring... it sets new performance standards in touring smoothness and comfort.'

The Suzuki president wasn't alone in thinking this. In a February 1973 article for the UK's *Motor Cycle Mechanics*, Alan Baker (BSc[Eng]) wrote: 'Within only a few years... no keen motorcyclist will buy a machine with a reciprocating power unit, the rotary will be the thing.'

---

*   Reports vary as to whether the bike on which Sheene had his accident was the three-cylinder TR750 or square four RG500. I have referenced UK weekly *MCN*'s report dated Wednesday 5 March 1975, published two days after the event, which states the machine was a '750cc Suzuki'; as does motorcycle historian Mick Walker's book, *Suzuki Production Motorcycles 1952-1980*.

**   For the first and only time, Britain could boast that it in 1976 it had the reigning world champions on both two and four-wheels in Barry Sheene and James Hunt - 500cc motorcycle and Formula One driver's champions respectively.

The RE-5 was not the first rotary-powered motorcycle. Indeed, Suzuki was not even the first of the Big Four Japanese manufacturers to produce one. Kawasaki also had a rotary under development. Codenamed the X99, engineers got as far as a working prototype comprising a water-cooled engine installed in a chassis using Z1 running gear. In 1972, Yamaha exhibited at that year's Tokyo Show the RZ201CCR, a 660cc liquid-cooled twin-rotor Wankel. With its black, white-pinstriped fuel tank, chromed side-panels, air-box and radiator, tan-coloured dual seat, twin front disc brakes, high bars and massive engine with large polished covers, the RZ201 was certainly eye-catching. However, Yamaha never put the bike into production.

Before long, Suzuki probably wished they had done likewise with the RE-5.

THE ROTARY: POWERPLANT OF THE FUTURE

First patented in 1929 by Felix Wankel, the German engineer had conceived his alternative to the piston-driven internal combustion engine a decade earlier when he was just 17-years-old. During the war, he worked on rotary disc valves for the engines powering the German navy's torpedoes. In 1951, Wankel went into partnership with the German car maker and motorcycle manufacturer NSU* Motorenwerke AG - originally to collaborate with the company's research chief Dr Walter Froede to develop rotary valves for their two-stroke engines - but very soon, on what would become the rotary engine. NSU was one of the world's largest (and oldest) motorcycle manufacturers. Their bikes had a reputation for high-quality construction and advanced designs (the 1952 NSU 250cc single-cylinder Supermax featured an overhead camshaft, leading link forks and pressed-steel frame, with racing versions winning the 250cc World Championship in 1954 and '55).

Wankel's engine - dubbed *Drehkolbenmotor* or DKM - consisted of a triangular-shaped rotor with convex sides. The rotor was sealed at its apexes, corners and at both ends, and rotated inside a peanut-shaped chamber within a housing circling in the same direction as the rotor, but at a different speed. By 1957, Froede and his colleagues had a 125cc-chambered prototype of Wankel's DKM engine up and running and generating 29bhp at 17,000rpm.

Whilst Wankel's arrangement for sealing the rotor undoubtedly worked, the DKM engine's rotating housing made it impractical. NSU therefore developed the *Kreiskolbenmotor* (KKM). In the KKM, the housing remained static, and it was this version of the rotary engine that NSU promoted as the Wankel. Yet whilst it made its namesake wealthy, Dr Felix Wankel was not himself fully persuaded of the KKM engine's advantages.

The automotive industry, however, was attracted to the rotary; a power unit that, although operating on the four-stroke cycle of induction, compression, combustion and

---

* The initials NSU stood for *Neckarsulm Strickmacschinen Union*: Neckarsulm being the town where the company began its initial business of making knitting machines. They later branched out into producing bicycles, before making their first motorcycle in 1901 by installing a Swiss-made 1.5hp Zedel engine into a standard bicycle frame. By 1903, NSU were manufacturing their own single-cylinder and V-twin engines.

exhaust, was simpler than a conventional four-stroke motor (dispensing as it did with pistons, valves and springs, connecting rods, camshafts, and pushrods). NSU made a succession of lucrative agreements licensing the technology to other manufacturers, including Ford, General Motors, Citroën, Curtiss-Wright, Daimler-Benz, Fichtel and Sachs, and Mazda in Japan.

In late 1959, NSU were compelled to release details of the Wankel engine's current state of development following the recently-appointed American licensee, Curtiss-Wright, announcing details of *'their'* revolutionary new engine. This prompted the press to speculate that NSU would have an air-cooled Wankel-engined motorcycle available by 1962. Moreover, after an expensive foray into small-car manufacturing with its rear-engined Prinz, NSU really needed to maximise its returns on their investment in the Wankel, as they ceased manufacturing scooters and motorcycles in 1963 to focus on expanding car production following the post-war boom in automotive ownership.

At the Frankfurt Motor Show in September that year, NSU launched the first Wankel-engined car. Fitted with the KKM unit, the Spider was an open-topped version of the Prinz, but the Spider proved both costly and unreliable. The single rotor, water-cooled engine suffered ignition problems, overheating, and rotor failure as the metallised carbon seals broke up.

NSU changed the materials it used to seal the twin rotors on the Ro80 they launched five years later - from carbon to cast iron alloy. They also switched the housing's working surface from hard chrome plating to a nickel and silicon carbide deposit. The seals, however, continued to fail, as did the rotor bearings, which were prone to seizure; and fuel consumption could dip to as low as 10mpg. To make matters worse, in 1968 the German press published a survey of Ro80 owners. The report revealed that 75 per cent of the 191 respondents had had their engines replaced under warranty.

For many engineers, NSU's travails were analogous to the pioneering days of the early reciprocating combustion engine. Despite these setbacks, motorcycle manufacturers saw that they had much to gain from a motor that could be lighter, more compact and smoother running than the up-and-down motion of a piston engine. A rotary motor has a longer power 'stroke' (270 degrees of shaft rotation compared to a reciprocating engine's 180 degrees). Rotary motors have flatter torque curves. They have fewer parts than a piston engine. With no reciprocating parts, there are none of the out-of-balance forces that produce vibration. And, moreover, their rotating parts can be dynamically balanced. MZ, Van Veen, Hercules in Germany (sold in the UK under the brand name 'DKW'), the four Japanese marques, and BSA/Triumph in Great Britain, all obtained licences to develop a rotary-powered engine.

In 1960, German supplier Fichtel and Sachs took out a licence with NSU to manufacture the Wankel engine's specialist components and develop a fan-cooled single rotor unit for generators and snowmobiles. To offset the high cost of their licence - which escalated in price according to power output, not engine capacity - the Nürnberg-based factory were keen to build and supply to other motorcycle manufacturers complete engines. In 1970, they displayed the DKW/Hercules W2000 at that year's Cologne Show. Based on Sach's largest rotary motor (the single rotor 294cc unit), the Hercules' engine was mated to the transmission from a BMW R27 in a chassis in which the motor acted as a stressed member.

More than a year earlier, in June 1969, the BSA/Triumph group took up an offer from NSU to purchase a licence from them for £129,000 to manufacture and develop a rotary engine capable of between 35-60bhp, performance levels the British combine knew Fichtel and Sach's licence with NSU did not cover. (It helped the cash-strapped BSA that a very large British manufacturer had volunteered to pay the high costs of developing a Wankel motor!)

In 1972, under a licence to Wankel which cost them £180,000, Yamaha caused a sensation at the Tokyo Show when they unveiled their twin-rotor 660cc RZ201. Like the Sachs' units, the RZ passed the fuel charge through its rotors to keep them cool. Unlike the air-cooled Sachs, however, the Yamaha's housing was liquid cooled.

Suzuki Build A Rotary

In the meantime, Suzuki had already started its research and development on the rotary, beginning in the mid-Sixties. In early 1970, they took out a licence with NSU, and by late 1971, *Cycle World*'s Jack Yamaguchi reported in his column 'Reports from Japan' that work on a rotary-engined prototype was progressing well, Hamamatsu having despatched four development engineers to West Germany in February to 'obtain the necessary know-hows'.

Suzuki's engineers, applying what they learned in Germany, developed a water-cooled unit with - according to reporter, Jack Yamaguchi - a 'Twin tandem rotor engine with a chamber capacity of 500cc (equivalent to a 1000cc normal piston engine). I gather,' revealed Yamaguchi, 'Suzuki is aiming at January 1972 for its release of the first Suzuki Wankel cycle'.

In fact, the RE-5 had just a single, three-vane rotor, and it missed its rumoured release date by almost three years.

In charge of the RE-5 project team was Shigeyusa Kamiya. As official 'Head of Suzuki's Rotary Division', he was responsible for both engine development and selecting basic chassis components. Under Kamiya's direction, engineers developed a rotor whose three apexes each featured a centre seal flanked by two smaller, spring-loaded outer seals. The rotor tips were lubricated by a two-stroke-style injector pump from oil supplied by an underseat plastic tank (which a doubled as a rear-drive chain oiler). A rotary oil pump driven off the contact-breaker shaft delivered lubricant at pressures of around 100psi to the engine and the rotor's internals, the cooling oil helping draw away excessive heat.

Between Suzuki signing the licence agreement with NSU and RE-5s rolling off the Hamamatsu production line five years later, Kamiya's project team worked hard to develop solutions to the technical problems that had dogged NSU's Ro80 rotary-engined automobile. Key amongst their challenges was sealing.

The team eventually overcame seal wear using CEM (Composite Electro-chemical Material), a plating process comprising a revolutionary, diamond-hard, corrosion-resistant nickel-silicon carbide on the rotor's apexes; and Ferro-Tic for the apexes' seals (a material combining sintered ferrous alloy with titanium carbide whose key property is that its wear-rate is twelve times better than cast-iron). The team even developed its own manufacturing and surface-plating technology in order to produce the accurate and durable surface necessary for the inner face of the rotor housing.

A substantial amount of the team's research and development work was spent overcoming both the considerable heat generated by a rotary engine (a rotary's combustion chamber has a large surface area relative to its volume, which draws heat very quickly from the fuel and air mixture) and the stark contrasts in temperature between the intake and exhaust ports. Unlike a conventional four-stroke engine, the induction and exhaust ports are separated in a rotary engine, creating massive heat differentials between the cooler inlet and the hot outlet sides.

Kamiya's team developed an array of solutions. These included a cooling system that warmed the induction area by transferring the heat of the combustion process over from the exhaust side, and fitting a finned exhaust manifold and double-walled twin exhaust downpipes, the interiors of which were made of stainless steel. Each header featured a Ram Air duct at the front to draw in cool air, remove heat and reduce noise.

In order to avoid uneven distribution of heat distorting the rotor housing as a result of the combustion chamber's long narrow shape, the large water jacket surrounding the housing incorporated deflectors to direct coolant from the chamber's hotter areas toward its cooler ones. To temper the hot-running rotor, oil was forced through at high pressure, then directed to the sump before being pumped through an oil cooler and re-circulated back to lubricate the rotor's bearings and on again through the rotor. The RE-5's water-cooling system shared many of the components Suzuki fitted to the three-cylinder GT750. However, whereas the two-stroke's electric fan was largely redundant, the rotary's - primed to cut in above 106°C and cut out below 100°C - was absolutely vital.

In all, the RE-5's lubricating and cooling systems boasted three oil supplies (one to lubricate the rotor tips, the supply tank for which also metered oil to the final-drive chain; another to cool the rotor, its bearings and the rest of the engine; and a third for the GT750-sourced five-speed gearbox); an oil cooler; an electric-thermostatically-controlled fan; water cooling; and twin double-skinned exhaust headers with air ducts.

Ignition and carburetion were no less complex.

The RE-5's ignition was provided by Capacitor Discharge Ignition (CDI), described by Suzuki in its promotional literature as the 'finest ignition system for large touring machines', benefits of which included 'a very hot spark, reducing plug deposits and extending plug life'. The spark plug itself was tipped with platinum. To ensure a smooth transition from high to low-speed running, the RE-5 had two sets of contact breakers. The main contact breaker circuit was opened and closed by dual lobes. This meant that instead of every rotor face receiving a spark, only alternate rotor faces did so. To overcome the high engine-braking forces generated by the rotary on a closed throttle, the second set of breakers, operating off a single-lobe, came into play when a vacuum sensor detected that the rider had rolled off the accelerator.

Fuelling was delivered via a single, two-stage twin barrel vacuum-operated constant-velocity Mikuni carburettor. It weighed 5lbs, featured 10 different jets, 15 air-bleed systems, two chokes (18 and 32mm), and required five control cables to operate its two small primary ports (for slow-speed running), large single port (for high-speed motoring), and CCI-style system for lubricating the rotor tip seals.

The results of all this complexity would prove decidedly mixed.

THE DKW AND VAN-VEEN ROTARIES

In September 1974, the RE-5 made its public debut at the International Show in Cologne (importers from across the world had enjoyed previews of the new bike during visits to Suzuki during the summer to learn about the anticipated 'Rotary Revolution'). Also making their debuts at the show that year were Honda's revolutionary one litre flat-four sports-tourer, the GL1000 Gold Wing, and two other Wankel-powered motorcycles: Germany's own Hercules/DKW W2000 (now available for sale to the public following its appearance as a prototype at the Cologne Show four years earlier to promote Sachs' rotary engine to manufacturers for use as a proprietary motor) and, from Holland, Van Veen's OCR 1000.

Unlike the RE-5's clean-sheet-design, never-before seen powerplant, both of the European motorcycles could demonstrate a degree of provenance. Hercules' fan-cooled Fitchel Sachs unit had seen several years' service powering snowmobiles and various 'specials' like the British 300cc air-cooled single rotor Roto Gannet or the French Advancer. Since unveiling the prototype W2000 at Cologne in 1970, Hercules had made a batch of fifty units for testing. In 1974, having by then replaced the prototype's BMW chassis and shaft drive with their own duplex frame, Hercules became the first manufacturer to put a Wankel-powered motorcycle into production.

The OCR 1000 was the brainchild of Dutch entrepreneur, Henk Van Veen. Importer of Kreidler mopeds and Johnson outboard motors, both lucrative enterprises for him in his native Holland, Van Veen decided in 1971 to build the world's most exclusive motorcycle. Unveiled to the press three years later, his first prototype utilised the Mazda rotary engine housed in the frame of a Moto Guzzi 850. Intended to be available in kit form, it was, according to *Classic Bike Guide*'s Dirk Melkebeek, 'downright ugly'.

The man responsible for Kreidler's racing frames, Jaap Voskamp, designed a new frame, development work on which was carried out by Joep Brokemans. Front and rear suspension units were developed by Koni to Van Veen's design. German car maker Porche designed the rotary's four-speed transmission. The sports car company also tested the motorcycle's shaft drive system, which had been developed by the factory at Duderstadt in West Germany contracted to build the complete machine to the Dutch company's specification.

Featuring twin oil-cooled rotors (hence, OCR), the liquid-cooled engine was the result of a joint venture between NSU and the Citroën-owned subsidiary, Comotor, and had seen service in the German car maker's Ro80 and the French company's Birotor GS. With two chambers each displacing 498cc (giving the engine a total volume of 996cc), the Van Veen developed 98.5ft-lbs between 3,500-5,000rpm and 100bhp at 6,000rpm (60 of those horses generated at just 3,000rpm). Moreover, the factory claimed that with modifications to the engine's peripheral ports and by swapping the stock 32mm Solex carburettor for a twin-choke Weber, the unit was capable of 150bhp.

Former 50cc GP racer Jos Schurgers was responsible for the Van Veen's styling. Its combination of green and black-panelled bodywork, and simple, low-key graphics managed to make the OCR 1000 appear both substantial yet elegant; whilst the strategically-blacked out components, and kohl-black downpipes and silencers, conspired to disguise the machine's considerable 562lbs bulk (644lbs fully laden).

The Van Veen's equipment levels also impressed (as well they might given its cost: £5,500 - twice the price of the next most expensive motorcycle available at the time). The OCR's spec sheet included: electronic ignition; electric fuel pump; dual front and single rear hydraulically-operated disc brakes; hydraulic clutch; stainless steel exhausts; light alloy rear swinging arm; Cardan shaft drive with CV joints; Koni gas-damped hydraulic front and rear suspension; alloy wheels with V-rated Pirelli 18 inch endurance-racing tyres front and back. An optional extra included a Schurgers-designed full fairing.

However, despite its ultra-smooth motor, a top speed of 224kph (139mph), acceleration of 0-100kph (62.14mph) in 3.6 seconds and 200kph (124.28mph) in around 16 seconds, the OCR's 19-28mpg fuel consumption meant that, even if ridden carefully, the bike's 4.75 gallon fuel tank restricted range to just 130 miles, seriously hampering its long-distance touring capability. By the time the OCR 1000 finally went on sale in 1976, the impact of the oil crisis, crippling development costs, and Citroën and NSU's buy-outs by Peugeot and Audi respectively, forced the two car makers to abandon the Wankel engine after building only 50 Comotor engines.

Out of a planned production run of 2,000 sold units in the second year, Van Veen built just 38 complete machines, retail prices for which rocketed from £5,500 to £7,000 in the space of a year.*

---

* Nearly forty years after the last OCR 1000 rolled off the line in Duderstadt, Germany, Dutchman Ger Van Rootselaar, a rotary-engine aficionado, who had negotiated a deal to buy the Van Veen factory's remaining stock, unveiled plans to produce a batch of ten more bikes in 2010. Rootselaar and Citroën enthusiast Andries Wielinga, and Wielinga's friend Dirk Knip as head of the new company's public relations, in partnership with the Dutch frame maker Nico Bakker, built ten OCR 1000s from Rootselaar's stock of unused Comotor engines. Each bike was built to be as original as possible, but with some sensible upgrades to components such as tyres - Michelin Macadams in place of the original machine's Pirellis. Rootselaar's team also developed new rotor seals and refinished all engine component faces to prevent even the smallest oil leak. The post-Millennium OCRs retailed at €85,000, excluding VAT (over £75,000).

Rotaries From East And West Go Head To Head

A few weeks after the RE-5's appearance at the Cologne Show in September, 24 motorcycle journalists gathered in Los Angeles on 1 October 1974 to take part in the press launch in America of the RE-5. In a six-day road-trip designed to showcase the new bike's role as a long-distance tourer, Suzuki provided half-a-dozen machines for the journalists to take on a journey from California to Arizona, run in relays of 250 miles. Starting in the US's second largest city, Los Angeles, the group headed out to Phoenix nearly 400 miles away. After arriving at the Arizona state capital, the riders turned the bikes round and lit off back to the Pacific coast and the Californian city of angels, a Cessna Citation jet-plane on hand to shuttle them back and forth.

All six bikes survived the trip intact, without any breakdowns. Journalists were impressed by 'the first practical new power concept in ninety years', with *Motorcyclist*'s Bob Greene praising the RE-5's 'butter-soft' engine impulses and the Suzuki's exhaust note, which he was pleased to learn sounded more like a motorboat than a two-stroke (or worse still, an electric motor). It all seemed to augur well for the rotary's future.

In February 1975, the UK's *Bike* magazine published the world's first comparison test of rotary-engined motorcycles. A few months earlier, Sachs-DKW (UK) Ltd's sales manager Dennis 'Doc' Johnson and public relations officer Peter Grove had phoned the magazine's offices to invite them to visit the factory in Germany and ride home one of the first three W2000s headed for Britain. With the launch of three rotary-powered motorcycles at Cologne in the autumn, the magazine sensed a story.

A phone call to Suzuki elicited their help in bagging an RE-5 to take part in the test, only for *Bike* to be told later that it would not now be available until mid-December - past the magazine's deadline for the February edition's colour pages, and just when the copy for the issue was due to go the printers. 'Suzuki were most co-operative, however,' recalled *Bike*'s assistant editor Bill Haylock, 'and let us have a bike to photograph before the test, although the machine was a non-runner which meant static shots only.'

The magazine then phoned Norton.

Probably more hopeful than expectant, *Bike* asked if they could 'have a brief spin' on the British Wankel-powered prototype, explaining that they were not intending to compare it directly with the W2000 or RE-5. Norton stunned the magazine by telling them that they could, if they wished, borrow the bike for a weekend.

'We'd got all the machinery lined up, all brand spanking new, and promising to be very different to anything we'd ridden before,' recounted Haylock. 'Of course, there was no telling what disasters might occur in Germany...'

After a long journey across Europe in a Transit minibus and an equally long evening taking in the delights of night-time Nuremberg, Haylock, John Robinson from *Motorcycle Mechanics* and *Motor Cycle*'s Stewart Boroughs, as well as photographer Frank Reynolds, the Doc and Peter Grove, following a restorative breakfast of strong black coffee, emerged the next morning - 'blinking in the daylight' - to visit the Nuremburger Hercules Werke factory where the W2000 was built. At the time of *Bike*'s visit, DKW was building

W2000s on a temporary assembly line set up in a corner of the plant whilst a new factory was under construction in readiness for volume production later that year.

The factory already produced a quarter of a million bicycles and 100,000 mopeds and 50cc motorcycles a year; but as Hercules technical director Herr Rudolph Brunner explained, Hercules - Germany's largest and the continent's oldest two-wheeler manufacturer - had ambitions to make inroads into the big bike market.

During their tour of the factory, the British journalists witnessed components being 'stamped, ground and welded', and were impressed by the quality of the work, especially the electric welding, which was done by hand. Even in their unpainted state, Haylock thought the frames 'looked really neat'.

The British visitors learned from Herr Brunner that the Sachs factory at Schweinfurt supplied the W2000's engine, and that DKW/Hercules was so confident of its long-term reliability that their promotional material for the American market asserted that it was good for 100,000 kilometres (approximately 62,000 miles).

The journalists' first ride aboard the W2000 took place in the factory yard, where the very first blip of the throttle proved an 'instant revelation'. The engine's smoothness was simply remarkable. But the complete absence of vibration made observing the factory's warning not to exceed 5,000rpm for the first few hundred miles very difficult and testers had to keep a careful eye on the Hercules' electronic rev counter. Haylock noted that with the engine's axis of rotation being in line with the motorcycle's direction of travel, the W2000 generated a torque effect similar to a BMW, although much less pronounced; that engine tick-over was fast and uneven; finding neutral was near impossible with the engine running; and the motor's hollow cases caused metallic ringing, although the rotary was still less noisy than 'the jangling of most two-strokes'. He admitted, however, that he was surprised by the sound emitted by the W2000's twin megaphones. Whereas he was expecting a 'whining scream' to emanate from a motor he described as looking like something from *Star Trek*, Haylock was momentarily stunned by the exhaust's 'deep, crisp bellow... more pleasant than any two-stroke, but at the same time not really like a four stroke'.

After their tour of the factory and their first acquaintance with the W2000, Hercules laid on a meal in the evening at a restaurant overlooking the prettiest and oldest parts of Nuremberg. As the British contingent dined, their Bavarian hosts insisted they sample one of the city's very special brews - a smoked beer matured in oak casks whose insides have first been charred.

Not surprisingly, given the night's reveries, the group were decidedly unenthusiastic when they embarked on their 400 mile ride from Nuremberg to Hamburg early the next morning.

Heading north along the autobahn at an indicated 80mph (a true speed of around 72mph) with the engine turning a steady 5,000 revs, Haylock's bike performed flawlessly. But the two rotaries ridden by *Motorcycle Mechanics* writer John Robinson and *Motor Cycle*'s Stewart Boroughs suffered occasional and inexplicable losses of power, and both fell behind, their bikes struggling up hills as their still-tight motors overheated. Then, one hundred miles or so out of Nuremberg, Boroughs' bike snapped its chain, which jammed itself between the gearbox sprocket and the W2000's clutch actuating lever.[*] With no Allen key included in the bike's miserly toolkit, Boroughs was unable to remove the side casing, and the bike had to be towed to a garage where the attendant loaned the journalists the Allen key they needed to extract the casing's fasteners. Fortunately, the box of spares the factory had provided included a spare chain.

It was now three o'clock in the afternoon. The three journalists had expected that by that time they would have been booking themselves in to their hotel in Hamburg. Instead, the delay meant they were still more than halfway from their destination - and just to add to their woes, the light of the winter's day was fading. Thankfully, the headlight DKW fitted to the W2000 included a very effective Bosch quartz-halogen 60 watt main beam, which illuminated the otherwise dark and unfamiliar roads of a foreign country quite brilliantly.

They finally arrived in Hamburg at around eight in the evening, too tired to do anything but retire early after the interminable boredom of a 400 mile straight-line slog along German Autobahns.

The Thursday morning broke cold and grey on the dank and miserable cobbled streets of the Reeperbahn. 'Hearing the disgruntled grumblings over the breakfast table about getting stung for seven quid a drink, and live sex shows that turned out to be flaccid fiascos,' reported Haylock, 'I was glad I'd had an early night.'

What remained of the morning was spent riding around a traffic-clogged Hamburg attempting to take action shots of the W2000. Then it was on board the ferry for the 20 hour journey home.

Once back in England, and away from the tediously straight German autobahns, a patch of good weather allowed Haylock to finally explore the W2000's handling. In his estimation, the machine's large-diameter spine-tube frame, duplex upper and lower rails (under which was slung the Wankel 'power pod'), Ceriani suspension, Metzeler tyres, and the bike's lack of bulk, combined to make the DKW 'one of the most faultless handling bikes I've ridden, on all road surfaces'.

It wasn't, however, without its peculiarities. The DKW's hard cornering capability was limited only by - on left handers - the centre stand, and on right handers, the silencer and footrest. Finding neutral amongst the W2000's six gears remained just as elusive in Blighty as it had back in DKW's factory yard; the bike's long gear selector required the rider to let it return to the central position after each shift (something Haylock confessed someone with a more delicate touch than he might not actually deem a problem - alternatively, they could just reposition the W2000's adjustable footrests).

The single 300mm chromed cast iron brake disc and Italian-made Grimeca calliper up front did a superb job of retarding the bike, whose top speed the magazine had clocked

---

[*]   Hercules replaced the exhibition bike's BMW gearbox with a six-speed unit and a final chain drive lifted off a Penton 400 dirt bike.

at 96mph, three miles an hour up on the maker's claimed maximum speed. From a standing start, the 294cc W2000 ran the quarter-mile in 16.25 seconds, and 0 to 60mph in just under seven-and-a-half seconds. But although the similarly-sized Yamaha RD250 could run the quarter in 15.90 seconds, *Bike* considered straight comparisons on cubic capacity meaningless. For Haylock, the more appropriate yardstick by which to judge the W2000 was probably the BMW R60/6. And against its southern Bavarian rival, he felt the DKW could more than compete - not just on performance, but comfort and quality also. Indeed, as the *Bike* scribe noted in his test report: 'Those neat cast alloy indicators even have BMW stamped on the lens!' From its electronic tachometer (when most manufacturers fitted mechanically-driven rev counters), through to DKW's extensive fitment of Allen screws; from the quartz-halogen headlamp to the luggage rack; the build quality and the evident craftsmanship, even if one discounted the novelty of its unconventional powerplant, the W2000 was, in Haylock's opinion: 'an outstanding machine in its own right'.

He just didn't like its styling.

Nice Clothes, Shame About The Engine

At £1,195, the Suzuki RE-5 cost £278 more than the DKW rotary, and £313 more than its three-cylinder stablemate, the GT750. Bill Haylock acknowledged that the RE-5 was smoother than its two-stroke sibling, but questioned if it was £300 smoother.

He was, however, unequivocal on other matters. He hated the RE-5 engine's looks. 'It's an untidy mess,' he wrote, comparing it to 'those Hillman Imp-engined bodge ups.' He also voiced his unease at Suzuki's interpretation of the rotary-engine concept. Haylock acknowledged that the RE-5 was certainly an 'incredible machine', but with two ignition systems, two cooling systems, two lubrication systems, and a two-staged twin-choke carburettor, the Wankel engine's advantages of simplicity and lightness had been lost in a 'maze of plumbing'; the motor 'buried under a mass of appendages'. In trying to produce the best Wankel-engined motorcycle, Haylock denigrated the RE-5 as an example of 'status technology'.

He continued in this splenetic vein, pouring scorn on some of the Suzuki's more contrived styling licks, such as the tubular instrument binnacle. Adopting mock marketing-speak to deride Suzuki's own sales materials, Haylock imagined a conversation between a potential buyer and fictitious salesman: 'That "strange bit of green plastic", as you describe it sir, is the instrument panel cowl. What's it for? Well, er, you'll notice sir, how the combination of spherical and straight line design elements conveys a forceful impression of smoothness and speed...'

Yet later, Haylock confessed to thinking the styling 'pretty neat', and the dark blue, silver-flecked paintwork superb - 'but, God,' bewailed the writer, 'that engine's a hideous lump'.

After collecting the bike from Suzuki GB's Croydon headquarters, and acclimatising himself to its considerable weight, he praised the ride, comparing it to the GT750 with which the RE-5 shared its front suspension and twin disc brakes ('one of the best brakes you'll find on a stock bike - fantastically powerful'). The RE-5's transmission also reminded him of the 750: clunky when shifting between the widely-spaced first and second gears, 'but nice 'n' smooth through the rest'.

On light throttle openings and with the engine running on just the primary choke, the motor felt very tame, even woolly, without the low-speed snatch of Suzuki's 750 flagship; and despite the RE-5 feeling six-feet wide when snaking through the centre of the South Circular traffic, it acquitted itself far better than Haylock had anticipated - although, unless the final drive chain was set up really tight, the combination of the heavy-duty chain and small engine sprocket created a 'bloody awful clattering' at certain speeds. 'It's annoying,' Haylock lamented, 'because the Wankel's smoothness emphasises any roughness in the transmission.'

And that smoothness was at its most turbine-like holding the throttle above 4,000 rpm (following a trace of vibration felt as a buzz through the footrests from 3,500 revs). It was apparent, too, when shutting off the throttle.

Haylock attributed the Suzuki's 'perceptibly smoother and more powerful engine deceleration than the DKW' to the RE-5's two-lobe contact breakers. (John Nutting reported that when *Motor Cycle* tested the RE-5 that: 'Until the ignition cut in a fraction of a second after shutting the throttle, quite considerable engine braking effect showed, sometimes with a discernible squeal from the tyre in low gears.' However, he then added, 'But then there came a deathly silence when the engine ran on without any braking effect at all.')

Heading north to Snowdonia for a weekend building stone walls, once Haylock had left the M1 at the M6 junction to pick up the A5 for North Wales, and with the traffic finally thinning out, the RE-5's weight began to work in its favour. Cruising at 80mph revealed the RE-5's strengths: its comfort; and its excellent straight-line stability at high-speeds as a result of the Suzuki's 61 inch long wheelbase.

Switching on the Suzuki's lights as the winter sun faded showed its headlamp to be 'good by normal bike standards'. It didn't, however, match the brilliance of the DKW's halogen lamp. The RE-5's cylindrical rear light, unusually for a Japanese bike, Haylock pointed out, developed an electrical fault and failed halfway through the test.

On the A5's twists and turns, the bike surprised Haylock by how adeptly it handled the bends approaching Betwys-y-Coed. The well-damped rear suspension coped just fine, only floundering if pushed really hard on fast curves when a quarter of a ton of top heavy machinery began to tell on the rider.

Haylock, however, reserved his most vitriolic comments for the 'nasty' Japanese tyres and their wet-weather performance. He and the bike hit rain as they crossed the border from England into Wales. On the pass down from Lake Ogwyn to Bethesda near Bangor, the RE-5 began to wriggle over cats-eyes or white lines and road markings. Even careful application of the otherwise weak rear brake (Haylock called it 'feeble') could induce the tyres to writhe. Wet weather riding was made more uncomfortable still by delay from the front discs when wet (and which - as Haylock found on the journey home - if applied too hard in the dry on anything other than a smooth surface could incite the bike's front end to dance and hop).

Get the correct combination of throttle, banking and braking, however, and the RE-5 could be hustled through the bends gracefully. Take the wrong line, though, and the bike would protest, bucking and weaving as the rider tried to correct their error.

High petrol consumption marred the RE-5's touring credentials. Haylock was forced to stop three times during the course of his 200 mile trip.

Motor Cycle journalist John Nutting's review of the RE-5 echoed most of Haylock's findings. Like Haylock, Nutting noted the vibration from the driveline, a symptom, he explained, of a small 14 tooth engine sprocket, which was necessary in order to make room for the heavy $^3/_4$ inch pitch rear chain (the same size, incidentally, as the one Kawasaki fitted to the 900cc Z1). He, too, praised the RE-5's steering on smooth dry roads, but he criticised the RE-5's bulk, its top heaviness and the adverse effect this had on the bike's handling - particularly in the wet, on tyres and with front disc brakes whose performance deteriorated markedly on damp surfaces.

Nutting described the bike's fuel consumption as appalling. In his view, it seriously handicapped the RE-5's ability as a long-distance tourer. An overall figure of 30mpg, and just 40mpg even with a careful throttle hand, gave the RE-5 a range of less than 110 miles. Tank capacity before the low fuel warning light came on was just 2.5 gallons - around 90 miles before reserve. The bike consumed engine oil at a rate of 400 miles per pint, whilst the tank, which also supplied lubricant to the rear chain, got through oil at a rate of 530 miles per pint.

But it wasn't all bad. He liked the riding position. And although the RE-5 was neither faster over the quarter mile nor on top end compared to its sibling the GT750 (*Motor Cycle* recorded a 14.2 second standing quarter at 91.5mph for the Rotary against the three's 13.5 seconds at 99.5mph; and two-way mean speeds of 110mph to 119.8mph respectively), Nutting remained impressed by the Rotary's 'stump-pulling power' at low revs. From its peak torque at 3,500 rpm through to the 7,000 rpm redline, the RE-5's throttle response was simply 'startling' - at the twist of the grip, the bike 'really stretched a rider's arms'. Indeed, it pulled so hard that it could tackle 1-in-3 hills at just 1,500 rpm in bottom gear.

To conflate two separate but related points from Messrs Nutting and Haylock: the RE-5 offered barely more performance than a Suzuki GT550, but at around the same price as a Kawasaki Z1. Haylock felt that the DKW's combination of German and Italian components, and its wholly European construction, meant it was far better suited to UK riding conditions than the RE-5, which he said was 'obviously tailored for the States'. Nutting thought similarly - that the RE-5 was 'aimed at the American long distance tourer who would find the utter smoothness and comfort a boon [as long as] he did not mind stopping for fuel every 100 miles'.

Indeed, it was both the German and the Japanese rotaries' thirst for fuel which led Haylock to conclude that whilst neither were 'as thirsty as some two-strokes in the their respective performance categories… consumption figures of 40mpg for the DKW and 30mpg for the Suzuki do not bode well for the future of the Wankel engine in motorcycling'.*

~ ~ ~

Haylock was right. The 1970's flirtation with rotaries proved short-lived. Hercules built just 1,784 rotary-powered motorcycles before they stopped production: not because the bikes were poorly designed, but because they missed their monthly sales quota by 25 units.

A little over a year after launching the RE-5, following poor sales, Suzuki replaced the original 'M' model and released the 'A' version of the RE-5 in mid-1976. The factory discarded the first-year model's themed tubular rear-light assembly, spherical indicators and the circular console with its modish flip-up cover, and replaced them with more conventionally-styled components, similar to those fitted to the GT750. But the makeover made little difference. Sales failed to cover the massive costs Suzuki had incurred developing the rotary technology and building a bespoke new factory to produce the RE-5.

In 1978, after producing just 6,000 machines (of which only around 200 were imported into the UK) at a cost rumoured to total several millions, Suzuki ceased production of the RE-5. The factory's foray into rotary-engined motorcycles had nearly crippled the company. Their next new bike just had to succeed.

---

*   Haylock was not against Wankel engines in motorcycles *per se*. After riding the Norton twin-rotor prototype, the writer said: 'I've realised the rotary does have a place in motorcycling, and can still be a sophisticated and faultless power unit.' He praised the Norton's lack of bulk, light weight and simplicity. But it saddened him to ponder on how the British industry had failed once again to grasp yet another opportunity.

Postscript: Norton continued to develop air-cooled and water-cooled versions of the rotary engine. During the 1980s, they issued 588cc examples to the police and military for assessment, and to help them develop the concept under hard service. However, it wasn't until Dennis Poore died and his company passed into new ownership that Norton released the bike to the public in the form of the Classic.

Under the leadership of Brian Crighton, the rotary - wearing firstly the black and gold colours of their sponsor John Player Special, then later Duckham - notched up racing successes; initially with the air-cooled version, then later with a water-cooled layout.

16

THE HONDA GOLD WING

A BIKE BUILT LIKE A CAR, DESIGNED IN JAPAN AND MADE IN AMERICA

'Create the King of Motorcycles'
(Soichiro Honda's brief to the Gold Wing project team)

Soichiro Irimajiri

HONDA DESIGN A GRAND TOURER

In the autumn of 1972, at around the time the Kawasaki Z1 made its first public appearance at the Motorcycle Show in Cologne in September, and its British debut two months later at London's Earl Court Motor Show in November, 6,000 miles away in Japan, Soichiro Irimajiri, had gathered together some of Honda's best engineers to brief them on their next project in a committee room at the Honda factory in Waco. Irimajiri was the man who had headed the team that designed the company's five- and six-cylinder GP racers and he relayed to his colleagues his boss and company founder Soichiro Honda's wishes to design a new flagship. Honda wanted to create a new 'King of

Motorcycles'. It was to be the biggest, the fastest and the very best grand tourer that any manufacturer had ever built, one that would uphold the company's reputation in the face of mounting competition.

Soichiro Honda's use of the phrase, 'King of Motorcycles', was interesting. Four years earlier, at a meeting in Japan with the head of Honda's Californian office, Bob Hansen, Soichiro Honda had used those same words to describe the groundbreaking CB750, which, at the time of Hansen's visit, was still in development and under wraps. Honda evidently intended to make a similar impact with this new flagship as they had with the CB750.

However, since its launch at the Tokyo Show in 1968 the CB750's mantle had slipped. In 1968, Kawasaki introduced the world's fastest accelerating production motorcycle, the H1 500 triple, followed two years later by the even faster 750 H2, winner of *Cycle* magazine's 1973 superbike comparison test. In 1971, Suzuki unveiled its own superbike, the GT750 two-stroke triple, a turbine-smooth liquid-cooled grand tourer. The following year, Yamaha announced the TX750, a counter-balanced 360 degree twin-cylinder tourer.

Manufacturers outside Japan were no less busy. BSA and Triumph's release of their 750 triples put them marginally ahead of Honda in being the first to the market with a modern multi-cylinder motorcycle. Within just a few years, Moto Guzzi, Laverda and Ducati expanded their model line-up to include large-capacity machines also. Some marques elected to evolve their company's long-standing engine formats rather than introduce revolutionary new ones. Harley-Davidson in America, for example, remained faithful to its overhead-valve big-inch V-twins; whilst BMW punched out their shaft-drive boxer twin to 750cc.

But the newly crowned and undisputed heavyweight champion of them all was the 903cc Kawasaki Z1 launched in 1972. Indeed, as *Bike* magazine's Mark Williams put it: 'The [Honda] 750 Four, for so long the best machine in the world is now old, and dated... The King is dead. Long live the King.'

Irimajiri's team's response was a one-off engineering exercise, codenamed the M1. Also known as the AOK, the M1's engine had six cylinders arranged horizontally in two opposing banks of three (similar to a BMW's boxer engine). Displacing 1,470cc, the over-square motor had a bore and stroke of 72 by 60mm respectively. Unlike the BMW, whose shaft-driven rear wheel assembly the prototype appeared to have borrowed, the M1's engine was liquid-cooled. Valves were actuated by a single-overhead camshaft above each of the engine's two banks of cylinders, whilst fuelling was taken care of by a single downdraft twin-barrelled carburettor boasting Venturis of 29mm and 27mm. These fed into an automotive-like cast inlet manifold. Power was transmitted via a single-plate dry clutch. Despite a very low compression ratio of 8.0:1, output was 80bhp at 6,700rpm. Those figures put the M1's mildly-tuned 1,500cc flat-six engine in the same ball park as the four-cylinder Z1.

The M1 was a similarly strong performer, capable of 130mph (210kph) and 12 second standing quarters. Not surprisingly, the flat six was exceptionally smooth-running.

Given the prototype's modest 58.25 inch wheelbase, credit for the M1's reportedly stable handling was attributed to its very low centre of gravity - a by-product of the engine's layout. The chassis comprised a double-cradle frame with CB750-like engine mountings, topped off by a 21 litre fuel tank. The prototype's transmission, shaft-drive, and rear wheel hub, its silencers, and even its seat, all appeared to have been sourced from a BMW donor bike; whilst the forks, front wheel, headlamp and clocks looked like the team had transplanted them straight off a CB750. Tyres were period-sized 4.00 x 18 inch rear and 3.25 x 19 inch front. Remarkably, the bike weighed just 484lb (220kg).

But even in its mongrel and roughly finished state, it was clear to Irimajiri's team that the prototype's engine was simply too long to permit a comfortable riding position. 'The M1,' said Honda, 'was built to find out what was possible.' The six-cylinder layout was shelved, and a new team was appointed to develop a flat-four, which they decided was a more practical engine configuration than the six.[*] Toshio Nozue replaced Irimajiri to head up the new assignment (codenamed Project 371). Essentially a chassis designer, Nozue's *curriculum vitae* listed the off-road Honda Elsinore 250cc two-stroke and the landmark CB750 amongst his achievements.

Inspired by Honda's winged logo, the M1 was re-named the Gold Wing.[**]

DECIDING ON ENGINE LAYOUT

Honda himself believed that the CB750 was at the capacity limit of what was acceptable to consumers. As a result, artist impressions and styling mock-ups depicted 750cc motorcycles - concepts like the Gold Wing GX750, X-1 750, and GL 750 Four. But to earn the title 'King of Motorcycles', it became clear that the bike had to displace more than the Kawasaki Z1 900, the Moto Guzzi V7, and the BMW R75/5 (and, from 1973, the 900cc R90S). The Gold Wing also had to be more powerful than Harley-Davidson's FLH-1200 Electra Glide, which, though powered by an antiquated pushrod V-twin, enjoyed a huge following and an enviable reputation for luxurious long-distance travelling courtesy of its well-appointed saddle-seat, and its standard-equipment panniers, windscreen and running-boards. Both the BMW and the Electra Glide exerted a powerful influence on the Gold Wing's project team, whose direction was steering increasingly toward grand touring. However, neither bike offered Project 371 a complete blueprint.

---

[*]   Flat-four-powered motorcycles had been tried before, with limited success. In England, Royal Engineer, Colonel H.C. Holden was marketing a liquid-cooled flat-four motorcycle as far back as 1900. Between 1933 and 1938, German manufacturer Zündapp produced the K800, an air-cooled 791cc side-valve flat-four. Weighing 400lbs and capable of 78mph, the K800 featured pressed-steel girder forks and frame, equipped with mounting points to fit a sidecar. The Gold Wing wasn't even the first water-cooled shaft driven four-cylinder motorcycle. In West London, the Wilkinson Sword Company (of razor-blade fame) produced the Wilkinson TMC (Touring Motor Cycle). Dubbed the 'Two-wheeled Mercedes', the hand-built liquid-cooled shaft driven side-valve inline four was available in small numbers from 1909 to 1916. Originally 848cc, it grew to 996cc in 1913 to improve its suitability for hauling a sidecar.

[**]   The GL1000's name was variously written in press reports and dealer adverts as 'GoldWing' - one word, with a capital letter 'W' - exactly as displayed on the machine's side-panel; or occasionally as a single word - Goldwing - with just an initial cap; or, most commonly, as two separate words - Gold Wing - just as it appeared in Honda's publicity materials (both those printed in Japan for the company's English-speaking markets, and written in American/English - hence 'tires' not 'tyres' - and as printed by Honda UK in England for its domestic British market).

The R90S, whilst quicker and lighter than the FLH1200, at just 451lbs (205kg), found its appeal in the States was hamstrung by its gross loading limit - especially when compared to the far greater carrying capacity of the Electra Glide.

The air-cooled boxer twin engine had a lineage dating back to 1923. With its crankshaft running lengthwise with the bike, the flat twin's engine layout aligned itself perfectly for running a shaft-propelled final drive (although blipping the throttle at rest, chopping the throttle too quickly, or accelerating hard, induced a disconcerting torque reaction that made the bike twist on its axis). The BMW's more European all-round capability and emphasis on fast-sports touring, its relatively low volume production and high purchase price, together with the US's unendingly straight highways, meant its attraction was confined to a small *cognoscenti* of riders. Harley-Davidson's appeal, on the other hand, was in Honda's view, too closely associated with counter-culture groups such as hippies and Hells Angels. With the Gold Wing, Honda intended to create the first *über* tourer - and, with it, a whole new market.

As with Project 371's antecedent, the flat-four's horizontally opposed layout required water-cooling to ensure the rear cylinders did not overheat. Also like the M1, the new engine's two valves per chamber were opened and closed by a single-overhead camshaft atop each bank of cylinders. Unlike the six-cylinder prototype, however, the flat-four deployed the common automotive practice of toothed rubber belts to drive the camshafts (at the time, the only production motorcycle to use the arrangement was Moto Morini on its 3½, a sporty 350 V-twin). Sourced from Honda's car division, the 17mm rubber Gilmer timing belts (installed in a dry chamber at the front of the Gold Wing's engine) were identical to those Honda fitted to the Civic.

Although the production version of the Gold Wing went on to incorporate many ground-breaking features, Toshio Nozue's team abandoned several others along the way. Project 371's engineers, for example, experimented with fuel injection. However, they rejected it for fear that riders would not be able to effect roadside repairs. Automatic transmission was rejected on grounds of size and weight, as too was an electronic hydraulically-operated centre-stand. The team also experimented with anti-lock braking, but the technology of the time made such a system impractical.

As the Gold Wing was Honda's first production motorcycle to feature shaft final drive, Toshio Nozue's team of engineers devoted more time developing this component than any other. To test the strength of the driveshaft, the team would set the bike rolling. Then, as it was coasting along at 30mph in neutral, they would slam the bike into first gear, causing the rear wheel to hop violently. But basic as the method was, and brutal as it may have seemed, meting out such punishment provided engineers with valuable empirical data. In fact, so important was the Gold Wing to Honda (it was, after all, the factory's first significant new model since the CB750), testing at the Tochigi development centre was extended beyond the usual eight months to a full year, as the project team explored the prototype's limits and capacities, its strengths and its weaknesses. Riders noted that the machine's low centre of gravity greatly aided its ability to resist cross winds, where it remained reassuringly stable, but that its weight counted against it when trying to haul the bike onto its wheels if lain on its side after a fall.

Meanwhile, press rumours about the new bike's engine layout were rife. The media speculated that the new Honda would be 'a huge V6' or 'an enlarged conventional powerplant much like the CB750'. The Gold Wing's debut in Cologne in 1974, and Honda's unveiling of a pre-production prototype to US dealers at their convention in Los Angeles late that same year - all part of a strategy whereby the factory released the bike separately in each of its foreign markets in order to garner maximum publicity - may have scotched the more fanciful rumours about the new machine's engine configuration, but its appearance did not end the assumption that the Gold Wing was a softly-tuned long distance tourer. This, in spite of the bike boasting several features suggesting more sporting aspirations.

Whilst the machine exhibited at Los Angeles differed slightly from the GL1000 K0 that went on sale the following year (the factory dropped the display model's self-cancelling indicators, and replaced the radiator cap), *Cycle* magazine wryly observed that the prototype's specification should 'have been a tip-off'.

Indeed so. Eighty horsepower at 7,000rpm (the same as the 1,500cc AOK prototype, but delivered 300 revs higher up the range); a one-litre four-cylinder engine (actual displacement, 999cc); four 32mm Keihin constant velocity carburettors; triple disc brakes and floating twin-piston callipers; lightweight aluminium wire wheels and Bridgestone Superspeed tyres, H-rated for sustained 132mph cruising and developed specifically for the Gold Wing. At 595lbs, (645lbs wet) the GL1000 was the heaviest bike to come out of Japan. In fact, only the Harley-Davidson Electra Glide was bigger.

Veteran automotive journalist, L.J.K. Setright reported in his column 'Cog-Swapping' in the August 1975 issue of *Bike* magazine that Honda spent £500,000 developing the Gold Wing's rear tyre (although project leader Toshio Nozue always denied those rumours). And though the Gold Wing's 4½ inch wide 4.50H 17A rear tyre - considered exceptionally broad at the time - was said to be inspired by the Electra Glide's tyre sizes, the reason Nozue's team opted for a 17 inch rear wheel was actually more prosaic: to keep the GL1000's seat height low.

But it was the Gold Wing's engine that took centre stage. Ironically, in designing the King of Motorcycles, Nozue's team turned to the world of cars for their inspiration. Studying the very best in contemporary automotive design, Honda's engineers examined BMW and Chevrolet motors. But for the Gold Wing's engine, they followed the example of German sports-car maker Porche with its flat-six and split the GL1000's crankcases vertically at the centre. The crankshaft fixing arrangement, however, was all Honda's.

THE GL1000: SUPERBIKE PERFORMANCE IN A CAR-LIKE PACKAGE

The Gold Wing was the company's first water-cooled motorcycle. As is normal for a liquid-cooled motor and common practice in the automotive industry, Honda cast the

GL1000's cylinders into the crankcase halves. This reduced manufacturing costs, but made replacing piston rings considerably more difficult.

Three bearing caps, each clamping down on a 40mm crankshaft main bearing, fastened the crank to the offside engine case. Stripping down the engine entailed removing the right (or nearside) crankcase half and sliding it off the nearside bank of pistons. Because of the position of the main bearing bosses, removing the offside bank of pistons involved first unbolting their connecting rod caps before taking the whole of the rod and piston assembly out through the top of the cylinder. Complex as it was, the trade off was that the GL1000's motor-industry-inspired engine promised Superbike performance with automotive-like reliability and service schedules beyond those of any other motorcycle.

The Gold Wing's shaft drive represented another first for a Honda production motorcycle (and for Japanese manufacturers also, as a driveshaft through the centre of the swinging arm was previously a feature associated with the European makers, Moto Guzzi and BMW). Rumours of shaft drive on a Honda had been circulating in the media several years before the GL1000 hit the showrooms. When *Bike* magazine pitted the CB750 against the Z1 in late 1973, after recalling the early 750's history of breaking drive chains, and noting that the K3 test model's larger chain was still only capable of a disappointing 3,000-4,000 miles service under hard use, consultant editor Mark Williams pondered if 'News of a shaft drive Honda Four perhaps means that Honda are forgetting compromise answers to drive train problems.'

Shaft drive, however, did not eliminate potential drive train problems. The disconcerting torque reaction of shaft-driven BMW flat twins and large-bore Moto Guzzis was caused by the driveshaft compressing the motorcycle's rear suspension as the bike tries to rotate around the engine's spinning crankshaft. Piston layout and a crankshaft's position was not the cause, they just influenced the side to which the bike twisted - and that was invariably opposite the engine's direction of rotation. Nor did torque reaction intrude during all riding conditions, largely confined as it was to abrupt opening and shutting off of the throttle (for example, when blipping the accelerator at standstill).

Be that as it may, Honda's engineers were determined to tackle such quirks. Their solution was to cancel out the torque reaction by attaching a flywheel to the back of the alternator. The flywheel and alternator spun on a shaft containing rubber inserts to cushion the noise. As the shaft was coupled to the crankshaft by a straight-cut gear rather than a chain, the alternator rotated in the opposite direction and at a slightly higher speed to the engine's crankshaft, thereby countering the torque generated by the spinning crank.

The result was impressive. As *Bike* magazine's Bill Haylock noted, even after blipping the Gold Wing's throttle, he could detect 'no trace of that lurching torque reaction, known so well to BMW and Guzzi owners, because,' he explained, 'the Honda's contra-rotating alternator compensates for it.'

Key to its success was the Gold Wing's charging system. Unlike the CB750's 'excited-field' alternator, which only generated the electricity needed at any given time, the GL1000's 300 watt fixed-rate alternator delivered current that only varied with engine speed. Excess or unwanted current was returned to the frame where it dissipated as heat via an electronic valve. On the face of it, this aspect of the GL's technology appeared to be a retrograde step. In fact, generating electricity at a steady rate avoided sudden fluctuations in demand on the Gold Wing's alternator, thus cleverly minimising variations imposed on the alternator's contra-rotating flywheel. The result was, just as Haylock could attest, GL riders could blip the throttle without the motorcycle twisting sideways beneath them.

Engine width was 26 inches (compared to a CB750 motor's 21½ inches). To keep its wheelbase within manageable proportions, the GL's clutch and gearbox sat underneath the engine. Although its gear ratios were identical to the CB750, and both bikes shared similar selector mechanisms, very few parts were actually interchangeable between the two machines. It was the same with the Gold Wing's wet multi-plate clutch. It, too, looked like a straight lift from the CB750 (but with friction plates courtesy of the CB450 twin and springs that had earlier seen duty on the old CB72). A Morse-type Hy-Vo primary chain (rather than the more common roller-link type) ran from a sprocket situated near the crankshaft's offside main bearing to a matching sprocket on the transmission shaft, which lay underneath and parallel with the crankshaft. A Hy-Vo countershaft incorporating a rubber-cushioned sprocket in the centre drove the outer clutch hub.

The GL's five-speed gearbox transferred locomotive power to the rear wheel via a spring-loaded shock absorber situated between the rear of the engine and swing-arm axle, where it connected to a universal joint (commonly referred to as a 'U-joint'), similar to those found on cars. Running on needle roller bearings, the joint was protected by a rubber boot, but neither the U-joint nor the BMW-like rear drive unit (which in the Gold Wing ran in tapered roller bearings to the Beemer's ball bearings) had provision to inject grease. It was an omission which *Cycle* magazine cited as their 'single cause for service-orientated concern'. From the U-joint, Honda ran the Gold Wing's driveshaft through the centre of the right-hand - that is, the offside - swinging arm tube to a spiral bevel-gear rear drive hub. At 3.40:1, the GL1000 K0's gearing meant its rev counter needle remained steadfastly stuck in the lowest quarter of the tachometer dial most of the time.

Yet, if the Gold Wing was geared too high for sidecar or trailer-towing duties, slowing down the engine paid enormous dividends in reduced maintenance and wear. This, of course, led to greater reliability, which, over time, cultivated trust, as Gold Wing owners learned that they could embark on long-distance journeys confident that the GL would not break down and leave them stranded out in the Boondocks.

Valve and camshaft mechanisms were almost identical to those of the CB750; each of the Gold Wing's banks of cylinders activated by what was effectively half of a 750 Four's camshaft. These were driven by a pair of toothed belts housed at the front of the engine. Recommended service intervals between adjustment of the belts (whose tension was controlled by a pair of spring-loaded pulleys) was set at 24,000 miles. Setting the tappet clearance was done by adjusting a conventional screw and lock nut.

With thermostatically-monitored liquid-cooling controlling the rate of piston-to-cylinder expansion, Honda's designers could maintain an almost constant operating engine temperature of between 176-182° Fahrenheit (with an auxiliary electric fan kicking in if coolant temperature exceeded 210°F). This allowed Nozue's team to work to far tighter tolerances, and led to the only otherwise remarkable feature of the Gold Wing's pistons and connecting rods - the omission of gudgeon pin retainers. Necessary to accommodate the greater clearances required in an air-cooled engine, the GL got by without them. Instead, its wrist pins were a press fit into the connecting rod's small end. Ignition came courtesy of old fashioned battery, coils and contact breakers (two sets of points, each firing two cylinders).

Housing the Gold Wing's flat-four engine was an all-welded duplex tubular steel frame, with a detachable rail on the near-side to facilitate engine removal. Up front, Honda fitted new telescopic forks. At 37mm in diameter, the Gold Wing's stanchions were 2mm beefier than the CB750's to cope with the GL's near 170 lbs greater weight (647 lbs with fluids to the original 750 Four's 480 lbs). Twin floating brake callipers were mounted behind the fork legs to assist steering.

Holding things up at the rear were twin shock absorbers, adjustable only for spring preload, and a wide 17 inch aluminium wheel rim. Both front and rear wheels featured a novel hollow square-section around the bead areas, in a move designed to save un-sprung weight. At the rear, the rim was laced to a hub that was actually narrower than the item worn by the Gold Wing's 750cc sibling. This positioned the spokes almost vertically; and, being the bent-type rather than the more robust straight pull-through design, they were prone to failure, unable to handle the GL's weight and power.

With twin 10.75 inch discs up front, the rear wheel's larger 11.6 inch stainless steel disc and higher spec dual opposed-piston brake calliper seemed a curious mix. However, the Gold Wing's rear-end bias in the braking department would prove influential, with other manufacturers - including BMW - following suit.

But the Gold Wing's signature feature (apart, of course, from its flat-four engine) was its dummy tank. Using the ignition key to unlock the spring-loaded top lid gave riders access to a small glove box, the air filter, and the filler cap for the 4.2 gallon (19 litres) under-seat fuel tank. Positioning the tank between the frame tubes helped centralise the machine's mass and lower the bike's centre of gravity, but it necessitated fitting a car-type, mechanically-driven fuel pump to ensure a consistent fuel supply; and - in a first for a motorcycle - a tank-mounted electric fuel gauge (because unscrewing the filler cap to inspect how much petrol was left was impractical on the move). After popping the lid, the sides fell away to reveal fuses and electrics on the left, and the coolant tank and emergency kick-start lever behind the panel on the right (the kick-starter was also necessary to set the timing).

Available in Candy Antares Red or Candy Blue Green with discrete gold pin-stripes on the dummy tank, chrome mudguards front and rear, and black U-shaped headers and silencers[*] with chrome accents on the end-tips and bolted-on heat shields, the launch model's styling was modest and understated. Press reaction to the Gold Wing proved mixed.

A Tourer For The American Highways

In their April '75 piece on the GL1000, *Cycle World* described it as 'a prestige machine and a winner... it is nimble for its weight, as smooth as good Scotch, and as quiet as time passing.' Rather presciently, they predicted that it 'may soon be the touring machine on American highways.'

That same month, rival magazine *Cycle* observed: 'The GL's low center of gravity gives it an extremely responsive feel for a machine that weighs close to 650lbs. The only time the rider notices the difference in feel from one of the 750s, which weigh about 125lbs less, is when the big bike is muscled through a series of tight switchback turns.'

Cycle's test bike also proved remarkably quick. Before it retired with a fried clutch, the GL recorded a 12.92 second standing quarter. *Cycle* had tested only two other bikes that posted quicker times: the Kawasaki Z1 and its stablemate, the 750 H2 two-stroke triple (which, by 1975, had been dropped from the range).

The UK's *Motorcyclist* magazine wrung 127mph from their test bike, with the rider lying prone over the tank. *Bike* magazine declared the Gold Wing was 'one of the fastest bikes we've tested, on top speed and acceleration' - 120.96mph, 0-60mph in 6.22 seconds, and the standing quarter in 13.125 seconds. Tester Bill Haylock said the GL's engine kicked out enough power 'to catapult you towards the horizon with thoroughly indecent haste accompanied by the shriek and smell of incinerated rubber.'

Haylock was most amazed at the sheer 'effortlessness of it all'. Much of that he put down to the complete lack of vibration, and the engine's ability to deliver all its power smoothly right up to the 8,500rpm redline. The bike, he said, 'just surges forward like an avalanche when you twist open the taps, and then gets noticeably more hectic as the needle approaches the 7,000rpm power peak.'

And yet he hated it.

Haylock, owner of a Ducati 450, dismissed its maker's claims that the GL was the most advanced bike ever made. 'In truth, the Gold Wing is a very conventional motorcycle,' he wrote. 'It is remarkable not so much for technological innovations, as for the change of course it represents, away from traditional motorcycle technology and into line with contemporary automobile technology.'

He damned the dummy tank as a waste of space, displaying 'the worst of Japanese gizmo-mania'. He thought the fuel gauge 'worse than useless'. He derided the engine's

---

[*]   Through a combination of the camshafts being driven by belt rather than a mechanically-noisier chain, and a water-jacket deadening engine clatter, together with a very large, highly efficient exhaust system, the maker was able to claim that at 77 decibels, the Gold Wing was one of the quietest bikes ever made - quieter even than Honda's own CB750, which at 80.5 Db(A) was the quietest in *Cycle* magazine's Superbike Comparison test just two years earlier.

30mpg fuel consumption, which limited fast motorway riding to just 110 miles. On fast bends, he said the Gold Wing under-steered; whereas on slow bends it over-steered, and felt like it was about to flop on its side.

The Gold Wing's biggest sin, according to Haylock was its weight: 'I think there is no excuse for a bike to weigh much over 500lbs…' The BMW R90S was almost 200lbs lighter, he pointed out, '… and is a much better motorcycle because of it.' (Months earlier, Haylock had voiced similar sentiments even before he had encountered the Gold Wing in the flesh, when he cynically suggested to fellow *Bike* journalists eying photographs of the GL that the magazine should assemble 'a special Big Fatso Giant Test'.)*

Honda UK responded by refusing to supply *Bike* any test machines for over a year and cancelling all advertising with the magazine.

In Britain, the Gold Wing retailed at £1,599. Its price in the US was $2,895, where Honda pitched the GL just above the Kawasaki Z1's $2,475 price tag, but below the BMW R90/6's $3,395 and the Electra Glide's $3,555.

In August 1975, following a month-and-a-half-long comparison test of the best touring motorcycles on the market, *Cycle* magazine declared the GL1000 joint winner alongside the BMW R90/6, the bike that had been a key influence in Project 371's development. Also among the challengers was another major role model for Toshio Nozue's project team, the Harley-Davidson FLH 1200. The eight-bike line-up comprised the H-D Electra Glide, Honda Gold Wing, Moto Guzzi 850T, Norton 850 Interstate, Kawasaki 900 Z1, Suzuki GT750-M two-stroke triple and RE-5 rotary. In such refined company, it was perhaps not surprising that the venerable Electra Glide finished in last place.

HONDA LAUNCH A LONG-DISTANCE TOURER AT THE TT RACES

Honda projected first-year sales of 60,000 units for the Gold Wing. They sold 5,000. Significantly, 4,000 of those were in America. In his book *Honda Gold Wing*, motorcycle journalist Ian Falloon, examined some of the reasons for the GL's initially slow take up, in Britain, at least. He attributed some of the blame to the location Honda chose for its UK launch in June 1975 at the Isle of Man TT.

Whilst the annual event is certainly a festival dedicated to motorcyclists, many of whom travel great distances to be there, the Island's fast mountain roads were arguably not the most suitable venue at which to showcase the Wing's credentials as a long-distance tourer.

Honda had shipped three GL1000s to the Island for journalists to sample on the $37^3/_4$ mile course during TT week. *Motor Cycle Mechanic*'s John Robinson even got to borrow

---

* In an interesting turn of events given the Bavarian maker's influence on the Gold Wing's development (and Haylock's lauding of the German twins as a stick with which to beat the GL1000), shortly after Honda launched the Wing, the motorcycling press reported rumours that BMW were 'on the verge' of producing a flat-four themselves. Representatives of the German company denied this, dismissing sightings of such a vehicle as a couple of Honda 'hack' bikes undergoing evaluation whilst wearing BMW fuel tanks.

the very machine which Honda had hired legendary British racer Geoff Duke to ride around the famous circuit in a few days' time. In a half-page piece summarising his four hours with the bike, Robinson was decidedly ambivalent in his assessment: 'While Honda have not bettered BMW's standards the flat-four doesn't fall flat on its face.'

Bike magazine's editor Mike Nicks was 'agreeably surprised' by his IoM ride on the Wing (doubly surprising given the magazine's later criticism). He confessed to not liking the GL when he brought it back after his first early Sunday morning lap of the Island. Determined not to be the first tester to crash a Gold Wing, he approached the 'famed Mountain Circuit' with some trepidation, distrustful of its Bridgestone tyres' ability to cope on roads peppered with damp patches. Feeling 'awkward and cumbersome', the bike confirmed his poor expectations. Still, he found 'the engine was smooth, and in fact the general ride was very similar to the 750 water-cooled Suzuki triple in that it was strangely reminiscent of the plusher varieties of V8 engined American sedans'.

A second circuit of the Island, but this time with others around 'to act as pacers' revealed virtues Nicks hadn't noticed on his first lap. The Honda tracked well. It was deceptively fast, approaching the Creg public house at 100mph with 2,500 revs to spare, and easily quick enough to keep up with a Z1 rider. Where Nicks expected the Wing's back end to pitch and yaw in spots like Quarry Bend, the GL's handling and rear suspension remained perfectly controlled.

Dave Minton, on the other hand, reporting for the UK's *Motorcyclist* magazine, described the US-spec machine that he and attending British journalists rode during TT week as 'unbelievably unstable'. Honda's Press and Publicity Officer, Allan Robinson - 'a rider of no mean ability himself', according to Minton - tried desperately to convince hacks that the American versions were 'in no way representative of the European one expected shortly.' Robinson, however, knew none of them believed him. It was perhaps inevitable, then, that in the reports testers filed on their return, they dubbed the GL a two-wheeled motor car (the headline *Bike* magazine put above Haylock's critical review), and christened it the 'Lead Wing'.

Falloon also considered the influence on British buyers of Haylock's coruscating article. He concluded, however, that whilst it remains the review of the Gold Wing most people remember, Haylock's lament on the direction he feared Japanese manufacturers were taking motorcycling clearly did little long-term damage to sales. Falloon acknowledges, though, that Haylock's test and Honda's withdrawal of its advertising with *Bike*, one of the UK's biggest selling motorcycle magazines at the time, 'may have affected the acceptance of the Gold Wing in the British market'.

The Wing's public acceptance was a point to which Dave Minton kept returning in his report published in *Motorcyclist* one month before Bill Haylock's review appeared in *Bike* magazine. Minton warned readers that the Gold Wing's 'velvety' power, its silence, and the bike's stability could give riders attracted to its glamour a false sense of security. A machine which, with rider and 'a few extras', tips the scales at over half a ton, 'positively states the definite limitations of tubular steel frames and telescopic front forks'. Yet Minton didn't blame Honda. It was the buying public, he said, who demanded traditional technology. Honda was 'cornered into disguising what radical changes they have been able to introduce... by public traditionalism'.

Minton concluded his report by saying: 'the Gold Wing is what could turn out to be an historic motorcycle'. It was not, he asserted, the technological breakthrough its makers claimed, however. He hoped, though, that it represented the peak of 'old school' technology. Indeed, he anticipated a time when public attitudes had evolved enough that they would accept an 'Automatic' version!

Classic Bike's Jim Stanley blamed the Wing's initially disappointing sales on Honda's advertising campaign, which promoted the GL as an all-rounder instead of focussing on its capabilities as a long-distance tourer. Certainly, sales materials for the Gold Wing suggest the factory wanted to cover all bases: 'Super Tourer or Superbike. It Just Depends on the Way You Ride It,' was the headline to one glossy, full-colour eight-page brochure. Inside, it read: 'The powerful 999 cc engine, 5 speed gear-box and good handling let it run along with the most highly regarded superbikes.'

Registrations took off in the Wing's second year, with sales soaring to over 20,000 in 1976. In the four years between its launch in 1975 and the release of the K4 version in 1979, Americans bought 97,000 GL1000s. The bike had found its market. Or perhaps the market had found the Wing, because according to Falloon, people in the US who bought the Gold Wing probably didn't read motorcycle magazines anyway. Owners were typically middle-aged, middle-class, and white-collar. With higher-than-average disposable income, they could not only afford the Wing's high purchase price, they could also lavish money on aftermarket accessories. In America, the Wing's biggest market, GL owners soon earned the nickname 'Wing Nuts'.*

Such was the Wing's success in the States, that Honda transferred production to the US. On 10 June 1979, Honda America opened a new 260,000 square-foot manufacturing plant in Marysville, Ohio (population: 7,500). Costing $93 million, the factory's production capacity was 60,000 motorcycles a year (initially, building Elsinore CR250Rs only), but on that first day of production, 64 workers built just ten motorcycles. On 1 May 1980, the new generation Wing, the GL1100, rolled off the Marysville assembly line. At first, numbers were low - just 150 bikes a day

---

    *   The Gold Wing's initially slow, then steep rise in sales, the specific constituency who embraced it, the groundbreaking nature of the machine, and the propensity of owners to adapt the bike, all demonstrate aspects of what the former Washington Post business and science reporter Malcolm Gladwell described in his book *The Tipping Point* as features of how an idea or product can go 'viral'. Like a virus, social epidemics are driven by a few exceptional people. The choices and tastes of society's outliers, a discriminating minority whom Gladwell calls Early Adopters, are noticed by others who become key agents in spreading the virus. These include 'Connectors', sociable and influential individuals who know lots of people and are good at bringing them together to share common interests. 'Mavens' are not salesmen, but they are knowledgeable and keen to teach or pass on what they know. 'Adapters' see what the outliers are doing and adapt it for more general consumption. 'Salesmen' are the market's mavens, promoting the idea to a wider audience until it 'tips' into the mainstream and general acceptance. In the Gold Wing's case, sales rocketed from just 5,000 units in its first year, to more than 20,000 machines just a year later. By the Millennium, Honda had sold half a million bikes, and the American Gold Wing Riders Association had become the world's largest one-model motorcycle club with 72,000 members.

compared to 1,000 machines per day in Japan. Also, most of the Wing's components were manufactured in Japan and only assembled in Marysville. Over time, however, that would change, especially following the opening of the engine plant in nearby Anna, Ohio five years later. Yet, as modest a start as those first 150 American-built Gold Wings were, they heralded a new chapter in the story of the King of Motorcycles.*

~ ~ ~

As Honda looked east toward America when designing its super tourer, Japan's second largest motorcycle manufacturer, Yamaha, turned its gaze westward for inspiration. To build a sports-tourer to rival the German BMW, Mitsui decided that what they needed was a European perspective.

---

* In 1980, Honda upped the Gold Wing's engine capacity from one litre to 1,100cc, increasing it a further 100ccs four years later. In 1988, they replaced the GL's flat-four motor with a 1,500cc flat-six, bringing the Gold Wing's evolution full circle. In 2000, Honda unveiled the fifth-generation Wing - the GL1800. Seven years in development, the 1,832cc flat-six was the ultimate in luxury two-wheel touring. A massive 1,100 watt alternator was necessary to power a slow-speed electric-driven reverse system; two digital 3-D fuel injection maps, and a single 3-D digital ignition map for each cylinder (which retained the original bike's SOHC and two-valve layout); a 16-bit CPU and motor-actuated throttle-operated cruise control system; built-in radio with intercom and automatic volume control blasting sound out of two 25 watt speakers built into the instrument console, plus a Panasonic CD player (with optional six-disc changer) and twin 25-watt rear speakers with passenger audio control.

17

THE YAMAHA XS750

A JAPANESE MOTORCYCLE MADE TO APPEAL TO THE WORLD'S BIGGEST MARKET - EUROPE!

'Blue Sky'
(The term Yamaha applied to its concept of 'clean-sheet' design)

Japanese Dogu figure

BUILDING A PROFILE OF THE MARKET

Yamaha's European Project Co-ordinator, Paul Butler, was sitting having a quiet drink at an Amsterdam Café. To his fellow patrons, his interest in the cars and motorcycles outside probably seemed merely idle, a distracting diversion. However, as Butler explained in a 1977 interview with *Bike*'s Editor, Mike Nicks: 'You can learn an awful lot just sitting in a boulevard café and watching the traffic go by.'

'It's the way bikes are used that give you many ideas on the machines people want to ride. You also find local ways of use that have major influences on people's dreams. The chopper influence still affects American biking. Theirs is a more laid-back image, whereas in Europe motorcycling is more sport-influenced, and endurance racing has quite an effect on bikers because the endurance machines relate closely to road bikes.'

But Butler didn't just take his influences from observing traffic over a coffee. He was a habitué of events such as the Isle of Man TT, the *Bol d'Or* in France or Laguna Seca in California where he could mingle with 'grass roots bikers'. 'We keep our eyes open and our ears to the ground, talking to people, maintaining contacts, and collating motorcycle magazines and newspapers from all over Europe and America,' he told Nicks.

Butler was part of the 60-strong team that made up Yamaha NV. Established in 1970 in Amstelveen (Amsterdam) to co-ordinate operations amongst Yamaha's 13 Western European importers, NV acted as the factory's bulk buyer in Europe. The arrangement simplified things for Tokyo and helped eliminate duplication. Yamaha was the only one of the Japanese manufacturers to operate such a centre. Meanwhile, with big bike sales virtually static in the USA, at the same time as sales in Europe were on the rise, both markets were now nearly equal in value. It meant that where the American arm once dominated motorcycle design, NV now had an increasingly powerful say in new model planning.

Every four months, engineers and product managers from Europe and America met with their counterparts from Japan to review the company's five-year product plan. Those attending would propose new models and consider new designs. The meetings were reportedly pretty heated affairs, 'enlivened by table thumping and hair tearing as the various factions attempt to get their particular dream projects accepted'. Bringing to the table the fruits of his coffee-fuelled observations, Butler and his colleagues would present the assembled executives with the results and findings from the dozen or more contracts the European arm had placed with universities, contractors or one-man concerns, whom Yamaha NV had commissioned to explore new technologies or systems (Yamaha's DT range of trail bike's cantilever rear suspension was perhaps the best known example to emerge from such an arrangement).

Yamaha NV could also bring to bear market research, such as the results of their recently completed consultation with journalists and trade and industry representatives, that they had cross-referenced with findings from a study NV had commissioned with 500 French motorcyclists. The research allowed Yamaha to build a profile of motorcyclists - what types of bikes they buy, what brand, what engine displacement they prefer, their age and income. The insights they gained helped them determine an engine's appeal to the market they may be seeking to penetrate.

In addition, Yamaha NV also conducted its own small test programme. Using Dutch enthusiasts instead of factory employees (to ensure they secured truly objective assessments), riders racked up 500 kilometres a day on two motorcycles. To maintain a 'fresh supply of criticism', test riders were replaced every two months. NV even purchased machines made by their competitors, running them for more than 10,000 kilometres to find out how they compared.

Thus armed, NV would attend the four-monthly planning meetings tooled up to argue the European position.

On the table for discussion at one of these meetings was Yamaha Motor Company's 'Blue Sky' concept sketches for a new sports-tourer. The sketches were the work of GK Design, a Tokyo-based design company who produced drawings for all of Yamaha's Blue Sky ideas. Accompanied by engineers from the factory, GK were frequent visitors to Europe as part of fact-finding missions into a market for which they might find themselves designing products.

Working from a brief supplied by Yamaha setting out the market requirements the new machine had to satisfy, GK took a blank piece of paper and began drawing. Their object was to 'extend the group's imagination'. Their approach, however, went beyond merely satiating the appetites of an industrial machine. GK Design's guiding philosophy to any product they developed was summed up in the Japanese word *dogu*.[*]

The Ancient Philosophy Of *Dogu*

As GK Design explained in their corporate brochure, the company was founded to 'extract the power and the energy that *dogu* possesses for people's lives'. *Dogu* permeates all man-made objects intended to enhance life, imbuing on both maker and user physical and mental well-being. In a densely populated country with few natural resources, and a rising demand for more and more products, the company believed that only through the creativity of its people and their countrymen's 'tradition of developing a rich life by utilising wisdom in design and innovation' could Japan overcome these combined threats to individuals and civilisation.

Amongst the engine designs GK presented Yamaha for the proposed new sports-tourer was a Moto Guzzi-style transverse V-twin; a BMW-like boxer flat-twin; a huge double-overhead camshaft in-line four; and a trio of three-cylinder layouts: a very car-like water-cooled longitudinal triple, and two quite different air-cooled DOHC transverse three-cylinder powerplants - one with the cam drive running between cylinders one and two, the other with the camshafts driven from the offside end of the crankshaft.

Following GK's presentation of its Blue Sky concepts, the factory then considered each layout's place in the market, concluding that the flat and V-twin configurations were too closely associated with BMW and Moto Guzzi, both of whose shaft-drive engines suffered problems with torque reaction. They analysed the manufacturing costs, and legislative obligations to produce each design. They studied the weight and size, and the creative opportunities each layout offered stylists (eliminating as they did so the least suitable configurations), before eventually settling on the optimum engine layout for what they had intended from the outset would feature shaft final drive. For Yamaha's new sports-tourer, that turned out to be the transverse in-line triple with twin cams driven by a cam chain off the crank running along the offside of the engine.

---

[*] Dating between 10,000 and 2,300 years old, the *dogu* (or *dogū*) are clay figures produced by the Jōmon people of Neolithic Japan. *Dogu* are thought to represent the spirits with whom the prehistoric Jōmon shared their forest world in harmony with the seasons. Since their rediscovery in the 20th Century, the ancient *dogu* have proved potent sources of inspiration to generations of Japanese artists.

A triple, however, was not what Yamaha had set out to build. The factory initially planned to design an across-the-frame four based on their XS500 twin. With Honda offering a range of multis from the seminal CB750 through to the jewel-like CB500 and CB350 fours, Kawasaki their all-conquering 900cc Z1, and Suzuki rumoured to be developing a four-cylinder motorcycle also, Yamaha thought it too should field a transverse four-pot multi. Yamaha USA disagreed.

A transverse three-cylinder engine promised the best combination of performance, smoothness, lack of bulk, and - most importantly - distinctiveness in a market increasingly populated by fours. There were, of course, other four-stroke three-cylinder motorcycles on sale at the time Yamaha were formulating their plans: the BSA/Triumph 750s and the Italian Laverda one-litre triples. However, the British machines lacked sophistication; the Italians were aiming the expensively-priced Laverda at the high-end of the market; and neither of the European triples sported shaft final drive.

The factory nevertheless remained unconvinced. They were finally persuaded, however, by the fact that it was possible to adapt the tooling for the now obsolete TX750 twin and use the TX production line to manufacture a three-cylinder 750 instead.

With the layout now decided, artists produced sketches of how the complete motorcycle might look. Early styling sketches for the XS750 show a lean, lithe profile with lots of spaces surrounding the engine, redolent of a British vertical twin (although Yamaha were adamant that at no point did the company actively pursue that look). What they did expend considerable effort on was developing a smooth line between the seat and the XS750's fuel tank.

The next stage was to produce full-size mock-ups made from wood and clay. The studio's early experiments were faithful renderings of the first styling sketches. Photographs taken at the time show how successfully the modellers had translated the flat, two-dimensional depictions of a lithesome machine into a three-dimensional nimble-looking, bare-boned motorcycle. Fitted with wire wheels and front and rear suspension from the factory parts bin, the roughly-hewn engine sat centre stage, with many of the hallmarks of the production motor already evident. The model captured the slim and Spartan styling of the sketches, and the smooth unbroken lines of the seat and tank. However, by the time the studio produced the final mock-up, the team's thinking had evolved. It still wore wire wheels, but the newest iteration of the XS750 departed quite considerably from the sparseness of the initial interpretation, as Yamaha made a conscious decision to give the triple a solid, compact appearance.

The challenge now facing the project team's engineers was how to turn the drive of the transverse triple's across-the-frame crank through 90 degrees, whilst maintaining the engine configuration's winning asset - its lack of bulk. Their solution was to position the five-speed gearbox's output shaft *under* the input shaft, then transferring the drive from the output shaft to bevel gears mounted on an intermediate shaft (sited where the output shaft normally resides). The bevel gears turned the driveline round by 90 degrees. As big and sturdy as it was, the arrangement nevertheless succeeded in keeping the engine compact.

MARRAKESH EXPRESS

Unveiled at the 44th Milan Motorcycle Show in November 1975, the Yamaha XS750 attracted a lot of attention. The machine on display had silver-coloured seven-spoke cast alloy wheels (although it was actually Yamaha's RD400C two-stroke twin that became the first production bike ever to feature alloy wheels as standard equipment). The single polished circular engine covers either side of the engine contrasted sharply with the otherwise inky blackness of the powerplant, transmission and driveline. The 750-3's silver fuel tank and side-panels sported graphics reminiscent of that season's RD350B's livery (and was considerably flashier than the panelled-designs of the triple that went on sale the following year). *Bike* magazine's Mike Nicks reporting from the Milan Show compared the display model's forward-tilted engine and sweeping three-into-one exhaust system to that of the Triumph Hurricane of a few years earlier, but disparaged as 'typically Japanese' the Yamaha's single silencer - which he called 'ugly' - and the bike's 'vast handlebars'.

Nicks felt, however, that 'overall the bike has definite appeal'.

European journalists finally got to test ride the new machine a year later when Yamaha NV invited around 50 motorcycle hacks to join them in Morocco for the early November press launch of the factory's new range of four-stroke two-wheelers. Amongst the ten Britons present were Vic Barnes reporting for *Motorcyclist Illustrated*, Mike Nicks for *Bike* magazine, and *Motor Cycle Mechanics* magazine's John Robinson.

Their billet during the four-day bash was the very classy Club Mediterranée (which Barnes described as a 'sort of up-market French Butlins'), situated in the centre of Marrakesh. The test fleet, however, was gathered at the club's leisure facility, Club Ranch, located at the edge of town.

'My first sight of the XS750 impressed me,' wrote Barnes. The Yamaha was, the journalist decided, 'a Japanese bike with a marked degree of cosmopolitan character.' He liked the styling - not 'a superfluous line anywhere.' He deemed the tank logo 'almost perfect.' He admired 'the curving sweep of the colour scheme complementing the shape and size perfectly' and felt the side panels and tailpiece gave the triple's cosmetics excellent balance (Barnes was particularly pleased to note the absence of 'those awful, pseudo racing, vertical stripes Yamaha have recently used').

Threading their way through the morning traffic of Marrakesh, ten bike-mounted European motorcycle journalists had to quickly adjust to the undisciplined antics of the locals. Proceeding warily, they found themselves steering to avoid traditionally-dressed Arabs whose awareness of their approach was obscured by their flowing robes. Beasts of burden proved another hazard as donkeys strayed blindly into their path. Jay-walking urchins also seemed oblivious to their presence. Eventually, however, the obstacles of the city and its kamikaze inhabitants were put behind them, and the ten test bikes headed out toward open Moroccan countryside to follow the 70 mile route Yamaha NV had mapped out to take the riders through a wide variety of terrains.

Before long, the convoy's half dozen 250s and 360s fell behind as the faster and more powerful shaft-drive triples began to pull away. Setting the pace was *Bike* magazine's Mike Nicks. Barnes and Robinson, also aboard 750s, followed 'at an even and safe distance'. In his report of the trio's test ride, Barnes painted colourful vignettes of their North African sojourn. Like when they rounded a long sweeping left-hand bend, and the three gave a wide berth to a three-ton truck packed with a 'herd of scraggy, wide-eyed goats' (a sight which Barnes found inexplicably amusing); or how he blinked in disbelief at the wide, smooth tree-lined road that lay before them, running straight as an arrow off into the distance, 'stopping, it seemed, only at the horizon...'

It was on this road that Barnes observed Nicks flick his wrist and toe the gear lever down twice, as he dropped from top to third. Barnes quickly followed suit. 'The acceleration of the big triple,' he recounted, 'whilst not exactly earth shattering was rapid enough and immensely satisfying - probably as good as most other 750s currently available.' Almost flat out at an indicated 183kph (114mph), the journalist glanced at his machine's vibration-free mirrors to see that Robinson - whose bike was conspicuously faster than Barnes' bike - was closing in on him, and quickly. He therefore slowed and waved him by. Then, tucking into Robinson's slipstream, the 6 feet 3 inch Barnes lay as flat and prone as the triple's otherwise comfortable layout would allow. The speedometer's needle swept round the clock, stopping just shy of the 190 kph mark (Robinson's bike topping out at 193 kph or 117 mph). Barnes was certain that with more miles on the odometer - the test machines had less than 700 miles under their wheels - and 96 octane instead of the Moroccan 86 octane-grade petrol, the triple would better these figures.

As the road narrowed and began to wend its way through villages and across the occasional intersection, the Atlas Mountains visible through the clear, still Moroccan air, the three riders found themselves flat out round a fast curve when they suddenly encountered about a dozen unattended sheep. Nicks swerved to avoid the main herd, but a lone sheep, seeking to rejoin its companions, bolted across the path of his already banking Yamaha. Barnes and Robinson hit their brakes together. 'The callipers of my front twin discs clamped fibre against steel,' recalled Barnes, 'the front fork dipped and the single disc back brake steadied the whole, rapidly decelerating plot.'

Barnes and Robinson went from the ton to around 40 mph in a matter seconds. Under 'the severest possible braking,' Barnes wrote, 'the Yam held its line magnificently... it all seemed so easy and controlled.' Nicks bike, however, broke into 'a mini tank-slapper'. The *Bike* journalist, though, managed to quickly bring the triple's front end back under control, before accelerating away seemingly unperturbed by the incident.

They later stumbled upon Alpine-like roads, which swooped, climbed and dived through the foothills of the North African mountain range. With the adrenalin surging and confidence in his mount and his riding abilities running high, Barnes pushed himself and his steed to the limit. 'The XS750 took all I could dish out in its stride, comfortably and with margin to spare.'

He deemed the handling superb. 'Line chopping at high speed was good,' Barnes reported, 'and steering was taut and precise. The Bridgestone tyres gripped well and only once did I detect any movement from the back end and that was on a smooth, tar-oozing right hander.'

Even flat out with the bike cranked over in a tight bend, the Yamaha remained 'rock steady' - not something you could say of previous Yamahas, said Barnes, which in similar circumstances displayed 'a tendency to try and get back up again.' The XS750's handling on the other hand was 'impeccable'. Indeed, the triple was, Barnes concluded, 'The best Japanese bike I've ridden.'

An avowed fan of BMW's boxer twins, Barnes paid the Yamaha the compliment of comparing the XS750 very favourably to the Bavarian-made tourers. He also answered the question he said that every road tester should ask after lavishing so much praise on a test bike: Would I buy it? The answer was an unequivocal yes.

Bike named the XS750 their Bike of the Year. Its £1,399 price tag, impressive specification and 119mph performance explained in their view, BMW's recent price cuts. The magazine also awarded Yamaha's Marrakesh event their Press Launch of the Year, an accolade guaranteed to irritate L.J.K. Setright. The magazine's venerable columnist had commented in *Motorcycle Sport* on the degenerate behaviour of some of his fellow journalists during the Moroccan sojourn (which *Bike* put down to the ingestion of certain local substances). The whole episode was classic gonzo journalism as pioneered by the celebrated American writer, Hunter S. Thompson, in which the exploits of the reporter becomes the story.

YAMAHA MOVE QUICKLY TO FIX THE TRIPLE

Problems began to emerge soon after the triple went on sale. The XS750D - the 'D' indicating its model year (1977) - suffered premature primary chain wear, a gearbox that could slip from top to first unexpectedly, piston ring failure, and partially seized centre cylinders due to inadequate oil supply. Straight from the crate, the triple was remarkably smooth, but its expensive-to-replace and difficult-to-set-up contact breakers, if neglected, could lead to rough running, with some bikes even suffering cracked frames where the tightly-packaged engine was allowed to 'settle' at its three mounting points.

It was also slow. With quarter mile times nudging 14 seconds, the Yamaha was over a second slower than its Honda and Suzuki rivals (not surprising given its modest 60bhp and a power-sapping driveline which reduced this to nearer 52bhp at the rear wheel).

Yamaha addressed most of the mechanical failings under warranty or through upgrades* incorporated in the mid-year release in 1977 of the '2D' model, and with the

---

*   Yamaha released the original XS750 so late in the 1976 sales season that they assigned it a 1977 'D' suffix. However, such was the factory's urgency to ameliorate the triple's shortfall in performance that they rushed out a stop-gap model during the same D-denoted sales season, differentiating its halfway-house status by labelling it '2D'. Yamaha produced four standard versions of the XS750: The very rare Japanese-only C model with a three-into-one exhaust; the D and 2D models (the D running from engine and chassis number 1J7-00101 and the 2D -the first version of the XS750 to go on sale in the UK - from 1J7-100101); and the E and F models from 1978 and '79 respectively, both of which they produced in factory-custom versions (prefixed SE and SF).

XS750E the following year. With the 2D, Yamaha dropped the launch model's three-into-one exhaust system in favour of a more symmetrical twin silencer arrangement, which, together with revised cam profiles, increased the triple's midrange power. The changes combined to raise engine power from 60bhp at 7,500rpm to 64bhp at 7,200 revs, and knock half a second off the Yamaha's quarter-mile time. The new exhausts also improved ground clearance on the right-hand side, and helped give the bike a more balanced look (ironically, just as Honda began to fit single-silencer systems to their F series of multi-cylinder bikes).

The introduction of the E in '78 saw the contact breakers give way to trouble-free electronic ignition; a doubling of the triple's oilway diameter to four millimetres; and the oil pump's efficiency uprated by nearly half. At the same time, changes to the cylinder head, carburettors, airbox, exhaust system and further revisions to the cam timing, alongside raising the engine's compression ratio from 8.5:1 to 9.2:1, helped increase power by 6 per cent. Output was now a more competitive 68bhp at 8,000rpm. With more power and a reduction in gearing in the centre gearbox, the E was markedly quicker over the standing quarter mile compared to the D. In fact, with the XS now capable of performing standing quarters in less than 13 seconds, the triple could at least stay in the hunt with most other 750s of the day. Its top speed also improved on its predecessor (by 6mph).

As the manufacturer's sales brochure proclaimed, 'This year [1978] Yamaha engineers have gone all-out for extra performance from the XS750, and have made modifications that have resulted in substantial horsepower and speed gains.' The leaflet went on to explain, 'Thanks to this horsepower increase they have been able to lower the final drive ratio to get improved acceleration without sacrificing top end power. Quite the opposite!' declaimed Yamaha. 'Yamaha engineers have extracted so much extra power from the XS750 that top speed has increased despite the drop in gearing that achieves better acceleration.'

Except that whilst the D loped along at the legal limit at just over 4,300 revs in top gear, the E felt altogether more frantic, with a discernible buzz above 6,000rpm.

In a November 1977 article, the US magazine *Big Bike* looked like it was set to write a piece demolishing the new triple. The item kicked off by condemning the D model as 'wretched' and compared the XS750E to the droid R2D2 from that year's summer blockbuster, *Star Wars*. However, after belabouring the sci-fi analogy to the point of tedium, the magazine concluded that the big Yam demonstrated 'functional dualities'. According to them, the triple was: 'The commuter that likes to travel. The perfect bike for the tourist with no particular place to go'. The Yamaha was unpretentious, and without affectation, they said, its uncomplicated design dazzlingly efficient and versatile. Yet, *Big Bike* observed, none of that diminished the bike's personality.

In a comparison test published in 1977, the UK magazine *Superbike* pitted the Yamaha against the Trident T160. NVT had ceased production of the Triumph triple, so the magazine had to approach dealers to find a machine for their test. In the end, Terry

Allwood of Hasting Motorcycles lent *Superbike* his own personal ride. But in a largely elegiac paean to the Triumph, much to his regret and against all tester Mike Scott's expectations, he actually ended up preferring the XS750.*

Less than eighteen months later, when *Bike* magazine conducted a test comparing the XS750E with its 750cc Japanese-built rivals, for the first time in a decade, such a line-up no longer included a Honda CB750.

SUPERBIKE 7 SOLE SURVIVOR

Of the ten motorcycles that took part in *Cycle* magazine's first two 'Big 7' superbike comparison tests in 1970 and 1972, only one of the ten was still in production by the time Yamaha released the XS750E in 1978. Remarkably, given its poor placings in both tests, that sole survivor was the Harley-Davidson XLCH1000. Out-dated and out-pointed, the Sportster outlasted a line-up comprising the BSA and Triumph 750 triples, the Kawasaki H1 500 and H2 750 three-cylinder two-strokes, the Honda 750 and Kawasaki 900 fours, the Ducati and Norton 750 and Suzuki 500 twins.

The first of the ten to go out of production was the bike that, together with its Triumph cousin, ushered in the modern era of multi-cylinder superbikes - the BSA Rocket 3. Small Heath ceased production of the triple in January 1972, followed by the Trident in April 1976. One year later, the Trident's NVT stablemate, the Norton Commando, also bowed out after a decade-long production run and a total of 55,000 machines built since its launch at Earls Court as the 750 Fastback Commando ('Fastback' on account of its fibreglass tailpiece).**

All in all, it wasn't a bad run for a bike that Norton had only intended to be a two-year stop-gap model.

---

*   Correspondence from outraged readers filled nearly three quarters of the magazine's subsequent letters pages. Gunners Bowyer, Bishop and Dunning of Nuneaton took exception to the caption above the double-page portrait of the XS750 and T160. Instead of reading 'Yamaha's XS750 shows what the Trident might have been', the three believed it ought to have read: 'Triumph's Trident shows what the XS750 Yamaha might become, if lucky'. They suggested that *Superbike*'s sales figures would improve if the magazine featured 'less Jap-crap and more beautiful British'. Mart the Bag from Kidderminster thought *Superbike* had it in for the Trident because 'the T160 wasn't as flash as the Yam, or hasn't got a super-cheapo black-painted engine'. He and his British bike-riding friends were, he wrote, 'disappointed with the fight our representative put up', accusing the magazine of comparing 'a new Yam in tip-top condition' against 'a T160 that was not up to standard'.

Xenophobia aside, Mart may have had a point. Jim Turner from Hastings wrote in to say that he owned the very Trident *Superbike* had tested. He, too, had been disappointed at the bike's performance, eventually asking Terry Allwood at Hastings Motorcycles to investigate. Allwood discovered that the bike had been fitted with a rogue batch of oval barrels.

**   Mike Jackson, one-time salesman and manager for Greeves and AJS, whom Dennis Poore had despatched to head-up Norton Villiers' Los Angeles operations, told *Classic Bike Guide* that the Americans much preferred the Roadster to the Fastback (Norton shifting 20 Roadsters for every Fastback). 'Although these were boom days,' recalled Jackson, 'we never ran out of Fastbacks!' The man behind the famous slogan 'Lotta Torque About Norton', which he had worked up with service manager Brian Slark over coffee one morning in 1971 (after Slark's remark: 'Hey MJ, these Nortons have so much torque'), Jackson joked that they might have done better had they charged buyers $1,500 for the hugely popular 'Lotta Torque' stickers they had printed as giveaways and thrown a Fastback in as the freebie!

18

NORTON COMMANDO TOPS THE FIRST SUPERBIKE 7

AND POORE NABS THE INSIDE COVERS FOR THE NORTON GIRLS

'Lotta torque about Norton'
(Strapline to US adverts)

Tony Benn

NORTON LAUNCH THE COMMANDO: *MCN* MACHINE OF THE YEAR

As Norton's new 750cc twin, the Commando, rotated slowly on its turntable beneath the spotlights of the Earls Court Exhibition Hall at London's annual motorcycle show, Dennis Poore looked on beamingly. It was September 1967. The head of the one-year-old Norton Villiers Company knew that the machine receiving the press and public's plaudits wasn't actually a runner (it had no engine internals). In fact, the bike did not even exist just thirteen weeks earlier.

Born in Paddington, London, in 1916, shortly before his father was killed in the war that cost the armies of the British Empire the lives of 956,000 of its troops,

Eton and Cambridge-educated Roger Dennistoun Poore - or 'Dennis' as he was more usually known - would see military service himself during the second of the Twentieth Century's global conflagrations. After the war, Poore enjoyed some success racing for the Connaught team on the international Grand Prix circuit. He was, recalled Norton's Long Beach, California service manager, Brian Slark 'a very educated, well-spoken man, very bright with figures'. Described as a 'dashing man about town' and a well-dressed city gent with offices in the lee of St. Paul's Cathedral, Poore would become Chairman of Manganese Bronze Holdings (MBH), a company that supplied ships' propellers to the likes of Cunard. In 1966, he was hailed as the saviour of the British motorcycle industry when MBH bought out Associated Motor Cycles (AMC) and established Norton Villiers from AMC's raked over ashes.

Poore chose to promote the Norton name over AMC's stable of other marques, like AJS or Matchless. But the asset he prized most from the takeover was a new 800cc double-overhead cam, unit-construction engine called the P10. Designed originally as a 650 by AMC's Charles Udall (ex of Velocette), the engine grew to 785cc and was being readied for production when AMC failed. Poore appointed former Rolls-Royce employee Dr. Stefan Bauer to develop the concept, which had got as far as a working prototype called the P800. Housed in a standard Featherbed frame with Norton Roadholder forks, the P800 proved mechanically noisy mainly due to its inordinately long cam chain. The motor was also difficult to assemble and the unit was prone to oil leaks. Poore, however, wanted to exhibit a feasible prototype at September's 1967 Earls Court Motorcycle Show.

He also wanted to have the machine in production the following year.

Even after a complete redesign by Tony Denniss, John Favill and Bernard Hooper and re-designated the Z26, there was just one problem: the new engine was no better than Norton's ancient pushrod parallel twins whose design went back more than three decades. Engine vibration from the new powerplant was as bad as other twin-cylinder motors, whilst power output was no better. In bench testing, the unit also suffered repeated failures.

By late summer 1967, the project team decided to abandon the '800' on cost grounds. A prototype double-overhead cam twin cylinder engine developed at Woolwich showed promise, but became a casualty of Norton's move to Andover and management's fears that it would take too long to put into production. John McDermott, who had joined Norton in 1967 (and later to be editor of *Motorcyclist Illustrated* magazine), found the prototype abandoned at Woolwich and rode it for three months before a director instructed him to destroy it, ignoring the future journalist's plea that the factory donate it to the Beaulieu motor museum. The project team elected instead to develop a new frame to house Norton's tried and tested 750 Atlas engine. Based in Wolverhampton, to distance them from the problems at Norton's Woolwich assembly line, the team's brief was to quell the big twin's uncomfortable and destructive vibrations. The bike also had to look good. Bauer's assistants Bob Trigg and Bernard Hooper, both ex-Villiers engineers, are credited with finding the solution.

Norton had experimented with rubber-mountings before, installing a Dominator engine in a Featherbed frame. However, due to the lack of positive side location, the arrangement caused the chain to peel off under acceleration. Bauer, however, denounced the McCandless brothers' legendary frame, whose strength he said, relied on the engine and gearbox. Rubber-mounting, Bauer contended, would compromise the whole structure and, to the design team's surprise, he discarded it. Hooper and Trigg would simply have to design a new frame.

Christened 'Isolastic', the lightweight spine-type duplex frame (it weighed just 24lbs) treated the engine, gearbox, transmission and rear swinging arm as one unit (dubbed the 'power wheel' by engineers). The vibrations from the vertical twin-cylinder engine were isolated (hence 'Iso') from the main cycle parts by mounting the whole unit in rubber bushes (from which the innovative system derived its trademark name's last two syllables).

Wolff Olins, a London-based consultancy firm whose previous work included designing liveries for British Oxygen and Camden Borough Council, won the commission to style the Commando and give Norton a new image (Poore wanted a bike with a unique identity, one that would make it stand out in the market place). A relation of Poore's knew Wolff Olins' titular founder, Wally Olins. Olins, who had formed the agency in partnership with Michael Wolff, therefore tendered for the project. Their pitch proved successful and Norton later sent over a prototype for them to work on. However, because the agency's office at 81 Parkway in Camden was so small, stylist David Bristow was compelled to work on the bike in the street (covering up the prototype with a sheet if the weather turned wet). Whilst the agency's styling of the prototype's tank, tail fairing and even its orange seat won popular acclamation, the green sphere adorning its fuel tank (in the spot where the maker's name was more conventionally located) generated considerably less enthusiasm.

Devised by Michael Wolff, his intention for the Green Dot was to create a motif Norton might use on a range of franchised apparel. The agency suggested, for example, Norton Villiers sell motorcycle gloves sporting the Green Dot. Other applications could include deploying green balloons to identify the Norton team's pits at race meetings. Dennis Poore understood the concept, but Norton Villiers management evidently did not. They told Wolff Olins that Norton Villiers was a motorcycle manufacturer, not a textile factory turning out branded gloves and clothes-wear.

Roger Jordan, who, just two days after Bob Trigg started, joined Norton on the first day of March 1967 to work in the Wolverhampton drawing office, remembered leaning on the rail curtaining off the exhibition stand at Earls Court the following September, pleased at the remarks he heard show-goers making about the new model. He was especially gratified to overhear Triumph's Chief Designer Brian Jones (formerly of Bracebridge Street himself) observe: 'A lot of thought had gone into the design of the Commando.' The prototype also generated considerable publicity on the other side of the Atlantic when Wolff Olins displayed the Commando at the British Design Show in New York.

A six-month long period of development followed the prototype's appearance at Earls Court. Jordan was present in Wolverhampton when the first working prototype arrived on the back of a trailer from Woolwich. He persuaded Bernard Hooper to let him run the bike in over the weekend. 'What an exhilarating time, slowly increasing the throttle openings until the full performance of the uprated Atlas engine was on tap,' Jordan recalled nearly a decade later for the UK magazine *Motorcyclist Illustrated*. 'The vibration was still noticeable,' he remembered, 'but the handling was excellent.'

Testing and development continued throughout the early part of 1968. Also moving up from Woolwich to the Midlands was Bill Brooker. Brooker was engaged full-time road testing the prototype. A 'gentle giant' of a man, according to Jordan, the development team responded to Brooker's repeated suggestions to move the footrest and gear lever further apart - only to discover after they made the alterations that Bill took size 16 shoes! An enthusiastic supporter of the project, Bill would ride without boots to demonstrate the effectiveness of the Isolastic system.

What Jordan called 'productionising' the Commando was carried out back in Woolwich where Norton planned to manufacture their new flagship. The final production prototype then underwent thousands of miles of testing. Enthusiasm for the new model was high throughout the company, and there was never any shortage of pilots. Riders ranged from Norton directors to staff and included the likes of William Colquhuon, John Hudson, John McDermott and Peter Williams.

Elsewhere, however, concerns remained that Norton couldn't possibly better their Featherbed frame. Such fears were allayed shortly after the Commando went on sale in April 1968. The British public voted the Commando *Motor Cycle News'* Machine of the Year for five years running.

But at the time the Commando first went on sale, its maker's profile in America amongst 20- to 35-year-old purchasers was, by contrast, very low. Mike Jackson, an expatriate Brit who NVT sent to America to run Norton's Los Angeles subsidiary, told *Classic Bike Guide* that none of this key demographic knew of the marque's racing success at Daytona (where Norton were four time-winners) or at the Isle of Man (where they were victors of 38 TTs).

Something had to be done. In 1968, during a three-week fact-finding mission to the US (in which Poore also undertook difficult negotiations with Norton's American distributor, Joe Berliner, to establish Norton Villiers Corporation [NVC] as the brand's exclusive distributor in five western states), Dennis visited the offices of the US's two biggest motorcycle magazines: the New York-based *Cycle World* (*CW*), where he met the magazine's founder, Joe Parkhurst; and editor Cook Neilson at *Cycle* magazine's base in Costa Mesa, California. With motorcycle magazines in the US exerting considerably more influence on sales than their British counterparts (three quarters of people who purchased motorcycles over 500cc bought *Cycle* or *CW*), Poore was keen to learn as much as he could from Neilson and Parkhurst. The Englishman established an immediate rapport with the two Americans, impressed that both understood exactly what he was trying to achieve with Norton Villiers (making them, in Poore's view, amongst the first senior people in the world of publishing he had met to actually do so).

THE NORTON GIRLS

On his return to London, Poore approached Les Nappin. Nappin was an account executive for one of the City's top advertising agencies and had produced leaflets and ads for the Commando. A gifted copywriter and designer, Poore offered to help Nappin set up his own studio and promised to provide him with regular work from Norton. Although Nappin knew nothing about motorcycles, he did know about advertising.

Instead of promoting Norton's impressive racing lineage, he and Poore created a series known as the Norton Girls ads. The adverts were an instant hit, popular with 90 per cent of its intended audience. Crucial to their success was their position - the inside cover page of both *Cycle* and *Cycle World*. Moreover, Poore had secured the slot permanently.

If the BSA/Triumph combine, who had occasionally booked that slot themselves, were unhappy at Poore's coup, the Japanese manufacturers were positively apoplectic. By 1969, Honda, Kawasaki, Suzuki and Yamaha had large capacity motorcycles of their own to promote, a booming US market to win over, marketing budgets to spend, and were regular bookers of up to five or six page full-colour advertisements. Yet, no matter how great the inducements, or how much time he spent defending his arrangement with Norton, Joe Parkhurst honoured the deal he had made with Poore: Norton kept their inside cover, simply changing the image every three to four months.

Each ad comprised a full-colour photograph of a Norton Commando with a girl sat astride, laid in front or stood behind the bike. The girls, usually blonde and long-haired, were always fully clothed and dressed as if habitués of Biba* in mini-skirts, hot pants, turtle-neck sweaters, patchwork-suede jackets and thigh-length boots. The models stared straight to camera, their gaze fixed on the reader, capturing his attention. Bike and model were always static. Some ads featured two bikes, such as a Roadster and an Interstate, with two girls decorating the set. Most images were shot against a blank studio backcloth; just occasionally the picture comprised an exterior shot. (One such picture features a leggy blonde sat side saddle on a gleaming black Norton Interstate parked in front of sand dunes, the girl's lilac shirt outside her purple wide-legged trousers, hair and outfit looking vaguely windswept by the sea breezes!)

Yet, whilst the designers claimed that the ads were deliberately un-provocative (certainly, the girls' wardrobe is very much Carnaby Street sophistication), the ad copy lent itself to more libidinous interpretation. For example, one early advert depicted a 750 Roadster, in front of which lay a blonde in a short red dress (colour coded to match the bike's bodywork). The girl is leaning on her elbows looking straight into the camera and out of the page toward the reader. The copy reads:

> *You probably saw this masterpiece of shape and pace through the glint of plate glass, or in*
> *a magazine, maybe being handled by a friend or even worse by someone you don't know.*
> *Long before your eyes laid her you knew that somewhere sometime you would meet for that*

---

*   Biba was a fashion boutique whose founder, Barbara Hulanicki, was cited by journalist John Crosby in the *Daily Telegraph* article that coined the phrase Swinging London' as one of the 'people who make London swing'.

never surpassed experience. You wanted a high flyer with scintillating looks... that could hold on tight even during the wildest inclinations... Of course, she can also be easy and gentle like a purring pussy cat, as smooth in motion as a ski on virgin snow - but only if you're man enough to move fast with her when you both get turned on.

Most photo-shoots took place in a studio in London and lasted about two days. Norton technician Richard Negus, however, recalled one memorably protracted session on a beach in Sussex. Undertaken in Arctic conditions, it dispelled forever any illusions Negus had harboured about the glamour of advertising.

Photo-shoots are notoriously frenetic affairs, but Nappin, who Mike Jackson described as 'an oasis of calm', planned out every shoot beforehand. He selected the girls' wardrobes, built several sets in different colours, and made sure that a Norton engineer was present with fuel tanks and panels in every livery listed in the manufacturer's catalogue for the sales season they were promoting. The photographer would shoot the female model in different outfits, against different colour schemes, and next to differently kitted-out motorcycles. As she changed garments, the engineer would swap out the bike's tank and bodywork. However expensive the campaign was (and it was) one ad in just a single month's issue of *Cycle* cost Norton as much as three Commandos - the phenomenal response to the ads made it worthwhile. Mike Jackson told *Classic Bike Guide*: 'According to a restricted circulation poll, the Norton ads consistently drew the widest response of any brand'.

After the copy, and adjacent to the Norton logo, each ad urged readers who wanted more information or literature to contact the magazine. *Cycle* then passed the enquirer's details to the advertiser. By including the addresses of both the Berliner Motor Corporation and NVC alongside the territories they each covered, Norton could split the advertising costs and the magazine was able to sort out to which organisation they should pass the enquiry. As Berliner was the exclusive importer and distributor for 43 States in the East, South and Mid-West, *Cycle* would forward a response from Florida, for example, on to their Hasbrouck Heights address in New Jersey; whereas they would direct a reader from San Francisco to Norton's office on Paramount Boulevard in Long Beach where NVC managed the import and distribution for the seven West Coast states of California, Arizona, Nevada, Oregon, Washington, Hawaii and Alaska. Even from those last two states ('about as lively as the Shetlands', was Jackson's summary of the business they each generated), NVC still received coupons by the sackful.

With the American sales season starting in March, Norton had to ensure that their ads promoting the coming year's models were ready in time to appear in *Cycle* and *Cycle World*'s April issues, both of whom operated on a 90-day lead-in time (which explains why their coverage of the Daytona races held in March never appeared before June). Not only that, it was essential that the April issue carried road tests of the factory's new offerings. It was a problem all the British motorcycle manufacturers wrestled with. Norton's answer was to have the Wolverhampton plant assign a small team of dedicated engineers to the task. They would hand-build the new models, which then had to be run-in and shipped to the US by early December. By Christmas, machines would have to be in London for Les Nappin to shoot the ad for the April issue (although those bikes did not necessarily have to be runners).

Almost inevitably, problems occurred. Shipments went astray or machines were damaged in transit, road testers crashed test bikes, and components failed. None of that, however, could be allowed to stand in the way. All that mattered was that the new bike received a great review in the all-important April editions.

And, as we have already seen in previous chapters, few reviews helped raise a bike's profile in the States more than *Cycle* magazine's very first superbike comparison contest.

In autumn 1969, editor Cook Neilson came up with idea of pitting the 'seven strongest motorcycles available for sale in the world' against one another. The Superbike 7 were the machines *Cycle* thought best embodied the traits a buyer focussed purely on a motorcycle's performance might themselves choose.

The magazine invited seven manufacturers to take part. (Two factories, Benelli and BMW, applied to take part even though *Cycle* hadn't actually invited them!)

In the end, Neilson settled on a shortlist comprising the three-cylinder BSA and Triumph 750s, the Harley-Davidson XLCH1000 Sportster, the Honda CB750/4; the Kawasaki 500 MACH III two-stroke triple, the Suzuki T500 Titan two-stroke twin, and the 750 Norton.

Neilson and *Cycle*'s technical editor Jess Thomas decamped from their New York base to the warmer climes of southern California for a few weeks (a move which probably influenced the magazine's eventual relocation there in 1971). The venue they selected for testing was Orange County International Raceway (OCIR) near Los Angeles.

Manufacturers could field one bike from their 1969 range. The bike had to be stock. *Cycle*'s rules did, however, permit company engineers to install components that were factory-listed options and assemble their challenger by hand. They were allowed to bring spare parts along with them - although they had to provide copies of published factory specification sheets - and be on hand at each of the track sessions.

After a series of tests comprising lap times, braking, and acceleration, the magazine tore down each engine and transmission to verify the motor was to manufacturer's published spec and that all components were standard or factory options. A couple were found to be running non-standard parts and their 'cheats' were duly exposed.

Staffers ranked the high-piped Commando S the easiest bike of the group to ride fast. It also proved the quickest of the seven down the Orange County drag strip after posting a time of 12.69 seconds over the quarter mile (the Trident was runner up with 12.78 seconds). With a best of 12.98 seconds, the Honda trailed a fraction behind the Harley's 12.97 - until *Cycle* disqualified the Sportster for cheating. 'It had huge, carved-out ports,' the magazine revealed. The test bike, they disclosed, had 'a larger inlet valve than stock ($1^{15}/_{16}$ inch which will be standard on the '70 models), and a quarter-speed racing oil pump.' Milwaukee subsequently withdrew all advertising.

The Norton placed third with its 103.68mph terminal speed at the end of a quarter mile (the Kawasaki 500 topped the group with 104.40mph, followed by the Trident with 103.92). The Commando was second fastest round the OCIR track with a lap time of 45.5, just four tenths of a second slower than the joint winners, the Honda and BSA 750s who tied with a matching lap time of 44.9 seconds. The Triumph came in fourth on 46 seconds dead, followed by the Harley (46.5), then the Kawasaki (46.7). The Suzuki posted the slowest lap time (48.5 seconds).

The Honda, the heaviest bike of the seven, had the strongest stoppers; the drum-braked Norton the worst (the CB750 pulled almost half as many Gs again as the last placed Norton). And yet, after all of the tests, by the end of contest staffers were unable to declare an overall winner. Instead, because there were so many variables, *Cycle* concentrated on the contestants' comparative performances in the various challenges, pointing out the best and worst, and, crucially, why.

With *Cycle* having over 450,000 subscribers and being perhaps the most influential publication on the market, the Commando's performance in the world's first superbike comparison test provided Norton with fantastic exposure. NVC ordered 10,000 reprints of the 16 page article (which they had to specially commission as the original printing plates were no longer available), and headlined all their West Coast ads with the Norton's '12.69 Second' quarter-mile time.

Originally intended as a stop-gap model, the Commando went on to enjoy a ten-year production run, during the course of which Norton made it available in a dizzying variety of forms. These included the model that launched the range in 1967, the Fastback, and a long-range version of the Fastback, the LR, a low volume model distinguished by its 3½ gallon fuel tank and its seat which dropped the original Fastback's tank-hugging projections at the front. There was the lean and lithe Roadster, and the heavyweight Interstate (421lb to 496lb respectively); the S and SS-model high-piped scramblers; the half-faired John Player Special (in 850 and 750 homologation versions); and the preposterous 750 and 850 Hi-Riders. Engine capacity went from 750 to 850cc (actually 828cc) in 1973; electric start and left-hand gear changing arrived in 1975 when NVT unveiled the new Commando Mk III and Trident T160V at a joint trade and press launch at Ragley Hall in Warwickshire that March.

For 1972, Norton also briefly offered buyers standard and high-powered versions of the Commando. The higher spec engine, known as the Combat, was Poore's idea and it proved an expensive disaster.

THE COMBAT ENGINE DISASTER

By 1971, the Commando desperately needed to replace its front drum brake. Rivals Triumph had successfully adapted the AP Lockheed cast iron calliper that car makers British Leyland fitted to the Mini Cooper. However, Norton's engineers deemed the item too heavy. Lockheed also offered a lightweight aluminium version, popular with racers; but that, Norton decided, was prohibitively expensive. And besides, neither calliper - cast iron nor alloy - looked right on the Commando. So, working in close collaboration with Lockheed, Bob Trigg and his designers developed a bespoke calliper and brake system for application on the Commando. The new purpose-built system looked good and Lockheed agreed to let NVT manufacture most of the components at Norton's Wolverhampton plant.

However, following detailed analysis of the costs for producing the new front binder, it was evident that the Commando's retail price would have to rise next year - and dramatically. Poore decided, therefore, that on purely marketing grounds, the increased cost should bring with it higher performance. He instructed his engineers to tune the engine. This sportier motor, which Poore decreed should have its power hiked by around 10 per cent, would only be available on the disc-brake model. Distinguished by its black barrels, the Combat engine, as it became known, sported fiercer cam profiles and higher compression ratios compared to the standard, drum-braked model (whose barrels retained their silver finish), which Poore demanded Norton should continue to sell alongside the high-spec versions.

Despite his engineers' protestations that the Commando's engine was already operating at its limit and that the plant's ancient machinery was simply not up to the task, Poore - who understood that upgrading the engine was a highly marketable, minimal-cost means of recovering the expenditure the factory had incurred tooling up for the new disc brake - overrode his technicians' advice. 'To his credit, though, and from the outset', Mick Jackson told *Classic Bike Guide* for a series of articles recalling his Norton years, 'Poore consistently stated he would assume responsibility'.

Norton introduced the Combat engine in 1972, the year NVT launched the Interstate. With power output raised to 65bhp - seven more than the original Commando - as a result of higher compression (from 8.9:1 to 10:1), engineers should have combined the Combat's hike in power with a stronger bottom end. Sadly, as they failed to do that, problems with the new engine soon emerged.

In an effort to re-establish Norton in Germany, Andover's newly-appointed importer, Gerd Korner, ordered a large batch of Interstates. The long-legged tourer with a large-capacity fuel tank seemed just the bike to take on BMW in its own backyard. Certainly, buyers reading the German-language version of Norton's new catalogue (the design and content of which Dennis Poore himself had had a hand in) could be forgiven for thinking NVT's new tourer could match the Bavarian twin on the autobahn and that it could soak up any punishment Germany's long-distance riders might mete out. The inconvenient truth, however, emerged in mid-April when reports of Combat engine failures started to surface. Nor was the problem confined to Germany. Combat-spec motors were failing by the dozen in other markets too. Fortunately, the standard motor represented about a quarter of the '72 season's sales and proved as reliable - or at least no more troublesome - than the previous year's Commandos. Indeed, NVT's head at Norton's Los Angeles subsidiary, Mick Jackson, credited the carry-over drum-brake model as the reason the factory survived the Combat debacle.

As NVT's Design Office and Research and Development team frantically sought a solution, their colleagues in Norton's Service Department were busy replacing broken Combat engines and placating hordes of irate owners, Keith Blair, NVT's sales chief for France, Italy and Spain foresaw - even before it had gone into production - that the Combat engine might prove problematic. He therefore persuaded many of his dealers to order the standard specification motor (Blair's prescience ameliorating quite considerably the scale of the recall).

Having moved to Australia in February 1971 to take up a post as Norton's service manager (and later Spares Manager), the former draughtsman Roger Jordan soon found himself in the thick of it. 'The eagerly-awaited Combat machines were a disaster,' he told *Motorcyclist Illustrated*, 'and I was soon up to my eyeballs in main bearing failures. The cost of new bearings (£5) and labour to replace them (£20) accounted for most of the profit on a new bike then, but worse, the name of Norton was being dragged down lower.'

In America, Norton's largest market, reports of failures were miniscule compared to the rates suffered in Europe. Norton's respected global service manager John Nelson put that down to the superior quality of the fuel available in the US. In Wolverhampton, on the other hand, MD John Pedley oversaw more than 1,500 new Commandos taken back down the assembly line to have their engines removed, their crankcases split, the offending '2S' profile cams and rogue main bearings replaced, and each motor rebuilt with softer camshafts and Superblend bearings. Each machine was then returned to the Testing & Rectification centre, and from there on to despatch (where many found themselves heading back to dealers in the UK from whom the machine had been returned to the factory in the first place).

The whole affair ended up costing Norton more than a £1 million to rectify.

The Commando lasted another five years. The end finally arrived when production of the venerable twin ceased in October 1977 with the 850 Mk III. The bike by then was, according to Roger Jordan, a pretty well sorted machine. It boasted disc brakes both front and back and an electric start as standard (the American-made Prestolite - Press to Light). Power output was an actual 51.5bhp (Norton claimed 58bhp), and when *Bike* magazine tested the very last of the Interstate models against a Honda CB750K7, they found that 'despite its four cylinders and totally different concept to the British machine, [the Honda K7] is surprisingly similar in its touring outlook to the Commando'.

Performance was also similar: the Honda topping out at 110.29mph with the rider sitting up (and an estimated 115mph with the rider flat out); with the Commando reaching 101.23mph (111.16mph with the rider prone). On the drag strip the K7 was quicker over the quarter mile - an estimated 13.9 seconds compared to the Norton's estimated time of 14.9. The difference between the two machines, however, didn't come down to mere seconds. In truth, the two were separated by decades.

Just ten years earlier, the Honda was a clean-sheet design. The Commando's powerplant, by contrast, could trace its roots back to 1949 and Bert Hopwood's 500cc Dominator engine. Over successive decades, Hopwood's half-litre twin rose in capacity from 500cc to 600cc; morphed into the 650 Dominator, the 750 Atlas, and then later the 750cc Commando. Even when Norton increased displacement to 850, the Commando retained the four-speed gearbox AMC fitted to their bikes as far back as 1956.

And yet *Bike* magazine felt that the Commando's demise was premature. It was still selling well despite NVT's high asking price of £1,317 - for just £82 more buyers could purchase the shaft-drive Yamaha XS750 triple, which the magazine described as 'surely one of the most refreshing Japanese designs in recent years'. Tester Graham Sanderson suspected demand for the last 1,400 machines to roll out of the Marston Road plant would be keen (fuelled as much by 'nostalgia and misplaced patriotism,' he thought, as 'the desire to own as good a British machine as there's likely to be in the immediate future'). It was especially sad, Sanderson thought, to see the Commando phased out before it had reached its 'development summit'.

NVT, however, was now in the hands of the receivers. When, in 1975, the Government withdrew its £4 million export credit guarantee, which NVT had been using as working capital, it was clear that Wolverhampton had to close. Poore eventually ended production of the Norton Commando in 1977 and emptied Marston Road and Small Heath of around two million pounds' worth of Commando, Trident, BSA and Triumph spares and transferred it all to their Andover site in rural Hampshire, making it NVT's worldwide service centre. It meant that Norton Villiers Triumph was no longer a motorcycle manufacturer, just a parts supplier and distributor.

It was not the outcome Poore had intended.

POORE'S DILEMMA

When the Conservative government approached him in 1972 and proposed he take on the dying BSA/Triumph combine and merge it with his own comparatively healthy Norton and Villiers brands, an initially hesitant Poore realised that such a conglomerate would 'carry more weight' with parts suppliers. The DTI also offered Norton's parent company, Manganese Bronze Holdings, BSA Group's profitable non-motorcycle engineering operations for the bargain price of £3½ million. These included BSA Guns (hence, BSA's piled arms logo), and Carbodies Limited, makers of London's iconic black cabs. The DTI would also provide a cash injection to the new Norton Villiers and Triumph combine of £4.8 million (with MBH match-funding the sum).

Moreover, following Meriden's recent reduction in staffing levels as a result of 300 staff accepting voluntary redundancy, employee levels were much more closely aligned to production and demand and the Motorcycle Division produced a surplus for April '73 of £390,000.

It seemed a sweet deal. Even so, Poore knew that if he chose not to accept it and the politicians nationalised BSA/Triumph, it would leave Norton vulnerable. His first objective was to stem BSA/Triumph's enormous losses (the combine was haemorrhaging money at a rate of nearly £4 million a year). Poore's rescue plan involved reducing the number of plants from three to two, thereby making immediate savings on overheads.

Production of the Commando would continue at Norton's Wolverhampton factory, whilst manufacture of the Bonneville would transfer from Meriden to Small Heath. Triumph's Coventry plant was to close. Under the plan, the former BSA plant at Small Heath - which Poore saw as the more modern of the two factories due to its greater number of overhead conveyors and timed component-delivery systems - would produce 10,000 Tridents and 35,000 Bonnevilles; Wolverhampton would turn out 15,000 Norton Commandos. (In 1971, consultants had also advised BSA to consolidate production by shutting down one of the main plants. Their plan, however, proposed closing Small Heath, buying components from external suppliers instead of BSA manufacturing them themselves, and retaining Meriden, which they felt was better positioned to accommodate the proposal.)

Poore denied rumours suggesting his reasons for shutting Meriden were because of the militancy of its unions and that wages were higher there than at Small Heath and Wolverhampton (although a 1990 study attributed the difference to Triumph's higher profitability and the resultant sense of greater self-worth amongst its workers). In fact, Poore was tasked by the Government under the terms of the Industry Act to save an industry, not jobs. When, at a model launch, he was accused by a reporter of being an asset stripper, Poore's retort was to ask the journalist archly: 'What assets do you actually mean?'

Poore's scheme had the support of the Heath Government, and the Department of Industry agreed to handle the repercussions. However, after Poore's misjudged announcement of the planned closure at that fateful lunchtime meeting in the Meriden canteen which precipitated the blockade, the Industry Minister Christopher Chataway's response complicated an already rapidly unravelling situation.

He insisted Poore should not call in the police. The Minister was anxious to avert 5,000 workers from nearby factories descending on Meriden amidst rumours that they were mobilised and ready to arrive by the coach load within an hour of any police action.

The Minister also instigated discussions with the Meriden workforce. As *Bike* journalist Mike Nicks observed a short time later, the move gave 'the sit-in an air of legality'. Chataway, however, was anxious to avoid the highly militant unions shutting down the Midland motor industry in sympathy with the plant's occupiers.

In February 1974, Tony Benn replaced Chataway to become the new Secretary of State for the Department of Industry after Harold Wilson surprised pollsters and beat Ted Heath and the Conservatives to form a minority Labour government. Seven months into their year-and-a-half-long sit-in, blockading workers now knew they had someone in Whitehall to champion the co-operative (even if Benn's Cabinet colleagues did not necessarily share his zeal).

The new Minister (whom the satirical magazine *Private Eye* dubbed 'Benn and the Art of Motorcycle Maintenance' after Robert M. Pirsig's cult philosophical novel *Zen and the Art of Motorcycle Maintenance* published that same year) immediately arbitrated an agreement between an exasperated and growingly litigiously-inclined Poore and the Meriden plant's occupiers to release more than a thousand Triumph twins locked inside the factory, which NVT desperately needed in order to supply its product-starved dealers.

By June, Benn had assuaged Small Heath workers' concerns regarding his support for a Meriden co-operative at a meeting he hosted in the House of Commons between NVT and the two sites' union convenors. One month later, Benn announced in Parliament that he had negotiated a settlement: The Government would loan the Triumph Co-operative £4.2 million (a sum which, because it was below £5 million, precluded a full Commons debate that the minority Labour Government would almost certainly have lost). They would also provide Meriden with a grant of £750,000. NVT would receive most of the money in payment for selling the factory, plant, machinery and manufacturing rights for the big Triumph twin to the Meriden-based Co-op.

From a pre-blockade workforce of 1,750 in September 1973, by the following July just 500 Meriden staff remained, the rest having drifted away over the course of the lock-ins two winters. By Christmas, only 280 were left. Of those, the Co-op could only offer enough work to 200. Their first task was to produce much needed spares.

Registered as Sinova Motors Ltd, but trading as the Meriden Motorcycle Co-operative (with NVT as its distributor in a two-year deal giving Poore's company the right to market 1,500 right-foot and 48,000 left-foot gear-change models through its worldwide dealer network), initial production rates for the fledgling business were only around 125 Bonnevilles a week.

Although Benn continued as Industry Minister following that year's second General Election (when voters returned to Britain's polling stations in October 1974), he retained the post for only nine more months. In a Cabinet reshuffle carried out in June 1975, Harold Wilson moved Benn to Energy and replaced him at the Department of Industry with Eric Varley.

Just three months before leaving the DTI, however, Benn had commissioned an independent assessment of Britain's motorcycle industry, its prospects, and options for a viable future. Published as a House of Commons paper in July 1975, The Boston Consulting Group's findings made sombre reading for the newly-appointed Industry Minister, Eric Varley.

THE BOSTON REPORT - STRATEGIES TO SAVE AN INDUSTRY

Titled *Strategy alternatives for the British motorcycle industry*, the 121 page report opened with an outline of the industry's decline, the underlying reason for which Boston attributed to 'a concern for short term profitability' during the 1960s. The consultants described how, over the course of the decade, British manufacturers had retreated from an increasing number of displacement categories, unable or unwilling to confront Japanese competition. As the British withdrew from the 175cc, 250, 350, 500 and finally 650cc categories, the Japanese 'progressively developed volumes and experience in ever larger displacement classes...' until all that remained to the British were those segments of the market to which the Far East had not yet challenged its hegemony. By the end of the Sixties, the only sector left to the British was large-capacity motorcycles. As the higher-displacement category had enjoyed rapid growth over that same period, it meant they had been able to maintain its output of approximately 80,000 units a year. Fatally, however, where the British strategy up till then had been to withdraw from a segment when confronted by Japanese competition, British manufacturers' error this time was their failure to introduce new models in the one category remaining to them.

In 1969, half of the eight models displacing between 450cc to 749cc on sale in the US were British, the UK boasting a 49 per cent market share of the segment. Four years later, and by 1973 only two of the ten models available were British built, and Britain's market share in the USA had fallen to just 9 per cent. But although Britain remained well established at home and in the States - the country which represented more than 70 per cent of the world's market for superbikes - the British motorcycle industry was not nearly so well ensconced elsewhere. With the report's authors predicting that America's consumption of superbikes was approaching saturation point, Boston anticipated that growth in the superbike segment would only come from those markets where British industry was *not* well established - and even then, despite the fact that in the seven years up to the report's publication (1975), global sales of superbikes had expanded by 40 per cent, they predicted that by 1980 the sector's worldwide sales was set to settle at around ten per cent. Yet between 1969 and 1973, volumes for British bikes had stayed at around 30,000 units a year in this segment, whilst Japanese volume in the over 450cc category grew more than eightfold in that period - from 27,000 to 218,000.

With manufacturers spending around 2 per cent of sales revenue on advertising, the Japanese manufacturers' greater volumes meant that Honda's expenditure, for example, was $8,100,000 in 1972 compared to British industry's total outlay of just $1,300,000.

The fact was that British factories' ageing plant and labour-intensive manufacturing methods precluded high-volume production.* According to the report's authors, the British factories were unable to produce parts 'to the close tolerances required for a reliable final product'. In Wolverhampton, for example, the factory's output of 18 bikes per man year made it the most productive of Britain's motorcycle factories - yet as many as 60 per cent of the machine tools were more than twenty years old.** Net fixed investment per man was about £1,300. Honda, by contrast, invested £5,000 per man and output at its Suzuka factory was around 350 motorcycles per man year.

---

* In his study of BSA's post-war decline, Joe Heaton argues that Britain's tax system in the 1950s 'discriminated against capital expenditure on plant and industrial buildings'. The tax deductions companies could claim against depreciation on plant were low whilst nominal tax levels were high. Tax policy gradually became more progressive during the 1960s until by the time BSA collapsed, whilst corporation tax was high (52 per cent), businesses could write off 60 per cent (and later 100 per cent) of expenditure on plant and machinery in mitigation. However, that shift came too late for BSA.

** Boston based their figures for Wolverhampton's productivity rate of 18 motorcycles per man year on 1975 volumes (18,000 machines). This bettered Small Heath's rate for 1975 of 10 units per man year (10,500 bikes), and Meriden's of 14 motorcycles per man year (based on the 1972-73 season when the factory produced 28,000 machines). The British factories' figures were comparable with both their European and US rivals. Moto Guzzi/Benelli, for example, with 40,000 motorcycles at a rate of 13 - plus 20 mopeds - per man year; BMW with 25,000 vehicles at 20 machines per man year; and Harley-Davidson with 38,000 and 15 units per man year (although that figure included a three-month strike).

The contrast to the Japanese factories, however, was startling. Honda produced a combined total of two million units at their Suzuka and Hamamatsu factories - an estimated 106 bikes plus 21 cars per man year; Yamaha 1 million motorcycles at 200 units per man year; Suzuki 800,000 motorcycles at a rate of 114 bikes per man year; and Kawasaki's Akashi factory's 300,000 motorcycles at 159 bikes per man year.

The Boston report outlined three strategy options. The first two required massive investment if the industry was to achieve greater productivity and remain competitive on price. The medium-volume strategy would realise 40,000 motorcycles a year and required an investment in the order of £38 million. The high-volume option called for an investment of £51 million to achieve annual outputs approaching 70,000 units made up of three-models. The range would comprise 500, 750 and 1,000cc machines - 'designed to come off the same transfer machinery'.

But even the least expensive strategy still required an investment of £15 million to deliver production runs of 17,000 bikes a year. This low-volume option would utilise existing technology and techniques concentrated on two superbike models - a 750cc and a 1,000cc machine. Manufacturing would take place in one factory (which, due to its size, Boston suggested should be Small Heath).

Dennis Poore, meanwhile, met with the DTI's new Secretary of State and told him he now needed £30 to £40 million to run a three-factory arrangement (Meriden, Small Heath and Wolverhampton). The sum was more than double the figure he had presented Varley's predecessor, Tony Benn.

The Government withdrew its £4 million export credit guarantee, money NVT had been using as working capital. Poore had no choice but to call in the receivers and in August 1975, NVT went into liquidation. Staff at Wolverhampton immediately staged a sit-in, which meant Poore now had TWO plants operating as workers' co-operatives! Small Heath, too, went into receivership and was rapidly wound down.

Re-emerging as NVT Engineering, the newly-formed company promptly wound down the Wolverhampton site at the same time as it assembled a batch of 500 Commandos there between June - when the workers finally bowed to the inevitable and ended their sit-in - and September 1976. Those 500 machines were followed by another 1,500 bikes by September the following year, and a considerably smaller number in Andover the year after that. In 1977, the company cleared out Marston Road and Small Heath of BSA, Commando, Trident, and Triumph spares and transferred around two million pounds' worth of components to Andover, now NVT's international service centre.

The move to Andover closed the book on the Commando's ten-year production run. More significantly, the Commando's demise also marked the end for Norton as a motorcycle manufacturer. Established in 1898 by James Lansdowne Norton to make it one of the world's oldest motorcycle marques, Norton now just stored, supplied and distributed spare parts.

This left a much reduced Triumph as Britain's only volume motorcycle manufacturer. Yet, in 1978, and against competition from showroom rivals such as the Yamaha XS750 triple (*Bike* magazine's 1977 Bike of the Year), Honda's 'bomb-proof' K7 and F2 successors to the original Dream Four, and Suzuki's new four-cylinder GS750 (introduced one year earlier to deserved acclaim), Meriden's twin-cylinder Bonneville managed to outsell them all. Improbably, one in three 750s bought in Britain that year was a Triumph, making the T140 the country's best-selling 750.

FOUR MORE BOW OUT

Two other Superbike 7 contenders now also out of production were the two-stroke triples from Kawasaki - the 500cc H1, and the outright winner from 1972's contest, the 750 H2 - Kawasaki having dropped them in 1975 and '76 respectively. Both were casualties of rising fuel costs and increasingly restrictive emission regulations in Kawasaki's biggest market, the US. But the H1 and H2 also fell afoul of changing expectations from customers whose tastes were shifting away from smoky, raw, gas-guzzling two-strokes. It was a trend hastened by manufacturers who had seen sales figures that showed buyers still wanted performance, but in a motorcycle that was easier to live with. Performance now had to be in a package that was also comfortable, reliable and civilised.

Suzuki's Titan 500cc two-stroke twin, a bike *Cycle* magazine themselves admitted they should *not* have included in 1970's inaugural Superbike 7, evolved over a ten-year life span from its first incarnation as a premium-priced torquey half-litre street (and successful road) racer to its eventual role as a budget-bike all-rounder. Time and trends, however, eventually caught up with the famously bullet-proof 500 twin in 1977 when Suzuki quietly dropped the GT500 from its range (by which time the twin had enjoyed various appellations during its lifetime, including 500/5, Titan, Cobra and T500).

Although it finished fifth in *Cycle*'s 1972 follow-up to its superbike comparison test, staffers nevertheless declared the Ducati 750GT 'the bike everybody wanted to ride home, points total or no'. The victor earlier that year of the first 200 mile race at Italy's Imola circuit, Ducati's desmodromic valve-operated race bike (based on the spring-valve 750GT roadster introduced the previous year), was soon being outclassed in F750 by its Japanese rivals. The factory's canny chief designer Fabio Taglioni therefore proposed a new engine displacement: 860cc. The larger capacity was intended to help the long-legged Ducati compete in endurance races for which the bike was better suited. As a result, the 750GT - its flowing lines styled by Italjet founder Leopoldo Tartarini - was superseded in 1974 by the Giorgietto Guigiaro-styled 860, which abandoned its predecessor's rounder shapes for a modern, squarer-edged look.

Runner up in the second of *Cycle*'s head-to-heads (with a tally of 399 points out of a possible 400), the Kawasaki Z1 was denied victory by its 750 sibling's winning total of 399.6. Yet it was the second-placed bike - not the outright champion - that represented the future of superbikes in the Seventies.

Even so, by 1978 the bike *Cycle* described as 'the frontier-stretching Kawasaki 903cc Z1' had ceded its crown to a successor, the Z1000, which the factory had introduced a year earlier (1977). Bigger, heavier, and more civilised than the Z1 (and its Z1A, B and Z900 variants), the new one litre bike was in fact slower than its antecedents, as manufacturers focused on civility and manners instead of drag light performance. This was one shift, however, that did not go down well with some observers.

In a special issue dedicated to Kawasaki, *Superbike* magazine's feature editor Michael Scott pronounced the 'Mighty Z1000, crowned King of Superbikes' a slob. Kawasaki's new flagship was a 'corpulent cat'. Once 'the most exciting, pre-packaged thrill in motorcycling,' the Z1 had, according to Scott, 'gone flabby.' It had gone soft, he moaned, had been civilised, and - what seemed particularly irksome to the journalist - 'idiot-proofed'.

Last One Standing

That left the Harley-Davidson Sportster as the only bike to take part in *Cycle* magazine's first two 'Big 7' superbike comparison tests that still remained in production when Yamaha released the XS750E. Introduced two decades earlier in response to competition from the lighter, nimbler and faster imports from Britain, the XLCH became the quickest bike *Cycle* had ever tested when their '69-model 883 Sportster ran a 13.73 second standing quarter, despite being an archaic design even when new. Yet the Milwaukee-built V-twin still managed to outlast its more modern Orange County combatants: the BSA and Triumph 750 triples, the Kawasaki H1 500 and H2 750 three-cylinder two-strokes, the Honda 750 and Kawasaki 900 fours, the Ducati and Norton 750s and Suzuki 500 twins.

Considered a muscle-bike when Harley launched the Sportster in 1957, this quintessentially American expression of the maxim 'there's no substitute for cubic inches' could trace its origins to a humble 10 x 15-foot wooden shed in turn-of-the century Wisconsin and an empty soup can.

19

HARLEY-DAVIDSON

THE MOTOR COMPANY'S EARLIEST DAYS, H-D PETITIONS THE US GOVERNMENT, AND MILWAUKEE LAUNCHES THE SPORTSTER - H-D'S ANSWER TO ITS LIMEY RIVALS

'These machines separate the men from the boys'
(Part of a letter presented as evidence before the US Tariff Commission)

Arthur Davidson

William S. Harley

BILL HARLEY AND HIS FRIEND ARTHUR DAVIDSON BUILD A BIKE

By 1901, 20-year-old draughtsman William 'Bill' Sylvester Harley and his boyhood friend Arthur Davidson, a pattern maker and the youngest of four brothers, had been mulling over the notion of a motorised pedal bicycle for some time. Bill was the son of Cambridgeshire-born English emigrants, William Harley and Margaret Scott. Arthur was also of British descent, his grand-parents having left Scotland for America in 1858 with their six children in tow. Bill had worked in a Milwaukee bicycle factory since the age of 15, but following a long discussion with Emile Kruger, a fellow draughtsman who had done what he and Arthur had up till then only talked about, the two friends decided to draft in the assistance of a mutual friend, Ole Evinrude. A small-engine enthusiast, Evinrude helped them refine the primitive carburettor they had fashioned from an old tomato-soup can.* (Ole would later find fame building out-board motors).

The plan was to construct a vehicle that would take them to their favourite fishing hole quicker than they could pedal their bicycles. Their first attempt at constructing a motorcycle consisted of a simple De Dion-type single-cylinder motor installed in a push-bike frame. The result proved reliable, but the 10 cubic inch (165cc) engine dispensed barely enough power to propel the bike along on anything other than perfectly level ground.

Arthur Davidson wrote to his brother Walter, a machinist working on railway locomotives in Parson, Kansas, and invited him to test ride the new motorcycle. On arrival in Milwaukee, Walter, who was planning to return to the Brew City anyway to attend his older brother William's wedding, was probably taken aback when his brother and his friend explained that the bike was in pieces and that Bill and Arthur had hoped Walter would assemble the machine before he took it for a ride! That delayed ride would prove life-changing. As Walter put together the petrol-powered two-wheeler, he took the opportunity to study the De Dion-style power unit. As a machinist himself, he appreciated its qualities and the close tolerances to which it had been constructed. With the bike now built, Walter took it out for a spin - and discovered that he was a born rider.

Walter immediately moved back in with his family and approached the Chicago, Milwaukee and St. Paul Railroad Company where his father and his recently-married brother William worked, securing a machinist's position to help his brother Bill and Arthur Harley in their enterprise. Their ambitions had now shifted from selling motorised bicycles as a mail-order kit, to designing and constructing complete motorcycles - Bill Harley draughting the designs, Arthur Davidson making the patterns, Walter acting as the machinist and mechanic, and William, the eldest of the Davidson brothers, acting as both consultant and occasional fabricator (utilising the Chicago, Milwaukee & St. Paul Railroad's tool-room to surreptitiously produce components from Arthur's patterns). Constructed in a cellar workshop situated beneath the family home, the first bike they manufactured had a single-cylinder motor housed in a cycle frame powered by an engine with a carburettor fashioned from an empty tin of tomato soup. Output, however, remained puny, so for the second prototype they increased the flywheel's diameter from 5½ inches to 11 inches. They also enlarged the engine's bore and stroke to 3 inches and 3½ inches respectively.

This engine was much stronger and easily capable of tackling hills and inclines. But it was clear to Bill from his years working for Milwaukee's Meiselbach Bicycle factory that the bicycle's 'diamond-shaped' frame to which they had attached the motor was simply too weak. The boys therefore devised a frame of their own. The new frame had its main tube loop under the engine and was a vast improvement. Margaret Davidson,

---

*   Accounts vary on the contents of the can Arthur Harley and Bill Davidson used to craft their first carburettor. Some sources cite tomatoes, others tomato juice. I have opted for the Davidson family's own version of the legend - tomato soup - which Walter Davidson's granddaughter cites in her fascinating book *Jean Davidson's Harley-Davidson Family Album*.

however, had had enough of the mess and the noise her sons and their friend Bill were bringing into her house and ordered them out of the basement. To keep the peace, her husband, William C. Davidson Senior, purchased and erected a 10 x 15 ft wooden shed in the family's back garden, across whose door the eldest of the Davidson sisters, Janet (who worked in her uncle's store designing monograms for fine linens), scrawled in large, crudely-painted capital letters the legend: 'HARLEY DAVIDSON MOTOR CO.'*

The trio were now full-time motorcycle manufacturers. They nicknamed their first production model the Silent Gray Fellow. Dubbed 'Fellow' to suggest a reliable and trusted travelling companion, they opted for a light grey livery, with pin-striping and hand-painted logo courtesy of Janet. Fitted with a muffler designed to quieten the noise from the engine, the bike boasted a 25 cubic inch (410cc) three horsepower single-cylinder motor inclined slightly forward in its loop frame. Typical of motorcycles at the time, the engine did not have a gearbox or starter. Instead, pedalling gears were fitted. The rider would place the bike on its rear stand and rotate the pedals to start up the engine and set the machine in motion. Once underway, the bike could cruise at around 25mph. Most noticeable was the engine's distinctively large crankcase, which it needed to house the 11 inch flywheel. Inlet valve actuation was automatic (insofar as it was operated by the suction of the piston descending in the cylinder, a common arrangement for engines at that time). The rear wheel was driven directly off the engine by a long belt.

Bill Harley and the Davidson brothers launched their first production motorcycle in 1903, building two bikes for paying customers over the winter of 1903-04 (one of which they sold to Bill and Arthur's schoolyard pal, Henry Meyer).** Indeed, 1903 turned out to be quite a propitious year for launches. Across seven countries - Austro-Hungary, Britain, France, Germany, Italy, Sweden and the United States - more than 80 new motorcycle marques sprang up (most notably, Sweden's Husqvarna).

Turn-Of-The-Century Pioneers

Out on the North Carolina coast late that same year, 800 miles north-east of Milwaukee, two brothers from Dayton, Ohio, assisted by five locals (who included lifeguards from the nearby Kill Devil Hill's lifesaving station), propelled a flimsy-looking home-made aircraft on a trolley along a wooden rail. Moments later, with 32-year-old Orville Wright lying prostrate at the controls and his elder brother Wilbur steadying the plane by its wing, their wooden and canvas flying machine jettisoned its trolley and was airborne.

---

   *   The shed still exists, preserved on the grounds of Harley-Davidson's massive modern-day factory in Milwaukee, a reminder of the company's modest origins.

   **   In his unauthorised history *At the Creation: Myth, Reality, and the Origin of the Harley-Davidson Motorcycle,1901-1909,* professional historian Herbert Wagner presents evidence which challenges Milwaukee's official line that the first Harley-Davidson was manufactured in early 1903. Wagner makes a persuasive case that it was built later than that. He examined H-D's own numbering system, which labelled the machine built for 1905 as Model 1. He cites as evidence that the Motor Company itself marked its Golden Anniversary in *1954,* not 1953.He quotes adverts from 1913 and 1919, which - like those of H-D's rivals at the time - embellish how long the company had been making motorcycles; and presents extracts from transcripts of William S. Harley's evidence in a court case, in which the company's co-founder denied responsibility for the misleading ad copy yet refused to condemn the H-D staff who had authored the wording.

Rising 15 feet into the cold December skies above Kitty Hawk beach, the Wright Flyer, as the brothers christened it - named after one of the bikes they made and sold in their Dayton bicycle store, not in tribute to their plane's aeronautical properties - it travelled just 40 yards before coming to rest on a sand dune. It was the world's first powered flight and it lasted less than 12 seconds.*

Six months earlier, on 13 June 1903, in Wisconsin's neighbouring state of Michigan, 39-year-old Henry Ford also made history (in spite of his famous assertion that history was 'bunk'). That Saturday night, he and eleven investors held their first stockholders' meeting. Three days later, on June 16, they filed papers of incorporation at the State Capitol in Lansing to establish the Ford Motor Company (Ford reputedly declining the offer of a local doctor to join the founders as that would have brought their number to thirteen).

Just five years earlier, not even 30 working cars existed in the whole of the US. Yet a year later, in the first four months of 1899 alone, American investors put up $388 million in start-up capital for new car makers. The result was that in a little over a decade there were 700 automobile factories in the United States.

It was a similar story for motorcycles. By 1911, around 200 motorcycle brands were being made in America.

All this happened without any infrastructure to support petrol-driven vehicles (neither two- or four-wheel). There were no petrol stations, and no road-management systems such as traffic lights. Drivers had neither driving licences nor insurance. There were no road maps. Indeed, as late as 1905, not one mile of paved rural highway existed in America even though by 1900 there were 8,000 motor vehicles, a figure which rose to nearly half a million by 1910 and doubled to two million in the five years to 1915. The federal government thought building highways was a state matter; the states were fearful of subsidising what might turn out to be a mere fad (resulting in 20 states in 1912 spending no money whatsoever on highway construction).

What roads did exist were little more than dirt tracks. In summer, they were baked hard and so rough that they could break an axle; in winter, the tracks would turn to mud and become impassable. Large swathes of Kansas and Nebraska had no roads at all. In hilly terrain such as the Rockies, to avoid fuel starvation, car drivers found they had to reverse up inclines so that the gasoline would flow back toward the engine. One early automotive pioneer from Vermont, Dr Horatio Nelson Jackson, accompanied by his dog, Bud (wearing goggles like his human companions), became a hero in America when in 1903 he and Jackson's mechanic made the first Transcontinental crossing from sea to shining sea in just 65 days in their open-top Winton twin-cylinder automobile.

Inevitably, America's automotive infrastructure soon began to catch up. Licence plates appeared in 1901. In 1905, the Automobile Gasoline Company of St Louis

---

* The Wright brothers made three more flights that blustery 17th December day. The longest lasted just under a minute and covered a distance of 852 feet. As they discussed a fifth attempt, a sudden gust of wind lifted the plane and bounced it across the dunes, wrecking its rear ribs and engine mountings and bringing to a halt any further test flights. The Wright Flyer never flew again and spent the next 25 years hidden under dust sheets in a shed back in Dayton.

introduced the first of a chain of gasoline stations; four years after Sylvanus F. Bowser invented an effective fuel pump, which he called a Filling Station (its use as a term for gas stations only becoming commonplace some two decades later in the 1920s).

Things were progressing just as quickly at Harley-Davidson (an appellation arrived at through mutual agreement, each concurring that the alternative naming order - 'Davidson-Harley' - didn't have the same ring to it).

The Four Founders

In 1904, C.H. Lang of Chicago opened the first Harley-Davidson dealership, selling one of Arthur, Bill and Walter's first three production bikes. In 1904, the trio hired their first full-time employee. On Independence Day of that year, a Harley-Davidson came first in a 15 mile race in Chicago with a winning time of 19:02. Production at the fledgling company, meanwhile, was expanding. Unclear what to do with their mounting proceeds, they banked it in a canning jar in the pantry, hidden behind tinned peaches and string bins. However, a maid employed to tidy after them found their cache and stole all the money. Fortunately, a bachelor uncle, James McLay, a Scottish-born beekeeper who lived in seclusion in nearby Madison overlooking Lake Mendota, loaned them his life savings so that they had the money to build a bigger factory. Measuring 28 x 80 feet, they moved into their spacious new premises on Chestnut Street (now Juneau Avenue) in 1906.* Now employing six full-time staff, output that year reached 49 motorcycles. Bill Harley, however, knew that if the company was to progress, they needed to develop a more advanced approach to production, and better and more improved designs. He therefore enrolled himself at Wisconsin University, located some 80 miles away, to pursue a degree course in engineering. The following year, the eldest of the Davidson brothers, 37-year-old William A. Davidson, quit his job as a foreman and railroad toolmaker to join the Motor Company as its works manager. On Tuesday 17th September of that year, the company was incorporated, its stock shared four ways between the founders.** Production in 1907 tripled as output rose to 152 units, trebling again in 1908 for a second successive year.

Meanwhile, Walter's successful campaigning in endurance competitions added to the company's growing reputation for building ruggedly dependable machines. Whilst all four founders viewed racing as a costly distraction from their primary business of building and selling motorcycles, they saw events in which simply finishing - irrespective

---

* In 1994, the US Government listed the Juneau Avenue site of H-D's corporate headquarters on its National Register of Historic Places.

** All seventeen H D employees bought stock in the new company, launched amidst a depressed stock market. Indeed, 1907 was a particularly difficult year for Harley-Davidson's founders to start up in business. In March, panic selling 'roiled the Stock Exchange', followed in October, by a stock market panic and a bank crisis that nearly wiped out New York city's finance houses (half of whose collateral on their massive loans to buy stocks and shares was backed by securities, leaving banks with few cash reserves to deal with any sudden runs). After stock prices collapsed (leading to ruin for many and a spate of suicides amongst speculators and depositors) it took the intervention of the Wall Street banking titan John Pierpont Morgan to steady things. It would be the last occasion when one man would yield such power. Henceforth, it would fall to federal government to intercede in financial crises.

of whether that included coming first - was showcase enough of their product's reliability in those early pioneering days.

Of Harley-Davidson's four founders, former railroad engineer Walter Davidson was the team's most gifted motorcyclist. In 1907, he was one of only three competitors to achieve a perfect score when he completed the 400 mile, two-day endurance event from Chicago to Kokomo, Indiana (and back again to Chicago).* At the Seventh Annual Federation of American Motorcyclists' (FAM) Endurance and Reliability Contest in June 1908, Walter and his box-stock single-cylinder belt-drive 30 cubic inch Model 5 scored a perfect 1,000 points (plus an additional five points for both man and machine's outstanding consistency) when he successfully completed the 190 miles from Catskill, New York to New York City in the Long Island Endurance Run. Walter was so confident of his mount that he carried no additional spares (unlike some competitors whose factory riders had cars in tow loaded with spare components). In what many consider America's first national motorcycle competition, the punishing rural roads eliminated 15 of the 61 starters by the end the contest's first day. Harley's victory earned him the FAM's diamond medal, as according to them: 'During the two days of the contest, he varied by eight minutes from the exact schedule, which places him so far in advance of all others as to leave his qualification for the award beyond dispute.' Bill Harley's win was significant in other ways, too. An authorised history of Harley-Davidson marking the company's eighty-fifth anniversary said: 'Many believe [Walter's] perfect score on one of only three H-Ds in the contest put the motorcycle on the map.'

Three days later, Walter added still more lustre to the company's reputation by setting the FAM economy record when he eked 188.23 miles out of a gallon of gasoline from his Harley-Davidson.

He became the company's first president. Despite his lack of formal business training, Walter's facility in the role grew - such that, in later life, he was appointed a trustee of Milwaukee's hugely successful Northwestern Mutual Insurance Company and a director of the state's largest bank, First Wisconsin. He had a reputation for honesty, almost to a fault. On one occasion, after checking the bill following a business lunch in a New York hotel, he deducted the cost of his own meal and claimed expenses for just those of

---

*   Also held that year was the very first Isle of Man Tourist Trophy (TT) motorcycle race. On 28 May 1907, 25 riders lined up for the start of that inaugural event, Aimed at testing competing machines' reliability and fuel consumption, the course consisted of a 16 mile circuit that began in St John's, before finishing ten laps later back at St John's. Just 12 riders completed the race. After covering a distance of 158 miles, Charlie Collier riding a Matchless crossed the line first with an average speed of 38.2mph, 11 minutes ahead of second-placed Jack Marshall riding a Triumph. Collier's winning Matchless averaged 94.5mpg.

Interviewed many years later by Geoff Davison for the Triumph Owners club magazine *Nacelle*, Marshall recalled the problems he encountered negotiating Creg Willey's Hill on his clutchless, single-gear Triumph: 'Those who had pedals, pedalled fit to bust. Those who hadn't frequently jumped off and ran.'

The island's topography wasn't the only challenge. 'Our main troubles were punctures, broken belts, broken or stretched exhaust valves, seized engines and crashes,' Marshall told Davison. 'We did find our compulsory toolkits very useful.' Riders carried final drive belts and at least one spare inner tube around their waist.

Riders apparel was commonly long leather trench or raincoats (with some sporting rubber ponchos). To keep down the dust on Manx's unpaved roads, organisers sprayed the course with an acid solution, which soon reduced competitor's clothing to tatters.

his guests. Another time, he allowed Harley-Davidson's race chief in the Thirties, Hank Syvertson, to travel to Los Angeles on board the luxurious Super Chief locomotive - only if Syvertson paid the additional $12 himself. Yet he was also incredibly generous, a man described as 'giving disproportionately to charity'.

Walter's younger brother, Arthur Davidson, was also a capable rider. The smallest of the four, Arthur, a patternmaker when he and Bill Harley constructed their first motorcycle, had emerged as an inspired marketing man (for example, when in 1913 the company promoted their motorcycle's durability by advertising that their very first machine had racked up 100,000 miles in a decade's service on its original main bearings). Arthur's most enduring contribution to the company, however, was establishing its dealer network. Starting in the Northeast, Arthur rode from town to town demonstrating the bike. Always a good storyteller, and with just his brother's success in the nationally-sanctioned endurance event as the company's only solid claim to fame, he managed to convince people to sell his company's motorcycles and become H-D dealers. Arthur's marketing nous and Walter's achievements resulted in the company selling its first motorcycle for police duty in 1908 when they delivered a Silent Gray Fellow to the Detroit Police Department (home turf of car giants General Motors and Ford!). It was the beginning of Harley-Davidson's long association with police departments across America (encapsulated for generations of cinemagoers by countless Hollywood movies featuring a motorcycle cop lurking behind a roadside billboard on the outskirts of town, from the back of which he would emerge - sirens wailing - to chase the bad guys fleeing in a black sedan!).

Arthur became the company's secretary and sales manager, retaining a strong bond with H-D's dealerships. He believed very firmly that the success of the company relied on the well-being of its dealers: 'A Harley-Davidson dealer,' he decreed at meetings with either dealers or factory staff, 'must make money.' An outdoors man, Arthur later became a gentleman farmer (purchasing many of his prize stock of Guernsey cattle from the founder of Harley-Davidson's chief domestic rival, the Indian Motorcycle Company!). A philanthropist, he donated time, money and part of his Waukesha County estate in west Milwaukee to the American Boy Scouts movement.

The eldest brother, William A. Davidson, had forsaken the relative security of the railroad to throw his hand in with his siblings, Walter and Arthur, and Arthur's friend Bill Harley. A family man with responsibilities, William joined them in the automotive industry at a time when, still in its first decade, the sector's future - even for automobiles - remained uncertain.

He became H-D's works manager, purchasing plant, presses and machinery for the nascent company, whose output was expanding at dizzying speed. A big man, William was affectionately known by his employees as 'Old Bill' because of his paternalism; perhaps no better symbol of which was a small black notebook he carried in his pocket. In it, William kept the names of welders, machinists, toolmakers, and assembly-line staff to whom he had loaned money to tide them over till payday. However, he rarely collected on whatever debts he was owed. A keen hunter and angler, William shared his brother, Arthur's, love of the outdoors. And though he boasted that 'my office door is always open', he would point visitors who overstayed their welcome to a large barrel of peanuts he kept in the corner of his office, inviting them to: 'Grab a handful on your way out'.

Bill Harley was one year older than his boyhood pal Arthur, and from an early age, something of a fixture in the Davidson family home. He was the only one of the four founders to graduate from college, and during his near 40 year tenure as the company's chief engineer and treasurer, he oversaw the design and introduction of several classic models. An expert rider, Bill Harley performed well in endurance competitions aboard some of Harley-Davidson's very first motorcycles, but his first love was the outdoors - something he really only found time to enjoy in his late twenties when the demands of a burgeoning company began at last to stabilise. Taking a Leica 35mm camera mounted on the stock of a gun, Harley would retreat into the woods surrounding the Wisconsin lakes and photograph the birds and water fowl. From the prints, he would produce sketches and copper etchings, which he often gave to friends and family as gifts.

As capable and popular as the 500cc single-cylinder Model 5 undoubtedly was, the long distances riders travelled meant its top speed of around 45mph left many owners wanting more power. But, rather than scrap the single's proven design, Bill Harley elected instead to use it as the basis of Harley-Davidson's next model. By grafting a pair of singles onto a beefed-up crankcase, Bill intended to create a stronger engine. The resulting V-twin, however, proved no faster than its donor single and after building just 27 of them in 1909, the company quickly withdrew the 4 horsepower 49 cubic inch (803cc) twin from sale.

Although it had retained the single-cylinder model's primitive suction-operated valves, Harley's first V-twin nevertheless managed to break new ground in other areas. It introduced twist-grip throttle control, and was their first bike to feature leading-link front fork suspension. In 1911, following a period of further development, H-D launched its newly incarnated V-twin. Known as the F-Type, Bill Harley had replaced the Model 5's automatic valve-actuated mechanism with a pushrod-operated system. Power output for the new V-twin had jumped to 7hp, giving it a top speed of nearly 60mph (bettering its single-cylinder stablemate by around 15mph). Like many of its pioneer contemporaries, the F still employed gravity-fed lubrication and fixed belt drive.

However, in 1912, with the launch of its 61 cubic inch Model XBE V-twin, Harley-Davidson dropped the hand-controlled belt tensioner which disengaged power from the rear wheel, and introduced the first commercially-successful motorcycle clutch. Housed in the rear-wheel hub, the new mechanism let the rider come to a halt and take off again without having to re-start the engine. In 1915, Harley introduced an automatic oil pump and a three-speed gearbox, together with the optional extra that year of electric lighting plus gear-driven magneto-generator. Production soared. Sales topped 3,000 machines in 1910, 5,000 the following year, and 9,000 the year after that. When hostilities in Europe broke out, the factory's output exceeded 16,000 motorcycles.

MILWAUKEE GOES TO COURT

Half-a-century after Harley-Davidson launched its first V-twin, the factory released the XLH Sportster. It was Milwaukee's response to an invasion by European rivals flooding the US market with faster and lighter motorcycles, culminating in 1952 with Harley-Davidson's request to the United States Tariff Commission to increase levies on foreign imports. By then, however, all four Harley-Davidson founders were gone. First to pass on was H-D's works manager, William 'Old Bill' Davidson, considered by many to be the heart of the company.

When Harley-Davidson signed its first union pact on 19 April 1937, William, who had fought against the move, took it as a personal defeat. Two days later, he was dead. He was just 66. Although William suffered with diabetes, his son, William H. Davidson (later to become president of the company) believed that losing his battle to keep the unions off his shop floor hastened his father's demise.

Walter Davidson passed away aged 65 on 7 February 1942. Eight years later, on the evening of 30 December 1950, the youngest of the brothers, Arthur Davidson, was killed alongside his wife in an automobile collision. Arthur was 69. He had survived by seven years his boyhood friend and co-founder, Bill Harley, who had remained an active member of the AMA and an energetic player of handball right up to his death in September 1943, aged just 62.

In January 1951, just days after Arthur Davidson's fatal car crash, Triumph announced the formation of its Baltimore-based east coast factory depot, Triumph Corporation (or TriCor, as it became known). Bill Johnson, president of Johnson Motors Inc., formed 14 years earlier in California to service the US's west coast, was appointed Vice President of the new corporation. His brief was to support TriCor's President, 48-year-old Coventry-born American émigré Dennis McCormack 'in coordinating the efforts of the two associated companies in promoting still further the popularity of Triumph motorcycles and rendering even greater assistance to the Triumph dealer organisation throughout the United States' (in truth, however, Johnson's role in TriCor was little more than titular).

The news about TriCor and Triumph's plans to introduce a 'left-' and 'right-side' presence in the States came as a shock to Milwaukee.

By 1950, 40 per cent of motorcycle sales in the US were now imports. In 1950 alone, Triumph had tripled its exports to America to 2,800 motorcycles. Harley-Davidson therefore felt understandably threatened when they heard about Triumph's announcement of its new factory branch. Then, just a few weeks after TriCor's grand opening, Triumph decided that because they had cancelled its popular annual service school and dealer convention in Baltimore in order to concentrate on launching their new eastern depot, they would invite more than 200 dealers from across the USA to the 1951 Daytona races to attend a banquet at the swanky Daytona Beach Bath and Tennis Club.

Edward Turner was also present. In response to a New York dealer's question about whether Meriden could satisfy the demands of its growing network in America, the Triumph chief answered: 'We will have enough machines for you in 1951. We will have enough in 1952. No sensible person will commit himself beyond that period. Triumph's new branch in this country is proof that we have faith in both our ability to produce, and your chaps' ability to sell them.'

Supporting Turner's contention was the fact that the market for motorcycles in America seemed barely tapped. Whereas in Britain one person in every hundred owned a motorcycle, in America only one in six hundred did.

Alarmed at what they saw as yet more encroachment into 'their' market, and the still more worrying news in March '51 that Triumph's owner, Jack Sangster, had sold the thriving Coventry company to the world's largest motorcycle manufacturer, BSA (who in 1950 had produced almost 50,000 machines), Harley-Davidson orchestrated a concentrated letter campaign by its dealers. H-D followed this up in June 1951 with a petition to the United States Tariff Commission urging them to levy higher duties on foreign-made motorcycles.

The charge Milwaukee filed with the Federal Trade Commission was against all British bike importers, whom they accused of 'dumping' motorcycles onto the US market. Harley-Davidson's lawyer, Martin Paulsen, sought a fourfold increase to the 10 per cent tariff then in place. In addition to a 40 per cent levy on all British imports, he wanted British motorcycle imports restricted to no more than 10 per cent of the manufacturing output of the American domestic market (essentially, Harley's own production figures).

Harley claimed that the English had not created a market, but stolen an existing one by selling machines at a quarter to nearly a third of the price of a Harley-Davidson as a result of the British Government's devaluation of the pound in 1949. Milwaukee contended that as price was the sole criteria for customers when purchasing a motorcycle, domestic makers were disadvantaged by foreign manufacturers.

Joining forces to oppose Harley's complaint were the newly-formed Triumph Corporation and its barely ensconced President, Dennis McCormack; Triumph's West Coast distributor, JoMo and its President (and TriCor's Vice-President), Bill Johnson; BSA's Hap Alzina and Rich Child; and Fred Stote, President of the Indian Sales Corporation. (Stote's presence was not as improbable it might at first seem, given that the majority of Indian's sales comprised a stable of British marques, including AJS, Matchless, and Norton.)

The hearings opened on 18 September 1951. Testifying for the plaintiff were long-standing Harley dealers Dud Perkins and Earl Robinson (of San Francisco and Detroit, respectively), and Triumph's first major US importer (and now Harley-Davidson dealer), Bronx-based Reggie Pink. Pink, who had enjoyed success competing across the eastern states in early hill climbs, fuel-efficiency contests, and endurance events on board lightweight British two-wheelers, had, as a dealer during the Twenties and Thirties, offered his customers up to nineteen motorcycle marques. Makes included Ariel, Calthorpe, Dunelt, JAP, New Imperial, Norton, OK Supreme, Scott, and Velocette, as well as the American-made Indian. But the marque he featured in his catalogue above all others back then was Triumph - with Turner's 1938 Speed Twin his outlet's most requested pre-war model.

To demonstrate to the commission the differences between the two countries' offerings, examples of British and American machines were wheeled into the building's elevator and transported up to the third floor. Machines presented to the commission included a brand new Triumph 6T and a Vincent V-twin. The room - including officials from the Tariff Board - broke into laughter, however, when the hearing learned that only the Harley was too big to fit in the lift car, and that it had to be dismantled in order to get it inside the elevator cage.

Triumph dealer, Charles Pusey, from Washington DC, generated further amusement (and more damning evidence against Harley) after he read out a letter from a customer: 'When I was struggling with the Harley and asked a certain well-known Harley enthusiast for some advice in "mastering the monster", his answer was, "These machines separate the men from the boys." Shortly after that, I was separated.'

Even in reports of the hearing from those sections of the American motorcycling press previously protective of their domestic manufacturers, such as *Motorcyclist* magazine (who had suppressed the results of war-time races where Harley or Indian had been beaten by a foreign marque), were unconvinced by Milwaukee's argument: 'The Harley-Davidson Company is being injured not by competition,' reported Rosemary Arctander in October 1951, 'but by its own lethargy in failing to improve its obsolete models - the 45 was introduced in 1929 and the 74, in the mid-Thirties - and both have remained virtually unchanged since then.'

Nine months after the hearings finished on 27 September, the commission announced its decision. On 16 June 1952, the Tariff Board rejected Harley's complaint, arguing that British manufacturers were supplying a middleweight market that America's domestic motorcycles makers had elected to ignore.

Milwaukee had evidently already reached the same conclusion. In December 1951, Harley-Davidson announced the launch of a new model. They had for some years been developing an all-alloy, 60 degree ohv V-twin, with high cams and twin carburettors. However, the bike which replaced H-D's 45 cubic inch (750cc) *three*-speed flathead V-twin WL45 (a model Milwaukee introduced a mere 32 years earlier), was a *four*-speed 45 cubic inch flathead V-twin called the K-model. Even more oddly, having gained a gear and replaced the WL's hand-operated gear lever with a foot-shift (thereby bringing the K in line with its modern English rivals), H-D's new model retained its predecessor's prehistoric side-valve motor. Sporting a low-slung frame, hydraulically-dampened front forks and swing-arm rear suspension, the K was, according *Old Bike Journal* magazine's Bob Rimel; 'one of Harley's most manageable and forgiving motorcycles.' However, Milwaukee's answer to foreign interlopers produced just 30bhp and weighed 100lb more than most British middleweight motorcycles. Not surprisingly, then, it was a good deal slower than the smaller displacement 650cc Triumph (and even Meriden's half-litre T100). Where a Triumph Thunderbird could top the ton (100mph), the K was barely capable of exceeding 80mph.

Sales were disappointing. Even when, two years later, Harley punched the motor out to 55 cubic inches (883cc), bringing power output to 38bhp - a hike of 12 per cent - the

K still could not compete with the Thunderbird. But the accompanying makeover the K received along with its increase in displacement offered customers a preview of what Harley would launch in just a few years' time.

THE SPORTSTER

In 1957, Harley-Davidson celebrated its Golden Anniversary. It proved a landmark for H-D in another regard, too, as it was in that same year that Milwaukee introduced its XLH Sportster. Based on K-series' running gear and powerplant, the Sportster's biggest obvious difference was atop the engine department, which now featured overhead valves - an arrangement H-D had originally introduced back in 1936 with its 61E 'Knucklehead' (the sixty-one denoting the one litre V-twin's capacity in cubic inches; the Knucklehead sobriquet a result of the rocker boxes' resemblance to the knuckles of a clenched fist).

The new engine featured larger valves, aluminium tappets, polished ports, domed pistons, a 7.5:1 a compression ratio, a massive three-inch bore and near four-inch stroke, a unit-construction four-speed gearbox, roller main bearings, constant-mesh clutch, and generator and battery-coil ignition. And yet, in spite of producing 40bhp (at 5,500rpm), the first Sportster still could not beat the 650cc Limeys. However, it could at least now match them. A year later, Milwaukee raised the XLH engine's compression to increase power to 55bhp. This made the Sportster truly competitive - in a straight line, anyhow. And, in a makeover inspired by the Spartan purity of the stripped-down homologated competition version, the XLC racer, the road-going XLCH Sportster* gained its signature profile courtesy of the factory-installed 2.2 gallon (10 litre) fuel tank lifted straight off its 125cc stablemate, the Hummer (a single-cylinder two-stroke based on the pre-war DKW).**

With its staggered high-level exhausts, 'peanut' tank, and bare-boned appearance, which placed the engine centre stage, the new-look Sportster outsold the dowdy XLH two to one. The model itself, however, was not an immediate hit, and throughout the Sixties fewer than one in every five Harleys sold was a Sportster.

The Sportster's 883cc displacement continued unaltered until 1972, when the factory increased engine capacity to one-litre (61 cubic inches), actually 997cc. During the preceding years, Milwaukee had converted the Sportster from 6 to 12 volt electrics and auto-advance ignition in 1965 (replacing the manual-retard magneto, which, if set incorrectly, could launch a rider into the air and over the handlebars should the motor suddenly backfire as they attempted to kick-start the motorcycle into life); and swapped from a Linkert carburettor to a Tillotson in 1966, and later a Bendix (a carburettor originally used on tractors) as fitted to the '72 model. Notwithstanding the electric start the milder XLH version of the Sportster received in 1967, the jump in capacity was the biggest change Harley had made to the XLCH's engine. The Sportster's performance, too, had also remained largely static. In 1967, *Cycle*'s test Sportster ran a standing quarter

---

*   From 1959, Harley-Davidson offered Sportsters in two variants: the H model and the CH model (CH standing for 'Competition Hot').

**   The DKW was offered to the Allies as part of Germany's post-war reparations (it appeared in Britain as the BSA Bantam).

in 14.41 seconds, at the end of which the bike was travelling at 92 miles an hour. A year later, and the magazine's '68-edition test bike was posting 14.3 second quarters at 91mph. However, the XLCH became the quickest bike *Cycle* had ever tested when their '69-model 883 Sportster ran a 13.73 second standing quarter.

The magazine managed to better this the following year, when staffers in *Cycle's* very first Superbike 7 comparison test ran an XLCH down the OCIR drag strip in 12.97 seconds at a terminal speed of 102.15mph. Unfortunately, *Cycle* later disqualified the Sportster for cheating.

When the magazine returned to Orange County two years later during the summer of 1972 for the follow-up to its hugely popular group comparison test, almost half of the twenty-two standing quarter-mile runs the Sportster performed that late August day were in the 13.5 second area. The one-litre V-twin had been the last of the seven competitors to go before the Raceway's drag strip staging lights. According to *Cycle*, the Sportster's California-compliant silencers - necessary to meet that State's newly-in-force 86.6 decibel limit - seriously impeded the '73 edition XLCH's 'high-rpm horsepower capabilities' (despite the bigger engine's gains in horsepower, which raised power output from 59 to 61bhp). Thankfully, its 'gargantuan low-end torque' remained undiminished - an impressive 52 ft-lbs at 3,800rpm. Unfortunately, the strangulated Sportster ran out of urge at the upper reaches of its power band. Nine of its runs hit terminal speeds in the region of 98mph, with seven runs posting trap speeds of some 99mph. The H-D Sportster's best time was 13.393 seconds at 99.88mph.

The Harley-Davidson was doubly let down by its Goodyear tyres, which either would spin uselessly off the line during drag-strip testing, or squirrel during hard cornering. Testers, however, deemed the Sportster's suspension excellent. Its brakes also performed well in track tests, despite the front binder dragging after a few laps. Other complaints included an uncomfortably hot oil tank, which jabbed into the rider's right leg; an erratic tachometer, which complicated consistent gear-changing; and a continuously blinking oil-pressure warning light.

The magazine concluded that the one-litre Sportster 'was clearly not as potent as its 833cc 1970 predecessor had been (12.97 seconds and 102.15mph). But it was just as clearly more legal' (an allusion, perhaps, to the XLCH's quieter silencers and its disqualification from *Cycle's* first comparison test two years earlier).

When *Bike* magazine in Britain tested an XLCH1000 alongside a Harley FX Super Glide that same summer in the course of a 2,500 mile road trip across America, testers Terry Krueger and Chris Hodenfield declared the Sportster a 'musclehead' and a 'bike like no other [which] must be learnt thoroughly'. Their article described the testers' evident delight at mastering the arcane rituals of successfully firing up the beast:

Stand up on the kickstart. Give it a half-stroke prime, then open the fuel petcock and turn the key. No choke unless it's extremely cold weather. Only a crack of throttle. Get the front cylinder on the compression stroke. Then summon up all that Black Belt Kickstart Karate energy and lunge like hell. Couple of those manoeuvres and you've got a running engine.

The pair also related how they had to acclimatise to the Sportster's handling characteristics. The XLCH demanded the rider 'Take Charge'. Only by physically *throwing* the bike into turns would the Sportster's pilot - to quote the author's Zen-like phrase - 'extract joy'. In a berserk dash to keep up with a Honda and Suzuki 750 on a run through Californian mountain roads, the journalists found themselves attacking broad sweeping turns at between 60 and 70mph, 'the XLCH tracking as true as a raging locomotive'. However, after heeling over its tall *iron* engine, they found that the Sportster could suddenly and disconcertingly tip over a couple of degrees further. In the heat of contest the testers soon overlooked this trait - until more veteran H-D riders cautioned the British scribes of the Sportster's propensity to 'drop to the floor altogether'.

And although the testers deemed the XLCH's low-speed handling satisfactory, the Sportster - whilst 'terrific' in the cut-and-thrust of traffic - did not take kindly to stop-start riding. Under stop-go conditions, the engine would overheat, die, and refuse to restart. *Bike* did wonder if the problem was confined to their particular test bike, which they revealed had seized a piston just a day after they had collected it.

Factory mechanic, Jim Wismer, asked if the writers had ridden the bike for long stretches without occasionally backing off the accelerator. (As the Harley had a friction-roll throttle with no snap-back return springs, the rider is able to wind the twist-grip right back and leave it there. The downside with that, though, is that the engine doesn't get a break and a chance to suck oil up the bores and lubricate the cylinder walls.)

Krueger and Hodenfield assured him that they hadn't, suspecting instead that the cause of their Sportster's poor health was more likely the thrashings the test bike had suffered at the hands of other magazines (*Bike*'s review coming along late in the testing season).

In the space of just a few hours, Wismer's mechanics had removed the XLCH's front cylinder, re-bored the barrel .0025 thou - dispensing with the usual niceties of balancing the motor - put it all back together, and had the engine up and running again. And although the bike ran lustily enough, it remained temperamental in traffic, and the engine was so noisy that gas station attendants would ask the journalists to switch off the motor while they filled up its 2.5 gallon tank - which, with the Sportster drinking fuel at a rate of 30mpg, meant riders were switching to reserve every 60 miles.

THE LAST OF THE OLD-TIME SUPERBIKES

The Sportster's weight disadvantage, at least when compared to its English competitors, had, by the end of the Sixties, all but disappeared since the advent of the new multi-cylinder superbikes from Britain and Japan. In *Cycle* magazine's first superbike showdown, the XLCH - at 453lbs with an empty tank, but a normal amount of oil - was actually only the *fourth* heaviest bike on test. It was lighter than the Honda 750/4 (480lbs), the BSA Rocket 3 (475lbs), and the Triumph Trident (470lbs). Only the Norton, the Kawasaki MACH III and the Suzuki 500 twin weighed less (404lbs, 390lbs and 387lbs respectively).

It was a similar story two years later when *Cycle* ran its follow up test and pitched the 1973 season's crop of superbikes against one another. The Sportster now tipped the scales at 487½lb. It still occupied fourth place, but this time it came in a whopping 54½lb lighter than that year's heaviest contender, the Kawasaki Z1 - double the difference that had separated the Sportster and the previous showdown's heaviest entrant, the Honda 750.

With its hike in displacement, new steering head casting, much-improved (Japanese-made) front forks and silencers, and a new Kelsey-Hayes hydraulic front disc brake, *Cycle* noted that the Sportster 'has changed more between 1972 and 1973 than it has between any other two model years'. Yet the XLCH still retained the very same qualities that had 'made it one of the world's most popular motorcycles since its introduction in 1957: it's big, demanding and masculine, and it projects the image of a bruiser'.

But it was clear to *Cycle* staffers and everybody else that the Sportster's performance *image* did not match its performance *figures*. In a *Bike* magazine 'Hall of Fame' retrospective published in 1980, Phil Wade, a Harley Riders Club President, described how, for almost a decade, 'H-D had a winner, advertised as the Number One'.

The Sportster, Wade wrote, could reach speeds of 120mph 'straight from the crate,' and reminded readers that in the Sixties, it held 'the fastest single-engined motorcycle world record on Bonneville Salts'. That, however, was then. 'The Sportster,' Wade conceded, 'belongs to the romantic age of motorcycling. Better your motorcycle says mean machine than have a spotless garage floor. Harleys have engines, Jap bikes have motors.'

Yet even back in 1972, *Cycle* dismissed such views. The Sportster and the Kawasaki 750 'are the last two legitimate, old-time Superbikes... and even the Mach IV shows signs of civility'. But the magazine, whilst praising the Sportster for strides it had made controlling its noise levels - the XLCH was one of only three contestants from the seven that came under California's 88dB limit - was considerably less charitable about its absolute performance, which *Cycle* described as 'rather shoddy'. Moreover, they concluded that 'what performance it does deliver comes at a pretty high price'. By their calculation, the XLCH was the most expensive bike in the test per point earned - $5.54 to the winning Mach IV's $3.50.

None of that seemed to matter, however. The factory sold 20,000 Sportsters in 1973. The bike had carved out quite a following amongst customers who placed more value on how the bike looked and felt over its ultimate performance. Milwaukee would leave the race for ever more power for others to pursue.

20

THE HORSEPOWER WAR HOTS UP

THE JAPANESE RELEASE THE CBX1000, GS1000, XS1100, AND Z1-R, THE ITALIANS A ONE-LITRE TRIPLE DEVELOPED ON THE BACKROADS OF RURAL WORCESTERSHIRE... AND KAWASAKI LAUNCH THE Z1300

'Meet The Megabikes'
(*Bike* magazine cover - March 1978)

Joan Claybrook

HONDA BUILD A BIKE TO POLE-AXE ITS RIVALS

Los Angeles, California, 1976: hidden amongst the maze-like corridors and passages of an airport motel, a small, but select group of journalists from the motorcycle press were gathered in a meeting room. With them were representatives from American Honda, and research and development staff from Japan and the US. It was late in the afternoon and they were there at the request of Tadashi Kume, Honda's Director of R&D.

Speaking directly to his assembled audience, Mr Kume wasted no time coming to the point: 'What do you think of Honda motorcycles?' he asked. Figuring that such an important man had not crossed the Pacific Ocean simply to glad-hand them, the American journalists responded candidly.

They did not pull their punches.

'Hondas embody the soundest engineering in all of motorcycling,' they answered. 'They have proven to be reliable. They're beautifully finished, and they all perform well. But it seems to us that Honda's current offerings are not really new. The 750 has been with us since 1969. The 550-Four is essentially the same bike it was in 1971, and we haven't seen much significant progress on the 450 twins either. The 360 has been adequate but not much more.'

Appearing to warm to their role as a critical friend, the scribes related their strong and heart-felt concerns. 'We suspect that something has changed at Honda since the late Sixties. Back then, your bikes were replaced frequently with ones which were genuinely better. But during the past several years the company seems to have grown static, conservative. It no longer moves as fast or reacts as quickly as it once did.'

In a statement tinged with disappointment, the journalists told Kume: 'Everyone looks to Honda for new expressions, new ideas, new solutions; but recently, Honda has been plodding along. Certainly progress has been made,' they acknowledged, 'but progress is not the same thing as excitement.'

Then, perhaps emboldened by the sense that none of what they were saying seemed news to Mr Kume, the journalists concluded their robust summary: 'Hondas,' they informed him, 'are no longer exciting.'

Mr Kume clearly concurred. Honda needed to produce something that would pole-axe the opposition. He returned to Japan after his meeting with the Americans determined to give them what they wanted.

HONDA TURN TO ITS GP RACING PAST

Two years later, just before sun-up on 24 October 1977, Honda unveiled the result to *Cycle* magazine in a secret preview at Willow Springs Raceway in California, (about an hour's drive north of Los Angeles).

Honda's own dealers were not scheduled to see the new bike for a full month yet (at dealer meetings in Hawaii and Japan). In fact, the bike had not even been shown to Honda's Directors in Tokyo. Normally, once the designs for a new model were complete and the prototype up and running, the Honda Research and Development Company (which Mr Soichiro Honda had made independent of the Motor Company back in 1960) would present the new machine to the parent company's senior executives first. Somehow, though, American Honda had intercepted the new flagship before it reached Tokyo. This was why *Cycle* found itself in the 'howling wilderness' of Willow Springs, far away from prying eyes, with just Honda engineers, technicians, and a film crew from American Honda for company.

American Honda was anxious to avoid information or photographs getting out and ruining the surprise for dealers. Security at the track, therefore, was tight. (The following day, Tuesday 25 October, movie-stars Gene Hackman and Paul Newman were turned away when they arrived to race their cars, with Newman's airplane making two attempts to land on Willow's straight before eventually giving up and turning back.)

It is 6:45am and still dark. The air is sharp and cold as the journalists gather trackside to get a glimpse of - as well as bag a ride on - the new flagship from Honda (which, if it isn't being ridden or filmed, American Honda are keeping hidden under tarpaulins). One of the four mechanics in attendance warms up the big engine. The journalists therefore hear the bike before they see it (*Cycle* described it as emitting a 'whistling Porche-like snarl'). As the sun crests the horizon, the hacks have gravitated close enough by now to make out the vehicle's shape. What they see before them is jaw-dropping. Struggling to maintain their aura of studied calm, their eyes cannot help but alight on the engine: a six-cylinder, air-cooled tower block of a powerplant boasting 1,047cc, *four* overhead camshafts and 24 valves. Set against velvety-matt black side panels, gold and red-centred geometric lettering announce the leviathan's name:

CBX

The CBX's project leader was 37-year-old Shoichiro Irimajiri. Back in the Sixties when he was still only in his twenties, Irimajiri had designed Honda's legendary World Championship-winning 250 and 297cc six-cylinder GP engines. Boasting 24 valves and twin-overhead cams, with a red-line of 20,000 revs, race mechanics had to heat the oil before starting the engine because it did not run below 8,000rpm.[*] He was also responsible for the factory's watch-like 125cc five, and the 23,000rpm twin-cylinder fifty.

As Irimajiri explained: 'When we were racing, we were up against the four-cylinder two-strokes built by Yamaha and Suzuki. Cylinder multiplication was the only way we could be competitive. That's why we built the Five, and the two Sixes. The CBX-Six is a direct descendant of those engines. That's one reason it only took a year and a half - we had the engine technology from our GP racing experience.'

What Irimajiri described was, in fact, a summary of the Honda way. Unlike Western corporations who commonly recruit their top executives from outside the organisation, Honda's policy from the outset was to promote from within. Right up to the end of the 1970s, the company valued proven ability and performance over formal qualifications. Consequently, before the company would let its engineers loose on designing products for the public, Honda blooded them on its racing projects.

---

[*]   With Phil Read's astonishingly fast Yamaha RD56 two-stroke twin threatening to end Honda's three-year stranglehold on the 250 championship, the factory decided the 250/6 - which they had intended to introduce in 1965 - must instead be ready to replace Rhodesian-born Jim Redman's RC162 (a 45bhp 250cc four) by the series' penultimate round: the Italian GP. Producing an incredible 53bhp at 16,500rpm, and with a top speed of around 150mph, at its debut at Monza, the eight-speed 250/6's engine overheated, allowing Read's RD56 to pass Redman and win Yamaha their first world championship.

At the Belgian and East German GPs the following year, Redman's 250/6 recorded a faster race average than Mike Hailwood's race-winning 500cc MV Agusta, and the South African achieved the first 100mph lap on a 250 at 1965's IoM TT. In 1967, Hailwood achieved still greater glory on the Six, which now displaced 297cc, produced 65bhp at 17,000rpm, all from a bike that weighed a little over 250lb. He won every race he entered at that year's IoM, breaking lap records in each. By season's end, he had finished well ahead of Agostini riding the MV Agusta, racking up five consecutive wins in the 350 class, and finished ahead of Read's Yamaha by the narrowest of margins to take the 250 title for Honda also.

Having proved himself by designing the GP racers and Honda's Formula 1 and 2 car racing engines, Irimajiri was assigned to the company's research centre in Waco to work on the Civic and the CVCC automobile engines. This was during the period when Honda's focus was centred on its loss-making car arm (to the detriment in many people's eyes of its motorcycles* - the point journalists had put to Mr Kume in Los Angeles - but on whose profits the automotive side of the business nevertheless relied).

When, however, the Civic and CVCC projects were finished, Honda established a new research centre in Asaka where Irimajiri and his fellow motorcycle engineers were transferred to develop a new range.**

After returning to Japan following his meeting with the US journalists, Tadashi Kume's determination to silence Honda's critics converged neatly, therefore, with the advent of the Asaka research facility and its coterie of talented, young designers, engineers and stylists.

For the first six months of development, the team worked on the Six alongside a one-litre four. Although they had managed to coax 98bhp from the Four - just five horsepower shy of the Six's 103 brake horsepower (as measured at the crankshaft) - because of the Six's smoothness, unique feel, and engine sound, together with Irimajiri's understanding of the layout from his time developing the six-cylinder GP racers, Honda's R&D team felt a Six offered greater long-term potential.

Other aspects of the layout, however, received almost immediate support.

Multi-valve cylinder heads had featured on Honda's factory racers going back to the RC125 of 1959, when the company entered their four-valve, bevel-driven double-overhead cam 125cc twin into the Isle of Man Lighweight TT. It was Honda's very first international road-race competition, and although the Japanese riders lacked experience, the bike itself proved reliable enough to secure sixth, seventh, eighth and eleventh places. It was not the win Soichiro Honda may have craved, but the results were good enough to earn the manufacturer's team prize. Honda's success also challenged some long-held shibboleths. Confronting the 'popular fallacy' that the Japanese were 'copyists', *Motor Cycling* said: '... the Honda racer is, without doubt at all, basically original.'

With engine power linked to engine speed, the operational effectiveness of the valve assembly is crucial. Four lightweight valves, although twice as many in number, are easier to control than two large ones. The CBX project team also imagined that '24 Valves' emblazoned across the fuel tank gave the Six more marketable appeal.

---

*   In the winter of 1967-68, Honda announced that it was retiring from motorcycle racing. The factory had decided to channel its energies into its racing car project in an effort to garner, for their growing car business, the prestige and publicity Honda had generated in the previous six years from their two-wheeled success on the track. Suzuki had already declared that it was pulling out, blaming the spiralling engineering sophistication of competition motorcycles, the ever-increasing costs of which no longer translated into sales nor was relevant to its core business of manufacturing and selling motorcycles (so much for the old maxim that 'racing improves the breed', or Harry Sturgeon's adage: 'Win on Sunday, sell on Monday'). For Honda, who had never flinched at the cost of supporting a race team, the issue was more one of reputation. Unable to wrestle the 500 title from Italy's MV Agusta, and with Yamaha's V-4 some 15bhp more powerful than Honda's 250cc challenger, plus Suzuki enjoying dominance in both the 125 and 50cc classes, Honda could only view the 350 title with any degree of confidence. They therefore faced the unpalatable prospect of winning fewer titles than they had in 1967.

**   The first models to emerge from the Asaka facility were the three-valve 400cc twin-cylinder Hawks.

The first time Honda's Chief Designer, Norimoto Otsuka, saw the Six was the same day as the team decided to halt work on the Four and direct all their energies toward the Six. Otsuka was the man responsible for the styling of all Honda motorcycles sold in Europe and North America. 'The first time we laid eyes on it,' he told *Cycle* magazine, 'we thought, "great!" It was such a new bike, with so many new ideas and concepts. We knew it would be difficult. But we were all very excited about the possibilities, since it was such a big departure from anything we had done before, both in terms of its technical specifications and the kind of look and feel the bike had to have.'

The thorny problem of where to position the six-cylinder engine had brought Irimajiri and his eight-man engine development team into contact with Otsuka and his five-man team of designers. Otsuka's immediate impression was that the rider needed more knee room. His observation led to two significant engineering decisions. The first was to tip the engine forward by 33 degrees. The second was to angle the engine's bank of CV carburettors inward so that they formed a V pointing rearward along the motorcycle's centreline.

Reducing engine width was Irimajiri's key priority. Extensive studies of the engine's thermal properties and the team's research into how it conducted heat allowed engineers to reduce the distance between cylinder bore centres. Commonly, the ratio governing the distance between bore centres of a conventional air-cooled engine was at least 1.4 times the bore's diameter. In other words, the space between the bores is 40 per cent of the bore's width. In the CBX, Irimajiri brought that down to just 1.2. (Water-cooling might have permitted engineers to bring the bore centres even closer to one another, and reduce engine width still further, but would have added weight.)

Another convention in contemporary multi-cylinder engines was to place the alternator and the ignition system at opposite ends of the crankshaft. For the CBX, with its six cylinders arranged transversely across the frame, this arrangement was simply not feasible as it would make the crankcases impossibly wide. Irimajiri's solution was to drive them, not from either end of the crank, but from the middle instead, via a jackshaft.

Turned by a 34mm wide Hy-Vo chain driven by a sprocket machined into the centre of the crankshaft, one end of the jackshaft drove the alternator (which had its own clutch to insulate it from the engine's violent acceleration), whilst the other end ran the CDI ignition, the starter-motor gear, and transmitted power from the crank to the clutch and oil pump.

The jackshaft enabled the project team to contain the Six's engine width to a creditable 23.4 inches, resulting in a powerplant just two inches (50mm) wider than its four-cylinder CB750 stablemate. Designed to perform multiple functions and cope with a variety of forces, Honda's Project Leader told *Cycle* that the jackshaft was his favourite component.

But whilst a six-cylinder engine is inevitably wide, it is also inherently smooth. It was the layout's remarkable smoothness that allowed Irimajiri to reduce the counter-weights at either end of the crankshaft. This not only shaved off vital grams, but helped improve cornering clearance. By making the two outer bob-weights approximately half the thickness of the other ten, and cutting bevels around their edges to reduce the space they occupied in the lower crankcase halve, engineers were able to improve the angles at which riders could bank the CBX through a turn (a few degrees of which were sadly negated by a pair of case bolts projecting otherwise unobtrusively at either side of the engine, as *Cycle* discovered during track testing at Willow Springs).

Counter-intuitively, perhaps, designing the CBX's exhaust system to ensure it did not ground also benefited from the engine's multiplicity of cylinders. A one-litre Six fires more evenly than a one-litre Four. This meant that the engineers could make the Six's silencers smaller and angle them higher in order to avoid grounding. As *Cycle* testified:

> It all works. After two days of hot-lapping around Willow Springs there are no hero-scratches anywhere on the exhaust system, even though the sidestand foot and curb-feeler nuts at the end of the footpegs have been frequently scraped.

Over dinner, Honda's Chief Designer Norimoto Otsuka, Senior Research Engineer Minoru Sato, American Research and Development Administrator Ken Nakagawa, and the CBX's Project Leader Shoichiro Irimajiri described to journalists the aspirations of the team's young engineers for the new model's exhaust system and the extraordinary lengths they went to in order to achieve them. Honda had a justly enviable reputation for extracting horsepower from its systems. Their ambitions for the CBX, however, went far beyond the usual parameters of what one might expect from an exhaust's performance.

'From the beginning,' Irimajiri told the journalists, 'our Six produced a smooth jet-like exhaust note. But with an ordinary exhaust arrangement, it wasn't that close to a jet. We thought if we worked on it we could come up with a motorcycle sound that no one has ever heard before.

'So we sent some engineers to the Hyakuri Japanese Air Force base in Chiba prefecture. For ten days they tape-recorded the sound of Phantom jet fighters, and then came back and designed an exhaust system for the CBX that could duplicate that sound. When I heard it for the first time I was amazed; they had captured the Phantom sound perfectly.'

Sato, a former racer, added: 'I rode the bike at our Suzuka test circuit. We had the HERT Endurance racers out at the same time. It was crazy. The Six, with its Phantom exhaust, made me feel like I was going 200 when I was only going 100. The bike's sound had a feel - a noise quality and texture - completely different from anything I have ever experienced. It sounded better than the HERT bikes.'

After Sato finished speaking, Irimajiri picked up the tale.

'After that, we contacted Mr. Kume. We told him we had something we wanted him to hear. He came, he listened, and he said, "You've gone too far. The feeling of that noise is just too much. We cannot build motorcycles that sound like jet fighters."'

The team therefore shelved the exhaust with the fighter-aircraft acoustics, and replaced it with something more conventional. Even so, Irimajiri's engineers still managed to produce a system capable of quickening the pulse of any petrol-head by engineering its headers and baffles to make the bike sound like a Porche. (*Cycle*, however, allowed itself a moment to ponder the possibility that somewhere in Asaka's 'hospital-clean' research facility, an exhaust system gathers dust, which, if fitted to a CBX, would emit the 'transcendental whoop of a deadly weapon of war'.)

TACKLING THE CBX'S TWIN CHALLENGES OF WIDTH AND WEIGHT

The six-cylinder CBX presented Irimajiri and his team with two big challenges, quite literally. As the Project Leader was quick to explain to journalists, the first problem was how to contain a six-cylinder engine's width. Clever engineering solutions, such as the jackshaft and slimmer crankshaft bob-weights, helped ameliorate that particular issue. But now Irimajiri had to address his second biggest problem: namely, to reduce the CBX's overall weight.

Inside the engine, his engineers saved precious grams and ounces by fitting hollow camshafts; a lighter valve train - a four-valve arrangement being made up of much smaller, less-heavily stressed components than a conventional two-valver - and an all-aluminium clutch. They made further savings by casting the countershaft sprocket, alternator, oil pick-up housing and shift-linkage covers in magnesium. An exotic, ultra-light alloy that was becoming increasingly common on motocross machines, its appearance on the CBX was a first for a standard street motorcycle.

Sometimes, however, Irimajiri and Otsuka locked horns over the stylist's occasional advocacy of covers for some components. And although he was prepared to make a few concessions to the designer, such as tilting the engine forward or angling the carburettors inward, Irimajiri was utterly obdurate over ideas that compromised his mission to trim weight.

This quest to keep weight off had informed Irimajiri's approach from the beginning. To eliminate the unwanted bulk of a remote oil tank (as fitted to Honda's seminal multi-cylinder superbike, the CB750), Irimajiri decided at the outset that the Six's engine should be wet-sump.

Ironically, the engine's six-cylinder layout also helped. Instead of a quad of 250cc cylinders, the CBX's six cylinders - each one displacing around 175cc - were only three-quarters of the size of those found in a one-litre Four. The happy corollary of this was that its pistons could be smaller and lighter. In all other regards, however, the CBX's pistons were entirely conventional three-ring semi-slipper affairs, with flat-top crowns cast with cutaways to clear the inlet and exhaust valves. Each piston travelled up and down cast iron liners on forged steel, two-piece connecting rods, at speeds of up to 17.8 metres a second, the piston's light weight (and a Six's inherently shorter stroke compared to that of a four-pot motor of equal displacement) allowing the engine to rev to 10,000 rpm safely.

Conventional inner and outer springs - manufactured, as on all Hondas, by Nihon Hatsujo - controlled the valves. Valve lash was set by inserting discs of the requisite thickness in a recess above the tappet. For the 297cc racing Six, Irimajiri had deployed Winkler caps, just like those Kawasaki used on their Z650-Four (in which the shim sat inside a bucket between the top of the valve stem and the underside of the tappet). 'That,' Irimajiri told journalists, 'reduces valve assembly weight, but makes maintenance difficult. We had lots of time between GPs to remove the camshafts and adjust the valves. But with four cams and two cam chains, it didn't make sense on the CBX.'

The Six's arrangement was more like that of the Z1. What, then, of the Kawasaki's reputation for spitting shims, asked the journalists?

'That is caused more by valve float than anything else,' explained Irimajiri. 'Valve float can be restrained by using the lightest components possible, which was one of the reasons we have a four-valve engine.'

Irimajiri then revealed to journalists something of the team's punishing approach to testing their ideas: 'To see if we would have a problem in this area, we put an engine on the dyno and tested it to failure at 11,000 rpm. We had no problems with the valve train - a cylinder stud broke, after 30 minutes.'

He was much less expansive about other problems. Torsional vibrations from the unusually-long crankshaft proved one of Irimajiri's biggest headaches. Yet the issue was not new to him. As he told the assembled journalists, he 'had had experience here before.' He did not, however, go on to explain what he meant by that, or how he tackled the CBX's crankshaft issues.

As with the crankshaft, the CBX's camshafts also threatened to be inordinately long. This would have increased the likelihood of distortion during the heat-treating stage of manufacture. So, instead of producing two very long camshafts to drive each bank of 12 valves, Irimajiri chose to fit *four* camshafts: two inlet and two exhaust, each joined by an Oldham coupling (with each cam hollow to save weight). Also, instead of a single chain running under the crankshaft up to the top of the engine, across both camshafts and back down again, to avoid cam chain whip, the two cams each ran off their own 9.5mm Hy-Vo chain.

Other, more intractable, problems surfaced around combustion. In a perfect world, Irimajiri would have preferred straight inlet tracts, where one could trace a direct line through the centre of each carburettor and on to its respective port. Otsuka's requirement to angle the carburettors inward to accommodate the rider compromised that ideal. Only those carburettors feeding cylinders three and four - that is, the two at the centre - enjoyed an unobstructed gas-flow to the combustion chamber. Fuel and air from the two adjacent carburettors (cylinders two and five) had to negotiate a bend and slightly longer tract. Those supplying fuel to cylinders one and six suffered most. Furthest outboard, they had to flow fuel and air along even longer tracts and around even sharper angles. Irimajiri's workaround was to install tubes of different lengths inside the plenum chambers so that the distance that air travelled on its path toward the inlet valves was the same for each of the CBX's six inlet tracts.

Irimajiri described the CBX's carbs as 'the most sophisticated ever used on a street-going motorcycle'. Manufactured by Keihin, the gang of six 28mm CV carburettors had two unique features. The first was an air cut-off valve fitted to carburettor Number One and connected to the other five via a gallery, the purpose of which was to stop backfiring during sudden deceleration (it worked by closing off the air flow to enrich the fuel mixture when the intake vacuum reached a certain level). The second was an accelerator pump. Attached to carburettor Number Three and connected to its five sisters by another gallery, the pump squirted fuel to help smooth out acceleration.

Despite *Cycle* declaring that they had 'never experienced CV carburettors that work as well', Irimajiri could not disguise his frustration when he revealed to journalists at Willow Spring that breathing across the CBX's six cylinders was better in some than others.

Thus, to reduce flat spots and 'pinking'* his team also developed a state-of-the-art transistorised ignition system. Using magnetic pick-ups to control the advance curve automatically, the team tailored the pulser circuit's rise-time so that the actual degree of advance remained proportional to engine speed. In addition, the Six also deployed a mechanical advancer. Comprising three bob-weights, the system advanced the ignition through 25 degrees until the engine was spinning at 2,000rpm, at which point the advance cut out and retarded a couple of degrees. It resumed again at 6,000 to 7,500rpm, advanced to between 31 and 34 degrees at peak revs, and then stopped.

Making A 24 Valve, Four-Cam Six-Cylinder Bike Look Elemental

With the CBX's powerplant weighing 233lbs dry (57lbs more than the CB750's four-cylinder SOHC engine, 53lbs heavier than Kawasaki's claimed engine weight of 180lbs for the DOHC Z1, and over 100lbs more than a Triumph 650 twin's ohv engine unit), Irimajiri's weight-loss programme could not stop at the engine.

He opted against adding fripperies such as a fuel gauge, and audible-warning and self-cancelling indicators. The team employed plastic in place of steel for the mudguards and the seat base. The adjustable handlebars and footrests were made from forged aluminium. Originally, the top engine mounts were also made from alloy, but had to be replaced with steel after failing crash tests. Aluminium Comstars saved 4.4lbs over steel-spoke wheels, and tubeless tyres saved further weight by dispensing with an inner tube.** Triple clamps, top and bottom, were also fabricated from alloy. Less obvious weight losses were achieved by shaving the walls of the fork sliders and stanchions internally at the low stress points to reduce their thickness. The heavily braced diamond frame, which the project's clay modeller Yoshitaka Omori recalled was adopted almost from the outset when it was realised that the exhaust pipes would not clear a cradle frame's downtubes, dispensed

---

* 'Pinking' (also known as 'knocking') is the metallic sound caused by part of the air-fuel mixture spontaneously igniting inside the cylinder at the wrong time during the combustion engine cycle. Instead of the charge burning smoothly across the combustion chamber from the point of ignition, sometimes the charge can ignite ahead of the flame front to produce intense, high-frequency pressure waves, creating vibration and an audible knock from the top of the engine.

** The bike under test was a pre-production model and Honda told *Cycle* that there was still some uncertainty as to whether the production bike would wear tubeless tyres. This was due to the tyre manufacturer's concern around the rubber plug they supplied to fix punctures and its ability to remain in place given the speeds the CBX could hit.

with lower frame rails and used the mighty six-pot motor as a stressed-member, weighed just 29.4lbs.[*]

Weighing 585lbs (247kg) dry, that figure quickly climbed to just below 600lbs (272.1kg) when the CBX was loaded up with a full tank, oil and fluids.

Irimajiri's emphasis on Spartan utility was reflected in Otsuka's styling. Indeed, such was the spare simplicity of his lines that the CBX looked organic, as if it had never been styled at all.[**]

Cycle described the CBX's styling as 'lean and elemental' (not bad for a bike weighing nearly a quarter of a ton fully laden). The shape of the fuel tank was informed by the chassis, the ergonomic needs of the rider, and, of course, the tank's capacity. The twin-vented side covers were finished in functional matt-black, making the gold and red-lettered legend 'CBX' appear as if suspended in space.

The one flourish Otsuka allowed himself was the CBX's tailpiece. Yet as late as the middle of September 1976, with the bike almost ready to go into production, the CBX did not have a tailpiece. Its emergence, moreover, was not due to Chief Designer Norimoto Otsuka.

The design of the fuel tank and side-panels of the second-generation mock-up known as 'CBX-II' had been developed to the point where they now looked very like the components that would appear on the production model - but married to a dual seat similar to the saddle fitted to the SOHC CB750 Four. Yoshitaka Omori recalled the managing director of Honda Research and Development observing that the clay model lacked punch. 'Since we want this bike to make us Number One, can't you do something with it?' he asked.

With chief designer Minoru Morioka away in France working on drawings for the Euro-styled CB900F and CB750F, Oomori's boss, Hitoshi Ikeda, chief stylist for the original CB750/4, was under pressure to come up with something in Morioka's absence. However, according to Ian Foster in his definitive tome on the Six, *The CBX Book*, Omori recalled that Ikeda 'didn't know what to do, but had to take on the case anyway until Morioka came back from Europe.[***]

'I asked Mr. Ikeda if he would let me do what I liked with the bike,' recalled Omori, 'and he agreed to let me have a go at it.'

Omori made a winged tail cowl. When he presented it to Ikeda, the stylist instructed Omori to consult Shinji Kakutani from Honda's Blue Helmets in-house racing team to

---

[*]   *Cycle* questioned some of what they labelled Irimajiri's 'gram-pinching'. They levelled particular criticism at savings made on the frame, the shock absorbers, and the front forks. At 35mm in diameter, they felt the tubes were not substantial enough, and perhaps explained the CBX's tendency to do the 'hippy-hippy shake' when negotiating Willow Spring's Turn Fight at full bore.

[**]   Early styling sketches explored a café-racer styled Six with just three carbs. The concept featured a small handlebar fairing similar to the bikini fairing worn by the Moto Guzzi 850 Le Mans. The sketches depict one-piece bodywork, with the tank flowing into the detachable side-panels, seat base and tail unit. Like the Le Mans, the front of the seat hugs the back of the fuel tank. Later designs show a tank whose rear flanks curve and flow in an unbroken line down toward removable side-panels, in a style which presaged Honda's Euro-styled DOHC CB750F-A and 900F models that the factory introduced late in 1978.

[***]   Ian Foster quotes Omori's interview in Honda Motor Co. Ltd's *Honda Design (Motorcycle Part 1) 1957-1984*.

get his view. Ikeda, it seemed, was worried. He wanted to understand what effects the tail might have, and that it wasn't, as he had speculated with Omori, 'just a gimmick?'

Omori met with Kakutani in the factory's cafeteria and showed him the model. 'Of course, I never expected Mr. Kakutani to tell me it would be effective. But if I had said that then, I'd have ended up in even deeper trouble.'

Omori needn't have worried. 'Hey,' exclaimed the racer. 'That looks really sharp. That's the most important thing. Let's go with that.' Armed with Kakutani's ringing endorsement, Ikeda contacted Mr. Morioka in France to get his approval to proceed, only to learn that the designer was drawing up something similar for the CB900 and 750Fs.

The production version of Omori's winged cowl weighed just 5lb, was completely detachable, and the kicked-up spoiler resembled the deck wing on a Porche. It looked aerodynamic, as if designed to exert downforce to prevent the bike from becoming airborne. In fact, the CBX's tailpiece added absolutely nothing to performance (which, Otsuka pointed out to the journalists at Willow Springs, was also the case with the Porche).

What the tailpiece did do, however, was to *evoke* a sense of performance. Its presence helped make clear the machine's purpose, without caricaturing or deceiving the onlooker as to its function. Indeed, engineers had rejected the styling department's early attempt at an instrument console for the CBX because, as contemporary, handsome and informative as it was, they felt it simply did not *look* functional.

Otsuka therefore turned to aircraft and jet fighters for inspiration. Aeronautical instrument designers have one overriding goal: function. Pilots have a vast array of information to assimilate very quickly. Otsuka studied myriad cockpits, all the time absorbing the lessons of how aircraft designers arrange and display instruments: glare-free glass; bold, bright, clear numerals set against a black background; and broad white-tipped needles. Otsuka stripped it all back to the essentials. The result was a model of simplicity. As *Cycle* said: 'It looks easy. It was not.'

THE STRONGEST STOCKER

After two days of track testing, *Cycle* loaded the Six into the back of an unmarked white Ford van to transport it to aftermarket engine-parts maker, Webco, where they planned to run it on the company's dyno. Once there, Honda technicians unloaded the bike and wheeled it in through the shuttered side door of the dyno room where they connected it up to the pump. It took them almost two hours (although some of that time involved waiting for an NGK representative to arrive with a set of nine-series sparkplugs that Irimajiri wanted to install). By lunchtime, Webco's Jim Hughes had the figures. The CBX proved to be the 'strongest stocker' that Webco had ever tested - and by a significant margin.

With 1,000rpm still to go before it reached peak power, the Honda was producing six horsepower more than the Kawasaki Z1-R's maximum output. And Irimajiri was sure that the Six's figures were down on what they ought to be. He put that down to Webco's dyno not having the cooling capacity the CBX required to deliver optimum performance.

'On any multi, exhaust tuning is crucial,' he explained.

'Waves travelling down the pipes have to behave in a certain way if optimum performance is to be obtained. How those waves travel is determined by pipe length, pipe diameter and pipe temperature. If the exhaust system is overheated some of this tuning is lost; I believe that is what is happening here.'

On day four of testing, journalists and Honda's engineers repaired to Orange County International Raceway to find out how the CBX performed over the quarter mile. It was Thursday morning. They had arrived early: the journalists at 6:40am; the engineers a little later. The original plan had been to conduct drag-strip testing at Irwindale Raceway, but just 24 hours before they were due to turn up, they learned that Irwindale had been sold and that the site was to be turned into a brewery. They called OCIR, the only drag strip left in Southern California. Orange County said yes, but that they would have to get there for 7:30am as the Raceway was hosting a motorcycle jumping contest on Friday and that workers would be arriving at 9:00 to set everything up for the following day's event.

As they waited outside OCIR's locked gates, a truck loaded with straw bales turned up, and workers to set up the jump contest began to gather. It started to rain; not heavily, but they could see that it would soon. Tension mounted. Everyone anxiously checked either their watches or the sky. The CBX had to be on a plane the following day for an appointment in Japan. If journalists wanted to test how quickly the Six ran a quarter-mile, it was going to have to be this morning, or not at all.

The gates eventually swung open at 7:50 (OCIR's track officials had been stuck in traffic and delayed). Journalists, mechanics, and the guys gathered to set up tomorrow's jump-off surged in. After paying the fee to rent the circuit, signing the requisite documents, and getting the officials to turn on the clocks, one of the journalists hurriedly donned his leathers as the mechanics warmed up the Six's engine (the bike still hidden beneath its cover). As soon as he was kitted up, the leather-clad scribe ran to the strip's starting line, touched the tarmac to assess its wetness, and hurried back over to the CBX. The mechanics uncovered the machine and the journalist climbed aboard. After checking the engine had warmed sufficiently, he rode the bike to the strip's right-hand lane.

He cued up the CBX along the middle of the lane, twisted back the throttle, held the engine at 3,500 revs and then dumped the clutch. The CBX didn't move. It just sat there, its rear tyre spinning uselessly on the wet track.

They moved the bike across the lane, over to the right-hand edge where the surface was free of tyre rubber and the CBX's rear wheel could get more purchase. The rider brought the engine back to 3,500rpm and the bike catapulted off the line. Sheltering from the rain beneath an inadequate number of brollies, the Japanese had gathered around the start-line speaker to hear how the Six had performed on its first run. The numbers that came back were impressive: 11.976 seconds at 115.97mph.

The second run was better still. Holding the throttle open at 6,500rpm this time, and with their new launch point providing decent traction, the bike covered the quarter mile nearly a fifth of a second quicker at 11.783. Its terminal speed was faster, too; the bike crossing the line at a recorded 116.27mph. They launched at 7,500rpm for the third run and recorded a time of 11.657 seconds at 116.12mph.

And that was it. They had to abandon a fourth run, unable to control power from the engine because of a 'grabby' clutch. The mechanics took back the bike and cloaked it once again under a blanket of high security. By 8:20am, Honda and the journalists were gone. They left behind them a rain-sodden OCIR and the sound of hammering as workmen readied the circuit for the next day's jump contest.

Three weeks later, Honda and the journalists were back. The CBX had run 11.65 second standing quarters on a wet track. Everyone needed to know what it could do if it was dry. Determined to find out, they returned to OCIR.

There was a light headwind, but the track was dry. Their first two runs did not go well. The test bike had racked up 600 miles of street riding, and the engine refused to pull hard in the higher gears. They made a call to aftermarket manufacturer and supplier of high-performance parts, Action Fours, in Santa Ana, California. Action Four's owner, Jim Dickinson, arrived at the track armed with a set of NGK D8s. After swapping the new plugs for the Six's sooted-up items, the team resumed testing.

The bike made nine more runs. The best of these turned out to be its second run, when it posted 11.55 seconds at 117.49mph. Those numbers made it the quickest stock production motorcycle any magazine had ever tested. The Six's elapsed time (ET) was nearly two tenths of a second quicker than the next quickest bike and its speed at the end of the quarter bettered the Yamaha XS Eleven's fastest time by over two miles an hour. 'There is no doubt,' *Cycle* told readers in their February 1978 issue, 'the CBX Six is the hardest-accelerating production vehicle ever built.'

Two months later, *Cycle*'s biggest rival, *Cycle World*, declared the CBX 'the fastest bike we've ever tested' after the prototype they were reviewing reeled off a standing quarter in 11.46 seconds at a terminal speed of 117.95mph.

Eight months on, and after getting their hands on an actual production bike, *Cycle World* announced in their January 1979 issue that 'the CBX is still the fastest bike we've ever tested. In fact,' they went on, 'it's even faster than the prototype.' The assembly-line model bettered the prototype by fully one tenth of a second, *CW*'s test bike tearing up the drag strip in 11.36 seconds and crossing the quarter mile marker at 118.11mph.

The CBX also demonstrated equally remarkable top-end figures.

The previous summer, at the Motor Industry Research Association's test centre in Nuneaton, England, *Motor Cycle Weekly*'s John Nutting road tested one of the very first CBXs off the production line; and, after removing the Six's mirrors, tucking in low behind its clocks, gripping the left-hand fork leg flat-track-style, and assisted by a light tailwind, he achieved an electronically-timed one-way best of 139.19mph on the downhill run.

Joan Claybrook Speaks Out Against Musclebikes

It was performance like this that prompted US President Jimmy Carter's administrator of the National Highway Traffic Safety Administration (NHTSA), Joan Claybrook, to pay the Japanese motorcycle manufacturers a visit. In a speech to industry representatives, Claybrook denounced the factories' pursuit of horsepower, and for marketing machines to America too big and powerful to sell in their own country. In her first public statement on the US administration's policy on motorcycle safety, Claybrook gave a sharply-worded speech to the industry-funded Motorcycle Safety Foundation, admonishing them for promoting 'the new muscle motorcycles that are capable of going a quarter mile in under 12 seconds and top speeds, in stock condition, of more than 130 miles per hour'. Moreover, she said: 'the advertising tends to encourage riders to use all that awesome performance.'

In American Honda Bob Jameson's assessment, Claybrook was 'a well-meaning person, but she didn't know what she was talking about'. Maybe so, but by fixing her gaze through those famous horned-rimmed glasses of hers on manufacturers, she succeeded in making Honda nervous enough to delay the CBX's release (from its slated launch as a '78 season model to an early-release '79 model instead).

The CBX was, in fact, Honda's belated response to the horsepower wars being waged by the factories. But contrary to whatever Joan Claybrook might have thought, not all the combatants were based in Japan.

Laverda And The Slater Brothers

The winding rural road running between the English market town of Tenbury Wells and Collington village, passes weather-worn brick-built cottages and a patchwork quilt of farmer's fields before reaching Richard and Roger Slater's premises. Official importers of the Italian manufacturer Laverda, the brothers would send bikes out on a six-mile test ride to Tenbury. The B4214 linking Tenbury in Worcestershire and Bromyard in Hertfordshire is not an easy road to ride fast (several riders misjudged what lay beyond the next crest and ended up in a cabbage field). But the road has plenty of corners and provides a perfect shake down to test the results of the brothers' factory-supported development work on the Breganze-built twin-cam one-litre triples.

Launched initially as a 1,000cc SOHC prototype in Geneva in 1969, the show bike retained the Laverda 750 twin's chain-driven overhead camshaft, but gained an extra cylinder. The following year, Massimo Laverda* and his design and development chief,

---

*   Massimo's father, Francisco Laverda, launched the company's first motorcycle - the single-cylinder 75cc Motoleggera - in 1949. Producing 40bhp per litre and capable of running steadily at 43mph, the Laverda company distinguished itself by making their own engine and making it well. In 1951, the factory began racing. All four machines entering the Milan-Taranto race, which runs the length of Italy, finished. The following year, a Laverda came first in its class, and again, all the Laverdas that started the race completed it. The factory repeated its success in 1953, a Laverda finishing first in its class, with the marque making up the next thirteen finishers. It was around this time that the company started to offer sports versions of their models for sale to the public that were factory-tuned and ready-to-race. Lightweight motorcycles continued to be the mainstay of their motorcycle business (re-badged in the US as Garellis, and later as American Eagles), until they released their first large-

the brilliant and a self-taught engineer, Luciano Zen, redeveloped the prototype into a 120 degree, *double*-overhead cam triple, its twin cams driven by a toothed-belt running on the outside of the cylinders.* Narrowly-angled valves were adjusted by a shim and bucket mechanism, similar to the arrangement Kawasaki would later deploy on the Z1. Zen and Laverda tucked the reworked machine's starter motor behind the cylinders, and positioned its belt-driven generator out front.

Supporting the new bike's built-up crankshaft was a quartet of roller bearings, an outrigger bearing inside the primary cover, and a roller bearing opposite it over on the timing side. Even so, problems soon arose when cranks began to fracture as a result of the rocking-couple vibration characteristic of a triple engine's pistons phased to fire 120 degrees apart. Swapping to a crankshaft which had its centre piston out of phase with the two outer pistons fixed that (the arrangement also provided the triple with its signature '1-2-3-miss' exhaust note); and an alternator mounted on the end of the crankshaft replaced the previous prototype's front-mounted generator.

Released in 1973, the 980cc 3C made an immediate impact. The 3CE, a derestricted factory-tuned version of the 3C developed by the Slater brothers for the British market (the 'E' suffix standing for 'England'), became the fastest motorcycle that *Motor Cycle* had ever tested when it clocked a two-way mean of 133mph at the MIRA test centre. But Richard and Roger realised that they needed a stock bike with even more power if the triple was to maintain its supremacy in production racing, especially the Avon Roadrunner series.

In the summer of 1974, using the Heenan and Froud dynamometer on which the brothers prepared customer's bikes and press machines for magazine tests, and tuned Laverdas for production racing, Richard and Roger spent hundreds of hours pushing the Laverda 3C's engine output to more than 80bhp at the rear wheel (some 12 per cent up on the standard machine's 70bhp).

Tuning the 3C took place late in the afternoon. 'Roger would be stood there with his earplugs, and a clipboard,' Richard Slater told *Classic Bike* magazine's Ben Miller in 2012, 'I'd be round this side of the bike, leaning over with my hand on the throttle. There was no back wheel on the bike. Instead,' he explained, 'the gearbox sprocket drove the dynamometer via a long and completely unprotected chain. I remember thinking: "I could lose my head here." But health and safety hadn't been invented. The exhausts would

---

displacement motorcycle in 1968: a beautifully-made 650 twin. Looking very like a Honda CB77, Laverda produced less than a hundred examples before the factory immediately upped its capacity to 750cc. Available in GT and S formats, the 750 acquired its famous SF code in 1971 when Laverda replaced the original model's Grimeca brakes with their own more powerful drum brakes, which they promoted under the slogan *Syper Freni* ('super brakes'). Laverda followed the SF with a competition version - the SFC - a model which went on to dominate endurance races that year.

     *   The Italians' layout was remarkably similar to a working model Doug Hele had been road testing in Meriden around about the same time. Housed in a BSA Rocket 3 Mk II chassis, and deploying specially-made castings bolted onto the triple's barrels, the prototype's single-overhead camshaft ran off a toothed belt driven by a pulley situated where the contact breakers would normally reside on a standard A75 engine. The pulley was powered by a countershaft located where the exhaust camshaft once rotated, and the points relocated to the end of the inlet camshaft. 'It went well enough,' Hele told Mick Duckworth, author of *Triumph and BSA Triples*, 'but never actually gave more power than the standard engine. The valve gear was a bit heavy.' BSA, who, by that time were trading at a loss, shelved the project.

be glowing bright blue and I used to wear a white storeman's coat. I'd go to walk away and it would have melted to the exhaust.'

Leaving the dynamometer room's doors wide open to let in air, Richard recalled the noise of an un-silenced triple in full throat, downpipes glowing and engine spinning at 8,200rpm - and confessed sympathy for the family with three young children living in the nearby farmhouse.

The response Roger Slater received from the Laverda board meeting in Breganze on the day he suggested the factory should charge a premium over the already expensive 3C, however, was considerably quieter. 'Naturally, this went down like a lead balloon,' Roger recalled, 'and so I followed up by presenting the power readings from the dyno with the endurance cam, new pistons and our own interpretation of the exhaust system.'

His proposal was for the factory to build some of the UK-bound bikes to the Slater brothers' higher specification.* The model would require a new livery (Roger suggested orange)** and a name befitting its image. Scanning the faces around the table, Roger sensed everyone was viewing him now with growing suspicion.

'What might the name of this new machine be?' asked Massimo Laverda.

'Jota,' Roger replied.

'What the hell is a "Yota"?' chorused the board.

'It's a Spanish gypsy dance danced in rapid triple time,' explained Roger.

The response was explosive. 'A great roar of approving laughter went up, Roger remembered, 'and we left for a splendid two-hour lunch at *Al Torresan*.'

So Fast, It Surely Can't Be Standard

The Jota became the first over-the-counter production road bike to top 140mph, when, on August 10th 1976, *Motor Cycle* posted a one-way best of 140.04mph on MIRA's banked track. For the next few years, the Jota was the fastest production motorcycle on earth.

When, that same year, Pete 'PK' Davies won the first Avon/*Bike* Roadrunner Production Racing Championship's biggest class - the 1,000cc - aboard a Laverda Jota supplied by Roger Slater, there was not much that season that could live with the Italian triple. Three years later, following a disastrous season in '77 when PK suffered a fractured collarbone and five broken ribs early in the series after a fall at the Croft race track, and sustained a serious injury to his foot in a later round, his Jota was so fast in the '78 season that some doubted Peter's assertion that the engine was standard.

Bike magazine decided to test that claim and sealed Pete's engine with an ACU-approved seal immediately after the Jota finished the meeting at Carnaby. Apart from Roger carefully honing the barrels and valve pushers to replicate 5,000 miles of engine wear, the mileage at which the motor performs best, the magazine found everything was indeed completely stock.

---

*   The Slater brothers' specification included 4/C profile camshafts, 10:1 compression pistons and UK-made silencers with minimal baffling, which, together with right-foot gear selection, meant the machine was only legal for sale in Britain and New Zealand.

**   Launched in 1976, the original Jota came in green or red, then silver from 1977, and orange in 1978-79.

Punk Versus Prog

At the time of the Jota's release in 1976, the fuel crisis, tightening emission regulations, safety lobbyists, and changing customer expectations had all combined to civilise superbikes. The Jota, however, made no concessions to civility. Although the Slaters' aspiration was to succeed on the track, the Jota's raw, stripped-down approach mirrored the mood that summer of a new elemental movement in music and fashion that had emerged spitting and screaming on the streets and TV screens of Britain during the worst drought the country had experienced in 250 years.

Punk rejected the trappings and self-congratulatory pretentiousness of progressive rock. Exponents of punk preferred short, fast and furious power-chord numbers that expressed their generation's anger at the ruined landscape of Seventies Britain. The movement, however, began in New York.

Following a visit there to promote his and his partner Vivienne Westwood's line of torn T-shirts and bondage gear, Malcolm McLaren was entranced by the NYC music scene and bands like The New York Dolls and The Ramones. Looking like faded glam rockers, The Dolls were crude, antagonistic, cacophonous, self-destructive, and largely inept. The Ramones looked like hooligans (or *punks* to use the American vernacular for low-lifes, the term that became forever attached to this new musical form after the launch in December 1975 of an underground comic called *Punk*, the inaugural issue of which carried on its cover a cartoon of Lou Reed, the godfather of this genre of music).

After a brief stint managing The Dolls, McLaren returned to London where he persuaded some youngsters who used to hang around his Kings Road clothes shop to form a band. The lads, who hailed from nearby London estates, named the group The Sex Pistols (after McLaren's boutique SEX, and some free association on Malcolm's part to connote violence).

They recruited a regular habitué at the shop to be their lead singer, a pallid-looking kid with budgerigar-green hair (the result of a mishap after trying to dye his yellow hair blue), and a Pink Floyd shirt with the words 'I hate' scrawled in Biro above it. His name was John Lydon. Bright and articulate, the 19-year-old Lydon affected the mannered speech patterns of the Anthony Burgess character, Alex, played by Malcolm McDowell in the Stanley Kubrick film, *A Clockwork Orange*. But it was band-mate Steve Jones, a petty thief with a penchant for stealing the instruments of his musical heroes, such as David Bowie or Keith Richards, who, at Lydon's audition for the group, conferred the name that would go on to immortalise Lydon: 'You're fucking rotten,' he taunted (on account of the would-be singer's teeth).

At a time when bands usually ingratiated themselves before their audience, the Sex Pistols made it clear that they could not care less. At their first gig in November 1975, supporting Bazooka Joe for a show at St Martin's School of Art, the headliners pulled the plug on them during their set. Lydon (now Johnny Rotten), still wearing his *I hate Pink Floyd* T-shirt, together with the rest of the Pistols, simply walked off. They departed to not even a smattering of applause from the audience. Yet it didn't matter. As Lydon said, 'We didn't do it to be loved.'

The Jota represented a similar iconoclastic sensibility. The new megabike offerings from the Japanese manufacturers seemed baroque in comparison. They were the antithesis of the punk ideal of a visceral, stripped-back approach, and more akin to the self-indulgence of Lydon's *bête noir*, Prog Rock.

The Big Four were aware of the dilemma. In France, at the joint launch of their shaft-driven water-cooled V-twin, the CX500, and the company's new flagship six-cylinder CBX1000, journalists asked Honda's Japanese executives if the new wave of 140mph megabikes was in fact pointless. The executives smiled: Honda was simply responding to market forces, they replied, but knowing that their rivals each had their own flagship models in the pipeline, Honda could not allow itself to be left behind. 'We are hoping,' said Zenya Nakajimi, General Manager of Honda Europe's Liaison Office, 'for an end to the escalation.'

CBX Project Leader Soichiro Irimajiri confessed that Honda felt motorcycles were becoming too alike. Yamaha voiced similar concerns. In a piece about their new half-litre single, the SR500, their company magazine *Circuit* said: 'In an age where complicated multi-cylinder engines are commonplace it becomes increasingly difficult for a manufacturer to provide the public with that "something different" to fire up some new enthusiasm.'

For 'enthusiasm' read 'sales.' Registrations of motorcycles over 50cc dropped 5.77 per cent in Britain between January and October 1977 compared to the year before. That translated into nearly 9,500 fewer machines being sold. On the face of it, the drop seems small, but in an economic system reliant on growth just to stand still, it was significant. With Europe now the biggest market in the world for motorcycles, relative market share in the UK between the Big Four was important. Sales, however, were now spread more thinly - a consequence, ironically, of booming sales.

There had been a proliferation of new dealers, attracted to motorcycling due to an increase in two-wheeled vehicle registrations spurred on by the rising price of fuel, escalating travel costs, and all too frequent disruptions to public transport systems because of lightning strikes (some 10 million days were lost to industrial action in Britain in 1977, four times more than France and considerably more than the 86,000 days lost in West Germany).*

It was the bike trade, then, that needed new models to revitalise a now moribund sales scene.

In a piece for *Bike* magazine entitled '1978: Boom or Bust?' journalist Peter Watson attempted to make sense of it all. Anticipating the shape of things to come in the year ahead, he discerned several emerging trends. Watson noted the scramble by

---

* Typical of the problems British commuters faced was an oil tanker drivers' dispute that occurred in early 1979. The fuel shortages it created left Liverpool with just one petrol station open, and saw petrol rise in price from 75p to as high as £3 a gallon in some places.

manufacturers to release one-litre plus 140mph flagships, coining the term 'megabikes' to describe this new category.

Watson's fellow scribes seized on the term, and deployed the noun in the very next issue, when *Bike* reported from West Africa on the European launch of Yamaha's XS1100 four - or the 'Eleven' as it was called in the US - a bike Yamaha described as 'the largest in-line four cylinder, four-stroke in production'. When *Cycle* tested the Yamaha XS Eleven in January 1978, they declared the 1,102cc four was 'by a solid margin the fastest, quickest Superbike we've tested.' The magazine had only tested one other 'showroom-stock Superbike' that ran quarters in under 12 seconds - 'and that was barely, after several tries,' explained *Cycle*. 'Yamaha's Eleven didn't turn a time over 12 seconds.' Their test bike's best ET was 11.82 seconds; its highest terminal 115.38mph, which *Cycle* said reflected the XS1100's 'incredible top-end charge'. According to the magazine, the Eleven 'can outhaul the latest Kawasaki Z; provide more ride comfort than a Gold Wing or a BMW; achieve between 45 and 50 mpg; behave itself acceptably in the mountains; and only rarely needs maintenance'. In *Cycle*'s opinion: 'The Eleven is simply the most impressive street motorcycle our staff has yet tested.'

Not everyone wanted a megabike, however. In his look at the trends for the year ahead, Peter Watson welcomed, for example, the resurgence in the 500cc middleweight class and of big single-cylinder bikes (in both roadster and off-road guises). He saluted the advances in suspension technology. He also observed that motorcycle makers - in contrast with their counterparts in the automobile industry who seemed content to churn out 'faceless front wheel-drive hatchbacks' - appeared to be moving away from 'lookalike four-cylinder models'. With the Big Four's engineers capable of overcoming the problems inherent in any engine configuration, formats and layouts were now shaped by what their market research told them rather than the application of pure engineering principles. Sometimes, of course, this approach created its own problems. When, for example, Honda decided to twist the barrels on their CX500 transverse V-twin to prevent the rider's knees from hitting up against the cylinder heads, the move precluded overhead-cam valve actuation. This was similar to CBX Project Leader Shoichiro Irimajiri angling the Six's carburettors inward to accommodate Chief Designer Norimoto Otsuka's requirement to improve rider ergonomics.

The advent of the Honda CBX and rumours of a large-capacity six-cylinder motorcycle from Kawasaki seemed to support the sense that for the second half of the Seventies, the vision amongst Honda, Kawasaki, Suzuki and Yamaha now seemed less UJM (Universal Japanese Motorcycle) and more USP (Unique Selling Point).

It was not, however, quite the end of the across-the-frame four.

Suzuki Make A Four-Stroke

The captions said it all. Beneath a black and white photograph of the Kawasaki Z1000-A2 engine, *Bike* magazine's caption writer wrote: 'The Z1000 is still one of the most powerful motorcycles available', whilst the descriptor under an adjacent photograph of Suzuki's new one-litre four-pot motor read: 'Note the marked similarity between this GS1000 engine and the Kawasaki mill.'

The Peterborough-based magazine was reporting the results of its comparison test in which they put the new Suzuki GS1000 up against the bike nicknamed 'The King'. Even Hamamatsu acknowledged that the Kawasaki Z1000 provided Suzuki its template for their first four-cylinder motorcycle.

In late 1973, Suzuki's head of design, Masa Takashi Shimizu, approved a project to develop a low-emission four-stroke engine. The design team, led by Hiroshi Nakano, began work early in 1974 on a successor to Suzuki's line-up of three-cylinder two-strokes and their as yet un-launched RE-5 rotary-engined sports-tourer. Codenamed GX960, the new project had a lot riding on it.

In America, the Democrat Senator for Maine, Edmund Muskie, had sponsored a bill requiring automobile manufacturers to reduce exhaust emissions of new vehicles by 90 per cent within five years. The passing into law of the 1970 Clean Air Act meant that two-strokes were now living on borrowed time and would soon be outlawed in the US, Suzuki's biggest market.

The writing had been on the wall for two-strokes for some time, of course, which was why Suzuki had established a team in the late Sixties to examine low-emission alternatives. These included not only four-strokes, but the Suzuki two-stroke EPIC project, and a rotary engine-powered motorcycle. However, by 1973, it was clear that escalating fuel costs as a result of war in the Middle East and OPEC's oil embargoes did not auger well for the prodigiously thirsty RE-5, which was scheduled for release at the end of 1974. Developing the rotary technology and building a bespoke new factory in which to make it was crippling the company. Hamamatsu knew it needed a back-up plan.

Given such high stakes, Suzuki could not afford to gamble. Studying the form of the runners and riders in the market place, they borrowed from the best and opted for a four-cylinder, two-valve, twin-overhead cam configuration just like the layout that had brought rival maker Kawasaki so much success. Choosing proven technology as a template also helped Nakano's team expedite development.

But whilst team leader Nakano acknowledged the debt, the GX960 was not a slavish copy of the Z1. For instance, instead of sticking to the Kawasaki's displacement of 903cc, Nakano's team upped capacity to 960cc.

Then, at the end of 1974 - less than a year into the project - the Japanese government introduced new licence regulations limiting novice riders to 400cc. The change in legislation also imposed an upper limit for motorcyclists set at 750cc. As a result, in January 1975, the team suspended work on the GX960 project. In its place, the factory initiated a twin-track project to develop a 750 four and a 400cc twin, each sharing components such as valve gear, pistons, connecting-rods, main bearings, timing chain, sprockets and tensioners, oil pump and clutch pressure plate, as well as several design features.

The GS400 twin, for example, shared the 750 four's bore size of 65mm. Unusually for a four-pot multi at that time, the GS750 adopted a short stroke motor when its contemporaries were either over-square like the Z1 (66mm x 66mm), or, like the Honda CB750, long-stroke (albeit at 61mm x 63mm only ever so slightly).

Also unlike the Honda, both of Suzuki's first four-stroke engines supported their cranks using ball and roller bearings (the four-cylinder 750's nine-piece pressed up crank assembly boasting no fewer than six main bearings). Nakano's preference was to run the crankshaft in plain bearings, which would not only have been cheaper but have made the engine quieter. The reasons Suzuki elected to go with ball and roller bearings were partly due to their years of experience building two-stroke engines with built-up crankshafts, but also because the factory had neither the time nor the resources to invest in the crank grinding processes necessary to manufacture shell bearings. The result was a crankshaft that was heavy, expensive to manufacture, enormously strong, but which 'should', according to *Motorcycle Mechanics*' John Hartley, 'last forever'.

Early development models, however, were mechanically noisy. Nakano's team fixed that by improving engine tolerances and using rubber blocks between the cooling fins to prevent 'fin ringing' (a trick Suzuki had learned developing their two-stroke range). Eventually, the engine was strong enough to survive trials of mechanical endurance in which engineers ran it flat-out for the equivalent of 20,000 kilometres.

But it was the 750's chassis that set the new bike apart from its Japanese rivals. The duplex double-cradle frame was quite conventional, differing from its contemporaries only by dint of its larger diameter tubing and heavier gusseting around the steering head (angled, like its competitors, at 63 degrees). 19 inch and 18 inch wire wheels front and back also conformed to extant practice, whilst the swinging-arm was unusual for the day by pivoting on needle-roller bearings. Neutral steering, a well-balanced chassis, a relatively light weight of 492lbs dry - 5lbs under the CB750, and 20lbs less than Yamaha's XS750 - plus carefully-calibrated suspension front and rear, helped mark out the GS750's handling. It was, according to journalist John Nutting, 'a true turning point in Japanese motorcycle design'.

The GS was quick, too. When the UK weekly paper *Motor Cycle* tested Suzuki's all-new flagship in November 1976 and posted a one-way best of 125.29mph on MIRA's 1,000 yard timing straight, they headlined their road test: 'Suzuki's GS750 - it's simply the quickest 750 we've ever tested.' That beat the former record-holder, the Honda 750F1, by 2mph; it was only poor grip from the OE Bridgestone rear tyre that stopped the GS from becoming the quickest accelerating seven-fifty the paper had ever tested.

Earlier that year, a faultless shift mechanism helped the UK's *Motor Cycle Mechanics* wrest a 12.9 second standing quarter from their test GS750, placing it top on a table (*see opposite*) comparing the price and performance of the GS to its rivals.

MODEL	PRICE Inc VAT	MAX Speed	MPG Average	¼ MILE SS	WEIGHT Dry
Suzuki GS750	£1260	123	44	12.9	492lbs
Honda CB750F	£1295	110	41	13.5	498lbs
Suzuki GT750A	£1140	118	42	13.6	507lbs
Ducati 860 GTS	£1599	107	43	13.1	506lbs
Kawasaki Z750	£ 949	102	46	15.0	481lbs
Moto-Guzzi 850T3	£1699	109	54	15.1	495lbs

The GS was the quickest quarter-miler (and the only one of the six to break into the 12s). It had the highest top speed, was second lightest (only Kawasaki's Z750 twin scaled lighter), and third cheapest. The machine's one flaw was its brakes.

As Bob Goddard observed for *Motor Cycle Mechanics*: 'The Suzuki's single disc stoppers front and rear showed themselves to be barely adequate.' In the wet, he deemed them 'pathetic'. And when cold, 'the brakes,' he was shocked to learn, 'don't work at all.'

Brakes notwithstanding, press reaction to the three-quarter litre Suzuki was positive. Despite, or perhaps because of, its restrained styling, the GS750 went on to become a big seller for Suzuki and helped revive the company's fortunes.

It was no surprise, then, that Suzuki decided to capitalise on the 750's success and release what was essentially a one-litre version, which Hamamatsu unveiled as a prototype in Paris in 1978 (complete with an adhesive sticker on its side panel with the words 'World Champions' ringed by laurel leaves - a reminder to show-goers of Barry Sheene's successive world titles for Suzuki in 1976 and '77).

'A simpler motorcycle is a better motorcycle,' explained Suzuki's General Manager of Products and Planning, Mr Watanabe to the journalists from *Cycle*, *Cycle Guide*, *Cycle World* and *Motorcyclist* magazines at a preview for the US press held in Suzuki's Hamamatsu test centre 200 miles south of the Japanese capital. 'And our target,' he continued, 'was to improve the acceleration *and* the handling through simplification and weight reduction. Handling *is* just as important as engine performance.'*

After a 17 hour journey, beginning in Los Angeles and taking in the 120mph Bullet Train from Tokyo to Hamamatsu, *Cycle World*'s Tony Swan spent the first full day of his visit inside Suzuki's new and pristine-clean research, development and test centre, where he and his fellow journalists pumped the factory's assembled heads of division - including motorcycle design, product planning, chassis, and engine design - with questions about the new Four, whilst outside a gentle rain fell steadily. The group under interrogation includes company director, Mr Y. Nakano. Nakano told the Americans that the GS1000s that the factory had provided each of the magazines are 'possibly the fastest production motorcycles in the world'.

---

*   This scene is reconstructed from contemporary reports. The statement I ascribe to Mr Nakano is a direct quote as recorded by *Cycle Guide* (February 1978), which the magazine attributes simply to 'an executive'. A paraphrased version of the statement appeared in the April '78 issue of *Two Wheels*, wherein Editor Jeff Bridges names the speaker as the General Manager of Suzuki's Products and Planning Division, Mr T. Watanabe.

   The following day the skies were clear. The journalists convened at Suzuki's Ryuyo race course, just outside Hamamatsu on Japan's south-east coast. It was time for them to put Mr Nakano's claim to the test.

   A 25mph headwind was blowing directly into the faces of the hacks hunkering low over their test bike's handlebars as they hurtled down Ryuyo test-circuit's long straight. The winds made high-speed riding difficult. Adding to the journalists' troubles were the dragonflies inhabiting the grass verges surrounding Ryuyo's 4.2 mile track, which felt as big as a small bird when hit at high speed. One test rider reached 130mph. Swan, confessed to 'being somewhat less streamlined and more protective of life and limb', managed 127 (Suzuki's engineers told him that the GS was good for around 138).

   With no quarter-mile timing clock at Ryuyo, the Americans could only rely on their sense that the GS1000's linear power delivery and 'off-the-line quickness' supported Suzuki's projections of a sub 12 second standing quarter (amidst factory claims of 11.4 seconds achieved by a 120lb rider on a prototype). Unable to verify their impression, the journalists looked forward to taking the big Suzuki to the States and running it on the drag strips back home.

   What was beyond doubt even in Japan, however, was that the GS1000 featured the most sophisticated suspension ever seen on a production motorcycle up to that time. Air-adjustable front fronts allowed a near-infinite variety of adjustment - from plush to taut, depending on riding style. Suzuki recommended riders set air pressure within a range of between 11 to 17psi (but absolutely no more than 35psi). However, as the two valves were unlinked, it made equalising each fork leg difficult.

   For the initial few months of production, the GS1000 sported Kayaba twin-shock 3½ inch travel rear suspension, featuring - in a first for a road bike - adjustable spring preload *and* rebound (the former by a conventional five-position adjuster collar at the bottom of the shock; the latter via an engraved wheel at the top of the unit, protected from the elements by a rubber gaiter). The owner's manual warned riders to make sure that any adjustments they made to the rear units were accompanied by corresponding adjustments to the front suspension: a rider wanting to tune the suspension for a sportier ride and who set the rear units' springs and dampers to five and four respectively, should at the same time increase the air pressure in the front suspension to a firm 17psi; whereas a rider seeking comfort who set the forks at a more compliant 11psi, should adjust the Kayaba's rear springs and dampers to setting one. The press hailed these refinements as a sign that the Japanese makers were finally taking handling more seriously ('as important a prerequisite,' according to *Bike* magazine's Graham Sanderson, 'especially for hard riding Europeans, as power itself'). Moreover, within a few months of its release, in a move thought to ameliorate a price increase to something more realistic than the importer's original bargain-basement price tag, the factory switched GS's revolutionary shock absorbers for oleo-pneumatic units (the update also included self-cancelling indicators).

   The result of all this sophistication, according to *Motor Cycle Mechanic* magazine's John Robinson, was a ride and long-distance comfort 'comparable to that of a BMW'.

With the suspension configured more firmly, *Superbike*'s Dave Hamill described the GS as 'a formidable handler, capable of running rings against any other Japanese big bike... and even giving a few Italian bikers a thing or two to worry about.'

Contributing to the GS1000's excellent road-holding was a frame constructed of large diameter thin-wall tubing made from STKM-13A mild steel. Designed by Hisashi Morikawa (whose credits included the fine-handling RE5 and GS750 frames), it was both rigid and light - a mere 38.3lbs, making it just 1.55lbs heavier than its stablemate, the GS750's frame. And the GS1000's slenderness didn't stop at the chassis.

Although the GS1000 incorporated lessons learned from the 960 prototype, it actually owed more to the knowledge Suzuki had gained building the 750. The four-pot 997cc twin-cam engine came in at 199.5lbs, 10lbs lighter than the GS750's 209.5lbs powerplant. Engineers achieved this through lightening the crank a couple of pounds by using 'pork-chop' flywheels instead of its sibling's full-circle crank wheels, deleting the kickstart mechanism completely to realise a near four-and-a-half pound saving - one dividend of which was shorter crankcases - and careful paring down of the engine cases' casting webs. The result was that the GS750 weighed only 6lbs less than its bigger brother; the one-litre bike tipping the scales at a claimed 507lbs dry. 'That's a meaningful 33lbs less than the Kawasaki Z1000,' Suzuki declaimed in an advert for their new flagship, before fixing their other Japanese rivals in the crosshairs by pointing out that the GS1000 also weighed '3lbs less than the Yamaha XS750. And 64lbs less than the Honda GL1000'.

The GS1000's output of 87bhp at 8,000rpm was almost 20bhp up on its 750cc four-cylinder stablemate, yet the engine was no wider and only 1mm taller. And whilst the other Japanese one-litre multis all bested the big Suzuki on power, the GS's superior power to weight ratio helped it deliver near equal performance figures. Moreover, the Suzuki's much better handling made it a highly competitive track bike in production racing. In the British Avon Roadrunner series, Norfolk rider Mick James took his bog-stock GS1000 to second place in its very first season after securing wins at Cadwell Park and Carnaby. Over in the US, America Suzuki entered Yoshimura-tuned GS1000s in five AMA Superbike Production races. They led in all five; won three; and suffered just two DNFs (did not finish), due to bolts on the rear sprocket pulling out and an oil cooler failing.

The GS was the quickest motorcycle *Bike* magazine had ever tested down the quarter mile, tripping the lights at 11.92 seconds. It was second only to the Laverda Jota as the fastest bike they had ever tested on top speed (135.7mph to the Italian triple's 138.89mph). The magazine recorded these figures in a comparison test between the GS1000 and its maker's benchmark, and the industry's gold standard for more than half a decade, the Kawasaki Z1000 - which in *Bike*'s head-to-head, the GS comprehensively overhauled.

The Z1000-A2 under test, however, was no longer Kawasaki's performance standard bearer. That role now fell to the Z1-R, conceived as far back as 1974 by Kawasaki executive Graham Kirk under the codename Mark II. When the factory finally revealed the Z1000-D1, better known as the Z1-R, in late 1977 at the Paris show in the Parc Des

Exposition's huge halls, the bike was billed as the first production motorcycle to run 11 second standing quarters straight from the crate (11.95 seconds at 110.25mph to be exact). And the Z1-R laid claim to other firsts, too, including: the first large-displacement Japanese bike to run with 18 inch wheels front and back, and the first mass-market bike from Japan to sport a factory-fitted quarter fairing. It was also the first Kawasaki to feature a four-into-one exhaust system. But whilst the Z1-R's sharp lines may have lent it the appearance of lightness, it actually weighed 6lbs more than the basic Z1000.

Using the standard Z1000 as a platform, Kawasaki aimed to replicate the success of a niche version of their big four called the KZ900-B1 Ltd, hailed as the first factory custom when it was introduced in America in 1976 (true, if one discounts H-D's FX Super Glide or Craig Vetter's Triumph Hurricane of three years earlier).

Kawasaki executive Wayne Moulton had noticed a burgeoning market to supply owners seeking to make their Zs look more fashionable. In a move calculated to entice Harley riders and devotees of the 'chopper' look, Moulton persuaded Kawasaki to take 2,000 standard bikes from the assembly line, strip them of their stock bodywork and running gear, and re-clothe them for a limited run in bell-shaped silencers from the American aftermarket exhaust firm, Jardine, and a 'peanut' fuel tank that was 25 per cent smaller than the Z900-A4's. The Ltd also ditched the base bike's wire wheels for seven-spoke Morris cast aluminium wheels, and swapped its flat bench seat for a stepped 'King and Queen' seat.

If the Ltd reflected an American's take on his US countrymen's tastes, the Z1-R represented America's view of a European café-racer, as interpreted by Japanese engineers (the 'R' standing for 'Racer'). Available in a single colour scheme only, the Z1-R's light blue livery (officially known as Metallic Stardust Silver) was classy and understated - and reportedly influenced by Porche's silver paintwork - whilst the 2.9 gallon coffin-shaped fuel tank and angular bodywork took its cues from voguish Italian styling. That sense of the Z1-R being 'dressed in high style gear', as Kawasaki's brochure called it, extended to the rectangular chrome fuel-filler cap, which resembled an elegant cigarette case.

The Kawasaki's squared-off cockpit fairing (with its smoked Lexan screen) aped the 1974 BMW R90S boxer twin from Germany and half-faired John Player Special 850 Norton from Britain, as well as the 1976 Moto-Guzzi 850 Le Mans Mk I from Italy.

It was a trend also adopted in 1977 by Harley-Davidson stylist Willie G. Davidson for the all-black XLCR 1000 Café Racer. With 68bhp compared to the Sportster's claimed 61, the XLCR was Milwaukee's most powerful ever road bike.

STYLIST WILLIE G.

Willie G. Davidson is the grandson of Harley-Davidson Motor Company founder William A. Davidson (the former toolmaker at Milwaukee Road Railroad Company who was known to H-D staff as 'Old Bill'). Willie G had been working for Ford and Brooks Stevens as a professionally-trained designer before he joined the family firm in February 1963 as its styling director at the invitation of his father, company president William H. Davidson who brought his son in to head up H-D's newly-established styling department.

The first major project to emerge under Willie G's stewardship was the seminal FX Super Glide. The FX married the 74 cubic inches (1,200cc) engine and frame from the Electra Glide with the Sportster's lighter front forks, small headlamp and 19 inch front wheel (many owners, however, quickly junked the FX's fibre-glass 'boat-tail' rear end).

Willie's mix 'n' match approach to blending different components from H-D's model range to produce 'new' products plugged in to the zeitgeist of the time, copying as it did what customisers had already been doing to Harleys for years. Unveiled in 1969 and released the following year, the Super Glide started a new era for Harley-Davidson and is credited as the first 'factory custom'. Whilst not a runaway success in itself, the Super Glide opened the door for the best-selling Low Rider of 1977, a canny combination of old and new (and which revived the 1903-style script for the painted-on tank badge). The XLCR of 1977, however - Willie G and his assistant Louie Netz's interpretation of the European fashion for café racers - was much less successful (at the time of its release, at least).

The two brought in the owner of a nearby development shop, Jim Hauvert, to create a full-size mock-up of what at that stage H-D was calling the 'Black Sportster'. *Cycle World's* Jess Thomas was given a sneak peek at the concept bike in 1975 two days ahead of the prototype being air-freighted to Florida for an appearance at the Daytona show. Thomas dubbed the mock-up a 'black beauty', describing it as 'a sophisticated and functionally styled machine that refuses to abandon H-D's traditional gut-level, raw-boned, primal appeal'. Buyers disagreed. Its long angular tank and tailpiece, factory-fitted cast alloy wheels, the first Harley to have them, and its snaking 'siamesed' exhaust proved too radical for traditional H-D customers, whilst the XLCR's top speed of 110mph and UK price tag of almost £2,500 (compared to 130mph and £1,995 for a Z1-R) made it too slow and expensive for the rest of the market. After a run of only 3,133 machines (1,923 in 1977; 1,201 in '78; and just nine the following year) production of the all-black Café Racer ceased after just two years. Posterity, however, has been kinder to the XLCR than many of its contemporaries.

STILL CRAZY AFTER ALL THESE YEARS

Styling apart, in almost all other respects, the Z1-R was pure Kawasaki. The frame and engine were modelled on the previous year's Z1000-A1, but with more bracing around the headstock, a revised swinging arm to accommodate four needle-roller bearings instead of the two supporting the A1's rear fork, stiffer suspension, drilled brake discs and callipers moved to behind the fork legs. A new lighter, but ultra-rigid front mudguard was claimed to improve handling by bracing the front forks to prevent the wheel - now a seven-spoke alloy - from 'hunting.'

According to *Superbike* magazine's Steve Brennan, the changes resulted in the Z1-R's handling being 'a drastic improvement over the stocker'. The changes did not, however, entirely exorcise the new bike of the Z series' infamous high-speed antics. As Brennan would discover, the changes merely postponed them. 'One moment the bike is behaving itself with panache and style, and you begin to think that here is a new breed of Japanese motorcycle, one that actually handles,' mused Brennan, 'and [then] there you are, as if plunged into a time warp, wrestling with a bike that is just plain old oriental in habits and character, bucking like a bronco. The only difference is, no bronco ever threw off its rider at 95mph...' (*Bike* journalist Peter Watson, who had ridden the first Z1 sold in Britain and countless examples of its successors, described how his encounter with the Z1-R at its European debut in Paris felt like meeting a friend for the first time in months to find they had swapped their sweatshirt and jeans for a pin-stripe suit and brogues and their broad Liverpudlian accent for the Received Pronunciation of a BBC newscaster. Watson had that same sense of disorientation after seeing the Z1-R on display in the French capital. 'It looks like a parting of [the] ways,' the journalist opined, until something they do provokes an echo of the past to remind you that beneath the fancy new attire, the big Kawasaki was 'still crazy after all these years'.)

In an attempt to recapture the first of the line's raw performance, Kawasaki's engineers discarded the A1's 26mm Mikunis, which first saw service in 1976 on the Z900, and returned to the Z1's larger carburettor size of 28mm (and, as if to signal their intent, the original's black engine finish also made a return with the Z1-R, but this time using tougher, more durable epoxy black paint).* Engine output now reached 90bhp. Kawasaki declared its Z1-R the fastest bike they had ever built. The 12.31 second standing quarter that *Bike* achieved on a cold, blustery late winter's day made the Z1-R 'the fastest accelerating stock machine' the magazine had ever tested (until their GS1000 test bike overhauled it just four months later by breaking into the elevens).

And with Yamaha announcing a new four-cylinder, shaft-driven 1,100cc behemoth of their own, the King, it seemed, was under assault on all sides. Peter Watson, however, felt that the Z1-R was simply 'a facelift to keep the king going for a little longer' until Kawasaki launched its rumoured megabike later in the year.** Boasting six cylinders and displacing at least 1,200cc, pundits anticipated the new machine from the Big K would simply flatten the opposition. They also wondered where this was all headed.

---

*   In 1974, Kawasaki dropped the Z1's black engine finish and adopted an all-alloy silver finish from the Z1-A model onwards. This was due to complaints from owners in markets where the black engine paint was unable to withstand inclement weather conditions.

**   Z1-R sales were disappointing. In an effort to shift unsold stocks, Kawasaki Germany produced a version called the Z1000-S, which replaced the Z1-R's four-into-one exhaust system with the four-into-four arrangement from the Z900. In America, Kawasaki resorted to more radical measures. In 1978, Alan Masek, a former Kawasaki marketing director, set up Turbo Cycle Corporation and collaborated with the US company Turbo-Pak to produce the Z1-R TC, a turbo-charged version of the Z1000-D1. Fitted with modified versions of the Ray-Jay 370F40 turbocharger, the bike was only available through selected dealers. When sales of the Z1-R TC also proved slow, Masek had the bike's blue livery repainted in black with orange, red and yellow stripes (similar to the album cover of Pink Floyd's *Dark Side of the Moon*). Sales picked up. In all, about 80 machines were sold in the US and around 125 TCs worldwide. Producing between 105 to 165bhp depending on how much boost the owner dialled into the turbo's adjustable wastegate (up to a maximum of almost 27 psi) the Z1-R TC was capable of around 160mph (with *Old Bike Journal* magazine reporting one owner in America claiming a certified 8.4 second standing quarter at 157mph running with the factory-option wheelie bar). Kawasaki did not offer the bike with a guarantee. In 1980, following a worldwide production run of around 17,500 units, Kawasaki dropped the Z1-R after just two years.

A Bike For The Eighties

The Mediterranean island of Malta, with its pot-holed roads and 42mph speed limit, seemed the perfect venue for letting 70 motorcycle journalists loose on Kawasaki's new 140mph megabike. 'There was little chance of anyone taking the 1300 remotely near its limits,' observed *Superbike* magazine's Dave Hamill in his report of the Z1300's[*] pan-European press launch. 'This in turn meant there was little chance of the bike being slated, and reports would be confined to brief riding impressions and technical descriptions.' The point being, Hamill explained, was that prospective buyers would have enough information on the Thirteen to whet their appetites, but not enough to know its faults.

Unveiled to the world at the Cologne Show in September, 1978, and to British dealers a short time later at London's Hilton Hotel, Kawasaki had conceived the Z1300 back in 1973, just a year after they had launched the ground-breaking Z1. They initiated the project to develop an 'effortless' sports-touring machine, one which would ensure Kawasaki retained their lead as *the* performance-bike manufacturer. The design department sketched out various engine configurations, including an in-line six, a square-four, and longitudinal, parallel and V4 layouts to distinguish the new bike from the increasingly ubiquitous Japanese transverse fours (labelled by the media as UJMs - Universal Japanese Motorcycles), before the factory decided quite early on in the project to lay down some basic specifications for the bike that would be their range-leader for the 1980s.

Codenamed Model 203, Kawasaki's new flagship would displace 1,200cc. Final drive would be shaft. It would have six cylinders. Initially, engineers gave equal consideration to both air and water-cooled engines. However, their analysis of the respective systems' pluses and minuses persuaded the team to opt for liquid-cooling. Water-cooling would allow engineers to reduce engine width by bringing the bore centres closer together and by dispensing with cooling fins. It also helped minimise power losses incurred during long journeys and extended operation, reduced mechanical noise, and offered better temperature control (particularly important for a six's two centre cylinders).

But air-cooling still had its proponents, and in their determination to address one of its drawbacks, its lobbyists managed to shave the cooling fins back to a point where they were barely wider than the cooling jacket of the water-cooled system. Yet even when the decision to adopt water-cooling prevailed, its champions still faced the problem of where to locate the radiator.

Their first attempt saw the radiator sited under the seat, in the spot where the airbox normally resides. Another idea the team explored is revealed in a colour illustration depicting a bike with panniers and a half fairing similar to one of Craig Vetter's popular Windjammers, but featuring a radiator grill between the fairing's twin headlamps.

By December 1974, following exhaustive debate, they had finalised a sketched rendering of how the 203 should look. The radiator is deliberately compact as the

---

[*]   The Z1300 was known as the KZ1300 in the US.

designers wanted to retain something of the Z1's sporty image. It has the teardrop tank and duck-tail seat fairing of the Z900, and six silencers - three a side, ranged in a fan.

The team made careful studies of the machine's rider and pillion accommodation, its centre of gravity, and seat height. As they factored for rider comfort and ergonomics, the Model 203's wheelbase, overall height and weight, tyre size, and engine width combined to express a more touring orientation than that of its illustrious four-cylinder forebear. When they then built a mock-up of the sketch, their three-dimensional rendition simply confirmed the departure. They decided, therefore, to scrap everything and start again.

After more work, more drawings and a second mock-up - this one resembling far more closely the concept of a machine in the image of the Z1 - the designers knew they were getting closer to their goal. Their second iteration had a narrower engine, and leaner tank, seat and tail-section, but fuel capacity was just 10 litres.

In August 1976, the team had the first functional prototype ready. Testing, however, revealed several issues. One of these - excessive noise from the primary gears - Kawasaki's engineers were able to solve by replacing the gears with a Hy-Vo chain (or 'a "silent" cam chain' as the brochure put it). Unfortunately, the solution created a different problem: a wider crankshaft, putting Model 203's sporty direction into jeopardy once again.

Two more problems also surfaced: transmission shock and over-heating. The team overcame troubles with the prototype's transmission by fitting a rubber damper in the clutch, another in the rear hub, and metal-to-metal dampers in the jack and output shafts. Their solution to address coolant temperature rising alarmingly under idling was, however, particularly ingenious. Instead of increasing the size of the radiator, or installing a big and bulky fan - all of which would have compromised their aspiration for a compact system - Kawasaki's engineers expanded fluid capacity by fitting a remotely-mounted coolant tank, and developed a thin, thermostatically-controlled electric-driven radiator fan. This cut in if the coolant temperature reached 207 Fahrenheit, irrespective of whether the engine was running or not (thus preventing heat from the engine continuing to warm up the coolant when the vehicle was switched off). And, in place of conventionally-wound coils, the fan's motor ran off printed circuitry.

Each time the engineers made alterations to fix the issues that the functional prototype was throwing up, the designers made a new clay mock-up, all the time refining incrementally the bike's overall design. Yet, just as the mock-ups went some way to recapturing the original Z1's sporty image, the Model 203's project designers had built another mock-up, this one oriented much more toward touring. The finished bike's styling ended up an amalgam of the two, with its angular lines following the parallelogram styling first seen on the Z1-R, and now by Kawasaki's new 1,000 and 500cc fours launched in Malta alongside the thirteen-hundred. According to *Bike*, Kawasaki described its new look as soft edges and angular planes from tank to tail. 'This style helps optically shift focus onto the Kawasaki cast wheels and wide-section tyres, rather than emphasising the awesome engine.' So ran the factory line. *Bike*'s Dave Calderwood called it 'ugly'.

But even with The Thirteen's styling now settled, the team still had its riding position to sort. Just as Honda had found with the CBX, a bank of six individual carburettors can prove obtrusive. Kawasaki opted to fit three twin-barrelled carbs instead. Made by Mikuni, the carbs were constant-depression type with just one vacuum chamber serving a pair of venturis. Compact and materially frugal, the move from one carburettor-per-cylinder to one-per-pair gave the rider more knee room, thereby greatly improving the seating position. In addition, engineers helped the relation of seat to footrest by swapping the shaft drive over to the right so that they could re-locate the footrest mountings to a better position.

Rider comfort, but also roadholding and handling, informed the team's decision to upgrade the telescopic front forks to air-suspension. Topped up with the correct amount of oil, a pneumatic compression ratio of 2.3:1, and nearly 8 inches of travel, UK journalist L.J.K. Setright said they displayed 'the most superbly progressive action I have ever seen plotted for any motorcycle suspension'.

With Honda once again beating Kawasaki to the punch by unveiling their six first, and Yamaha's new 1,100cc four-cylinder flagship out-displacing the Big K's big fours, in January 1978, the team decided to raise the 203's engine capacity to 1,286cc.

They achieved the increase by adopting a bore to stroke ratio that was rare in car or bike engines. Piston stroke for the CBX measured 53.4mm against The Thirteen's 71mm, giving the Z1300 a bore to stroke ratio of 1.145:1 (38 per cent greater than the Honda CBX's 018:1). It meant that relative to its displacement, the Kawasaki Six had a comparatively small piston area, one consequence of which was a tall engine (and, of course, greater weight).

To offset the weight penalty resulting from a taller engine, Kawasaki's engineers reduced the front to back length of the crankcases by doing something that engineers would usually consider bad practice - they split the connecting-rods across The Thirteen's plain-bearing big ends at an angle. The reason for this was simple. Con-rods are usually split at their big end so that if an engine has to be dismantled, the rods and pistons can be withdrawn through the cylinder bores. By angling the split, the amount of space the front-facing side of a con-rod in motion requires to clear the crankcase is less than the swept area necessary for a conventional, horizontally-split con-rod.

To contain the height of the Z1300's already tall engine, the project team once again chose to defy convention by drastically reducing the length of The Thirteen's con-rods. Normally, the centre distances between the eyes of a con-rod's big- and little-ends measures twice the stroke of the piston. Some tuners, however, favour a shorter rod, believing that its greater rates of velocity to and from top-dead centre aid breathing. Fashionable at the time was a rod 1.8 times the piston's stroke as it helped shorten the cylinder block (resulting in a smaller, lighter powerplant).

With the Z1300's connecting rods only 1.68 times the length of the stroke, piston acceleration and its mean velocity were both very high. On the face of it, the Z1300's claimed power peak of 120bhp at 8,000rpm makes its engine sound positively lazy compared to the CBX's 105bhp at a more frantic 9,500rpm. However, at peak power, The Thirteen's pistons are travelling at 3,727 feet a minute, and accelerating at 3,291 G. The Honda's engine, by contrast, although turning 1,500 revolutions a minute faster to reach peak power, with its smaller bore, longer stroke, and shorter con-rods, is actually under much less stress than the slower-turning Z13. This is because the CBX's pistons cover nearly 400 fewer feet at peak power (3,328 ft/min compared to the Kawasaki Six's 3,727 ft/min).

And whilst The Thirteen produced considerably more torque than the CBX, the Z1300 did so across just 40 per cent of its working range (that is, between 5,000 to 8,000rpm), compared to approximately 60 per cent for the softer-tuned Honda Six. In truth, The Thirteen's inherently smooth six-cylinder engine disguised its comparative edginess. Honda's mix of a short-stroke engine with relatively long con-rods (2.14 times the stroke), coupled with a larger valve area (8.8 square inches compared to The Thirteen's 7 square inches), and more modest rates of valve opening, meant that whilst the CBX engine was certainly livelier, despite its higher crankshaft speeds, it was actually considerably less stressed.

Crucially, however, the CBX was not more powerful.

With a dry weight of 647lbs (296 kg) and 120 horsepower, the Z1300's power to weight ratio was 406bhp per ton, easily topping the 572lb CBX's 396bhp per ton. And although considerably lighter at 510lbs, with only 80bhp, the Benelli 900 Sei (Six) - which in its 750 form presaged both the Honda and Kawasaki when unveiled in 1972 - trailed the two Japanese machines with just 352bhp per ton.

The US market model of The Thirteen came with a 4.71 Imperial gallon (21.4 litres) fuel tank.* But the European versions** of the Z1300 were equipped with a 5.95 gallon (27 litres) tank. This meant that fully fuelled, with a gallon of oil and three-quarters of a gallon of coolant, The Thirteen's kerb weight climbed to well above 700lbs (add a rider and a pillion passenger and that figure rose to nearly half a ton).

The Z1300's six-cylinder engine made up 286lb of that (just one pound more than the kerb weight of a complete Kawasaki Z200). Yet such adiposity was not without its advantages.

The Thirteen's greater sprung mass comparative to its un-sprung mass contributed to the ride and roadholding qualities that won over L.J.K. Setright. As he explained in his technical analysis of the Z1300: 'The springing and damping media allow the suspension to work from the steady base which the relatively great inertia of the sprung mass gives

---

*   'And the KZ1300 runs on regular gas. A blessing at today's gas prices' extolled the breathless copy in a two-page advert in the June '79 issue of the US magazine *Motorcyclist* (which, coincidentally, had reported just a few pages earlier on President Carter's energy conservation proposals to reduce gasoline rations to motorcycles).

**   In all markets except Germany, engine output for the Kawasaki Z1300 engine was 120bhp at 8,000rpm. A voluntary 100 horsepower limit (which was in practice all but mandatory), limited the German version to 99bhp. Torque also dropped - from the all-market version's 85.3ft-lbs to just 75.2ft-lbs.

it.' He pointed out, too, that a heavy bike also maintains its stability when loaded with luggage that on a machine of more moderate mass would induce weaving.

Journalists attending the European launch in Malta, impressed by the big Kawasaki's chassis features - linked pneumatic front suspension and leading axle front forks, long-travel twin rear shocks for a smooth ride, needle-roller bearings for the box-section swinging arm, and a duplex cradle frame with dual-wall downtubes to the steering head - nevertheless seemed taken aback at The Thirteen's good low speed manoeuvrability. They also voiced surprise 'at how nimble such a gargantuan bike could be'. Nor did the Z1300's great weight seem to hold it up too much at the drag strip.

Motor Cycle Mechanics (*MCM*) recorded a 12.1 second standing quarter at the MIRA test circuit, posting terminal speeds ranging from 111mph to 113mph. Aware that others had got The Thirteen to run a fifth of a second faster, only tyre spin prevented them bringing their times down to match. (Kawasaki themselves claimed the Z1300 could run 11.7 second standing quarters, besting the manufacturer's claimed times for The Thirteen's shaft-driven stablemate the Z1000 ST and the chain-driven Z1000 Mk II by 0.4 and 0.1 seconds respectively.)

On MIRA's banked track, The Thirteen attained its predicted top speed of 139mph. 'Being wary of what banked corners can do to tyres,' recalled *MCM*'s test rider, 'I was going into the turn before the timing straight at about 110mph and using full power halfway through. With surprising comfort, the Kawasaki surged forward and came out of the turn like a stone from a slingshot.'

For *MCM*, between the two Japanese six-cylinder bikes, the CBX remained their big bike of choice 'as long as roads have bends in them'.* Ranged against the market's other heavyweights, the Z1300 was altogether different to 'the lazy old full dress Harleys... beats the GoldWing on just about every score and it's just a bit heavier, more powerful and generally *more* than the Yamaha [XS1100].'

Having questioned the need for machines like the Z1300, the magazine came away no longer asking 'Why?' but 'Why not?'

---

* In a production run lasting just four years (1978-82), Honda built a total of 41,229 CBXs (compared to more than a million units of their former flagship, the CB750). The Z1300 lasted ten years, selling around 20,000 (plus a further 4,000 Voyagers in the US, the full-dress touring version of Kawasaki's Six).

The majority of Honda's production run of its six-cylinder flagship - around 26,000 - were the silver CBX1000-Zs (the first and most powerful of the breed). The Maryland-built Model A followed in 1979 (almost all 3,000 of which were sold in the US with none officially imported into the UK). Resplendent in Candy Red, the A sacrificed absolute maximum speed for a stronger mid-range, the result of Honda revising the CBX's ignition and cam timing. In 1980, Honda introduced the Model B. Now available (officially) for the first time in black, more restrictive silencing and redesigned cams dented performance even further. The Pro-link mono-shock B and C Models followed in 1981 and '82. With a half-fairing, longer wheelbase, and a 54lb weight gain, Honda repositioned the last iterations of the CBX to a more clearly defined role of sports-tourer.

The Kawasaki Z1300 ran with three twin-choke carburettors for its 1979-1983 models, and Digital fuel injection thereafter. The change smoothed out the carburetted model's low-speed hesitancy, improved fuel economy (consumption went from 32-35mpg to 38-40mpg), increased power output to 130bhp, and raised maximum speed to 145mph.

End Of An Era

Bike magazine was far more apocalyptic (and apoplectic). They devoted almost a fifth of their September '79 issue to the Z1300, starting with an item called 'Megabikes: The Party Is Over.' Penned by Assistant Editor Steve Brennan, his three-page article examined the economics and history of the phenomena, which he pointed out did not start with the Japanese, but could be dated back to Henry Capel Lofft, a Major in the British army who in 1896 built a 1,047cc four-cylinder motorcycle. Brennan's article explained how the performance of superbikes from the Brough Superior through to The Thirteen had risen just as their price in real terms had fallen. This was followed by a two-handed piece entitled 'Z1300: End of an Era?' Accompanied by an illustration of a Z1300 being carried through a cemetery by four helmeted pallbearers, the nine-page article was prefaced with an introduction associating the timing of Z1300's introduction with West Germany's implementation of a 100 horsepower limit. L.J.K. Setright contributed a characteristically brilliant exposition on the bike's technical attributes, whilst an unapologetic polemic from Mike Nicks explored what he feared The Thirteen meant for motorcycling's future (which for Nicks did not include a machine so heavy that to change the front wheel, Kawasaki's engineers incorporated a jacking point into the engine sump).

The Z1300 arrived at the end of a tumultuous ten years, over the course of which each manufacturer had replaced their biggest-capacity model with a successor of greater displacement and power. Megabikes represented another step - albeit a bold one - in the march to still bigger and more powerful motorcycles. Many in the motorcycle press voiced concern, aware that the industry's pursuit and promotion of ever more powerful machines had powerful critics in government - including the National Highway Traffic Safety Administration's administrator Joan Claybrook.

They therefore viewed Kawasaki's 1.3 litre flagship as something of a nadir in motorcycle development. But, in fact, it was The Thirteen's co-debutantes at the European launch in Malta - the Z1000 Mk II and ST - that better symbolised the changes overtaking motorcycling.

In answer to journalists' questions as to why Kawasaki had produced chain *and* shaft-drive versions of the same one-litre four, the factory's response was that they were simply trying to satisfy 'an increasingly fragmented motorcycle public'.

The era of the one-model production bike owners adapted to reflect their tastes or riding style (either by swapping the handlebars or the whole rolling chassis for something from the likes of Rickman or Egli) was coming to an end. The era of the niche motorcycle was about to begin.

21

POSTSCRIPT

'A decade of grit and glamour'
(*Daily Telegraph* article by Neil McCormick: 'The Diamond Decades - The 1970s')

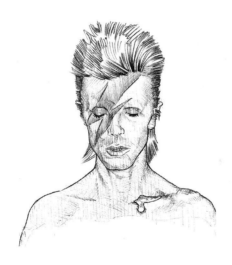

David Bowie

A DECADE OF STARK CONTRASTS

In a *Daily Telegraph* article commemorating Queen Elizabeth II's Diamond Jubilee and the six decades of her reign, Neil McCormick described the Seventies in terms of stark contrasts: from the disco dancers of New York's Studio 54 to the rebels of the 100 Club; the gritty realism of Roman Polanski's *Chinatown* (1974) to the space-age daydream of George Lucas's *Star Wars* (1977). 'It was a decade,' McCormick observed, 'defined by both a new realism and a new escapism. It was punk and glitter, grit and glamour...'

Much the same could be said of Seventies motorcycling. As the press lauded the technological *tour de forces* emerging from Japan - bikes like Yamaha's XS750 twin-cam shaft-drive triple (*Cycle* and *Bike* magazines' Machine of the Year in 1976 and 1977 respectively), or the Suzuki GS750 four (*Cycle*'s favourite 750 in the Class of '76') - the best-selling large-capacity motorcycle in Britain was the Triumph Bonneville, an overhead-valve pushrod twin based on a design dating back to the Thirties. And when readers voted the ground-breaking Kawasaki Z1 900 as *Motor Cycle News*' Machine of the Year for four successive years, the landmark four-cylinder marvel still did not manage to beat the five-year record (1968-1972) of the award's previous incumbent, the Norton Commando, a twin-cylinder motorcycle based on a 40 year-old design.

At odds with escalating fuel prices and greater traffic congestion - car ownership in Britain rose from 52 per cent in 1970 to 60 per cent by the end of the decade, as nearly 12,000 more vehicles a day flowed down its motorways and almost 1,500 more passed along its cities' main roads in 1975 than ten years earlier - motorcycle manufacturers developed ever larger, more powerful, faster and fuel-hungrier vehicles. And although bikes became cheaper in real terms, the energy costs to produce them began to rise.

Developed to satisfy a niche demand, one of the best-selling style of motorcycles towards the end of the Seventies were the oxymoronic 'factory customs'. Each of the Big Four Japanese makers produced a custom version of the 'standard' model. Kawasaki, who had kick-started the trend, labelled their custom range *LTD* (or *Custom*, somewhat unimaginatively in the case of the Z650). Yamaha called theirs *Specials*. In a 36 page magazine insert incorporating two four-page foldouts, a Yamaha advert promoting their 1978 season's range explained: 'The Specials come ready-to-wear. With all the individualistic touches, that usually take a lot of time and money to add yourself, already integrally designed into the machine.'

Nostalgia

Michael B. Crawford Ph.D, author of *Shop Class as Soulcraft: An Inquiry into the Value of Work* described such bikes as satisfying a longing 'for a lost authenticity'. For Crawford, the factory customs tapped into a motorcycle culture that still retained 'a dim remembrance of the more involving character of old machines.

This harking back was a trend Seventies historian Dominic Sandbrook observed was typical of a populace living in difficult and changing times. Britons in the 1970s immersed themselves in period dramas such as *Upstairs, Downstairs* or *The Onedin Line*, sitcoms like *Dad's Army*, Edith Holden's unlikely bestseller *The Country Diary of an Edwardian Lady*, or Laura Ashley clothes and wallpapers.

Triumph was quite unabashed about promoting heritage in its adverts. Occupying the coveted Norton-girl spot on the inside cover of *Cycle* magazine, a 1977 advert placed by NVT America piggy-backed the vogue for everything Fifties following the success of the film *Grease* (1978) and the hugely popular US TV show *Happy Days*. The ad depicted a leather-jacketed Fonzarelli-type character standing behind a T140, a girl dressed as a waitress from a 1950s diner on his arm. Behind the pair are a line of hot-rods. Paper-clipped at an angle to the top right of this air-brushed (literally) evocation of the Fifties is a black-and-white drawing, purportedly a photograph of a crinoline-dressed girl sat side-saddle on a Thunderbird. The bike is parked in front of two riders in white tee-shirts and bike jackets. It could be a scene from *The Wild One* or a snap from a family album taken 20 years previously.

'It was known as the Bonnie,' says the ad copy. 'The production hot rod of the motorcycle industry... And the guy who rode one knew he had the most responsive, best handling motorcycle ever built. Others have tried to copy the Bonneville for 20 years [step forward, Yamaha?], but haven't come close.'

And, just in case the use of the past tense had the reader thinking the Bonnie was extinct: 'Today, you can still enjoy the classic styling, the raw power and the unmatched handling that sets the legendary 750cc Bonnie apart.'

Unable to compete with the technology of its Japanese rivals, Triumph simply made capital of its old-fashioned craftsmanship. In a four-page ad in the February '78 issue of *Cycle* magazine (whose cover featured a photo of the Honda CBX1000 overlaid with a list of the Six's jaw-dropping specification), underneath a picture of a man's hands guiding a paintbrush across the top of a fuel tank was the caption: 'Each Triumph pinstripe for over 40 years has been painted by hand.' Meanwhile, the accompanying text issued a challenge to the reader's sense of self. 'It's always taken a special breed of man to fall in love with a Triumph,' read the copy. 'The kind of man who appreciates motorcycles designed, built and ridden by men, not computers.'

Kawasaki employed a similar device. In a 1977 advert for the Z1000-A1, copywriters got their retaliation in first.

'Z-1000. You may never master it completely,' acknowledged the strap-line in a knowing reference to the Big Z's family trait for wayward handling. 'But then, who wants a tame motorcycle?'

The showroom success of Suzuki's GS1000 suggested the answer was: quite a few.

Although the appetite for bigger street-bikes had been a characteristic of the Seventies, Neil McCormick's observation about the decade's duality applied here also. Between 1972 and 1976, the two best-selling models in America were the Honda CB750 and the Suzuki TS185.

SALES RISE AND ENGINES GROW

The Seventies' trend for bigger bikes coincided with the second of two phenomenal periods of growth in the numbers of people riding motorcycles. The first occurred between 1962 and 1967, when, according to the US Department of Transportation, registrations of new bikes climbed to 1.75 million in 1966 (up from 600,000 in 1962), before dropping back again to just over 600,000 by 1969, which commentators attribute to the war in Vietnam and the US Government's escalation of the military draft. In June 1965, President Lyndon B. Johnson had abandoned the pretence of American soldiers acting as 'military advisers' in Vietnam (deployed by his predecessor John F. Kennedy who increased their numbers from 500 to 10,000 in 1962), and committed US soldiers to ground combat: 390,000 by the end of 1966, rising to 550,000 by the beginning of 1968. By the end of Johnson's presidency in January 1969, 35,000 American soldiers had paid the ultimate price. Just over 58,000 US soldiers would die by the time Richard Nixon ended America's involvement in Vietnam in January 1973.

The second rise began in 1970, with figures from the Motorcycle Industry Council indicating that sales grew steadily in the US throughout the decade and on into the early 1980s.

In Britain, registrations of new motorcycles in 1975 rose 40 per cent compared to 1974, as Britons turned to two-wheels in the face of rising fuel prices and lightning strikes on UK transport systems.

And just as sales rose, so too did displacement. Back in the world's biggest market, sales of 600cc plus motorcycles trebled in 1969-70 alone. Kawasaki's best seller in the US during the early Seventies was the KZ400, whereas by the end of the decade it was their KZ650 and 750.

And yet the large-displacement bikes category that had for so long been Meriden and Milwaukee's exclusive preserve was being lost to the Big Four from Japan. In 1972, Yamaha's XS650 outsold Triumph in the 650 class (by 1971, BSA and Triumph's joint share of the US market had dropped to less than 7 per cent, as almost half of all motorcycles sold in America were made by Honda). By the end of the Seventies, Harley-Davidson's share of the big bike market had slid to just a third (and less than 24 per cent by 1983, when for the first time ever, Honda sold more big bikes than Milwaukee).

TROUBLE IN MILWAUKEE AND MERIDEN

Despite successes with models such as the limited edition Jubilee Bonneville produced to mark Queen Elizabeth II's Silver Jubilee in 1977* and the T140D Special, the Meriden Co-operative struggled throughout the rest of the decade. It finally limped to a close in 1983, when construction-industry magnate John Bloor bought the Triumph name and manufacturing rights after the Co-op when into liquidation. The Bonneville, however, lived on. Bloor granted Les Harris a licence to build T140 Bonnevilles to strict Meriden-specification at the parts manufacturer and supplier's factory near Newton Abbot in Devon.

Harley-Davidson had a similarly torrid decade. Rather than develop a lightweight of their own with which to take on the European and Japanese middleweight competition, Milwaukee's development committee decided it would be better to re-badge a foreign-made model and market it as an H-D. But declining to simply import and re-brand them, they elected instead to buy the Italian manufacturer, Aermacchi.

The 250 and 350cc Aermacchi-engined H-D American Sprints sold well, but they suffered indifferent build quality (separated by both language and the Atlantic Ocean, with factories located on different continents, Milwaukee was never able to solve the

---

*   With a price premium of £150 and half of all Silver Jubilee Bonnevilles sold never actually run as buyers immediately mothballed them, the T140J did very well for Meriden (not least because they resulted in far fewer recalls and warranty claims).

problem). The Italian tie-in boosted sales and turnover, but not profit. Meanwhile, Harley-Davidson's V-twins were becoming outliers in an expanding market. Dogged by financial problems, for the first time in its 65 year history, H-D decided to generate revenue by going public and floating the company on Wall Street (yet making sure to retain overall control of this still family-run firm - the family making up seven out of the nine-member Board). They invested the windfall on plant and machinery, and big budget advertising campaigns. The flotation stalled their financial troubles, but it did not cure them. After conceding that a takeover provided the only means of survival, in 1969 H-D accepted an offer by the American Machine and Foundry Company to buy them out. An engineering firm whose businesses included manufacturing the mechanisms in bowling alleys which reset the ten pins, AMF's Harley-riding chairman, Rodney Gott, saw H-D as important to his company's ambitions to extend its leisure businesses.

Motorcycle sales were booming, yet Milwaukee had produced just 27,000 machines in 1969. AMF's plan was to raise production - rapidly and dramatically. After investing considerable sums re-equipping H-D's six decades-old Juneau Avenue plant, AMF managed to more than double production of engines and gearboxes within the space of just three short years. With final assembly moved to its plant in York, Pennsylvania, AMF succeeded in raising output to 60,000 units.

Quality, however, suffered. So, too, did employee and dealer relations as AMF-era Harleys became a byword for poor workmanship and unreliability (Gott later confessed that AMF drove things at too fast a pace). AMF's Ray Tritten carried out a review of the business. His conclusion was that Milwaukee had underestimated its Japanese competitors, its marketing and engineering departments lacked professionalism, and its production processes were inefficient. He appointed former associate professor of engineering at Yale, Jeff Bleustein, to overhaul H-D's engineering department; and installed AMF man Vaughn Beals to take charge at Milwaukee with the immediate task of fixing Harley's long-term programme of new models.

Beals, who had graduated from MIT (Massachusetts Institute of Technology) with degrees in aeronautical engineering, took a two-track approach. In the short term, and to get the company through the next few years, Harley would develop its V-twins (the result would be 1983's Evolution - or Evo[2] - engine). The longer-term plan was much more ambitious - and considerably more expensive.

Launched in 1976, AMF put $10 million into a programme called NOVA, a project to develop a range of water-cooled engines. Harley's new-generation powerplants would be built around a modular concept, whereby a 500cc twin, a one-litre four, and a 1,500cc six shared key components such as transmission, valves and pistons. AMF, however, aware that Milwaukee was fully engaged developing the Evolution V-twin, and reluctant to underwrite the whole cost themselves, sub-contracted development to the German sports car-maker Porsche. But as the Seventies drew to a close, AMF's commitment to Harley-Davidson cooled. When the new chief executive Tom York joined, he rejected a team of consultant's recommendations that AMF give the NOVA project the green light (at an estimated cost of $60 to $80 million).*

In 1981, after more than a decade of pumping considerable sums of money into Harley-Davidson with little profit to show in return, AMF decided to sell its motorcycle division to H-D executives in a leveraged buyout headed up by Beals.

CANDY-COLOURED PEACOCKS

The Motorcycles of the Seventies shone particularly brilliantly amidst Britain's post-war shabbiness. Grand Victorian public buildings stood drab and oppressive, their stonework black from a century of coal soot; the brutalist concrete high-rises thrown up in the 1960s by the acolytes of *en vogue* French architect Le Corbusier were, like the brave new world of council planners, already crumbling, as refuse piled high in the streets, uncollected due to industrial action.

On Britain's roads, cars like the Morris Minor (launched in 1948 and still in production as late as 1972) came in battleship grey or army field-dress green. British Leyland offered every car they made - from the Austin Allegro to the Jaguar XJ6 - in brown or mustard (listed more cryptically as 'Sand Green' in the brochure). In the provinces outside of London, corporation buses were commonly painted in drab greens, dowdy blues, khakis or magnolias, depending on the civic livery of the particular conurbation they served.

Small wonder, then, that on a canvas made up of such dreary hues, the polychromatic motorcycles of the Seventies proved so alluring to glamour-starved Brits. Motorcycles like the Candy Lavender Suzuki GT750 and Candy Purple Kawasaki H2 stood out like those peacocks of Glam Rock, Marc Bolan and David Bowie. UK inflation may have reached a high of 25 per cent, union pay claims 30 per cent, and unemployment close to a million in 1975, but none of that mattered to transfixed young men eyeing these two-wheeled meteors like magpies might a bauble. Freed from National Service (which had ended early the previous decade), together with relaxations on hire purchase, plentiful jobs - both for the 8.4 per cent of the population who went to university and the ninety-per cent plus who did not but who could still find work in the old heavy industries - combined with the great strides made by the Japanese manufacturers in performance, reliability, functionality and affordability, plus liberal learner laws that permitted novices to ride 250cc motorcycles that were often sleeved down versions of larger models, all helped shape motorcycling's halcyon decade.

'To be young in that dawn might not have been very heaven,' wrote Alwyn W. Turner in *Crisis? What Crisis? Britain in the 1970s*, 'but sometimes it didn't seem too far off...'

---

*   In 1983, H-D revealed a working prototype of a V4 NOVA to selected dealers during Milwaukee's unveiling of the new Evo V-twin as part of company plans toward the introduction of a water-cooled V4 and V6 in 1985-86.

SPECIFICATIONS

'What'll it do, mister?'

I have compiled the information in this section from a variety of sources. My main source has been magazines from the period. However, details in previews, road tests and manufacturer's adverts published at the time a model was released often differ, particularly when it comes to performance. Take, for example, the Honda CB750.

In an article published in March 1969, a US magazine reported the Four's output was 'a whopping 75 horses at 9500rpm'. Most magazines, however, reported output as 67bhp at 8,000rpm. Yet, in a US advert for the CB750, Honda stated horsepower as '68 at 8,500rpm'. In still another Honda ad, the Four appears to have been gelded and become a '67 horsepower masterpiece from the master maker.' Similar variations can be found when it comes to top speed: from Honda's claimed 125mph to *Cycle* magazine's 131mph as reported in its August 1969 road test. Even the Four's wheelbase could vary (albeit very slightly: 57.3 inches to 57½ inches), as could its weight. A Honda magazine ad claimed it weighed 445lbs. It came in at 522lbs (dry) according to a *Cycle Guide* road test, whereas *Cycle* magazine's test machine had a 'curb weight' of 485lbs.

I have therefore listed figures that are most represented in the sources (apologies, therefore, if they should not accord with any well-thumbed road test you hold for your favourite model).

With the exception of the Harley-Davidson Sportster and Yamaha's XS750, I have provided specifications for the introductory model only. As Milwaukee first introduced the Sportster in 1957, with this a book about Seventies Superbikes, I felt it more appropriate to provide figures for the XCLH that took part in *Cycle* magazine's 1972 Superbike Comparison Test.

For the Yamaha triple, the specifications cover the XS750-2D. This was the model Yamaha introduced mid-way through the XS750's first year of production, as an upgrade to address the inaugural machine's performance problems.

1972 DUCATI 750 GT

ENGINE

Type	Air-cooled overhead-valve 90° L-twin, four-stroke
Capacity	748cc
Bore x stroke	80 x 74.4mm
Compression	8.5:1
Carburetion	Two Amal type R930/76 and 77
Clutch	Multi-plate clutch running in oil
Gearbox	Five-speed constant mesh

CHASSIS

Frame	Open double tubular-steel cradle, with crankcases acting as frame member
Front suspension	Marzocchi leading axle 38mm telescopic forks
Rear suspension	Twin Marzocchi, three-way adjustable for spring preload
Brakes front/rear	Front: 11.02 inch disc, twin-piston Lockheed calliper
	Rear: 7.87 inch single leading shoe drum
Tyres front/rear	Front: 3.25 x H19 L25 Michelin
	Rear: 3.50 x H18 S41 Michelin

DIMENSIONS

Weight	407lb dry (185kg)
Wheelbase	60.2 inches (1530mm)
Seat height	30.7 inches (780mm)
Fuel capacity	3.74 Imperial gallons, 4.49 US gallons (17 litres) plus reserve (0.35 Imp gall, 0.42 US gall, 1.6 litres)

PERFORMANCE

Top speed	124mph approx.*
0-60mph	N/A
Standing ¼ mile	13.289 seconds / 101.12mph**
Max power	49.9bhp at 7,114rpm, 43.2ft-lbs at 4,819rpm **
Fuel consumption	36mpg
Price new	UK: £842 US: $1,964*
Colour schemes	Bodywork: Blue, green, orange and red; or red with black decals; or black with white decals
	Frame: Black

*   *The Ducati 750 Bible* by Ian Falloon
**   *Cycle* magazine (December 1972)

1972 HARLEY-DAVIDSON XLCH 1000
SPORTSTER

ENGINE

Type	Air-cooled overhead-valve 45° V-twin, four-stroke
Capacity	1,000cc
Bore x stroke	81 x 96mm
Compression	9.0:1
Carburetion	One 42mm Bendix
Clutch	Multi-plate clutch running in oil
Gearbox	Four-speed constant mesh

CHASSIS

Frame	Duplex steel cradle
Front suspension	Two-way damped telescopic forks
Rear suspension	Twin gas-filled spring damper units
Brakes front/rear	Front: 10 x $2^{1}/_{8}$ inch disc brake with Kelsey-Hayes calliper
	Rear: 8 x 1.625 inch drum
Tyres front/rear	Front: 3.50 x 19
	Rear: 4.25 x 18

DIMENSIONS

Weight	$487^{1}/_{2}$lb wet (221kg)
Wheelbase	$58^{1}/_{2}$ inches (1486mm)
Seat height	28.75in (730mm)
Fuel capacity	2.7 Imperial gallons, 2.25 US gallons (12.3 litres)

PERFORMANCE

Top speed	120mph*
0-60mph	N/A
Standing ¼ mile	13.393 seconds / 99.88mph**
Max power	46.5bhp at 5,724rpm, 49.8ft-lbs at 2,602rpm *
Fuel consumption	42mpg average*
Price new	UK: £2,400** US: $2,025**
Colour schemes	Bodywork: Gloss black or Deep red**
	Frame: Black

---

*   John Warr (Warr's Harley-Davidson)
**   *Cycle* magazine (December 1972)

1974 HERCULES W2000

Marketed as DKW in the UK

ENGINE

Type	Fan-cooled, single rotor NSU/Wankel-type rotary
Capacity	Single chamber 294cc
Bore x stroke	N/A
Compression	6.5:1
Carburetion	Single Bing 32mm constant pressure type
Clutch	Wet multi-plate clutch
Gearbox	Six-speed constant mesh

CHASSIS

Frame	Duplex steel cradle
Front suspension	Telescopic forks with hydraulic damper
Rear suspension	Twin 5-way adjustable hydraulic spring damper units
Brakes front/rear	Front: Single 11.8 inch diameter disc
	Rear: 7.1 inch diameter, single leading shoe drum
Tyres front/rear	Front: 3.00 x 18in Metzeler
	Rear: 3.25 x 18in Metzeler

DIMENSIONS

Weight	386lb incl. 2 gallons of fuel (175kg)
Wheelbase	56 inches (1422mm)
Seat height	31 inches (787mm)
Fuel capacity	3.95 Imperial gallons plus 1 gallon reserve (22 litres)

PERFORMANCE

Top speed	96.36mph*
0-60mph	7.24 seconds*
Standing ¼ mile	16.25 seconds*
Max power	32bhp at 6,000rpm 24.5ft-lbs torque at 4,500 rpm*
Fuel consumption	42mpg average**
Price new	UK: £917 incl. VAT. US: $1,900
Colour schemes	Bodywork: Red and Silver
	Frame: Silver

*   *Bike* magazine (February 1975)
**   *On Two Wheels (Volume 3)*

1969 HONDA CB 750/4
DREAM FOUR

ENGINE

Type	Air cooled, transverse four-cylinder, 8 valve four-stroke
Capacity	736cc
Bore x stroke	61 x 63mm
Compression	9:1
Carburetion	Four 28mm Kehin-Seiki
Clutch	Multi-plate clutch running in oil
Gearbox	Five-speed constant mesh

CHASSIS

Frame	Duplex steel cradle
Front suspension	Honda two-way damped telescopic forks
Rear suspension	Twin gas-filled spring damper units
Brakes front/rear	Front: 11½ inch diameter disc
	Rear: 7 inch diameter, single leading shoe
Tyres front/rear	Front: 3.25 x 19in Dunlop F-3
	Rear: 4.00 x 18in Dunlop K87

DIMENSIONS

Weight	480lb (217kg)
Wheelbase	57½ inches (1455mm)
Seat height	31 inches (787mm)
Fuel capacity	4 Imperial gallons, 5 US gallons (18 litres)

PERFORMANCE

Top speed	125mph
0-60mph	5.3 seconds**
Standing ¼ mile	12.6 seconds*
Max power	67bhp at 8,000rpm
Fuel consumption	38-42mpg average***
Price new	UK: £679 19s 0d US: $1,495
Colour schemes	Bodywork: Candy Ruby Red or Candy Blue Green
	Frame: Black

*   Honda Advert
**   *Cycle* Magazine (August 1969)
*** *Motor Cycle Mechanics* magazine (June 1970)

1978 Honda CBX1000/6
Super Sport

ENGINE

Type	Six-cylinder DOHC 24-valve four-stroke
Capacity	1,047cc
Bore x stroke	64.5 x 53.4mm
Compression	9.3:1
Carburetion	Six 28mm Keihin VB28 constant vacuum
Clutch	Multi-plate clutch running in oil
Gearbox	Five-speed constant mesh

CHASSIS

Frame	Tubular steel backbone truss
Front suspension	Telescopic fork
Rear suspension	Dual shock absorbers
Brakes front/rear	Front: Twin 10.7 inch (276mm) discs
	Rear: 11½ inch (295mm) disc
Tyres front/rear	Front: 3.50 x 19 Dunlop F11
	Rear: 4.25 x 18 Dunlop K127

DIMENSIONS

Weight	545lbs dry (247kg)
Wheelbase	60.43 inches (1535mm)
Seat height	31.89 inches (810mm)
Fuel capacity	4.8 Imperial gallons (22 litres)

PERFORMANCE

Top speed	132mph (after ½ mile)*
0-60mph	N/A
Standing ¼ mile	11.39 seconds / 118.11mph*
Max power	103bhp at 9,000rpm (claimed)*
Fuel consumption	39.2mpg*
Price new	UK: £2,578 US: $3,998
Colour schemes	Bodywork: Silver or red
	Frame: Black

*   *Cycle World* magazine (January 1979)

1975 Honda GL1000 Gold Wing

ENGINE

Type	Water-cooled overhead cam flat-four-cylinder four-stroke
Capacity	999cc
Bore x stroke	72 x 61.4mm
Compression	9.2:1
Carburetion	4 x 32 Keihin
Clutch	Multi-plate clutch running in oil
Gearbox	Five-speed constant mesh

CHASSIS

Frame	Duplex steel cradle
Front suspension	Two-way damped telescopic forks
Rear suspension	Twin gas-filled spring damper units
Brakes front/rear	Front: Twin 11 inch (279mm) discs
	Rear: $11^1/_2$ inch (295mm) disc
Tyres front/rear	Front: 3.50 x 19 inch Japanese Dunlop
	Rear: 4.50 x 17 inch Japanese Dunlop

DIMENSIONS

Weight	595lbs dry (595kg), 645lbs wet (293kg)
Wheelbase	60.6 inches (1536mm)
Seat height	31.6 inches (802.6mm)
Fuel capacity	4.2 Imperial gallons, 5 US gallons (19 litres)

PERFORMANCE

Top speed	120.96mph
0-60mph	6.22 seconds
Standing ¼ mile	13.125 seconds
Max power	80bhp at 7,500rpm
Fuel consumption	35-40mpg
Price new	UK: £1,599 US: $2,895
Colour schemes	Bodywork: Candy Antares Red or Candy Blue Green
	Frame: Black

*   *Bike* magazine (January 1976)

1969 Kawasaki 500 H1 (MACH III)

ENGINE

Type	Air cooled, inline three-cylinder piston port two-stroke
Capacity	498cc
Bore x stroke	60 x 58.8mm
Compression	6.8:1
Carburetion	Three 28mm Mikuni carburettors
Clutch	Multi-plate wet clutch
Gearbox	Five-speed (transferable gear lever to left or right side)

CHASSIS

Frame	Tubular steel cradle
Front suspension	Ceriani-type telescopic fork
Rear suspension	Twin three-position spring adjustment
Brakes front/rear	Front: 8 inch (200mm)diameter, twin leading shoe
	Rear: 7 inch (180mm) diameter, single leading shoe
Tyres front/rear	Front: 19in x 3.25 Dunlop K77
	Rear: 18in x 4.00 Dunlop

DIMENSIONS

Weight	382lb claimed (174kg)
Wheelbase	55 inches (1397mm)
Seat height	31 inches (787mm)
Fuel capacity	3½ Imperial gallons, 4 US gallons (16 litres)

PERFORMANCE

Top speed	118mph*
0-60mph	N/A
Standing ¼ mile	12.8 seconds / 104.40mph**
Max power	60bhp at 7,500rpm
Fuel consumption	45mpg average
Price new	UK: £589 19s 11d US: $999
Colour schemes	Bodywork: White/blue decals or grey (not available in UK)
	Frame: Black

*   *Bike* magazine (July/August 1973)
**   *Cycle* magazine (March 1970)

1971 KAWASAKI 750 H2

ENGINE

Type	Three-cylinder piston port two-stroke, six bearing crank
Capacity	748cc
Bore x stroke	71 x 63mm
Compression	7.0:1
Carburetion	Three 32mm Mikunis
Clutch	Multi-plate clutch running in oil
Gearbox	Five-speed constant mesh

CHASSIS

Frame	Duplex steel cradle
Front suspension	Two-way damped telescopic forks
Rear suspension	Twin gas-filled spring damper units
Brakes front/rear	Front: $11^1/_2$ inch disc
	Rear: SLS 8 x 1.4 inch
Tyres front/rear	Front: 3.25 x 19
	Rear: 4.00 x 18

DIMENSIONS

Weight	435lbs dry (198kg)
Wheelbase	55½ inches (1409mm)
Seat height	31½ inches (800mm)
Fuel capacity	4 Imperial gallons, 4.8 US gallons (18 litres)

PERFORMANCE

Top speed	120mph*
0-60mph	N/A
Standing ¼ mile	12.49 seconds/106mph*
Max power	74bhp at 6,800rpm†
Fuel consumption	22mpg
Price new	UK: £754 US: $1,200
Colour schemes	Bodywork: Blue or orange
	Frame: Black

---

*   *Bike* magazine (March/April 1973)

1972 KAWASAKI 900 Z1
SUPER FOUR

ENGINE

Type	Four-cylinder, double-overhead cam four-stroke
Capacity	903cc
Bore x stroke	66 x 66mm
Compression	8.5:1
Carburetion	Four Mikuni VM 28SC
Clutch	Multi-plate clutch running in oil
Gearbox	Five-speed constant mesh

CHASSIS

Frame	Duplex steel cradle
Front suspension	Two-way damped telescopic forks, 5.5 inches travel
Rear suspension	Twin 5-way adjustable hydraulic, 3.2 inches travel
Brakes front/rear	Front: Single 11.7 inch diameter hydraulic disc
	Rear: 7.9 inch internal expanding drum
Tyres front/rear	Front: 3.25 x 19 Dunlop F6
	Rear: 4.00 x 18 Dunlop K87

DIMENSIONS

Weight	500lbs dry (230kg)
Wheelbase	58.7 inches (1490mm)
Seat height	31½ inches (800mm)
Fuel capacity	4 Imperial gallons, 4.75 US gallons (18 litres)

PERFORMANCE

Top speed	130.54 mph (mean)*
0-60mph	4.8 seconds**
Standing ¼ mile	12.386 seconds / 110.70***
Max power	82 bhp at 8,500 rpm, 54.2ft-lbs at 7,000 rpm
Fuel consumption	48mpg at 70mph
Price new	UK: £1,088 incl. VAT US: $1,895
Colour schemes	Bodywork: Candy maroon and orange or green and yellow
	Frame: Black

*   *Motor Cycle* magazine (August 1973)
**   *Motor Cycle* magazine (August 1973)
***   *Cycle Guide* magazine (September 1973)

1979 KAWASAKI Z 1300/6

ENGINE

Type	Liquid cooled, DOHC inline 6-cylinder, 12 valve four-stroke
Capacity	1,286cc
Bore x stroke	62 x 71mm
Compression	9.9:1
Carburetion	Three 32mm two-barrel Mikuni BSW32
Clutch	Multi-plate clutch running in oil, shaft final drive
Gearbox	Five-speed constant mesh

CHASSIS

Frame	Duplex tubular steel cradle
Front suspension	41mm telescopic forks, air-assisted fork, with compression damping
Rear suspension	Twin adjustable air-assisted units
Brakes front/rear	Front: twin 10.2 inch (260mm) diameter discs
	Rear: single 9.8 inch (250mm) diameter disc
Tyres front/rear	Front: 110/90V x 18 inch Dunlop tubeless
	Rear: 130/90V x 17 inch Dunlop tubeless

DIMENSIONS

Weight	710lb wet (322kg)
Wheelbase	62½ inches (1587mm)
Seat height	31.85 inches (809mm)
Fuel capacity	UK: 5.94 Imp. gallons (27 litre)/5.6 US gallons (21.2 litre)

PERFORMANCE

Top speed	139mph*
0-60mph	N/A
Standing ¼ mile	12.13 seconds / 114.1mph**
Max power	120bhp at 8,000rpm
Fuel consumption	37.7mpg**
Price new	UK: £3,249 US: $4,695
Colour schemes	Bodywork: Black, blue or dark green
	Frame: Black

*   *Classic Bike* magazine (July 2007)
**   *Motorcyclist* magazine (June 1979)

1976 LAVERDA JOTA

ENGINE

Type	Air-cooled double-overhead cam three-cylinder four-stroke
Capacity	981cc
Bore x stroke	75 x 74mm
Compression	10:1
Carburetion	3 x 32mm Dell 'Orto
Clutch	Multi-plate clutch running in oil
Gearbox	Five-speed constant mesh

CHASSIS

Frame	Welded duplex steel cradle with 2½-inch diameter spine
Front suspension	Ceriani telescopic forks
Rear suspension	Twin Ceriani spring damper units
Brakes front/rear	Front: Twin Brembo 11 inch discs
	Rear: Single Brembo 11 inch disc
Tyres front/rear	Front: 4.10 x 18 Dunlop TT100
	Rear: 4.25 x 18 Dunlop TT100

DIMENSIONS

Weight	522lbs with one gallon of fuel (237kg)
Wheelbase	58½ inches (1485mm)
Seat height	32 inches (812mm)
Fuel capacity	4¼ Imperial gallons, 5.1 US gallons (19 litres)

PERFORMANCE

Top speed	140.04mph best one-way, 137.8mph two-way mean*
0-60mph	N/A
Standing ¼ mile	12.96 seconds**
Max power	90bhp at 7,600rpm
Fuel consumption	42.6mpg*
Price new	UK: £2,465
Colour schemes	Bodywork: Silver, red or black
	Frame: Black

*   Superbikes of the Seventies by John Nutting - page72
**   Superbike magazine (September 1977)

1968 NORTON COMMANDO

ENGINE

Type	Air-cooled overhead-valve twin-cylinder, four-stroke
Capacity	745cc
Bore x stroke	73 x 89mm
Compression	8.9:1
Carburetion	Twin 30mm Concentric Amals
Clutch	Multi-plate clutch with large diameter diaphragm spring
Gearbox	Four-speed constant mesh

CHASSIS

Frame	Duplex tubular steel cradle, Isolastic engine mounting
Front suspension	Two-way damped 'Roadholder' telescopic forks
Rear suspension	Twin Girling exposed chrome spring damper units
Brakes front/rear	Front: 8 inch twin leading shoe drum
	Rear: 7 inch single leading shoe drum
Tyres front/rear	Front: 3.00 x 19 Avon
	Rear: 3.50 x 19 Avon

DIMENSIONS

Weight	395lbs dry (179kg)
Wheelbase	$56^3/_4$ inches (1442mm)
Seat height	31 inches (790mm)
Fuel capacity	3.25 Imperial gallons, 3.9 US gallons (15 litres)

PERFORMANCE

Top speed	116mph
0-60mph	5 seconds*
Standing ¼ mile	13.7 seconds / 98.6mph*
Max power	58bhp at 6,800rpm
Fuel consumption	61mpg at 50mph*
Price new	UK: £456 19s 4d · US: $1,457
Colour schemes	Bodywork: Orange tank and tailpiece, silver side panels
	Frame: Black

* *Motorcycle* magazine (11 Sept 1968)

1976 Suzuki GS 750

ENGINE

Type	Four-cylinder DOHC, 8 valve four-stroke
Capacity	748cc
Bore x stroke	65 x 56.4mm
Compression	8.7:1
Carburetion	4 x 26mm Mikuni
Clutch	Multi-plate clutch running in oil
Gearbox	Five-speed

CHASSIS

Frame	Duplex steel cradle
Front suspension	Two-way damped telescopic forks
Rear suspension	Twin gas-filled spring damper units
Brakes front/rear	Front: 11^1/$_2$ inch (280mm) disc
	Rear: 11^1/$_2$ inch (280mm) disc
Tyres front/rear	Front: 3.25 x 19 Bridgestone
	Rear: 4.00 x 18 Bridgestone

DIMENSIONS

Weight	492lbs dry (223kg)
Wheelbase	58.7 inches (1490mm)
Seat height	31 inches (787mm)
Fuel capacity	3.97 Imperial gallons, 4.75 US gallons (18 litres)

PERFORMANCE

Top speed	121.95mph*
0-60mph	N/A
Standing ¼ mile	12.98 seconds*
Max power	68bhp at 8,500rpm
Fuel consumption	38mpg*
Price new	UK: £1,260 US: $2,195
Colour schemes	Bodywork: Red or blue
	Frame: Black

*   *Bike* magazine (March 1977)

1977 SUZUKI GS 1000

ENGINE

Type	Four-cylinder double-overhead camshaft four-stroke
Capacity	997cc
Bore x stroke	70 x 64.8mm
Compression	9.2:1
Carburetion	4 x 26mm Mikuni
Clutch	Multi-plate clutch running in oil
Gearbox	Five-speed

CHASSIS

Frame	Duplex steel cradle
Front suspension	Pneumo-mechanical, 5.9 inch travel telescopic forks
Rear suspension	Twin Kayaba spring units, adjustable for damping and rebound
Brakes front/rear	Front: Twin 11 inch (279mm) discs
	Rear: 11 inch (279mm) disc
Tyres front/rear	Front: 3.50 x 19 Dunlop
	Rear: 4.50 x 17 Dunlop

DIMENSIONS

Weight	516lbs dry (243kg)
Wheelbase	59.3 inches (1505mm)
Seat height	32 inches (813mm)
Fuel capacity	4.2 Imperial gallons (19 litres) plus ½ gall reserve (4 litres)

PERFORMANCE

Top speed	135.7mph*
0-60mph	N/A
Standing ¼ mile	11.92 seconds*
Max power	87bhp at 8,800rpm
Fuel consumption	43mpg*
Price new	UK: £1,725 US: $2,749
Colour schemes	Bodywork: Red, blue or black
	Frame: Black

Bike magazine (March 1977)

1970 SUZUKI GT 750

ENGINE

Type	Three-cylinder liquid-cooled piston-port two-stroke
Capacity	738cc
Bore x stroke	70mm x 64mm
Compression	6.7:1
Carburetion	3 x 32mm Mikuni VM32
Clutch	Multi-plate clutch running in oil
Gearbox	Five-speed constant mesh

CHASSIS

Frame	Duplex steel cradle
Front suspension	Two-way damped telescopic forks
Rear suspension	Twin gas-filled spring damper units
Brakes front/rear	Front: Double-sided 200mm 4 leading shoe drum
	Rear: 180mm single leading shoe drum
Tyres front/rear	Front: 3.25 x 19 inch
	Rear: 4.00 x 18 inch

DIMENSIONS

Weight	472lbs (dry)*
Wheelbase	58 inches (1432mm)
Seat height	32 inches (812mm)
Fuel capacity	3.75 Imperial gallons, 4½ US gallons (17 litre)

PERFORMANCE

Top speed	107.27mph**
0-60mph	5.9 seconds**
Standing ¼ mile	13.87 seconds**
Max power	67bhp at 6,500rpm* 55.7ft-lbs @ 5,500**
Fuel consumption	44mpg average**
Price new	UK: £766. 10s. 0d US: $1,752***
Colour schemes	Bodywork: Candy Lavender or Candy Jackyl Blue
	Frame: Black

*   US Suzuki GT750J sales brochure
**   *Cycle World* magazine (February 1971)
***   *Suzuki Production Motorcycles 1952-1980* by Mick Walker
****Price for the GT750K

1975 Suzuki RE-5

ENGINE

Type	Liquid-cooled, NSU/Wankel-type rotary, single rotor
Capacity	Single chamber 497cc
Bore x stroke	N/A
Compression	9.4:1
Carburetion	Single Mikuni 18mm & 32mm HHD two-stage, two barrel
Clutch	Wet multi-plate clutch
Gearbox	Five-speed constant mesh

CHASSIS

Frame	Dual down-tube steel cradle
Front suspension	Telescopic forks with hydraulic damper
Rear suspension	Twin 5-way adjustable hydraulic spring damper units
Brakes front/rear	Front: Dual 11.6 inch diameter discs
	Rear: 7 inch diameter, single leading shoe drum
Tyres front/rear	Front: 3.25H x 19in 4PR
	Rear: 4.00 x 18in 4PR

DIMENSIONS

Weight (Dry)	507lb (230kg)
Wheelbase	59.1 inches (1,501mm)
Seat height	32½ inches (826mm)
Fuel capacity	3.7 Imperial gallons, 4½ US gallons (17 litres)

PERFORMANCE

Top speed	116.40mph*
0-60mph	6.25 seconds*
Standing ¼ mile	14.37 seconds*
Max power	62bhp at 6,500rpm (claimed)*** 54.9ft-lbs at 3,500rpm****
Fuel consumption	26-30mpg average*
Price new	UK: £1,195 US: $2,475
Colour schemes	Bodywork: Firemist Blue, Orange and Black
	Frame: Black

*   *Motorcycle Mechanics* magazine (December 1974)
**   *Bike* magazine (February 1975)
***   *Japanese Classics* magazine (May 1992)
****US advert (January 1975)

1973 TRIUMPH HURRICANE X-75

ENGINE

Type	Air-cooled, ohv transverse three-cylinder, 6 valve four-stroke
Capacity	740cc
Bore x stroke	67 x 70mm
Compression	9.0:1
Carburetion	Three 27mm Amal concentric
Clutch	Dry, single plate, diaphragm spring
Gearbox	Five-speed

CHASSIS

Frame	Dual-downtube steel cradle
Front suspension	Triumph-type telescopic fork
Rear suspension	Twin three-position spring adjustment Girlings
Brakes front/rear	Front: 8 inch diameter, twin leading shoe x 1.62-inches
	Rear: 7 inch diameter, shoe x 1.25-inches
Tyres front/rear	Front: 3.25 x 19 inch
	Rear: 4.10 x 18 inch

DIMENSIONS

Weight	444lb kerb* (201kg)
Wheelbase	60 inches (1524mm)
Seat height	32½ inches (826mm)
Fuel capacity	2 Imperial gallons approx, 1.66 US gallons (9.1 litres)

PERFORMANCE

Top speed	116mph*
0-60mph	N/A
Standing ¼ mile	13.31 seconds / 102mph*
Max power	60bhp at 7,250rpm
Fuel consumption	29mpg*
Price new	UK: £895 US: $2,295**
Colour schemes	Bodywork: Camaro Hugger Red
	Frame: Black

*   *Bike* magazine (March/April 1973)
**   *Motorcycle Classic* magazine (January/February 2010)

1969 TRIUMPH TRIDENT T150
BSA ROCKET 3 A75

Figures in brackets show A75 details where different to the T150

ENGINE

Type	Air-cooled, ohv transverse three-cylinder, 6 valve four-stroke
Capacity	741cc
Bore x stroke	67 x 70mm
Compression	9.5:1
Carburetion	Three 27mm Amal concentric 626
Clutch	Borg & Beck dry single plate diaphragm
Gearbox	Four-speed

CHASSIS

Frame	Tubular cradle
Front suspension	Triumph-type telescopic fork
Rear suspension	Twin three-position spring adjustment Girlings
Brakes front/rear	Front: 8 inch diameter, shoe width $1^5/_8$ inches
	Rear: 7 inch diameter, shoe width $1^1/_4$
Tyres front/rear	Front: WM2 x 19 inch/3.25 x 19 inch Dunlop K70
	Rear: WM3 x 19 inch/4.10 x 19 inch Dunlop K81

DIMENSIONS

Weight	468lbs/212kg (470lbs/213kg)
Wheelbase	58.1 inches/1473mm (56.25 inches/1429mm)
Seat height	31 inches/787mm (32 inches/813mm)
Fuel capacity	4.25 Imperial gallons, 5 US gallons (19 litres)

PERFORMANCE

Top speed	127mph*
0-60mph	5.6 seconds** (5.0)*
Standing ¼ mile	13.7 seconds / 98.46mph (14.0 / 103mph)*
Max power	58bhp at 7,250rpm
Fuel consumption	48mpg average
Price new	UK: £614 0s. 5d US: $1,765
Colour schemes	Bodywork: Aquamarine, Flamboyant Red or Blue
	Frame: Black

---

*   *Cycle* magazine (October 1968)
**   *Cycle World* magazine (October 1968)

1977 YAMAHA XS 750-2D

ENGINE

Type	Air-cooled DOHC three-cylinder, six-valve four-stroke
Capacity	747cc
Bore x stroke	68 x 68.6mm
Compression	8.5:1
Carburetion	3 x BS34 Mikuni
Clutch	Multi-plate clutch running in oil
Gearbox	Five-speed constant mesh

CHASSIS

Frame	Duplex steel cradle
Front suspension	Two-way damped telescopic forks
Rear suspension	Twin gas-filled spring damper units
Brakes front/rear	Front: Twin 270mm discs
	Rear: 270mm disc
Tyres front/rear	Front: 3.25 x H19
	Rear: 4.00 x H19

DIMENSIONS

Weight	511lbs (232kg)
Wheelbase	$58^3/_4$ inch (1492mm)
Seat height	33 inch (838mm)
Fuel capacity	$3^3/_4$ Imperial gallons, US: $4^1/_2$ gallons (17 litres)

PERFORMANCE

Top speed	117mph*
0-60mph	N/A
Standing ¼ mile	14.10 seconds / 97mph*
Max power	64bhp at 7,200rpm, 46ft-lbs at 6,000rpm*
Fuel consumption	41.0mpg overall*
Price new	UK: £1,660 US: $2,198
Colour schemes	Bodywork: Silver and black, maroon and red
	Frame: Black

*   *Classic Motorcycle Mechanics* magazine (March 2012)

1978 YAMAHA XS1100
US: XS Eleven

ENGINE

Type	Air cooled, DOHC transverse 4-cylinder, 8 valve four-stroke
Capacity	1,102cc
Bore x stroke	71.5 x 68.6mm
Compression	9.2:1
Carburetion	Four 34mm Mikuni CVs
Clutch	Multi-plate clutch running in oil, shaft final drive
Gearbox	Five-speed constant mesh

CHASSIS

Frame	Duplex tubular steel full cradle
Front suspension	Telescopic coil spring with three-pre-load centre-axle forks
Rear suspension	Twin 5 pre-load position sprung damper units
Brakes front/rear	Front: twin 11.73 inch (298mm) diameter discs
	Rear: single 11.73 inch (298mm) diameter disc
Tyres front/rear	Front: 3.50 x H19 Bridgestone
	Rear: 4.50 x H17 Bridgestone

DIMENSIONS

Weight	565lb dry (255kg)
Wheelbase	60.8 inches (1545mm)
Seat height	31.8 inches (808mm)
Fuel capacity	4.4 Imperial/5.3 US gallons (20 litres)

PERFORMANCE

Top speed	126mph*
0-60mph	N/A
Standing ¼ mile	11.82 seconds / 115.38mph**
Max power	95bhp at 8,000rpm
Fuel consumption	36.8mpg average**
Price new	UK: £2,005 US: $2,989
Colour schemes	Bodywork: Burgundy or Silver (Europe: black engine/US: silver engine finish)
	Frame: Black

*   *Cycle* magazine (January 1978)
**   *Motor Cycle Mechanics* magazine (October 1978)

THE BIG 7: SUPERBIKE COMPARISON TEST

CYCLE MAGAZINE (MARCH 1970)

Manufacturer	Model	¼ Mile ET (secs)	¼ Mile Speed (mph)	Lap Time (secs)	Brake Force (Gs)	Weight (lbs)
BSA	Rocket 3	13.14	102.15	44.9	1.04	475
Harley-Davidson	XLCH	12.97	102.15	46.5	1.19	453
Honda	750/4	12.98	102.27	44.9	1.45	480
Kawasaki	500/3	12.81	104.40	46.7	1.22	387
Norton	750 S	12.69	103.68	45.5	0.98	404
Suzuki	Titan	14.29	92.40	48.5	1.18	390
Triumph	Trident	12.78	103.92	46.0	1.08	470

THE BIG 7: SUPERBIKE COMPARISON TEST

CYCLE MAGAZINE (DECEMBER 1972)

Manufacturer	Model	¼ Mile ET (secs)	¼ Mile Speed (mph)	Lap Time (secs)	Brake Force (Gs)	Weight (lbs)
Ducati	750 GT	13.289	101.12	46.4	0.902	469
Harley-Davidson	1000	13.393	99.88	48	0.83	487
Honda	750/4	13.497	100.67	47	0.895	526
Kawasaki	750/3	12.283	110.29	44.5	0.922	469
Kawasaki	903	12.386	110.7	44.5	0.92	542
Norton	750	12.896	104.77	45.6	0.916	439
Triumph	Trident	12.718	106	45.3	0.889	497

BIBLIOGRAPHY

Books

Aamidor, Abe: *Shooting Star: The Rise & Fall of the British Motorcycle Industry* (2009, ECW Press)

Allen, Grahame and Hicks, Joe: *A Century of Change: Trends in UK statistics since 1900 - Research Paper 99/111* (21 December 1999, House of Commons Library)

Ayton, C.J.: *The Great Japanese Motorcycles* (1983, Charles Herridge Ltd)

Bacon, Roy: *The Illustrated Motorcycle Legends: Kawasaki* (1994, Sunburst Books Ltd)

Bacon, Roy: *Triumph Twins & Triples* (1981, Osprey Collector's Library)

Banham, Russ: *The Ford Century: Ford Motor Company and the Innovations That Shaped the World* (2002, Tenabi Books)

Bayley, Stephen: *Design Heroes: Harley Earl* (1992, Grafton)

Beckett, Andy: *When the Lights Went Out* (2009, Faber and Faber)

Benn, Tony: *Against the Tide - Diaries 1973-76* (1989, Century Hutchinson)

Bercuson, David J. and Herwig, Holger H.: *One Christmas in Washington* (2005, Weidenfeld & Nicolson)

Brogan, Hugh: *The Pelican History of the United States* (1985, Penguin Book)

Brook, Lindsay: *Triumph Motorcycles: A Century of Passion and Power* (2002, MBI Publishing)

Brooke, Lindsey and Gaylin, David: *Triumph Motorcycles in America* (1993, Motorbooks International)

Bryson, Bill: *Made in America* (1998, A Black Swan Book)

Chernow, Ron: *The House of Morgan: An American Banking Dynasty and the Rise of Modern Finance* (1990, A Touchstone Book by Simon & Schuster Inc.)

Cohen, J.M. and M.J.: *The Penguin Dictionary of Modern Quotations - Second Edition* (1980, Penguin Books)

Crawford, Michael B.: *Shop Class as Soulcraft: An Inquiry into the Value of Work* (2009, Penguin Books)

Crawley, Tony: *The Wordsworth Dictionary of Film Quotations* (1994, Wordsworth Editions Ltd)

Currie, Bob: *Great British MotorCycles of the Sixties* (1981, Tho Hamlyn Publishing Group Ltd)

Currie, Bob and Louis, Harry: *The Story of Triumph Motorcycles* (1975, Patrick Stephens Ltd)

Davidson, Jean: *Growing Up Harley-Davidson: Memoirs of a Motorcycle Dynasty* (2001, Veloce Publishing)

Davidson, Jean: *Jean Davidson's Harley-Davidson Family Album* (2003, Voyageur Press)

De Cet, Mirco and Kemp, Andrew: *Classic British Bikes* (2000, Abbeydale Press)

Duckworth, Mick: *Triumph and BSA Triples* (1997 and 2004, The Crowood Press)

Duckworth, Mick: *Honda CB750* (2003, Haynes Publishing)

Duncan, Paul and Eyman, Scott: *John Ford: The Complete Films* (2004, Taschen)

Ellis, Edward Robb: *A Nation in Torment: The Great American Depression, 1929-1939* (1970, Kodansha America)

Evans, Harold: *The American Century* (1998, Jonathan Cape/Pimlico)

Falloon, Ian: *Honda Gold Wing* (2001, Haynes Great Bikes)

Falloon, Ian: *The Ducati 750 Bible* (2006, Veloce Publishing)

Falloon, Ian: *The Essential Buyer's Guide: Ducati Bevel Twins* (2012, Veloce Publishing)

Forester, Tom: 'Do the British Sincerely Want to Be Rich?' (28 April 1977, *New Society*)

Foster, Ian: *The CBX Book* (2011, Ian T.A. Foster)

Frank, P. Aaron: *Honda Motorcycles* (2003, MBI Publishing)

Gladwell, Malcolm: *The Tipping Point: How Little Things Can Make a Big Difference* (2000, Little, Brown and Company)

Gould, Jonathan: *Can't Buy Me Love: The Beatles, Britain and America* (2007, Piatkus Books)

Grant, R.G.: *Flight: The Complete History* (2002, Dorling Kindersley Limited)

Haslam, Dave: *Young Hearts Run Free* (2007, Harper Perennial)

Heaton, Joe: *An Examination of the Post-Second World War relative Decline of UK Manufacturing 1945-1975, Viewed Through the Lens of the Birmingham Small Arms Company Ltd* (2007, Ph.D thesis, University of Birmingham)

Henshaw, Peter and Kerr, Ian: *The Encyclopedia of the Harley Davidson* (2011, Hermes House)

Hopwood, Bert: *Whatever Happened to the British Motorcycle Industry?* (1981, Haynes Publishing)

Howarth, Tony: *Twentieth Century History: The World Since 1900* (1979, Longman Group Ltd) - Brooman, Josh: *Second Edition* (1987, Longman Group Ltd)

Kane, Gerard: *Original Triumph Bonneville* (2000, MBI Publishing)

Kemp, Andrew: *Pocket Encyclopedia: Classic British Bikes* (2009, Abbeydale Press)

Kindleberger, Charles P.: *The World in Depression 1929-1939* (1987, Pelican Books)

Lacey, Robert: *Ford: The Men and the Machine* (1986, Pan Books Ltd)

Lindsay, Craig: *A Century of Labour Market Change: 1900 to 2000* (2003, Labour Market Division, Office for National Statistics)

MacDiarmid, Mac: *Classic British Bikes* (1997, Parragon Books)

MacKellar, Colin: *Yamaha Street Bikes 1955-2009* (2010, The Crowood Press)

Main-Smith, Bruce: *The Book of Super Bike Road Tests* (1972, Bruce Main-Smith & Co. Ltd)

Makins, Marian (Managing Editor): *Collins English Dictionary* (Third Edition updated 1995, HarperCollins Publishers)

Marr, Andrew: *The Making of Modern Britain* (2010, Pan Macmillan)

Marsden, Dave: *Original Kawasaki Z1, Z900 & KZ900* (1999, MBI Publishing)

Marwick, Arthur: *British Society since 1945* (Fourth Edition - 2003, Penguin Books Ltd)

McBride, Joseph: *Searching for John Ford: A Life* (2001, Faber & Faber)

McCann, Graham: *Morecambe & Wise* (1999, Fourth Estate)

McWhirter, Norris: *Guinness Book of Records: Edition 25* (1979, Guinness Superlatives Limited)

Moynahan, Brian: *The British Century* (1997, Weidenfeld & Nicolson)

Nelson, Edward and Nikalov, Kalin: *UK Inflation in the 1970s and 1980s: The Role of Output Gap Mismeasurement* (2001, Publications Group, Bank of England)

Nelson, J.R.: *Bonnie - The Development History of the Triumph Bonneville* (1979, Haynes Publishing)

Norman, Philip: *John Lennon: The Life* (2008, Harper)

Nossiter, Bernard D.: *Britain: A Future that Works* (1978, Deutsch)

Nutting, John: *Superbikes of the Seventies* (1978, Hamlyn Publishing Group Limited)

O'Brien, Michael: *John F. Kennedy: A Biography* (2005, Thomas Dunne Books, an imprint of St. Martin's Press)

Oxbury, Harold: *Great Britons: 20th Century Lives* (1985, Oxford University Press)

Posthumus, Cyril: *First Motorcycles - The Illustrated History of the Motorcycle* (1977, Phoebus)

Remus, Tim: *Triumph Motorcycles Twins and Triples* (1997, MBI Publishing)

Rosamond, John: *Save the Triumph Bonneville: The Inside Story of the Meriden Workers' Co-Op* (2009, Veloce Publishing)

Sample, Paul: *The Ogri Omnibus* (1981, Talisman Books Ltd)

Sandbrook, Dominic: *State of Emergency - The Way We Were: Britain, 1970-1974* (2010, Allen Lane, an imprint of Penguin Books)

Satchell, Tim: *McQueen* (1981, Sidgwick and Jackson Ltd)

Schumacher, Michael: *Francis Ford Coppola: A Film-Maker's Life* (1999, Bloomsbury Publishing Ltd)

Semmeling, Rob: *Racing Circuits Factbook* (2012, published online at www.wegcircuits.nl)

Semmeling, Rob: *Rennen, Races, Vitesse! American Road Courses* (2012, published online at www.wegcircuits.nl/AmericanRoadCourses.pdf)

Shipman, David: *Cinema: The First Hundred Years* (1993, Weidenfeld and Nicolson)

Sinclair, David: *The Pound: A Biography* (2000, Arrow Books)

Sintich, Claudio: *Road Racing History of the Triumph 500 Unit Twin* (2010, Panther Publishing Ltd)

Smith, Bill: *Armstrong Siddeley Motors: The cars, the company and the people in definitive detail* (2006, Veloce Publishing Ltd)

Sounes, Howard: *Seventies: The Sights, Sounds and Ideas of a Brilliant Decade* (2006, Simon & Schuster UK Ltd)

Thompson, Jon F. and Bonnello, Joe: *Ducati* (1998, MBI Publishing)

Turner, Alwyn W.: *Crisis? What Crisis? Britain in the 1970s* (2008, Aurum Press)

Un-credited author: *Social Trends* (Palgrave Macmillan available on www.knowuk.co.uk)

Vale, Matthew: *Norton Commando: The Complete Story* (2011, The Crowood Press)

Various authors (compiled by R.M. Clarke): *BSA & Triumph Triples Gold Portfolio 1968-1976* (Brooklands Books)

Various authors: *Cycle World on Suzuki Street Bikes 1971-1976* (Brooklands Books)

Various authors: *Cycle World on Triumph 1967-1972* (1993, Brooklands Books)

Various authors (compiled by R.M. Clarke): *Harley-Davidson Sportsters Performance Portfolio 1965-1976* (Brooklands Books)

Various authors (compiled by R.M. Clarke): *Honda CB750 Gold Portfolio 1969-1978* (Brooklands Books)

Various authors (compiled by R.M. Clarke): *Kawasaki Z1 900 Performance Portfolio 1972-1977* (Brooklands Books)

Various authors (compiled by R.M. Clarke): *Norton Commando Ultimate Portfolio* (Brooklands Books)

Various authors (compiled R.M. Clarke): *Suzuki GS1000 Performance Portfolio 1978-1981* (Brooklands Books)

Various authors: *On Two Wheels Volumes 1-4* (Orbis)

Viner, Brian: *Nice to See It, To See It, Nice* (2009, Simon & Schuster UK)

Wagner, Herbert: *At the Creation: Myth, Reality, and the Origin of the Harley-Davidson Motorcycle, 1901-1909* (2003, Wisconsin Historical Society Press)

Walker, Mick: *Honda Production Motorcycles 1946-1980* (2006, The Crowood Press)

Walker, Mick: *Suzuki Production Motorcycles 1952-1980* (2006, The Crowood Press)

Warner, Hannah: *Fascinating TV Facts* (2004, Virgin Books Ltd)

Wilkinson, Carl (Editor): *The Observer Book of Money* (2007, Observer Books, an imprint of Guardian News and Media)

Wilson, Hugo: *The Ultimate Motor-Cycle Book* (1993, Dorling Kindersley)

Wilson, Steve: *Triumph T120/T140 Bonneville* (2000, Haynes Great Bikes)

Wyatt, John: *Original Honda CB750* (1998, MBI Publishing)

The AA Atlas of the World (2005, Mairdumont and Automobile Association Developments Ltd)

Magazines, Newspapers, Periodicals, Supplements and Reports

Big Bike magazine (Hi-Torque Publications Inc.)

Bike magazine (EMAP National Publications Ltd)

Bike's Book of Superbike Road Tests - a Bike magazine special (1977, EMAP National Publications Ltd)

Bikes of the Seventies - a Classic Bike supplement (June 1994, EMAP National Publications Ltd)

British Bike magazine (Green Designs)

Classic Bike magazine (Bauer Media House)

Classic Bike Guide magazine (Mortons Media Group Ltd)

Classic Motorcycle Mechanics magazine (Mortons Media Group)

Classic Racer magazine (Mortons Media Group Ltd)

Classic Roadtests Revisited 1969-1983: The Motor Industry Research Association Files - a Classic Motorcycle Mechanics supplement (2011, Mortons Media Group Ltd)

Cycle magazine (Ziff-Davis Publishing Company)

Cycle World magazine (CBS Publications)

Education: Historical statistics - Standard Note SN/SG/4252 (2007, House of Commons Library)

Fast Classics magazine (Colin Schiller)

Harley-Davidson: 85 Years of Glory (1988, LEP Inc)

Honda Motor Co. Ltd: Honda Design (Motorcycle Part 1) 1957-1984

Insurance Institute for Highway Safety Status Report: Volume 13, No. 6 (8 May, 1978)

Japanese Bikes (EMAP National Publications Ltd)

Japanese Classics magazine (Roger Lee)

Japanese Classics: A Motor Cycle News Special (Autumn 1983, EMAP National Publications Ltd)

K News: Newsletter from Kawasaki Specialist Centres (1978, Intercity Publicity)

Los Angeles Times newspaper (Tribune Company)

Motorcycle Classics magazine (Ogden Publications Inc.)

Motor Cycle Mechanics magazine (East Midland Allied Press Ltd)

Motorcycle International's Classics: Great Motorcycles of the '60s and '70s (1987, Advanced Publishing Ltd)

Motor Cycle News weekly newspaper (Bauer Consumer Media)

Motorcycle Sport magazine (Teesdale Publishing Company Ltd)

Motorcycling Monthly magazine (IPC Magazines Ltd)

Motorcyclist magazine (Petersen Publishing Company)

Motorcyclist Illustrated magazine (Byblos Production Ltd)

Nacelle (the monthly magazine of the Triumph Owners Motor Cycle Club)

newZletter (the quarterly magazine of the Z1 Owners Club of Great Britain)

Old Bike Journal magazine (TAM Communications Inc)

Practical Sportsbikes magazine (Bauer Media)

Silver Machine magazine (Advanced Publishing Ltd)

Strategy Alternatives for the British Motorcycle Industry: A Report prepared for the Secretary of State of Industry by The Boston Consulting Group Limited (House of Commons report 30th July 1975)

Superbike magazine (Link House Magazines)

The Classic MotorCycle magazine ((EMAP National Publications Ltd)

The Independent newspaper (Independent Print Limited)

The Telegraph newspaper (Telegraph Media Group Limited)

Widening Participation in Higher Education: Analysis using Linked Administrative Data - IFS Working Paper W10/04 (2010, Institute for Fiscal Studies)

Websites

AMA Motorcycle Museum Hall of Fame (www.motorcyclemuseum.org/halloffame)

Art of the Motorcycle: Guggenheim Museum (www.pastexhibitions.guggenheim.org/motorcycle)

BBC Website - On This Day (www.news.bbc.co.uk/onthisday)

Bonhams (www.bonhams.com/cgi-bin/public.sh/pubweb/publicSite)

British Museum (www.britishmuseum.org)

Craig Vetter official website (www.craigvetter.com)

Farmers' Almanac: Weather History for Daytona Beach (www.frmersalmanac.com)

Find a Grave (www.findagrave.com)

Guardian newspaper (www.guardian.co.uk)

Harley-Davidson (www.harley-davidson.com)

Honda Worldwide History (www.world.honda.com)

Imola 200 by Don Emde (www.superbikeplanet.com)

Institute for Fiscal Studies (www.ifs.org.uk)

Insurance Institute for Highway Safety (www.iihs.org/externaldata/srdata/docs)

Met Office figures (www.metoffice.gov.uk/events/easter)

Motorcycle Classics (www.motorcycleclassics.com)

Motorcyclist (www.motorcyclistonline.com)

Motohistory (http://motohistory.net)

Museum of Broadcast Communications websites (www.museum.tv/)

Muskie, Edmund - Congressional Record (http://abacus.bates.edu/muskie-archives/)

RMS Queen Mary (www.queenmary.com/Statistics)

Science & Society Picture Library (www.scienceandsociety.co.uk)

Smithsonian National Air and Space Museum (www.nasm.si.edu/exhibitions/gal100/wright1903)

Social Trends - Motor Vehicles (www.knowuk.co.uk)

Sunrise times (www.timeanddate.com)

Telegraph newspaper (www.telegraph.co.uk/news)

Suzuki GT750 Owners Forum (www.kettleclinick.com)

Warr's Harley-Davidson (www.warrs.com)

Willow Springs International Raceway (www.willowspringsraceway.com)

INDEX